The Little Big
MEDITERRANEAN
BOOK

The Little Big Mediterranean Book
was created and produced by McRae Books Srl
Borgo Santa Croce, 8 – Florence (Italy)
info@mcraebooks.com
www.mcraebooks.com
Publishers: Anne McRae and Marco Nardi

Text by the Editors of McRae Books
Translation: Osla Fraser, Ailsa Wood
Editing: Helen Farrell
Photography: Lorenzo Borri, Keeho Casati, Walter Mericchi, Leonardo Pasquinelli, Stefano Pratesi, Stefania Talini, Studio Marco Lanza
Home Economist: Benedetto Rillo
Food Styling: Arianna Cappellini, Francesco Piccardi
Layout: Adina Stefania Dragomir, Sara Mathews
Repro: RAF Toscana, Florence - Fotolito Toscana, Florence

The Publishers would like to thank:
Bellini Più, Montespertoli (Florence)
Ceramiche Il Pozzo, Montespertoli (Florence)
Ceramiche Virginia, Montespertoli (Florence)
CIVE Vetrevia in Toscana. Cos.coop.r.l., Empoli
Il Nodo Ceramiche, Montelupo Fiorentino (Florence)

ISBN 88-89272-50-3

Printed and bound in Italy by Grafiche Industriali, Foligno

The Little Big
MEDITERRANEAN
BOOK

MᶜRAE BOOKS

CONTENTS

DRINKS

FRUTTISSIMO

Beat the yogurt, milk, and honey in a large bowl until smooth and thick. • Divide into three parts. • Process one part with the raspberries in a food processor or blender until smooth. • Process the second part of the yogurt mixture with the pineapple and banana. • Process the third part with the strawberries. • Pour a layer of the raspberry mixture into each glass. Top with a layer of the banana mixture and finish with the strawberry mixture. • Garnish with extra fruit.

8

Serves: 4

Preparation: 20'

Level of difficulty: 2

- **1 cup/250 ml plain yogurt**
- **1 cup/250 ml milk**
- **1 tbsp honey**
- **2 cups/250 g raspberries**
- **2 cups/250 g strawberries**
- **¼ pineapple**
- **1 banana, peeled and finely chopped**

LETTUCE AND PEA SMOOTHIE

Serves: 4–6

Preparation: 20'

Level of difficulty: 2

- **2 cups/250 g shelled peas**
- **1 quart/1 liter Vegetable Stock (see page 224)**
- **²⁄₃ cup/150 ml plain yogurt**
- **salt and freshly ground black pepper to taste**
- **1 head lettuce, rinsed and shredded**
- **²⁄₃ cup/150 ml heavy/double cream**
- **¹⁄₄ tsp red chile pepper**

Cook the peas in the boiling stock until tender.
• Transfer the peas and their cooking liquid to a food processor. Let cool slightly. • Process the peas (reserving a few to garnish) with the yogurt until smooth. • Season with salt and pepper. • Blanch the lettuce in boiling water for 1 minute. Drain. • Process the lettuce with the cream until smooth. Season with salt and pepper. • Spoon the lettuce mixture into 4–6 glasses. Top up with the processed pea liquid. Stir well. Garnish with the chile powder and peas.
• Serve at room temperature.

FRUITY RUM PUNCH

C ut the watermelon in two pieces (one larger). Cut the peel of the larger piece into a zigzag with a sharp knife. Remove the flesh with a melon baller (eliminating the seeds). • Put the balls of watermelon in a glass bowl and pour in any juice. • Pour the lemon juice into the watermelon shell, rubbing it into the cut edges, so that they do not turn black. • Cover with plastic wrap (cling film) and refrigerate until ready to use. • Take the remaining piece of watermelon and remove the seeds. Liquidize the flesh and add to the bowl with the melon balls. • Chop up the fruit and add to the bowl. • Drizzle with lime juice to prevent the banana from darkening in color. • Add a handful of mint leaves, the orange and pineapple juice, rum, Angostura, and grenadine. Cover with plastic wrap and refrigerate for 2 hours. • Use a slotted spoon to transfer two-thirds of the fruit to the empty watermelon shell. • Serve the fruit punch as a pre-dinner drink. • Serve the rum-flavored fruit salad in the watermelon shell at the end of the meal as a refreshing dessert.

Serves: 8

Preparation: 30' + 2 h to chill

Level of difficulty: 2

- **1 large watermelon**
- **juice of 1 lemon**
- **3 lb/1.5 kg mixed fruit (pineapple, mango, papaya, bananas, melon, strawberries, peaches, kiwifruit)**
- **⅔ cup/150 ml lime juice**
- **mint leaves, to garnish**
- **2 cups/500 ml orange juice**
- **2 cups/500 ml pineapple juice**
- **1⅓ cups/350 ml dark rum**
- **½ cup/125 ml white rum**
- **16 drops Angostura bitters**
- **16 drops grenadine (pomegranate syrup)**

SANGRIA

Place the peaches, apricots, plums, and melon in a large glass bowl. • Use a sharp knife to cut 4 or 5 long pieces of peel (yellow part only) from the lemons. Add to the fruit with the lemon balm and the cinnamon. • Squeeze the lemons and drizzle the juice over the fruit. • Pour in the cognac and wine and add the ice cubes. • Set aside until the ice has melted a little, then serve.

Serves: 8

Preparation: 25'

Level of difficulty: 1

- **4 peaches, pitted and sliced**
- **4 apricots, pitted and sliced**
- **4 red plums, pitted and sliced**
- **1 small cantaloùpe (rock melon), peeled and diced**
- **2 lemons**
- **twigs of lemon balm or verbena**
- **2 sticks cinnamon**
- **6 tbsp cognac**
- **1 quart/1 liter robust red wine**
- **about 20 ice cubes**

BLOODY MARY

Serves: 4

Preparation: 10'

Level of difficulty: 1

- **ice cubes**
- **2 cups/500 ml tomato juice**
- **½ cup/125 ml vodka**
- **1 tbsp lemon juice**
- **1 tsp Worcestershire sauce**
- **½ tsp Tabasco**
- **salt and freshly ground pepper to taste**
- **4 slender stalks celery, to garnish**

Fill a cocktail shaker one-third full with ice cubes. Pour in half of all the ingredients (tomato juice, vodka, lemon juice, Worcestershire sauce, and Tabasco). Season with salt and pepper. • Shake vigorously. Divide the drink between two glasses. • Repeat with the remaining ingredients. • Serve with the celery which, as well as being an attractive garnish, doubles up as a tasty appetizer.

FLORENTINE BLACK MAGIC

Warm the milk, sugar, chocolate, cinnamon, and allspice in a medium saucepan over low heat and stir until the chocolate has melted. • Cover and set aside to cool. • Transfer the milk mixture to a cocktail shaker, add the remaining ingredients, and shake vigorously. • Pour into four glasses and serve very cold.

Serves: 4

Preparation: 10'

Cooking: 10'

Level of difficulty: 1

- 2¼ cups/600 ml milk
- 1 tbsp superfine/caster sugar
- 3 oz/90 g semi-sweet/dark chocolate
- ¼ tsp cinnamon
- ¼ tsp allspice
- 5 tbsp rum
- 4 tbsp brandy
- grated zest of ½ lemon
- cracked ice

BRANDY ALEXANDER

Serves: 4

Preparation: 5'

Level of difficulty: 1

* **ice cubes**
* **½ cup/125 ml crème de cacao**
* **½ cup/125 ml brandy**
* **½ cup/125 ml heavy/double cream**
* **freshly grated nutmeg**

Put the ice cubes, crème de cacao, brandy, and cream into a cocktail shaker. • Shake well and strain into 4 cocktail glasses. • Grate the nutmeg over the top of each glass and serve immediately.

SAUCES

ROUILLE (FRENCH SAFFRON AND GARLIC MAYONNAISE)

Use a mortar and pestle to crush the garlic with the salt. • Transfer to a small bowl and season with saffron. Add the egg yolks and beat with a wooden spoon. Set aside for 5 minutes. • Add the oil in a thin, steady trickle, stirring constantly, until smooth and creamy. • Transfer to a small bowl and garnish with the saffron powder. • Do not make this recipe using unpasteurized eggs as they may contain bacteria, such as salmonella, which can seriously endanger your health.

Serves: 4–6

Preparation: 15'

Level of difficulty: 1

- **6 cloves garlic, peeled**
- **½ tsp salt**
- **½ tsp crumbled saffron threads**
- **2 pasteurized egg yolks**
- **1 cup/250 ml extra-virgin olive oil**
- **⅛ tsp saffron powder, to garnish**

18

MAYONNAISE

Serves: 4

Preparation: 15'

Level of difficulty: 1

- **3 pasteurized egg yolks**
- **salt to taste**
- **1¼ cups/300 ml extra-virgin olive oil**
- **6 tbsp lemon juice or white wine vinegar**

Beat the egg yolks with the salt until light and fluffy. • Add the oil in a thin, steady trickle, stirring constantly, until smooth and creamy. • When the mayonnaise is dense, stir in the lemon juice followed by any remaining oil. • If not using pasteurized eggs, place the egg yolks and lemon juice or vinegar in a double boiler over barely simmering water. Heat until the mixture reaches 160°F (80°C). This will destroy potentially harmful bacteria, including salmonella, that can be present in raw eggs. • Let the mixture cool a little then gradually beat in the oil and salt. • Store in an airtight container in the refrigerator.

SAUCE FOR CARPACCIO

Mix the mayonnaise and mustard in a small bowl. • Add the brandy and whisky and mix well. • Gradually fold in the cream until smooth and well blended. • Serve with carpaccio or bresaola.

Serves: 6–8

Preparation: 5'

Level of difficulty: 1

- 1½ cups/375 ml Mayonnaise (see page 19)
- 2 tbsp mustard
- 1 tbsp brandy
- 1 tbsp whisky
- 6 tbsp heavy/ double cream

MINT AND LEMON VINAIGRETTE

Serves: 4

Preparation: 15'

Soaking: 2'

Level of difficulty: 2

- 1 large organic lemon
- salt and freshly ground black pepper to taste
- 6 tbsp extra-virgin olive oil
- fresh mint leaves, to garnish

Remove the zest from the lemon with a sharp knife, without removing any of the bitter white part. Shred the zest finely. • Soak the zest in boiling water for 2 minutes. • Drain. This helps to release the flavor. • Squeeze the lemon and then strain the juice. • Beat the lemon juice, salt, pepper, and oil in a small bowl until smooth. • Add the lemon zest and mint and mix well.

PISTACHIO AND ORANGE VINAIGRETTE

Serves: 4

Preparation: 15'

Level of difficulty: 1

- ½ cup/90 g shelled pistachios
- 6 tbsp fresh orange juice
- 2 tbsp balsamic vinegar
- 4 tbsp extra-virgin olive oil
- salt and freshly ground black pepper to taste

Blanch the pistachios in boiling water for 3 minutes. • Use a slotted spoon to transfer to a cloth. Roll firmly under your fingers to remove the skins. Chop coarsely. • Beat the orange juice, balsamic vinegar, oil, salt, and pepper in a small bowl until the mixture is smooth and slightly thick. • Add the pistachios and mix well. • Serve with all types of salads and with steamed or baked vegetables.

PINE NUT SAUCE

C rumble the bread into a small bowl. Moisten with the vinegars. • Chop the bread, sugar, and pine nuts finely in a food processor or blender, gradually adding the oil a little at a time.
• Serve with poached or baked fish or boiled or roast poultry.

Serves: 4

Preparation: 10'

Level of difficulty: 1

- **1 slice day-old bread**
- **2 tbsp white wine vinegar**
- **1 tbsp cider vinegar**
- **1 tsp sugar**
- **½ cup/90 g pine nuts**
- **4 tbsp extra-virgin olive oil**

SCALLION VINAIGRETTE

Serves: 4

Preparation: 10'

Level of difficulty: 1

- **4 scallions/spring onions**
- **2 tbsp white wine vinegar**
- **salt and freshly ground black pepper to taste**
- **½ cup/125 ml extra-virgin olive oil**

Separate the green part from the white part of the scallions. Finely slice the white part and shred the green part. • Beat the vinegar, salt, pepper, and oil in a small bowl to make a smooth and slightly thick dressing. • Add the sliced scallions and mix well. • Sprinkle with the shredded scallions. • Serve with green salads or with boiled or steamed vegetables.

AÏOLI (FRENCH GARLIC MAYONNAISE)

Serves: 4–8
Preparation: 15' each
Level of difficulty: 1

C rush the garlic using a pestle and mortar or garlic crusher. • Place in a medium bowl and stir in the egg yolks and vinegar. • Add the oil in a thin, steady trickle, stirring constantly, until smooth and creamy. • Season with salt and pepper and drizzle with the lemon juice.

- 6 cloves garlic
- 2 pasteurized egg yolks, beaten
- 1 tbsp vinegar
- 2 cups/500 ml extra-virgin olive oil
- salt and freshly ground white pepper to taste
- 1 tbsp lemon juice

26

TAPENADE (OLIVE AND ANCHOVY SAUCE)

C hop the olives, capers, anchovies, and garlic coarsely in a food processor. • Season with pepper. Gradually stir in the oil followed by the lemon juice.

- 2 lb/1 kg pitted black olives
- 2 tbsp capers
- 4 anchovy fillets
- 1 clove garlic
- freshly ground black pepper
- ½ cup/125 ml extra-virgin olive oil
- juice of ½ lemon

WALNUT AND ANCHOVY SAUCE

D esalt the anchovies carefully under a trickle of cold running water. Drain well and pat dry with paper towels. • Place the anchovies in a small bowl and crush with the back of a fork. Stir in the walnuts. • Add the oil in a thin, steady trickle until well mixed. • Stir in the water.

- 3 oz/90 g salted anchovy fillets
- 2 cups/250 g finely ground walnuts
- ½ cup/125 ml extra-virgin olive oil
- 1 tsp cold water

PEPPER SAUCE

Crumble the bread into a small bowl. Moisten with the vinegar. • Place almost all the peppercorns (reserve a few to make the finished sauce more attractive) in a food processor with the bread and oil. Pulse until the sauce is smooth. • Add the reserved peppercorns. • Serve with steamed or baked vegetables and boiled and roast meats.

28

Serves: 4

Preparation: 15'

Level of difficulty: 1

- **2 slices day-old bread**
- **4 tbsp cider vinegar**
- **2 tbsp black peppercorns**
- **2 tbsp red peppercorns**
- **2 tbsp pink peppercorns**
- **1/2 cup/125 ml extra-virgin olive oil**

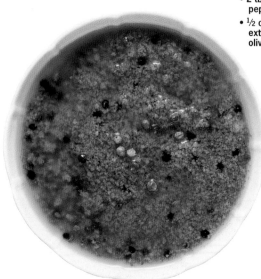

TARRAGON SAUCE

Serves: 4

Preparation: 15'

Level of difficulty: 1

- **2 slices white sandwich bread**
- **4 tbsp white wine vinegar**
- **1 small bunch parsley, tough stalks removed**
- **1 small bunch tarragon, tough stalks removed**
- **3 cloves garlic**
- **½ cup/125 ml extra-virgin olive oil**

Crumble the bread into a medium bowl. Moisten with the vinegar. • Process the bread, parsley, tarragon, and garlic in a food processor or blender until very finely chopped. • Gradually add the oil and pulse until smooth. • Serve with boiled or roast meat or poached or baked fish.

SAUCES

YOGURT AND TUNA SAUCE

D rain the tuna of its oil and place in the bowl of
a food processor or blender. Add the yogurt,
capers, tuna, salt, and pepper and chop until
smooth. • Serve this delicate sauce with
steamed or poached fish.

Serves: 4

Preparation: 10'

Level of difficulty: 1

- 4 oz/125 g canned tuna, packed in oil
- 1 cup/250 ml plain yogurt
- 2–3 tbsp salted capers, rinsed
- salt and freshly ground black pepper to taste

These are two classic Italian sauces. Both are served with fish. The olive sauce also makes a delicious spread for canapés.

30

BLACK OLIVE SAUCE

S hell the boiled eggs, cut them in half, and
remove the yolks. Place the yolks in a small
bowl. • In another small bowl, mix the olives,
parsley, capers, and garlic. Add the egg yolk,
vinegar, salt, and pepper and mix until creamy.
• Serve with steamed or poached fish.

Serves: 4

Preparation: 15'

Level of difficulty: 1

- 2 boiled eggs
- 15–20 large black olives, pitted and chopped
- 6 tbsp finely chopped parsley
- 1 tbsp salted capers, rinsed and chopped
- 2 cloves garlic, finely chopped
- 1 tbsp balsamic vinegar
- salt and freshly ground black pepper to taste

HAM AND APPLE SAUCE

Place the apples, oil, cheese, lemon juice, ham, and walnuts in the bowl of a food processor or blender. Chop until smooth and creamy. • Season with salt and pepper. • Serve with roast pork, boiled rice, or baked vegetables—this sauce is especially good with baked potatoes.

Serves: 4–6

Preparation: 15'

Level of difficulty: 1

- **2 Golden Delicious apples, peeled, cored, and chopped**
- **4 tbsp extra-virgin olive oil**
- **5 oz/150 g Fontina or Emmental cheese, coarsely grated**
- **4 tbsp lemon juice**
- **²⁄₃ cup/80 g chopped ham**
- **¹⁄₂ cup/50 g walnuts, shelled**
- **salt and freshly ground black pepper to taste**

HONEY AND ONION SAUCE

Serves: 6–8

Preparation: 5'

Cooking: 50'

Level of difficulty: 1

- 8 medium onions, finely chopped
- 1½ cups/375 ml water
- 2 tsp ras-al-hanout (North African spice mix)
- salt to taste
- 6 tbsp extra-virgin olive oil
- 2 tbsp honey

Bring the onions and water to a boil in a medium saucepan over medium heat. • Add the ras-al-hanout and season with salt. • Cover and simmer for 20 minutes. • Lower the heat and continue cooking for 15–20 minutes more, or until the liquid has evaporated and the onions have broken down. • Uncover and cook for 5 minutes over high heat, stirring constantly, until the sauce has reduced to a paste. • Add the oil and honey and cook for 5 minutes more. • Serve hot with roast meat or fish. It is also good with boiled rice or potatoes.

RED SAUCE

Place the tomatoes in boiling water for 1–2 minutes, or until the skins start to split. Plunge into cold water and leave for 2 minutes. Dry and carefully remove the skins. • Cut the tomatoes in half, gently squeeze out the seeds, and place cut-side down on a cutting board to drain. • Chop the basil, garlic, and onion in a blender or food processor. • Add the chile pepper, vinegar, salt, and tomatoes. Blend well. Remove from the blender and use a fork to beat in the olive oil. • Serve with boiled meats or boiled or roast poultry.

34

Serves: 4

Preparation: 15'

Level of difficulty: 1

- 1½ lb/750 g ripe tomatoes
- 5 leaves basil
- 2 cloves garlic
- 1 onion
- ½ tsp chile pepper
- 1 tbsp vinegar
- salt to taste
- 4 tbsp extra-virgin olive oil

PECORINO CHEESE SAUCE

Serves: 4

Preparation: 15'

Level of difficulty: 1

- **2 tbsp parsley**
- **10 leaves basil**
- **1 tbsp pine nuts**
- **1 hard-boiled egg, chopped**
- **3 oz/90 g aged Pecorino cheese, finely grated**
- **4 tbsp extra-virgin olive oil**
- **salt and freshly ground black pepper to taste**

Chop the parsley, basil, and pine nuts in a blender or food processor until smooth. • Use a wooden spoon to stir in the hard-boiled egg, Pecorino, and olive oil. Season with salt and pepper. • Serve with poached or baked fish or boiled or roast poultry.

ARTICHOKE SAUCE

36

Remove the tough outer leaves from the artichokes by snapping them off at the base. Cut off the top third of the remaining leaves. Cut the artichokes in half, removing any fuzzy choke with a sharp knife. Rub with the lemon. • Thinly slice the artichokes and place in a saucepan with the oil and onion. Sauté over medium heat for 10 minutes. • Add the mushrooms, garlic, and parsley and sauté for 5 minutes. • Increase the heat and add the wine and tomatoes. Bring to a boil and cook for 10 more minutes. • Stir in the butter and season with salt and pepper. • Serve with pasta or rice, or spread on slices of toast.

- 3 artichokes
- 1 lemon
- 4 tbsp extra-virgin olive oil
- 1 onion, finely chopped
- ½ oz/15 g dried mushrooms, soaked in warm water for 15 minutes, drained, and coarsely chopped
- 2 cloves garlic, finely chopped
- 1 tbsp finely chopped parsley
- 4 tbsp dry white wine
- 2 small tomatoes, peeled and chopped
- 1 tbsp butter
- salt and freshly ground black pepper to taste

TOMATO SAUCE

Serves: 4–6

Preparation: 20' + 1 h
to drain tomatoes

Cooking: 50'

Level of difficulty: 1

- 3 lb/1.5 kg firm-ripe tomatoes, coarsely chopped
- salt to taste
- 1 red onion, thinly sliced
- 2 cloves garlic, finely chopped
- 1 small bunch fresh basil, finely chopped
- 2 tbsp extra-virgin olive oil
- $^1/_8$ tsp sugar

Cook the tomatoes with $^1/_8$ teaspoon salt in a covered saucepan over medium heat for 5 minutes. • Transfer to a colander and let drain for 1 hour. • Return to the saucepan and add the onion, garlic, basil, oil, sugar, and salt. Cover and bring to a boil over medium heat. Simmer for about 40 minutes, or until the sauce has thickened. • Remove from the heat and run through a food mill or process in a food processor or blender until smooth. • Serve with pasta, gnocchi, rice, or baked potatoes. It is also good on toast.

MOUSSELINE SAUCE

Melt 1 tablespoon of butter in a casserole over low heat. • Add the flour and mix well. • Gradually add the stock, stirring constantly to prevent lumps from forming. • Cook for 3 minutes, stirring constantly. • Transfer to a double boiler over medium heat. • Add the egg yolk and beat well. • Add the remaining butter, 1 tablespoon at a time, beating well after each addition. • Add the chopped marjoram, cream, and lemon juice and stir gently until smooth and creamy. Garnish with the marjoram leaves. • Serve with poached fish or over boiled or steamed vegetables—it is especially good with broccoli or cauliflower.

Serves: 2–4

Preparation: 10'

Cooking: 15'

Level of difficulty: 2

- ²/₃ cup/150 g butter
- 2 tbsp all-purpose/plain flour
- 4 tbsp stock or milk
- 1 pasteurized egg yolk
- 2 tbsp chopped marjoram + extra leaves, to garnish
- 4 tbsp heavy/double cream
- 1 tbsp lemon juice

SICILIAN PESTO

Serves: 4–6

Preparation: 15' +
1 h to drain

Level of difficulty: 2

- **4 large tomatoes**
- **salt to taste**
- **3 oz/90 g blanched almonds**
- **2 cloves garlic, finely chopped**
- **freshly ground black pepper to taste**
- **1 small bunch fresh basil**
- **4 tbsp extra-virgin olive oil**
- **4 tbsp freshly grated Pecorino or Parmesan cheese**

Peel the tomatoes with a sharp knife. Quarter them and gently squeeze out as many seeds as possible. Sprinkle with salt and drain in a colander for 1 hour. • Rinse off the salt and dry well on paper towels. • Process the tomatoes with the almonds and garlic in a food processor until smooth. Season with salt and pepper. • Add the basil and 1 tablespoon of oil and chop until smooth. • Add the Pecorino and the remaining oil and mix well to make a smooth sauce. • Serve with pasta, gnocchi, or steamed or baked vegetables.

SPICY VEGETABLE SAUCE

Heat the oil in a medium saucepan over medium heat. • Add the flour and mix well. • Add the pickled vegetables, anchovies, chile pepper, and water. • Mix well and cook for 3 minutes. • Remove from the heat. • Serve with boiled meat or poached or baked fish.

Serves: 4

Preparation: 15'

Cooking: 10'

Level of difficulty: 1

- 4 tbsp extra-virgin olive oil
- 2 tbsp all-purpose/ plain flour
- 14 oz/400 g mixed pickled vegetables, drained and finely chopped
- 4 anchovy fillets, rinsed and chopped
- 1–2 fresh red chile pepper, seeded and finely chopped
- 2 tbsp water

PINE NUT AND ANCHOVY SAUCE

Serves: 4

Preparation: 10'

Level of difficulty: 1

- ½ cup/90 g pine nuts
- 2 tbsp capers, rinsed and drained
- 2 cloves garlic
- 4 anchovy fillets
- 1 small bunch parsley
- yolks of 3 large hard-boiled eggs,
- 1 tbsp white wine vinegar
- salt and freshly ground black pepper to taste
- 6 tbsp extra-virgin olive oil

Process the pine nuts, capers, garlic, anchovies, and parsley in a food processor until finely chopped. • Add the egg yolks and vinegar and process until purèed. Season with salt and pepper. • Beat in the oil to make a smooth sauce. • Serve with poached or baked fish or with steamed or baked vegetables.

43

VEGETABLE SAUCE

Sauté the garlic, onion, anchovies, carrot, zucchini, eggplant, and green beans in the oil in a large frying pan over low heat for about 5 minutes, or until the vegetables begin to soften. • Add the Marsala and let it evaporate. • Season with salt and pepper. Add the tomatoes and cook for 15 minutes. • Mash the canned beans with a fork until puréed. Add to the sauce and mix well. • Add the parsley and cook for 5 more minutes. • Serve hot with pasta, boiled rice, boiled or baked potatoes, freshly cooked polenta, or with couscous.

44

Serves: 4–6

Preparation: 20'

Cooking: 30'

Level of difficulty: 1

- **1 clove garlic, finely chopped**
- **1 small onion, finely chopped**
- **2 anchovy fillets, chopped**
- **1 carrot, peeled and chopped**
- **2 large zucchini/ courgettes, sliced**
- **1 small eggplant/ aubergine, peeled and cut into small cubes**
- **4 oz/125 g green beans, halved**
- **3 tbsp extra-virgin olive oil**
- **6 tbsp Marsala wine**
- **salt and freshly ground black pepper to taste**
- **generous 1½ cups/ 400 g peeled tomatoes, chopped**
- **½ cup/100 g canned borlotti or red kidney beans, drained**
- **2 tbsp finely chopped parsley**

WALNUT AND GORGONZOLA SAUCE

Place the Gorgonzola in a heavy-bottomed pan over very low heat and stir with a wooden spoon until creamy. • Remove from heat and add the lemon juice and walnuts. • Stir in the oil and yogurt to make a creamy sauce. • Serve with pasta, gnocchi, or boiled rice or as a dip with fresh vegetables (such as carrots, celery, radishes, scallions/green onions).

Serves: 4–6

Preparation: 15'

Level of difficulty: 1

- 6 oz/180 g creamy Gorgonzola cheese, cut into small cubes
- 2 tbsp lemon juice
- 12 walnuts, finely chopped
- 1 tbsp extra-virgin olive oil
- ⅔ cup/150 ml plain yogurt

WALNUT AND RICOTTA SAUCE

Serves: 4–6

Preparation: 40'

Level of difficulty: 2

- 1¼ cups/150 g walnuts, shelled
- 2 cloves garlic, finely chopped
- 3 slices bread
- 1 cup/250 ml water
- salt to taste
- 1 tbsp extra-virgin olive oil
- ¾ cup/180 g Ricotta cheese

Blanch the walnuts in boiling water for 1 minute. Drain and transfer to a cloth. Roll the nuts firmly under your fingers to remove the skins.
- Finely chop the walnuts and garlic in a food processor or blender. Reserve a few to garnish.
- Dip the bread in the water, squeezing out the excess moisture. • Add the bread to the walnuts. Season with salt and purèe. • Add the oil and Ricotta and process until smooth and creamy.
- Serve with pasta or baked potatoes.

SPICY TOMATO SAUCE

Serves:	4–6
Preparation:	10'
Cooking:	45'
Level of difficulty:	2

Cook the tomatoes, leek, zucchini, parsley, salt, pepper, 2 tablespoons of oil, and the chile pepper into a large saucepan over medium heat for 40 minutes. • Remove from the heat and let cool slightly. • Transfer to a food processor or blender and process until smooth. • Return the sauce to the saucepan. • Cook over medium heat for 5 minutes. • Remove from the heat and drizzle with the remaining oil. • Serve with pasta, gnocchi, rice, or steamed or baked vegetables.

- 2 lb/1 kg tomatoes, chopped
- 1 leek, chopped
- 2 zucchini/ courgettes, chopped
- 2 tbsp finely chopped parsley
- salt and freshly ground black pepper to taste
- 4 tbsp extra-virgin olive oil
- 1 fresh chile pepper, seeded and chopped

Serves: 6

Preparation: 10'

Level of difficulty: 1

BASIL SAUCE

- **1 large bunch fresh basil**
- **6 tbsp extra-virgin olive oil**
- **2 cloves garlic, finely chopped**
- **salt and freshly ground black pepper to taste**

Place the basil, oil, garlic, and salt in a food processor or blender and chop until very smooth. • Season with pepper. • For a traditional Italian pesto, add 2–4 tablespoons of pine nuts to the other ingredients before blending. • Serve with baked or poached fish, steamed or boiled vegetables, pasta, gnocchi, or rice.

MEAT SAUCE

Finely chop the carrots, onions, and celery together. • Sauté the chopped vegetables in the oil in a large saucepan over medium-low heat for 20 minutes. • Add the garlic and parsley and cook for 10 more minutes. • Add the beef and sauté over high heat until browned all over. • Add the wine and let it evaporate. • Stir in the tomatoes, bay leaf, rosemary, and lemon zest. Season with salt and pepper. • Cover and cook over low heat for 3 hours, stirring often. Add water or stock if the sauce begins to stick to the bottom of the pan. • Serve with pasta, rice, or polenta.

Serves: 6–8

Preparation: 30'

Cooking: 3 h 40'

Level of difficulty: 1

- **2 carrots**
- **2 red onions**
- **2 sticks celery**
- **½ cup/125 ml extra-virgin olive oil**
- **2 cloves garlic, chopped**
- **2 tbsp finely chopped parsley**
- **1 lb/500 g ground/minced beef**
- **¾ cup/180 ml dry red wine**
- **2 lb/1 kg peeled and chopped tomatoes**
- **1 bay leaf**
- **1 sprig rosemary**
- **small piece lemon zest**
- **salt and freshly ground black pepper to taste**
- **water or stock, if required**

HARISSA

S oak the chile peppers in a bowl of cold water for 1 hour. • Drain and transfer to a food processor. Add the garlic, cilantro, coriander, mint, caraway seeds, and salt. Process to make a smooth paste. • Gradually add the oil and pulse until well blended. • Transfer to a small bowl and garnish with a sprig of mint. • Use this fiery North African sauce to flavor soups or stews or serve with meat, fish, and vegetables.

52

Serves: 8–10

Preparation: 10' + 1 h to soak

Level of difficulty: 1

- 8 oz/250 g fresh red chile peppers, seeded
- 4 cloves garlic, finely chopped
- 3 tbsp finely chopped cilantro/ coriander
- 1 tbsp ground coriander
- leaves from 1 sprig mint
- 1 tbsp caraway seeds
- 1 tbsp salt
- 4 tbsp extra-virgin olive oil
- sprig of mint, to garnish

CHILE PEPPER OIL

Serves: 10–15

Preparation: 20' +
3 weeks to rest

Level of difficulty: 1

- **6–8 small hot red chile peppers**
- **6–8 cloves garlic, sliced**
- **1 tbsp rosemary leaves**
- **10 black peppercorns**
- **1 quart/1 liter extra-virgin olive oil**

Place the chile peppers, garlic, rosemary, and peppercorns into a large glass bottle with an airtight stopper. • Add the oil, seal, and let rest for 3 weeks. • The oil will remain good for several months. Store in a cool dark place. • Serve with homemade pizza, pasta, rice, or boiled or baked vegetables. Drizzle over toasted bread as a quick and tasty appetizer.

BÉCHAMEL SAUCE

Serves: 4–8

Preparation: 5'

Cooking: 10'

Level of difficulty: 2

- 2 cups/500 ml milk
- 3 tbsp butter
- 1/3 cup/50 g all-purpose/plain flour
- 1/4 tsp freshly grated nutmeg
- salt to taste

Heat the milk in a saucepan over low heat. Remove from the heat just before it begins to boil. • Melt the butter in a large saucepan over low heat. • Add the flour and stir with a wooden spoon. • Remove from the heat and add 4 tablespoons of the hot milk. Beat well with a whisk to prevent lumps from forming. • Gradually pour in the remaining milk, whisking constantly. • Return to the heat and bring to a boil over low heat. Cook for about 5 minutes, stirring constantly, until the sauce has thickened. • Remove from the heat. Season with nutmeg and salt.

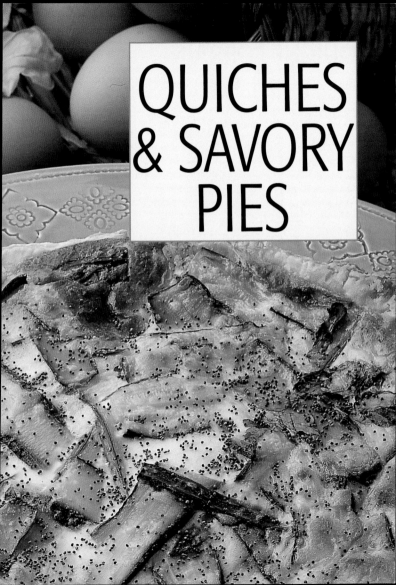

QUICHES
& SAVORY
PIES

QUICHE LORRAINE

Pastry: Sift the flour and salt into a large bowl and cut in the butter with a pastry cutter (or rub in with your finger tips), until the mixture resembles bread crumbs. • Gradually stir in enough water to make a smooth dough. • Shape into a ball and wrap in plastic wrap (cling film).

This is a classic French savory pie. It is named after the northern Lorraine region but is served all over France.

Refrigerate for 1 hour. • Preheat the oven to 350°F/180°C/gas 4. • Butter a 10-inch (25-cm) pie plate or springform pan. • Filling: Sauté the onion and pancetta in the oil in a small frying pan for 5 minutes. • Beat the eggs, egg yolks, cream, milk, salt, and pepper in a medium bowl with an electric mixer at high speed until frothy. • Roll out the pastry on a lightly floured work surface to $1/4$-inch (5 mm) thick. • Line the prepared pan with the pastry. • Sprinkle the base with the cheese and onion and pancetta mixture. • Pour in the egg mixture. • Bake for 45 minutes, or until golden brown and set. • Serve hot or at room temperature.

Serves: 6–8

Preparation: *30' + 1 h to chill*

Cooking: *50'*

Level of difficulty: *2*

PASTRY

- 2 cups/300 g all-purpose/plain flour
- ¼ tsp salt
- 1 cup/250 g butter, cut up
- 6 tbsp water

FILLING

- 1 onion, finely chopped
- 1 cup/125 g coarsely chopped pancetta or bacon
- 1 tbsp extra-virgin olive oil
- 2 large eggs
- 2 large egg yolks
- ¾ cup/180 ml heavy/double cream
- ¾ cup/180 ml milk
- salt and freshly ground black pepper to taste
- ⅓ cup/50 g freshly grated Emmental cheese

CHERRY TOMATO QUICHE

Pastry: Sift the flour and salt into a large bowl and cut in the butter with a pastry cutter (or rub in with your finger tips), until the mixture resembles bread crumbs. • Gradually stir in enough water to make a smooth dough. • Shape into a ball and wrap in plastic wrap (cling film). Refrigerate for 1 hour. • Preheat the oven to 350°F/180°C/gas 4. • Butter a 10-inch (25-cm) pie plate or springform pan. • Filling: Cut the cherry tomatoes in half and gently squeeze out as many seeds as possible. • Beat the eggs, cream, Ricotta, Parmesan, salt, and pepper in a medium bowl with an electric mixer at medium speed until well mixed. • Stir in the basil and oregano. • Roll out the pastry on a lightly floured work surface to $1/4$-inch (5 mm) thick. • Line the prepared pan with the pastry. • Pour the egg and cheese mixture over the base. Add the tomatoes one by one, cut side down, pressing them into the filling slightly. • Bake for about 45 minutes, or until golden brown and set. • Serve hot or at room temperature.

Serves: 6–8

Preparation: 30' + 1 h to chill

Cooking: 45

Level of difficulty: 2

PASTRY

- 2 cups/300 g all-purpose/plain flour
- $1/4$ tsp salt
- 1 cup/250 g butter, cut up
- 6 tbsp water

FILLING

- 15–20 cherry tomatoes
- 4 large eggs
- $1/2$ cup/125 ml cream
- $1/2$ cup/125 g fresh Ricotta cheese
- 6 tbsp freshly grated Parmesan cheese
- salt and freshly ground black pepper to taste
- 4–6 leaves fresh basil, finely chopped
- $1/2$ tsp dried oregano

ZUCCHINI AND ARUGULA QUICHE

Serves: 4

Preparation: 30'

Cooking: 55'

Level of difficulty: 2

- 8 oz/250 g frozen puff pastry, thawed
- 2 tbsp poppy seeds
- 6 zucchini/courgettes, with flowers attached
- 2 tbsp butter
- 2 eggs + 1 egg yolk
- salt and freshly ground black pepper to taste
- 1 bunch arugula/rocket, shredded
- 2/3 cup/180 ml heavy/double cream
- 8 tbsp freshly grated Parmesan cheese

Preheat the oven to 400°F/200°C/gas 6. • Butter a 10-inch (25-cm) pie plate or springform pan. • Place the pastry on a lightly floured work surface and sprinkle with 1 tablespoon of poppy seeds. Roll out into a thin sheet. • Line the prepared pan with the pastry. • Cover with a sheet of waxed paper and fill with pie weights or dried beans. • Bake blind for 20 minutes. • Trim the zucchini flowers and cut each one into 3–4 pieces. • Slice the zucchini thinly lengthwise. • Sauté the zucchini in the butter in a large frying pan over medium heat for 3 minutes. • Add the flowers and sauté for 5 minutes. • Beat the eggs and egg yolk in a medium bowl with an electric mixer at high speed until frothy. Season with salt and pepper. • Add the arugula, cream, and Parmesan. Mix in the sautéed zucchini and flowers. • Pour the mixture into the pastry case and sprinkle with the remaining poppy seeds. • Bake for 25 minutes, or until golden brown and set. • Serve hot or at room temperature.

LEEK QUICHE

Serves: 4–6

*Preparation: 30' + 1 h
to chill the dough*

Cooking: 45'

Level of difficulty: 2

PASTRY
- 1 cup/150 g all-purpose/plain flour
- $1/4$ tsp salt
- 4 tbsp butter, cut up
- 1 large egg

FILLING
- $1\frac{1}{2}$ lb/750 g leeks, finely sliced
- 2 tbsp butter
- salt and freshly ground black pepper to taste
- 3 large eggs
- 1 tbsp all-purpose/plain flour
- $2/3$ cup/150 ml heavy/double cream
- generous $3/4$ cup/200 ml milk
- $1/4$ tsp freshly grated nutmeg
- $3/4$ cup/90 g freshly grated Emmental cheese

Pastry: Sift the flour and salt into a large bowl. Use your fingers to rub in the butter until the mixture resembles coarse crumbs. • Add the egg and mix well to make a smooth dough. • Shape into a ball and refrigerate for 1 hour. • Filling: Sauté the leeks in the butter in a large frying pan over medium heat for 5 minutes until transparent. Season with salt and pepper and remove from the heat. • Beat the eggs, flour, cream, milk, and nutmeg in a large bowl. Season with salt and pepper. • Preheat the oven to 425°F/220°C/gas 7. • Butter a 10-inch (25-cm) quiche or pie pan. • Roll the pastry out on a lightly floured work surface to about $1/4$ inch (5 mm) thick. • Use the pastry to line the prepared pan. Prick all over with a fork. • Spread the leeks in the bottom of the pastry case. Pour the egg mixture over the top and sprinkle with the Emmental. • Bake for 40 minutes, or until golden brown and set. • Let rest for 5–10 minutes before serving. • Serve warm.

RUSTIC CHICKEN AND HAM PIE

Preheat the oven to 350°F/180°C/gas 4. •
Arrange the chicken, ham, onions, and shallots
in a baking dish. • Mix the stock with the cream in
a small bowl. Season with salt and pepper. • Pour
the cream mixture into the baking dish. Brush the
edges of the dish with the milk. • Roll the pastry
out into a thin layer and use it to cover the baking
dish. • Bake for 35 minutes, or until the pastry is
golden brown and puffed up. • If the pie darkens
too quickly, cover it with a sheet of aluminum foil
for the final 10 minutes of cooking. • Serve hot.

Serves: 4

Preparation: 40'

Cooking: 35'

Level of difficulty: 2

- 1 lb/500 g chicken
  breasts, cut into
  small pieces
- ¾ cup/90 g
  chopped ham
- 4 onions, finely
  chopped
- 3 shallots, finely
  chopped
- 1¼ cups/310 ml
  Chicken Stock
  (see page 226)
- ⅔ cup/150 ml
  single/light cream
- salt and freshly
  ground black
  pepper to taste
- 2 tsp milk
- 8 oz/250 g frozen
  puff pastry, thawed

SPINACH PIE

Serves: 6

Preparation: 25'

Cooking: 45'

Level of difficulty: 2

- **4 small onions, finely chopped**
- **6 tbsp extra-virgin olive oil**
- **1½ lb/650 g spinach, boiled, squeezed dry, and finely chopped**
- **1 tbsp finely chopped parsley**
- **1 tbsp finely chopped dill**
- **3 eggs, lightly beaten**
- **1 cup/250 g crumbled Feta cheese**
- **salt and freshly ground white pepper to taste**
- **10 sheets frozen phyllo dough, thawed**

Preheat the oven to 350°F/180°C/gas 4.
• Set out a 12-inch (30-cm) round baking pan.
• Sauté the onions in 3 tablespoons of oil in a large frying pan over medium heat for 8–10 minutes, or until lightly browned. • Add the spinach and sauté for 5 minutes. Transfer to a large bowl and let cool.
• Stir in the parsley, dill, eggs, and Feta. Season with salt and pepper. • Brush the phyllo sheets on both sides evenly with the remaining oil. Arrange five sheets of phyllo dough in the pan, trimming to fit. • Spoon in the spinach filling, spreading it evenly. Cover with five more dough sheets. • Use a sharp knife to make diamond-shaped cuts in the top five sheets of phyllo dough. • Bake for 25–30 minutes, or until golden brown and crispy. • Serve hot or at room temperature.

MUSHROOM AND ESCAROLE PIE

Pastry: Sift the flour and salt into a large bowl.
• Mix in the oil and enough water to make a
smooth dough. • Knead briefly on a lightly floured
work surface until smooth and elastic. • Shape into
a ball, wrap in plastic wrap (cling film) and
refrigerate for 30 minutes. • Preheat the oven to
400°F/200°C/gas 6. • Lightly oil a 9-inch (23-cm)
springform pan. • Filling: Sauté the onion in
2 tablespoons of oil in a large frying pan until
softened. • Add the mushrooms, cover, and cook
over medium heat for 15 minutes. • Add the
escarole, spinach, and marjoram. Season with salt.
• Heat the remaining oil in a saucepan. Add the
remaining flour and mix to make a paste. •
Gradually add the milk and cook over low heat for
5 minutes, stirring constantly. Season with salt.
Add the Parmesan and mix well. • Stir in the
mushroom mixture and the eggs, beating until the
eggs are well mixed in. • Divide the dough in half.
Roll it out on a lightly floured work surface into two
thin sheets. • Place one sheet of dough in the
prepared pan. Prick all over with a fork. • Pour in
the filling. Cover with the remaining pastry, sealing
the edges to enclose the pie. • Bake for about
40 minutes, or until golden brown. • Serve hot or
at room temperature.

Serves: 6

*Preparation: 45' + 30'
to chill*

Cooking: 1 h

Level of difficulty: 2

PASTRY
- 2²/₃ cups/400 g all-purpose/plain flour
- ¹/₈ tsp salt
- 5 tbsp extra-virgin olive oil
- 1 cup/250 ml warm water

FILLING
- 1 small onion, finely chopped
- 7 tbsp extra-virgin olive oil
- 10 oz/300 g chopped porcini mushrooms
- ¹/₂ head escarole, shredded
- 5 oz/150 g spinach leaves
- 2 sprigs marjoram
- ¹/₂ cup/75 g all-purpose/plain flour
- salt to taste
- 2 cups/500 ml milk
- ¹/₂ cup/60 g freshly grated Parmesan cheese

FISH AND SPAGHETTI PIE

Preheat the oven to 400°F/200°C/gas 6. • Set out a 9-inch (23-cm) springform pan. • Cook the spaghetti in a large pot of salted, boiling water until al dente. • Drain and set aside. • Sauté the swordfish, garlic, basil, and oregano in the oil in a large frying pan until the fish is tender. Season with salt and pepper. • *Use any firm-textured fish or seafood to create this delicious pie.* Add the bell pepper and spaghetti. • Roll the pastry out on a lightly floured work surface and use it to line the prepared pan. • Fill with the swordfish mixture and tomatoes. • Beat the eggs and cream in a large bowl. Season with salt and pepper. Pour the egg mixture into the pastry case. • Bake for 25–30 minutes, or until golden brown and set. • Serve hot.

Serves: 6

Preparation: 30'

Cooking: 40'

Level of difficulty: 2

- 7 oz/200 g spaghetti
- 5 oz/150 g swordfish, diced
- 1 clove garlic, finely chopped
- 1 small bunch basil, torn
- ½ tsp dried oregano
- 3 tbsp extra-virgin olive oil
- salt and freshly ground black pepper to taste
- 1 yellow bell pepper, seeded, cored, and diced
- 1 lb/500 g frozen puff pastry, thawed
- 15 cherry tomatoes, halved
- 2 eggs
- 8 tbsp single/light cream

PASTRY
- 4 cups/600 g all-purpose/plain flour
- 2 tsp salt
- 2 tbsp extra-virgin olive oil
- 1 cup/250 ml water

FILLING
- 2 lb/1 kg Swiss chard
- 2 tbsp finely chopped onion
- 1 clove garlic, finely chopped
- 1 tbsp finely chopped parsley
- ½ cup/125 ml extra-virgin olive oil
- 1 tsp finely chopped marjoram
- ¾ cup/180 g Ricotta cheese
- 5 tbsp heavy/double cream
- 1 tbsp flour
- 8 eggs
- salt and freshly ground black pepper to taste
- ½ cup/60 g freshly grated Parmesan cheese
- 2 tbsp butter

ITALIAN EASTER PIE

Preheat the oven to 375°F/190°C/gas 5.
• Set out a deep 12-inch (30-cm) springform pan. • Pastry: Sift the flour and salt into a large bowl. • Stir in the oil and enough water to make a firm dough. • Knead until smooth. Divide into 15 portions, 14 of the same size and one slightly larger.
• Filling: Cook the Swiss chard with the water clinging to the leaves for 5–7 minutes. Chop coarsely. • Sauté the onion, garlic, and parsley in 3 tablespoons of oil for 2 minutes until aromatic.
• Add the chard and cook for 5 minutes. Add the marjoram and let cool. • Mix the Ricotta, cream, flour, and 2 eggs in a large bowl. Season with salt and pepper. • Roll the larger piece of dough out to make a round large enough to line the base and sides of the pan. Place in the pan and brush with oil.
• Roll out six pieces of dough into 12-inch (30-cm) disks and place in the pan one by one, brushing with oil. • Spread with the chard and sprinkle with half the Parmesan. Drizzle with 2 tablespoons of oil and top with the Ricotta mixture. • Make 6 hollows in the filling. Place a pat of butter in each hollow, and break an egg into each, keeping the yolks intact. Season with salt and pepper, drizzle with oil, and sprinkle with the remaining Parmesan. • Roll the remaining dough into six 12-inch (30-cm) disks. Place them over the filling one by one. • Brush with oil and prick with a fork. • Bake for 50 minutes. • Serve at room temperature.

The original recipe was made using 33 sheets of pastry—one for each year of Christ's life.

ONION PIE

Sauté the onions in the butter over low heat for 25–30 minutes, stirring often, or until soft and golden brown. • Preheat the oven to 350°F/180°C/gas 4. • Set out a 12-inch (30-cm) quiche pan. • Lightly beat the egg in a medium bowl. Stir in the flour, followed by the milk, mixing well to prevent any lumps from forming. Season with salt and pepper. • Line the pan with the pastry. Cover with a sheet of aluminum foil, pressing it down carefully so that it adheres to the pastry. Fill with pie weights or dried beans. • Bake blind for 15 minutes. • Discard the foil and pie weights or beans and bake for 5 minutes more. • Spread evenly with the onion mixture and pour the egg and milk mixture over the top. • Bake for 20 minutes, or until golden brown. • Serve hot.

Serves: 6–8

Preparation: 30'

Cooking: 50'

Level of difficulty: 2

- **2 lb/1 kg onions, thinly sliced**
- **4 tbsp butter**
- **1 egg**
- **1 tbsp all-purpose/ plain flour**
- **1 cup/250 ml milk**
- **salt and freshly ground black pepper to taste**
- **8 oz/250 g store-bought short-crust pastry**

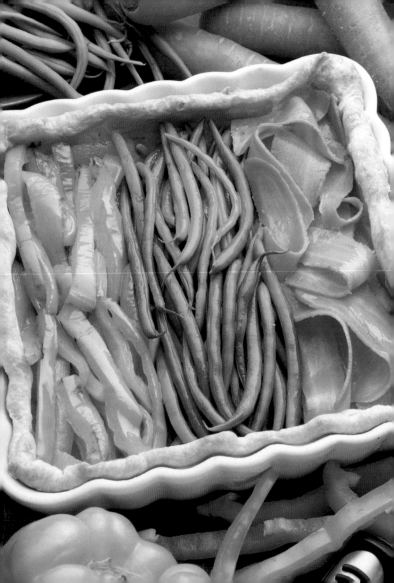

MIXED VEGETABLE PIE

Serves: 6

Preparation: 20'

Cooking: 1 h

Level of difficulty: 1

- 2 yellow bell peppers/ capsicums, seeded and cored
- 4 large carrots
- salt and freshly ground black pepper to taste
- 3 tbsp extra-virgin olive oil
- 8 oz/250 g green beans
- 2 tbsp butter
- ½ cup/125 ml dry white wine
- 8 oz/250 g frozen flaky pastry, thawed

Preheat the oven to 375°F/190°C/gas 5.
• Butter a 10 x 1-inch (25 x 2.5-cm) square pie pan. • Cut the bell peppers into thin strips and the carrots in ribbons. • Sauté the bell peppers and salt in the oil in a frying pan over high heat for 10 minutes. Remove the bell peppers and set aside. • Cook the green beans in salted, boiling water for 5 minutes, or until crunchy-tender.
• Drain and sauté the green beans in the same oil with a pinch of salt until softened. Remove from the pan and set aside. • Cook the butter, carrots, wine, and a pinch of salt in a medium frying pan until the liquid has evaporated and the carrots are softened. Set the carrots aside. • Roll the pastry out on a lightly floured surface and use it to line the prepared pan. Prick all over with a fork.
• Cover with a sheet of aluminum foil and fill with pie weights or dried beans. • Bake for 35 minutes. • Remove the foil and beans and bake for 10 minutes more. • Garnish with the vegetables and serve.

RICOTTA AND SAUSAGE PIE

Prepare the dough following the instructions on page 93. • After kneading, shape into a ball and place in an oiled bowl in a warm place for 1 hour. • Preheat the oven to 400°F/200°C/gas 6. • Butter a 9-inch (23-cm) springform pan. • Filling: Mix the Ricotta, sausage, Pecorino, and parsley in a large bowl. Season with salt and pepper. • Knead the risen dough on a lightly floured surface for 1 minute. • Break off about a third of the dough and set aside. • Roll the remaining dough into a 12-inch (30-cm) disk. Line the prepared pan with the dough. • Spread with half the filling, followed by a layer of egg. Cover with the remaining filling. • Roll the remaining dough into a disk as large as the pan and cover the filling. Seal the dish by folding the edges of the first sheet of dough over the second to make a border. • Prick the surface all over with a fork and dot with the lard. Cover with a cloth and set aside in a warm place for 30 minutes. • Bake for about 30 minutes, or until lightly golden. • Serve hot.

Serves: 6–8

Preparation: 40'

Rising time: 2 h

Cooking: 30'

Level of difficulty: 2

- **1 quantity Basic Bread Dough (see page 93)**

FILLING

- **1 cup/250 g soft Ricotta cheese**
- **4 oz/125 g cooked Italian sausage, diced**
- **3 cups/375 g freshly grated Pecorino cheese**
- **1 tbsp finely chopped parsley**
- **salt and freshly ground black pepper to taste**
- **2 hard-boiled eggs, sliced**
- **1 tbsp lard or butter**

TUNA AND SPINACH COUNTRY PIE

Prepare the dough following the instructions on page 93. • After kneading, shape into a ball and place in an oiled bowl in a warm place for 1 hour. • Filling: Cook the spinach with just the water clinging to the leaves until wilted. • Drain and squeeze out excess moisture. • Cook the cauliflower in a large pot of salted, boiling water until crunchy-tender. • Drain well. • Sauté the spinach and cauliflower in 2 tablespoons of oil in a large frying pan over medium heat for 3 minutes. • Preheat the oven to 400°F/200°C/gas 6. • Oil a deep 10-inch (25-cm) springform pan.
• Divide the dough into two unequal parts (about two-thirds/one-third) and roll out the larger piece into a $1/8$-inch (3-mm) thick round. Use the dough to line the prepared pan, slightly overlapping the edge. • Top with the spinach, cauliflower, cheese, tuna, and olives. • Roll out the smaller piece of dough to the same thickness and slightly larger than the diameter of the pan. • Place on top of the filling. Pinch the edges together, then fold them over toward the center and tuck under to make a neat rolled edge. • Brush with the remaining oil and prick with a fork. • Bake for 30–35 minutes or until the crust is golden brown. • Serve hot.

Serves: 4–6

Preparation: 45'

Rising time: 1 h

Cooking: 35'

Level of difficulty: 2

• 1 quantity Basic Bread Dough (see page 93)

FILLING
• 2 lb/1 kg spinach
• 1 medium cauliflower, trimmed, cut into small florets
• ½ cup/125 ml extra-virgin olive oil
• 7 oz/200 g Provolone or Mozzarella cheese, diced
• 6 oz/180 g canned tuna in oil, drained and flaked
• 12 black olives, pitted and coarsely chopped

ONION AND OLIVE PIE

Serves: 4–6

Preparation: 30'

Rising time: 1 h

Cooking: 50'

Level of difficulty: 2

- 1 quantity Basic Bread Dough (see page 93)

FILLING

- 2 lb/1 kg white onions, sliced
- 6 tbsp extra-virgin olive oil
- salt and freshly ground black pepper to taste
- 3 large eggs, lightly beaten
- ²/₃ cup/100 g freshly grated Parmesan cheese
- ½ cup/125 g soft creamy cheese (Caprino, Ricotta, cream cheese, Mascarpone)
- ½ cup/50 g green olives, pitted and halved

Prepare the dough following the instructions on page 93. • After kneading, shape into a ball and place in an oiled bowl in a warm place for 1 hour. • Filling: Cook the onions in 4 tablespoons of oil and a pinch of salt in a large frying pan over low heat for 15–20 minutes, or until soft and golden brown. • Let cool. • Add the eggs, Parmesan, soft cheese, olives, and pepper. Mix well. • Preheat the oven to 400°F/200°C/ gas 6. • Oil a deep 10-inch (25-cm) springform pan. • Divide the dough into two unequal parts (about two-thirds/one-third) and roll the larger piece into a ¹/₈-inch (3-mm) thick disk. Use the dough to line the prepared pan, slightly overlapping the edge. • Spread the filling over the dough.
• Roll out the smaller piece of dough to the same thickness and slightly larger than the diameter of the pan. • Place on top of the filling. Pinch the edges together, to make a neat rolled edge.
• Brush with the remaining oil. • Bake for about 30 minutes, or until golden brown. • Serve hot.

RICOTTA AND MORTADELLA PIE

P astry: Sift the flour into a bowl and make a well in the center. Add the salt, water, and oil and mix to make a smooth dough. • Preheat the oven to 425°F/220°C/gas 7. • Butter a 9-inch (23-cm) pie pan. • Break off one-third of the dough and set aside. • Roll out the larger piece of dough and use it to line the prepared dish. • Filling: Mix the mortadella and Ricotta in a large bowl. Add the eggs and season with salt and pepper. Mix in the Parmesan and Pecorino. • Spread the mixture in the pastry case. Roll out the remaining pastry to cover the pie. Moisten around the edges with water and seal, pinching the top and bottom together with your fingers. • Bake for about 35 minutes, or until golden and cooked through. • Let rest for 10 minutes before serving.

Serves: 4–6
Preparation: 35'
Cooking: 35'
Level of difficulty: 2

PASTRY
- 2 cups/300 g all-purpose/plain flour
- ½ tsp salt
- ½ cup/125 ml water
- 4 tbsp extra-virgin olive oil

FILLING
- 3 oz/90 g mortadella, chopped
- scant 1¼ cups/ 300 g Ricotta cheese
- 2 large eggs, lightly beaten
- salt and freshly ground black pepper to taste
- 2 tbsp freshly grated Parmesan cheese
- ½ cup/60 g freshly grated Pecorino cheese

Serves: 4	
Preparation: 30'	
Cooking: 45'	
Level of difficulty: 2	

BEEF AND ONION PIE

- 3 medium onions, finely chopped
- 6 tbsp extra-virgin olive oil
- 7 oz/200 g lean ground/minced beef
- salt and freshly ground black pepper to taste
- 6 sheets frozen phyllo dough, thawed

Preheat the oven to 400°F/200°C/gas 6. • Butter a 9-inch (23-cm) pie pan. • Sauté the onions in 2 tablespoons of oil in a large frying pan over medium heat for 8–10 minutes, or until lightly browned. • Add the beef and brown for 5–7 minutes. Season with salt and pepper. • Lay out the sheets of dough and cover with a damp cloth. • Place a sheet of dough in the pie pan, trimming to fit. • Top with a layer of the beef and onion filling. • Cover with another sheet of dough. Brush with oil. • Cover with another layer of filling. Repeat until all the filling is used up, finishing with a sheet of dough. • Bake for 25–30 minutes, or until golden brown. • Serve hot.

BROCCOLI AND SAUSAGE EMPANATA

Prepare the dough following the instructions on page 93. • After kneading, shape into a ball and place in an oiled bowl in a warm place for 1 hour. • Filling: Cook the broccoli in a large pot of salted, boiling water for 5 minutes, or until crunchy-tender. • Drain well. • Mix the broccoli, sausage, cabbage, salt, and chile pepper in a large bowl. • Knead 2 tablespoons of oil into the dough on a floured work surface. Roll the dough out on a lightly floured work surface ¹/₄-inch (5-mm) thick and cut out 2 large disks. • Line an oiled 9-inch (23-cm) baking pan with one of the disks and cover with the filling. • Top with the remaining disk of pastry and seal the edges well. Mix the remaining oil and water and brush all over the bread. • Let rest for 30 minutes. • Preheat the oven to 425°F/220°C/gas 7. • Bake for 45–50 minutes, or until golden brown. • Serve hot.

Serves: 6–8

Preparation: 30'

Rising time: 1 h 30'

Cooking: 55'

Level of difficulty: 3

- **1 quantity Basic Bread Dough (see page 93)**

FILLING

- **2 lb/1 kg broccoli florets**
- **8 oz/250 g sausage meat**
- **7 oz/200 g cabbage, finely shredded**
- **salt to taste**
- **¹/₄ tsp chile powder**
- **4 tbsp extra-virgin olive oil**
- **1 tbsp water**

FOCACCE
& BREAD

FILLED MINI FOCACCE

Serves: 4–6

Preparation: 30'

Cooking: 30'

Level of difficulty: 2

Preheat the oven to 350°F/180°C/gas 4. • Set out a large baking sheet. • Filling: Mix the Feta, Kefalotiri, eggs, dill, and mint in a large bowl. Season with salt. • Yogurt Pastry: Mix the flour, yogurt, and salt in a large bowl to form a smooth dough. • Roll the dough out on a lightly floured work surface to about $1/8$-inch (3-mm) thick. Cut into 3-inch (8-cm) disks. • Use a spoon to place the filling in the center of each disk. Fold in half and seal the edges by pressing down gently on them with a fork. • Arrange on the baking sheet and brush with the beaten egg. • Bake for about 30 minutes, or until golden brown. • Serve hot or at room temperature.

FILLING

- 1 cup/250 g crumbled Feta cheese
- 2 tbsp freshly grated Kefalotiri or Parmesan cheese
- 2 large eggs, lightly beaten
- 1 tbsp finely chopped dill
- 1 tbsp finely chopped mint
- salt to taste

YOGURT PASTRY

- 1²/₃ cups/250 g all-purpose/plain flour
- ¹/₂ cup/125 ml plain yogurt
- ¹/₂ tsp salt
- 1 large egg, lightly beaten

Serves: 4–6
Preparation: 20'
Rising time: 1 h
Level of difficulty: 2

BASIC BREAD DOUGH

- ½ oz/15 g fresh yeast or 1 (¼-oz/ 7-g) package active dried yeast
- 1 tsp sugar
- about ¾ cup/ 180 ml warm water
- 2⅓ cups/350 g unbleached or all-purpose or plain flour
- 1 tsp salt
- 2 tbsp extra-virgin olive oil

Mix the yeast, sugar, and half the water in a small bowl. • Let stand for 10 minutes, or until foamy. • Sift the flour and salt into a large bowl. Make a well in the center and pour in the yeast mixture, the oil, and enough of the remaining water to make a firm dough. • Place the dough on a floured work surface and knead until smooth and elastic. • Shape into a ball and place in a large bowl. Cover with a clean cloth folded in half and let rise in a warm place for 1 hour, or until the dough has doubled in volume. • Knead the dough briefly on a lightly floured surface just before using.
• Use as indicated in the recipes.

GREEN OLIVE FOCACCIA

Prepare the dough following the instructions on page 93. • After kneading, shape into a ball and place in an oiled bowl in a warm place for 1 hour. • Oil a large rectangular baking pan (a 10 x 15-inch/25 x 38-cm jelly-roll pan is ideal). • Place the dough in the pan and use your fingertips and knuckles to stretch it evenly over the bottom. • Sprinkle with the olives, garlic, mint, fennel, chile pepper, and salt. Drizzle with the oil. • Set aside in a warm place and let rise for 30 more minutes. • Preheat the oven to 350°F/ 180°C/gas 4. • Bake for about 30 minutes, or until the dough is golden brown and well cooked. • Serve hot or at room temperature.

Serves: 4–6	
Preparation: 20'	
Rising time: 1 h 30'	
Cooking: 30'	
Level of difficulty: 2	

- 1 quantity Basic Bread Dough (see page 93)
- 2 cups/200 g green olives, pitted and cut in half
- 3 cloves garlic, thinly sliced
- 1 small bunch fresh mint leaves
- 2 tbsp fennel seeds
- 1 red chile pepper, sliced
- ½ tsp salt
- 2–3 tbsp extra-virgin olive oil

FOCACCIA WITH ONIONS AND WALNUTS

Prepare the dough following the instructions on page 93. • After kneading, shape into a ball and place in an oiled bowl in a warm place for 1 hour. • Sauté the onions in the butter in a large frying pan over medium heat for 10 minutes, or until soft and golden. Season with salt and pepper and remove from the heat. • Heat the oil and the rosemary in a small pan over low heat for 3 minutes. Remove from the heat and set aside. • Oil a large rectangular baking pan (a 10 x 15-inch/25 x 38-cm jelly-roll pan is ideal). • Place the dough in the pan and use your fingertips and knuckles to stretch it evenly over the bottom. • Spread the onions over the dough. Sprinkle with the Gorgonzola and walnuts. Drizzle with the oil and rosemary. • Set aside in a warm place and let rise for 30 more minutes. • Preheat the oven to 400°F/200°C/ gas 6. • Bake for about 25 minutes, or until the dough is golden brown and well cooked. • Serve hot or at room temperature.

Serves:	4–6
Preparation:	25'
Rising time:	1 h 30'
Cooking:	35'
Level of difficulty:	2

- 1 quantity Basic Bread Dough (see page 93)
- 1½ lb/750 g onions, sliced
- 4 tbsp butter
- salt and freshly ground black pepper to taste
- 3 tbsp extra-virgin olive oil
- 1 tbsp finely chopped rosemary leaves
- 7 oz/200 g Gorgonzola cheese, crumbled
- ¾ cup/75 g chopped walnuts, toasted

BASIL FOCACCIA

Prepare the dough following the instructions on page 93, working the basil into the dough as you knead. • After kneading, shape into a ball and place in an oiled bowl in a warm place for 1 hour. • Oil a large rectangular baking pan (a 10 x 15-inch/25 x 38-cm jelly-roll pan is ideal). • Place the dough in the pan and use your fingertips and knuckles to stretch it evenly over the bottom. • Set aside in a warm place and let rise for 30 more minutes. • Preheat the oven to 400°F/200°C/gas 6. • Brush with the oil and sprinkle with the coarse sea salt. • Bake for about 25 minutes, or until golden brown and well cooked. • Serve hot or at room temperature.

Serves: 4–6
Preparation: 25'
Rising time: 1 h 30'
Cooking: 25'
Level of difficulty: 2

- 1 quantity Basic Bread Dough (see page 93)
- 6–8 tbsp finely chopped basil
- 2 tbsp extra-virgin olive oil
- 1 tsp coarse sea salt

GARBANZO BEAN FOCACCIA

Serves: 4–6

Preparation: 30' + 1 h to rest

Cooking: 30'

Level of difficulty: 2

- 1²/₃ cups/250 g garbanzo bean flour/chickpea flour
- 2 cups/500 ml water
- ½ tsp salt
- 2 tbsp extra-virgin olive oil
- freshly ground black pepper to taste

Sift the flour into a large bowl. Gradually add the water, stirring constantly, to prevent any lumps from forming. Season with salt. • Let rest for 1 hour. • Preheat the oven to 475°F/250°C/ gas 9. • Grease a 12-inch (30-cm) pizza pan with the oil. • Remove any foam from the surface of the batter with a spoon. Pour the mixture into the prepared pan. • Bake for about 20 minutes, or until lightly golden. • Season generously with pepper and serve hot.

FOCACCIA WITH TOMATOES, CHEESE, AND GREEN OLIVES

Prepare the dough following the instructions on page 93. • After kneading, shape into a ball and place in an oiled bowl in a warm place for 1 hour. • Oil a large rectangular baking pan (a 10 x 15-inch/25 x 38-cm jelly-roll pan is ideal). • Place the dough in the pan and use your fingertips and knuckles to stretch it evenly over the bottom. • Spread with the cheese. • Set aside in a warm place and let rise for 15 more minutes. • Preheat the oven to 400°F/200°C/gas 6. • Arrange the olives and tomatoes on top of the cheese. Season with salt and pepper and sprinkle with the oregano. Drizzle with the oil. • Bake for about 20 minutes, or until the dough is golden brown and well cooked. • Serve hot or at room temperature.

Serves: 4	
Preparation: 30'	
Rising time: 1 h 15'	
Cooking: 20'	
Level of difficulty: 1	

- 1 quantity Basic Bread Dough (see page 93)
- ¾ cup/180 g fresh creamy cheese
- 1½ cups/150 g pitted and chopped green olives
- 4 large tomatoes, thinly sliced
- salt and freshly ground black pepper to taste
- 1 tsp dried oregano
- 2–3 tbsp extra-virgin olive oil

MEDITERRANEAN FOCACCIA

Serves: 4

Preparation: 30'

Rising time: 1 h 15'

Cooking: 20'

Level of difficulty: 1

Prepare the dough following the instructions on page 93. • After kneading, shape into a ball and place in an oiled bowl in a warm place for 1 hour. • Oil a 12-inch (30-cm) pizza pan.
• Spread with the tomatoes and garnish with the olives and capers. Drizzle with 1 tablespoon of oil.
• Set aside in a warm place and let rise for 15 more minutes. • Preheat the oven to 400°F/ 200°C/gas 6. • Bake for about 20 minutes, or until the dough is golden brown and well cooked.
• Drizzle with the remaining oil and serve hot or at room temperature.

- **1 quantity Basic Bread Dough (see page 93)**
- **1 cup/250 g drained and chopped canned tomatoes**
- **8–12 black olives**
- **2–3 tsp salted capers, rinsed**
- **3 tbsp extra-virgin olive oil**

Serves: 4	
Preparation: 15'	
Cooking: 1 h	
Level of difficulty: 1	

QUICK OLIVE BREAD

- 1²⁄₃ cups/250 g all-purpose/plain flour
- 1 tsp baking powder
- 4 large eggs
- ½ cup/125 ml dry white wine
- ½ cup/125 ml extra-virgin olive oil
- 8 oz/250 g ham, diced
- 5 oz/150 g salt pork or lardons (fat bacon), diced
- 1½ cups/150 g thinly sliced pitted black olives
- 1¼ cups/150 g freshly grated Parmesan cheese
- salt and freshly ground black pepper to taste

Preheat the oven to 350°F/180°C/gas 4.
• Butter a 9 x 5-inch (23 x 13-cm) loaf pan.
• Sift the flour and baking powder into a large bowl. Make a well in the center and add the eggs, one at a time, stirring until just blended after each addition. Add the wine and oil and stir until smooth.
• Stir in the ham, salt pork, olives, and cheese. Season with salt and pepper. • Spoon the batter into the prepared pan. • Bake for about 1 hour, or until a toothpick inserted into the center comes out clean. • Cool the loaf in the pan for 15 minutes. Turn out onto a rack and let cool completely.

FILLED BREAD WITH OLIVES, POTATOES, AND TOMATOES

Serves: 4–6

Preparation: 30'

Rising time: 1 h

Cooking: 1 h 15'

Level of difficulty: 1

- 1 quantity Basic Bread Dough (see page 93)
- 1 large onion, finely sliced
- 6 tbsp extra-virgin olive oil
- 5 tomatoes, coarsely chopped
- salt and freshly ground black pepper to taste
- 1 lb/500 g potatoes, peeled and thinly sliced
- 1 cup/100 g pitted and chopped black olives
- $^1/_2$ cup/60 g freshly grated Pecorino or Parmesan cheese

Prepare the dough following the instructions on page 93. • After kneading, shape into a ball and place in an oiled bowl in a warm place for 1 hour. • Sauté the onion in half the oil in a large frying pan over medium heat for 2–3 minutes, or until softened. • Add the tomatoes and season with salt and pepper. Cook for 5 minutes. • Boil the potatoes in a large pot of salted, boiling water for 5 minutes. • Drain and add to the tomato mixture. Add the olives. • Preheat the oven to 400°F/200°C/gas 6. • Knead 2 tablespoons of oil into the dough on a floured work surface. Roll the dough out on a floured surface to $^1/_4$ inch (5 mm) thick. • Transfer to a large oiled baking sheet. • Sprinkle half the dough with the cheese and cover the filling, leaving a 1-inch (2.5-cm) border around the edge. • Fold the dough in half over the filling and seal the edges with your fingertips. • Mix the remaining oil with 1 tablespoon of water and brush all over. • Bake for 45–50 minutes, or until golden brown. • Serve hot.

APRICOT BREAD

Serves: 4

Preparation: 30'

Rising time: 2 h 30'

Cooking: 30'

Level of difficulty: 2

- ½ oz/15 g fresh yeast or 1 (¼-oz/ 7-g) package active dried yeast
- 1 tsp sugar
- ½ cup/125 ml warm water
- 2 cups/300 g all-purpose/plain flour
- ½ tsp salt
- 5 ripe apricots, halved
- 1 tbsp extra-virgin olive oil

Oil a 9 x 5-inch (23 x 13-cm) loaf pan. • Mix the yeast, sugar, and water in a small bowl. Let stand for 15 minutes, or until foamy. • Sift the flour and salt into a large bowl. • Stir in the yeast mixture to make a firm dough. • Knead the dough on a lightly floured work surface until smooth and elastic. • Shape into a ball and place in an oiled bowl. Cover with a cloth and let rise in a warm place for 2 hours. • Place the dough in the prepared pan and arrange the halved apricots on top. Cover and let rise for 30 minutes. • Preheat the oven to 400°F/200°C/ gas 6. • Drizzle a little oil over the surface. • Bake for about 30 minutes, or until risen and golden. • Serve hot or at room temperature.

If fresh apricots are out of season, make this delicious loaf using well-drained canned apricots.

ITALIAN FLATBREAD WITH CHEESE AND PROSCIUTTO

Sift the flour, baking soda, and salt into a large bowl. Mix in the lard and enough water to make a firm dough. • Knead the dough on a lightly floured work surface until smooth and elastic. • Return to the bowl, cover with a cloth, and let stand for 30 minutes. • Divide the dough into pieces about the size of an egg. Sprinkle with flour and roll into $1/8$-inch (3-mm) thick disks about 6 inches (15 cm) in diameter. Prick well with a fork. • Cook, one at a time, in a very hot griddle or cast-iron pan, without adding any fat. After 2–3 minutes, turn the flatbread and cook for 2–3 minutes more. • Stack the flatbread on a plate. Serve hot spread with cheese and ham.

Serves: 8–10

Preparation: 15' + 30' to rest

Cooking: 30'

Level of difficulty: 1

- 4 cups/600 g unbleached white flour
- 1 tsp baking soda
- $1/2$ tsp salt
- 6 tbsp lard, at room temperature, thinly sliced
- $1/2$ cup/125 ml warm water
- 8 oz/250 g fresh creamy cheese (goat's cheese, Mascarpone, Ricotta, Stracchino)
- 7 oz/200 g prosciutto/ Parma ham

BREAD RINGS

Serves: 12–15

Preparation: 45' + 20'
to rest the dough

Cooking: 1 h

Level of difficulty: 2

- 6²/₃ cups/1 kg all-purpose/plain flour
- 1 tbsp salt
- scant 1¼ cups/ 300 ml dry white wine
- 1 cup/250 ml extra virgin olive oil

Sift the flour and salt into a large bowl. Stir in the wine and oil to make a firm dough.
- Knead the dough on a lightly floured work surface for 15–20 minutes, until smooth and elastic. Cover and let rest for 20 minutes.
- Preheat the oven to 400°F/200°C/gas 6.
- Oil 3 large baking sheets. • Shape the dough into small batons, about ¹/₂ inch (1 cm) in diameter and 3 inches (8 cm) in length. Make into rings, pinching the ends together with your fingertips. • Cook the rings in small batches in a large pot of salted, boiling water for 2–3 minutes. • Remove with a slotted spoon and transfer to a clean cloth to dry.
- Arrange on the baking sheets. • Bake for 40 minutes, or until crisp and golden brown.

FIERY QUICK BREAD ROLLS

Mix the oil, tomatoes, olives, red pepper, and onions in a large bowl. • Add the flour, baking powder, and salt and stir to make a fairly firm dough. • Knead the dough on a lightly floured work surface until soft and smooth. Shape into a ball and let rest for 10 minutes. • Preheat the oven to 475°F/250°C/ gas 9. • Lightly oil a baking sheet. • Divide the dough into 10–12 balls and arrange on the baking sheet. • Bake for about 15 minutes, or until risen and golden brown. • Serve hot.

112

These spicy rolls hail from southern Italy. Substitute the red pepper with finely chopped rosemary, if preferred.

Serves: 8–10

Preparation: 30'

Cooking: 15'

Level of difficulty: 2

- generous ⅓ cup/ 100 ml extra-virgin olive oil
- 1 cup/250 g canned tomatoes, crushed with a fork
- 1 cup/100 g pitted black olives
- 1 tsp red pepper flakes or powder
- 2 onions, finely chopped
- 3⅓ cups/500 g all-purpose/plain flour
- 2 tbsp baking powder
- salt to taste

ZUCCHINI AND HERB QUICK BREAD

Preheat the oven to 350°F/180°C/gas 4.
• Butter a 9-inch (23-cm) springform pan.
• Slice the zucchini into very thin rounds and place in a large bowl. Season with salt. • Sift the flour and salt into a large bowl. • Mix in the eggs, butter, Parmesan, basil, thyme, parsley, and oil. Add the zucchini (and any liquid that has drained from them) and mix well. • Spoon the mixture into the prepared pan. • Bake for about 30 minutes, or until lightly golden. • Serve hot or at room temperature.

Serves: 6

Preparation: 20'

Cooking: 30'

Level of difficulty: 2

- 6 zucchini/courgettes
- salt and freshly ground black pepper to taste
- 2²/₃ cups/400 g all-purpose/plain flour
- 4 eggs
- 2 tbsp butter
- 1 tbsp freshly grated Parmesan cheese
- 4–6 leaves basil, torn
- 1 tbsp finely chopped thyme
- 1 tbsp finely chopped parsley
- 2 tbsp extra-virgin olive oil

BRAIDED CHEESE BREAD

Serves: 10–15

Preparation: 30'

Rising time: 2 h

Cooking: 30'

Level of difficulty: 2

- 1 oz/30 g fresh yeast or 2 (¼-oz/ 7-g) packages active dried yeast
- 1 tsp sugar
- 1 cup/250 ml lukewarm water
- 4 cups/600 g all-purpose/plain flour
- 2 tsp salt
- 2 cups/250 g freshly grated Pecorino or Parmesan cheese
- freshly ground white pepper to taste
- 1 large egg, lightly beaten
- 2 tbsp sesame seeds
- 2 tbsp poppy seeds

Mix the yeast, sugar, and half the water in a small bowl. • Let stand for 10 minutes, or until foamy. • Sift the flour and salt into a large bowl. Make a well in the center and pour in the yeast mixture and enough of the remaining water to make a firm dough. • Place the dough on a floured work surface and knead until smooth and elastic. • Shape into a ball and place in a large bowl. Cover with a clean cloth folded in half and let rise in a warm place for 1 hour, or until the dough has doubled in volume. • Turn out onto a floured surface and knead for 2 minutes. • Divide the dough into 4 balls. Roll each one into a 16-inch (40-cm) sausage. Fold each sausage in two and gently fold one over another to make a braid. • Place the braided dough, well spaced, on an oiled baking sheet. Brush with the egg. Sprinkle two braids with sesame seeds and two with poppy seeds. • Cover with a clean cloth and set aside in a warm place to rise for 1 hour. • Preheat the oven to 400°F/200°C/gas 6. • Bake for about 30 minutes, or the loaves are golden brown and sound hollow when tapped on the bottoms. • Remove from the oven and let cool slightly. • Serve warm.

PITA BREAD

Mix the yeast, sugar, and half the water in a small bowl. • Let stand for 10 minutes, or until foamy. • Sift the flour and salt into a large bowl. Make a well in the center and pour in the yeast mixture and enough of the remaining water to make a firm dough. • Place the dough on a floured work surface and knead until smooth and elastic, about 10 minutes. • Shape into a ball and place in a large oiled bowl. Cover with a clean cloth folded in half and let rise in a warm place for 1 hour, or until the dough has doubled in volume. • Preheat the oven to 450°F/220°C/gas 7. • Lightly oil two baking sheets. • Shape the dough into small balls, then stretch with your hands to make ¼-inch (5-mm) thick disks. • Place on the baking sheets. Spray with a little water. • Bake for 8–10 minutes, or until puffed and golden brown. • Cool on wire racks.

Pita bread is perfect with salad, cheese, and dips. For a classic touch, serve with Falafel (see page 204).

118

Serves: 8–10

Preparation: 30'

Rising time: 2 h

Cooking: 30'

Level of difficulty: 2

- 1 oz/30 g fresh yeast or 2 (¼-oz/ 7-g) packages active dried yeast
- 1 tsp sugar
- about 1½ cups/ 375 ml warm water
- 3½ cups/500 g all-purpose/plain flour
- 1 tsp salt

STARTERS

PROSCIUTTO WITH FRESH FIGS

Rinse the figs carefully under cold running water and pat them dry with paper towels. • Trim the stalks, then cut each fig into four, without cutting right through. Open the figs out a little and place them on a serving dish. • Lay the slices of prosciutto on top and serve.

Serves: 4

Preparation: 10'

Level of difficulty: 1

- **8–12 large green or black figs**
- **8–12 slices prosciutto/ Parma ham**

SALAMI WITH FRESH FIGS

Serves: 4

Preparation: 10'

Level of difficulty: 1

- **8–12 large green or black figs**
- **8–12 large slices salami**
- **fresh fig leaves, to serve (optional)**

Rinse the figs carefully under cold running water and pat them dry with paper towels. • Trim the stalks, then cut each fig into four. • Remove the rind from the salami. • If using, place the fig leaves on a large serving dish and arrange the salami and figs on top.

FIGS WRAPPED IN PANCETTA

Serves: 4

Preparation: 5'

Cooking: 20'

Level of difficulty: 1

- **12–16 ripe figs**
- **7 oz/200 g mild sliced pancetta**
- **12–16 bay leaves**

Preheat the oven to 300°F/150°C/gas 2. • Peel the figs, leaving them whole. Wrap each one in 2 or 3 slices of pancetta. Use a bay leaf threaded onto a toothpick to fix the pancetta. • Arrange the figs in a nonstick baking dish. • Bake for about 20 minutes, or until the figs are pink and a thick liquid has formed. • Transfer to serving dishes and pour the juices over the top. Serve.

PROSCIUTTO WITH CANTALOUPE

Wipe the cantaloupe with a damp cloth and cut it in half. Slice each half into 4 to 6 wedges and arrange them on a serving dish with the prosciutto. • If liked, cut the skin off the cantaloupe using a sharp knife and place the wedges of fruit back in the skins to serve.

Serves: 4

Preparation: 10'

Level of difficulty: 1

- 8–12 slices prosciutto/ Parma ham
- 1 medium cantaloupe/ rock melon

VENISON PROSCIUTTO WITH KIWI FRUIT

Serves: 4

Preparation: 10'

Level of difficulty: 1

- 1 bunch arugula/
  rocket, rinsed
  and dried
- 8 oz/250 g venison
  prosciutto, thinly
  sliced
- 6 kiwi fruit, peeled
  and thinly sliced
- 4 tbsp extra-virgin
  olive oil
- salt and freshly
  ground black
  pepper to taste

Arrange the arugula on a large flat serving dish. Place the slices of venison prosciutto over the top and cover with the slices of kiwi. • Mix the oil with salt and pepper to taste and drizzle over the prosciutto and fruit. Serve at once.

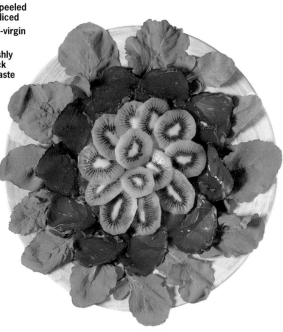

MIXED PROSCIUTTO AND DELI MEAT PLATTER

Remove the rind from the salami and the finocchiona. If you can't find finocchiona replace it with another large, tasty salami with a flavor that contrasts with the smaller salami.
• Arrange the prosciutto, salami, finocchiona, and sausages on a large serving platter. • This is a typical Tuscan appetizer; traditionally, the bread should be firm-textured and unsalted—the lack of salt contrasts beautifully with the salty garlic and herb flavors in the deli meats. • Serve with bowls of olives and pickles.

Serves: 4–6

Preparation: 10'

Level of difficulty: 1

- **4 oz/125 g finocchiona (fennel-flavored Tuscan salami) sliced fairly thickly**
- **5 oz/150 g prosciutto/ Parma ham**
- **4 oz/125 g salami**
- **6 small wild boar sausages**
- **1 lb/500 g sliced firm-textured white bread**
- **green or black olives**
- **Mediterranean pickles (capers, pickled onions, gherkins, pickled chile peppers, etc) (optional)**

POLENTA SLICES WITH ONIONS

Preheat the oven to 350°F/180°C/gas 4. • Sauté the onions in 4 tablespoons of oil in a large frying pan until light golden brown. • Season with salt and pepper. • Bake the slices of polenta for 5–10 minutes, or until they are dry and crisp. • Spoon the onion mixture onto the polenta slices and serve warm.

130

Serves: 4

Preparation: 10'

Cooking: 15'

Level of difficulty: 1

- 1 lb/500 g red or white onions, thinly sliced
- ¾ cup/180 ml extra-virgin olive oil
- salt and freshly ground black pepper to taste
- 8–12 slices cold Polenta (see page 350)

MEDITERRANEAN OLIVES

Serves: 8–10

Preparation: 15' + 4 h to stand

Level of difficulty: 1

- 10 oz/300 g mild green olives, pitted
- 1–2 cloves garlic, thinly sliced
- 1 small chile pepper, seeded and finely chopped
- 2 tsp dried oregano
- 2 bay leaves
- 4 tbsp extra-virgin olive oil
- 1 tbsp red wine vinegar

Place the olives in a small serving bowl and add the garlic, chile pepper, oregano, bay leaves, oil, and vinegar. • Stir well, then let stand for at least 4 hours before serving. This will enable the the flavors to mingle and penetrate. • The olives will keep for up to a week if stored in a tightly closed container in the refrigerator.

PANZANELLA (TUSCAN BREAD APPETIZER)

Slice the bread fairly thickly or break it into small chunks. Soak in a bowl of cold water for 5 minutes. • Drain the bread in a colander and gently squeeze out all the excess moisture. It should resemble large, damp bread crumbs. Transfer to a salad bowl. • Add the tomatoes, cucumber, onion, basil, vinegar, salt, pepper, and oil. Toss gently. • Refrigerate for at least 2 hours before serving. • Garnish with the basil and serve.

Serves: 4

Preparation: 20' + 2 h to chill

Level of difficulty: 1

- 1 lb/500 g day-old, firm-textured bread, preferably unsalted
- 4 ripe tomatoes, cut into small wedges
- 1 large cucumber, peeled and thinly sliced
- 1 medium red onion, thinly sliced
- fresh basil to taste
- 6 tbsp extra-virgin olive oil
- salt and freshly ground black pepper to taste
- 2 tbsp red wine vinegar

SALADE NIÇOISE (FRENCH TUNA, EGG, AND TOMATO SALAD)

Serves: 4–6

Preparation: 20'

Level of difficulty: 1

- 1 large lettuce heart
- 4 ripe tomatoes, cut into small wedges
- 1 large cucumber, peeled and thinly sliced
- 1 red bell pepper/ capsicum, seeded, cored and chopped
- 1 medium red onion, thinly sliced
- 15 black olives
- 8 oz/250 g tuna, preserved in olive oil, drained and crumbled
- 2–3 hard-boiled eggs, sliced
- 6 tbsp extra-virgin olive oil
- 2 tbsp red wine vinegar
- salt and freshly ground black pepper to taste

Wash the lettuce and dry well. Tear into large pieces and place in a large salad bowl. • Add the tomatoes, cucumber, bell pepper, onion, olives, tuna, hard-boiled eggs, oil, vinegar, salt, and pepper. Toss gently. • Serve at once.

BELL PEPPER CROSTINI

Cut the bell pepper into thin slices. • Sauté the anchovies with the garlic in 2 tablespoons of butter in a small frying pan until the garlic is pale gold. • Transfer to a bowl and set aside. • Sauté the bell pepper in the remaining butter in the frying pan until tender. Season with salt. • Spread the slices of bread with the anchovy mixture. • Arrange the bell pepper on top and serve warm.

134

Serves: 4

Preparation: 15'

Cooking: 10'

Level of difficulty: 1

- **1 large yellow bell pepper/capsicum, seeded and cored**
- **4–6 anchovy fillets**
- **2 cloves garlic, finely chopped**
- **6 tbsp butter**
- **4 large slices firm-textured bread, toasted**
- **salt to taste**

TOMATO AND OLIVE BRUSCHETTE

Serves: 4–8

Preparation: 10'

Cooking: 5'

Level of difficulty: 1

- 8 large slices firm-textured bread
- 3–4 large ripe tomatoes, thinly sliced
- 2–3 cloves garlic, whole
- 1 scallion/spring onion, sliced into small rings
- 12 black olives, pitted and sliced
- salt and freshly ground black pepper to taste
- 4–6 tbsp extra-virgin olive oil
- 1 small bunch fresh basil, torn

Toast the bread under the broiler (grill) or in the oven. It should dry out sufficiently to act as a rasp when you rub it with the garlic and should also be able to absorb the juice from the tomatoes without becoming soggy. • Rub each slice of toast all over with garlic. • Arrange the slices of tomato on top. • Top with the scallion and olives. Season with salt and pepper and drizzle with the oil. • Garnish with the sprigs of basil and serve.

CROSTONI WITH TOMATOES AND ANCHOVIES

Place the bread on individual serving plates. If liked, the bread can be lightly toasted in the oven so that it dries out enough to absorb the tomato juices without becoming soggy. • Use a large knife to spread the tomatoes on the bread, squashing them a little as you work. • Drizzle each piece of toast with 1 tablespoon oil and season with salt and pepper. • Top with the anchovies and serve. Do not leave the crostoni for too long before serving as they will become soggy and unappetizing.

Serves: 6

Preparation: 10'

Level of difficulty: 1

- **6 large slices firm-textured bread**
- **14 oz/400 g cherry tomatoes, coarsely chopped**
- **6 tbsp extra-virgin olive oil**
- **salt and freshly ground black pepper to taste**
- **6–12 anchovy fillets**

138

AVOCADO AND OLIVE CANAPÉS

H alve the avocado and remove the pit. Scrape out the flesh with a teaspoon and chop in a food processor or blender with the olives, almonds, garlic, and lemon juice to make a smooth cream. • Stir in the vinegar and oil. Season with the cinnamon and pepper. • Spoon the avocado cream into a pastry bag fitted with a star tip. • Squeeze the mixture out in rosettes onto the slices of bread. Garnish with the prawns and serve.

Serves: 6

Preparation: 15'

Level of difficulty: 1

- 1 avocado
- 7 oz/200 g green olives, pitted
- 4 almonds
- 1 clove garlic
- juice of ½ lemon
- 2 tbsp cider vinegar
- 1 tbsp extra-virgin olive oil
- ½ tsp ground cinnamon
- freshly ground black pepper to taste
- 6 large slices whole-wheat bread
- 18 small cooked prawns (optional)

CROSTINI WITH TUSCAN COLONNATA LARD

Serves: 4

Preparation: 15'

Cooking: 10'

Level of difficulty: 1

- 8 slices firm-textured bread
- 2–3 cloves garlic, whole
- 7 oz/200 g Colonnata lard, finely sliced
- ½ tsp dried oregano or 1–2 tsp finely chopped fresh oregano

Preheat the oven to 400°F/200°C/gas 6.
• Toast the bread in the oven until crisp and lightly browned. • Rub each slice of toast with garlic. • Lay the slices of lard on top and cook in the oven until the lard melts slightly. (If you cannot obtain the special Colonnata lard from Tuscany, use another highly-quality, seasoned lard.) • Sprinkle with oregano and serve hot.

TOMATO AND MOZZARELLA BRUSCHETTE

Serves: 4–8

Preparation: 15'

Cooking: 10'

Level of difficulty: 1

- 4 large ripe tomatoes
- 2 cloves garlic, finely chopped
- salt and freshly ground black pepper to taste
- 4 tbsp extra-virgin olive oil
- 12 oz/350 g Mozzarella cheese, sliced
- 8 large slices firm-textured bread
- 4–8 stalks chives, chopped

Preheat the oven to 400°F/200°C/gas 6. • Blanch the tomatoes in boiling water for 30 seconds. Drain and slip off the skins. Gently squeeze out as many seeds as possible. Chop the flesh coarsely. • Mix the tomato flesh and garlic in a small bowl. Season with salt and pepper and drizzle with the oil. • Spread the tomatoes on the bread and top with slices of Mozzarella. • Toast in the oven for 5 minutes, or until the Mozzarella has melted slightly and the bread is crisp and golden brown. Arrange on a serving dish and sprinkle with the chives. • Serve immediately.

CROSTINI WITH LIVER PÂTÉ AND FRESH GREEN FIGS

Serves: 6–8

Preparation: 25' + 1 h to chill

Cooking: 1 h

Level of difficulty: 2

- 1 shallot, finely chopped
- 1 clove garlic, finely chopped
- 1 cup/250 g butter
- 1 lb/500 g chicken livers, soaked in milk overnight
- 4 tbsp vin santo or dry sherry
- 4 tbsp dry white wine
- salt and freshly ground black pepper to taste
- 4 tbsp Vegetable Stock (optional) (see page 224)
- 6–8 large slices firm-textured bread, toasted
- 6–8 green figs, quartered
- 1 tbsp extra-virgin olive oil

Sauté the shallot and garlic in 1 tablespoon of butter in a large frying pan until golden. • Add the livers and cook over high heat until they change color. • Add 3 tablespoons of vin santo and the wine and let it evaporate. • Season with salt and pepper and cook over low heat for 40–45 minutes, or until the livers are almost falling apart, adding the stock (or water) if the sauce begins to stick to the pan. • Remove from the heat and chop in a food processor or blender with the remaining butter and vin santo until thick and smooth.
• Spoon the mixture into the center of a sheet of plastic wrap or aluminum foil and form into a sausage shape. • Refrigerate for 1 hour. • Serve in slices on the toasted bread. Garnish with the figs, drizzle with the oil, and season generously with pepper.

CLASSIC BRUSCHETTE

Preheat the oven to 400°F/200°C/gas 6. •
Toast the bread in the oven until crisp and
golden brown. • Rub each slice of toast with half a
clove of garlic. • Drizzle each slice with 1
tablespoon of oil and season with salt. Remember
to use only the best cold-pressed extra-virgin olive
oil, as everything in this dish depends on the quality
and freshness of the oil.

Serves: 4

Preparation: 5'

Cooking: 5'

Level of difficulty: 1

- **4 large slices firm-textured bread**
- **2 cloves garlic, whole**
- **4 tbsp extra-virgin olive oil**
- **freshly ground sea salt to taste**

CHICKEN LIVER AND MARSALA CROSTINI

Serves: 6–8

Preparation: 35' + 2 h to chill

Cooking: 20'

Level of difficulty: 2

- 1 lb/500 g chicken livers
- 1 shallot, finely chopped
- 3 bay leaves
- 2 tbsp butter
- 2 tbsp capers
- 6 tbsp marsala wine
- 1 long loaf firm-textured bread, sliced and toasted in the oven

Trim any connective tissue and discolored parts from the chicken livers and chop into small pieces. • Soften the shallot with the bay leaves in the butter in a large frying pan over medium heat. • Add the chicken livers and capers and cook over high heat for 10–15 minutes, or until the livers are cooked. • Transfer the livers to a plate. • Add the marsala to the cooking juices and cook over high heat for 3 minutes. • Discard the bay leaves. • Process the chicken livers and cooking juices in a food processor or blender until smooth. • Refrigerate for 2 hours. • Spread over the toast and serve.

SEAFOOD BRUSCHETTE

S oak the clams and mussels in cold water for
1 hour. Scrub the mussels. • Preheat the oven
to 400°F/200°C/gas 6. • Place the shellfish in a
large frying pan over medium heat and cook until
open. Discard any that do not open. • Extract all
the mollusks from the shells and set aside. • Heat
the oil in a large frying pan and sauté the parsley
and garlic for 5 minutes over low heat. • Turn the
heat up to high and add the shrimp, squid, and
cuttlefish and cook for 10 minutes, then add the
chopped tomatoes and cook for 5 more minutes.
• Add the clams and mussels, season with salt and
pepper, and cook for 2 minutes. Turn off the heat.
• Transfer the mixture to a food processor and
chop for 1 minutes. Leave the spread reasonably
chunky. • Toast the bread slices in the oven until
crisp and golden brown. • Spread the mixed fish
spread over the toasted bread and transfer to a
serving platter. • Serve warm.

Serves: 4–6

Preparation: 30' + 1 h
to soak the shellfish

Cooking: 25'

Level of difficulty: 2

- 7 oz/200 g clams,
  in shell
- 7 oz/200 g
  mussels, in shell
- 5 tbsp extra-virgin
  olive oil
- 6 tbsp finely
  chopped parsley
- 4 cloves garlic,
  finely chopped
- 4 oz/125 g
  shrimp/prawns,
  peeled and cooked
- 4 oz/125 g squid,
  cleaned and
  coarsely chopped
- 4 oz/125 g
  cuttlefish
  (optional), cleaned
  and coarsely
  chopped
- 4 small tomatoes,
  peeled and finely
  chopped
- salt and freshly
  ground black
  pepper to taste
- 12 small slices
  firm-textured white
  bread, toasted

ANCHOVY CROSTINI WITH HARD-BOILED EGGS

Serves: 6–8

Preparation: 10'

Level of difficulty: 1

- ½ cup/125 g butter, at room temperature
- 4 tbsp anchovy paste
- 3 hard-boiled eggs
- 1 long loaf firm-textured bread (a French loaf or baguette is ideal), sliced
- 2–3 tbsp salted capers, rinsed

Place the butter and anchovy paste in a small bowl and beat with a fork until smooth and creamy. • Shell the eggs and slice them with an egg-slicer, cutting the larger slices in half. • Cut the loaf into about 24 slices, spread them with a thin layer of butter and anchovy paste, and garnish with slices of hard-cooked egg and capers. • Arrange on a serving platter and serve. • If not serving immediately, keep refrigerated (but not for too long as they will become soggy and unappetizing after about 1 hour).

CLAM TOASTS

Soak the clams in a bowl of cold water for 1 hour. • Place the clams, 3 tablespoons of oil, and the whole clove of garlic in a large frying pan over medium-high heat. • Pour in the wine and cover until the clams have opened, about 5–7 minutes. • Remove the clams from the skillet, discarding any that have not opened. • Extract the clams from the open shells and place in a dish. Cover with a plate so they do not dry out too much. • Sauté the chopped garlic, parsley, and chilies in the remaining oil in a large frying pan over medium heat until the garlic is pale gold. • Add the tomatoes and cook for 15 minutes, or until the sauce has reduced. • Add the clams and stir well. • Top the bread with the clam mixture and serve.

Serves: 8

Preparation: 50' + 1 h to soak clams

Cooking: 20'

Level of difficulty: 2

- 2 lb/1 kg clams, in shell
- ²⁄₃ cup/150 g extra-virgin olive oil
- 1 whole clove garlic + 2 cloves garlic, finely chopped
- ½ cup/125 ml dry white wine
- 3 tbsp finely chopped parsley
- 2 dried red chilies, crumbled
- 5 tomatoes, seeded and finely chopped
- salt to taste
- 16 slices firm-textured bread, toasted

ANCHOVY AND GRUYÈRE TOASTS

Preheat the broiler (grill). • Cover each piece of toast with a slice of tomato and top with a quarter of the anchovies and olives. Sprinkle with the Gruyère. • Drizzle with the oil and season with pepper. • Broil (grill) the toasts about 5 inches (12 cm) from the heat source until the cheese is lightly browned and bubbling. • Serve hot.

Serves: 2–4

Preparation: 10′

Cooking: 10′

Level of difficulty: 1

- 4 slices firm-textured bread, lightly toasted
- 2 large ripe tomatoes, thinly sliced
- 4 anchovy fillets, chopped
- 20 black olives, pitted
- ¾ cup/90 g freshly grated Gruyère cheese
- 2 tbsp extra-virgin olive oil
- freshly ground black pepper to taste

BRUSCHETTE WITH CANNELLINI BEANS

Serves: 4–6

Preparation: 10' + 12 h to soak beans

Cooking: 1 h 30'

Level of difficulty: 1

- 1 lb/500 g dried white cannellini (or kidney) beans
- 4 leaves sage
- salt and freshly ground black pepper to taste
- 12 slices firm-textured bread, toasted
- 6 tbsp extra-virgin olive oil

Soak the beans in a large bowl of water for 12 hours. • Boil in a large pan of lightly salted water with the sage for about 1 hour 30 minutes, or until tender. Season with salt and pepper.
• Arrange slices of toast on individual serving plates and top with the beans, adding some of the cooking water as well to soften the bread.
• Drizzle with the oil and season with a generous grinding of pepper. • Serve warm.

SMOKED SALMON CROSTINI

Lay the smoked salmon slices in a single layer on a large serving dish, drizzle with the oil, and season with pepper (salt is not usually necessary because the smoked salmon is already quite salty).
• Add lemon juice if you wish to lighten the flavor.
• Let macerate for 20 minutes. • Preheat the oven to 425°F/220°C/ gas 7. • Toast the bread for about 5 minutes. It should not dry out too much but should be crisp on the outside and still soft inside. • Arrange the toast in a basket lined with a napkin and cover to keep it warm.
• Serve the smoked salmon and the toast and butter separately, so that your guests can help themselves.

In Italy, this dish is often served as one of several starters at elegant New Year's Eve dinner parties.

156

Serves: 8

Preparation: 10' + 20'
  to macerate

Cooking: 5'

Level of difficulty: 1

- **14 oz/400 g smoked salmon, thinly sliced**
- **4 tbsp extra-virgin olive oil**
- **freshly ground black pepper to taste**
- **1–2 tbsp fresh lemon juice (optional)**
- **1 lb/500 g white or whole-wheat (wholemeal) bread, thinly sliced**
- **7 oz/200 g best-quality butter**

TOMATO AND EGGPLANT DIP

Dice the eggplants without peeling and cook in salted boiling water for 30 minutes. • Cook the tomatoes with the oil, garlic, cumin, paprika, half the lemon juice, and salt and pepper in a medium saucepan over medium heat until the tomatoes begin to break down. • Drain the eggplant, pressing out the excess water. • Add the eggplants to the tomatoes. Mash with a fork and cook over low heat for about 20 minutes, stirring often, until all the liquid has evaporated. • Add the remaining lemon juice. • Let cool and serve with black olives and slices of toasted bread.

Serves: 6

Preparation: 20'

Cooking: 1 h

Level of difficulty: 2

- 2 lb/1 kg eggplants/ aubergines
- 1 lb/500 g tomatoes, peeled and coarsely chopped
- 5 tbsp extra-virgin olive oil
- 4 cloves garlic, finely chopped
- 1 tbsp ground cumin
- 1 tsp mild paprika
- juice of 1 lemon
- salt and freshly ground black pepper to taste

HAZELNUT SPICE MIX

Serves: 8–10

Preparation: 10'

Cooking: 10'

Level of difficulty: 1

- 1 lb/500 g sesame seeds
- 8 oz/250 g coriander seeds
- 4 oz/125 g blanched hazelnuts
- 4 oz/125 g cumin seeds
- salt and freshly ground black pepper to taste

Preheat the oven to 450°F/225°C/gas 8.
• Toast the sesame seeds, coriander seeds, hazelnuts, and cumin seeds separately for 5–10 minutes, or until lightly browned. Do not overcook. • Transfer to a food processor and chop coarsely. Season with salt and pepper.
• Serve with slices of bread or toast.

BLACK OLIVE AND ANCHOVY DIP

P lace the olives, anchovies, hard-boiled eggs, oil, 1 tablespoon of capers, the garlic, and oregano in the bowl of a food processor or blender. Chop until smooth. • Stir in the mustard and brandy. Taste the dip, seasoning with salt and pepper according to taste. Do not add salt without tasting since the olives and anchovies are already very salty and the dish may not require any extra. • Refrigerate for at least 2 hours. (This dish is best prepared the day before, so that the flavors can mingle and build. Take out of the refrigerator about 30 minutes before serving.) • Garnish with the whole capers and serve with freshly baked bread.

Serves: 6–8

Preparation: 15' + 2 h to chill

Level of difficulty: 1

- 1 lb/500 g black olives, pitted
- 8 anchovy fillets
- 2 eggs, hard-boiled
- 2 tbsp extra-virgin olive oil
- 1 tbsp salted capers + a few extra to garnish, rinsed
- 2 cloves garlic
- 1 tsp dried oregano
- ½ tsp hot mustard
- 2 tbsp brandy
- salt and freshly ground black pepper to taste

TARAMASALATA (GREEK COD ROE DIP)

Serves: 6–8

Preparation: 15' + 2 h to chill

Level of difficulty: 1

- **2 medium white potatoes, peeled and boiled**
- **5 oz/150 g cod roe**
- **1 small white onion, chopped**
- **$^2/_3$ cup/180 ml extra-virgin olive oil**
- **juice of 1 lemon**
- **salt and freshly ground black pepper to taste**
- **olives, parsley, capers, to garnish and serve**

Place the potatoes, roe, onion, oil, and lemon juice in the bowl of a food processor and chop until smooth. Add more oil if the dip is too thick. • Season with salt and pepper. • Transfer to a serving bowl, cover with plastic wrap and refrigerate for at least 2 hours before serving. • Garnish with finely chopped parsley and capers and serve with olives and freshly baked bread.

HOUMOUS

Serves: 6–8

Preparation: 15'

Level of difficulty: 1

P lace the garbanzo beans, tahini, garlic, lemon juice, and oil in the bowl of a food processor. Chop until smooth, adding enough water to obtain a creamy dip. • Season with salt and pepper. • Transfer to a serving bowl. • If liked, serve the houmous immediately but it will be tastier if refrigerated overnight. • Take out of the refrigerator 1 hour before serving. • Serve with pita bread.

- 2 (15 oz/450 g) cans garbanzo beans/chickpeas
- 3 tbsp tahini (sesame seed paste)
- 4 cloves garlic
- juice of 1 lemon
- 4 tbsp extra-virgin olive oil
- ½ cup/125 ml water
- salt and freshly ground black pepper to taste

EGGPLANT DIP

Serves: 6–8

Preparation: 15' + 1 h to chill

Cooking: 45'

Level of difficulty: 1

P reheat the oven to 400°F/200°C/gas 6. • Arrange the eggplants in a baking pan. • Roast for 45 minutes, or until the skin has blackened and the insides are tender. • Remove from the oven and let cool. • Cut the eggplants in half and use a spoon to scoop out the flesh. • Place the eggplant flesh in a large bowl with the garlic and use a fork to mash until smooth. • Mix the tahini and lemon juice in a small bowl. Pour in the water and season with salt. • Stir into the eggplant mixture along with the oil. • Refrigerate for at least 1 hour before serving.

- 2 large eggplants/ aubergines
- 3 cloves garlic, finely chopped
- ½ cup/125 ml tahini (sesame seed paste)
- juice of 2 lemons
- 4 tbsp water
- salt to taste
- 2 tbsp extra-virgin olive oil

TOMATO SORBET

B lanch the tomatoes in boiling water for 30 seconds. Drain. • Transfer to a food processor and process until smooth. • Strain the mixture through a colander to remove the seeds. • Mix the sugar and water in a medium saucepan. Bring to a boil and simmer over low heat to make a clear syrup. • Remove from the heat and let cool. • Mix in the strained tomato juice and lemon juice until well blended. Season with salt. • Pour the mixture into a ice-cream machine and freeze according to the manufacturer's instructions. • Spoon into individual dishes and freeze for 10 minutes. Garnish with sprigs of basil and serve.

If you don't own an ice-cream machine, pour the mixture into a freezerproof bowl and stir often.

166

Serves: 6–8

Preparation: 25'

Freezing: 4–6 h

Cooking: 20'

Level of difficulty: 2

- **2 lb/1 kg ripe tomatoes**
- **½ cup/100 g sugar**
- **2 cups/500 ml water**
- **juice of 1 lemon**
- **salt to taste**
- **1 bunch fresh basil, to garnish**

STUFFED BELL PEPPERS

Preheat the oven to 400°F/200°C/gas 6. •
Place the bell peppers in a roasting pan, skin-side down. Bake for 5 minutes. • Mix the capers, garlic, bread crumbs, parsley, raisins, pine nuts, oil, and salt and pepper in a medium bowl.
• Spread the mixture on the partly cooked bell peppers. • Bake for 10–15 minutes more, or until the filling begins to brown. • Serve warm.

Serves: 4

Preparation: 10'

Cooking: 20'

Level of difficulty: 1

- **4 medium yellow bell peppers/ capsicums, halved lengthwise and seeds removed**
- **2 tbsp salt-cured capers, rinsed and chopped**
- **2 cloves garlic, finely chopped**
- **¼ cup/30 g fine dry bread crumbs**
- **2 tbsp finely chopped parsley**
- **2 tbsp raisins, soaked in warm water for 1 hour, drained**
- **2 tbsp pine nuts**
- **½ cup/125 ml extra-virgin olive oil**
- **salt and freshly ground black pepper to taste**

BROILED BELL PEPPERS WITH ANCHOVY DRESSING

Serves: 4

Preparation: 25' + 1 h to rest

Cooking: 25'

Level of difficulty: 1

- 2–3 medium yellow or red bell peppers/ capsicums
- salt to taste
- 2–3 cloves garlic, thinly sliced
- 4–6 tbsp extra-virgin olive oil
- 8–10 anchovy fillets

Place the bell peppers whole under the broiler (grill) under a fairly high heat, giving them quarter turns as their skin scorches and blackens. This will take about 20 minutes, by which time the peppers will have released a lot of moisture. Wrap them in foil. Leave for 10 minutes and remove the skins. • Cut the bell peppers in half from top to bottom and discard the stalks, seeds, and the pulpy inner core. • Slice the bell peppers lengthwise into $1^1/4$-inch (3-cm) wide strips. Place in a colander, sprinkling each layer with a little salt. Let drain for at least 1 hour. • Sauté the garlic in the oil in a small frying pan over very low heat for 3–5 minutes until pale gold. • Add the anchovies, crushing them with a fork until they dissolve in the oil. Cook for 2 minutes more. • Transfer the bell peppers to a serving dish and drizzle with the anchovy dressing. • Serve at room temperature.

TZATZIKI-FILLED TOMATOES

Serves: 4–6

Preparation: 25' + 1 h to chill

Level of difficulty: 2

- **12 small ripe tomatoes**
- **salt and freshly ground black pepper to taste**
- **1 cucumber**
- **1 cup/250 ml Greek yogurt**
- **2 cloves garlic, finely chopped**
- **1 bunch mint, finely chopped**
- **2 tbsp extra-virgin olive oil**
- **1 tbsp vinegar**

Slice the tops off the tomatoes and set aside the "lids". Scoop out the flesh and seeds carefully. Sprinkle the insides with salt. • Drain the tomatoes cut-side down on paper towels. • Peel and grate the cucumber. Sprinkle with salt and drain in a colander. • Mix the yogurt, garlic, cucumber, and mint in a large bowl. Stir in the oil and vinegar and beat with a mixer at high speed until the yogurt has thickened. Season with salt and pepper. • Spoon the mixture into the tomatoes and top with the "lids." Refrigerate for at least 1 hour. • Serve chilled.

TOMATOES STUFFED WITH MUSHROOM CREAM

Slice the tops off the tomatoes. Scoop out the flesh and seeds carefully. Sprinkle the insides with salt. • Drain the tomatoes cut-side down on paper towels. • Chop the mushrooms coarsely. • Process the mushrooms with the tomato flesh, basil (reserve a few leaves to garnish), thyme, garlic, and oil until smooth and creamy. • Transfer to a large bowl. Mix in the Mascarpone, cream cheese, and mustard. Season with salt and pepper and mix well. • Stuff the tomatoes with the mushroom cream and refrigerate for at least 1 hour. • Garnish with the reserved basil leaves and serve chilled.

Serves: 4

Preparation: 30' + 1 h to chill

Level of difficulty: 2

- 8 medium tomatoes
- salt and freshly ground black pepper to taste
- 8 oz/250 g button or champignon mushrooms
- 1 bunch fresh basil
- 4 sprigs fresh thyme
- 1 clove garlic
- 2 tbsp extra-virgin olive oil
- 1/2 cup/125 ml Mascarpone cheese
- 2/3 cup/150 ml cream cheese
- 1 tsp mustard powder

FILLED GRAPE LEAVES WITH RICE AND LAMB

I f using fresh grape leaves, blanch in salted, boiling water for 30 seconds. If using preserved grape leaves, blanch in salted, boiling water for 4–5 minutes, then drain and rinse well. • Drain the leaves and lay on a clean cloth. • Place the rice in a medium bowl and cover with boiling water. Let

Grape leaves can be bought preserved in brine. If possible, buy fresh leaves in the spring and freeze. soak for 30 minutes. • Drain well and transfer to a large bowl. • Stir in the lamb, allspice, cinnamon, and 2 tablespoons of butter. Season with salt and pepper. • Lay the grape leaves out on a clean work surface, veined surface upward. • Divide the meat and rice mixture evenly among the leaves and carefully fold the leaves over to make parcels. • Place a layer of stuffed leaves seam-side down in a large saucepan. Cover with another layer. Repeat until all the stuffed leaves are in the saucepan. • Pour in the boiling water and bring to a boil over medium heat. • Simmer, covered, for about 1 hour, or until the leaves are tender and the rice is cooked. • Use a slotted spoon to remove the stuffed leaves and place them on a serving plate. Brush with the remaining 1 tablespoon butter and drizzle with the lemon juice. • Serve hot.

Serves: 6–8

Preparation: 50' + 1 h to soak

Cooking: 1 h

Level of difficulty: 2

- 12–16 fresh or preserved grape leaves
- 1¼ cups/250 g short-grain rice
- 1 lb/500 g ground/minced lamb (or beef)
- ½ tsp ground allspice
- ½ tsp ground cinnamon
- 3 tbsp butter
- salt and freshly ground black pepper to taste
- 2 tbsp fresh lemon juice

VINE LEAVES FILLED WITH MUSHROOM AND BEEF

Serves: 4–8

Preparation: 30'

Cooking: 30'

Level of difficulty: 2

- 1½ oz/40 g bread, crusts removed
- ½ cup/125 ml milk
- 10 oz/300 g porcini or white mushrooms
- 8–12 fresh or preserved grape leaves
- 1 clove garlic, finely chopped
- 6 tbsp extra-virgin olive oil
- salt to taste
- 10 oz/300 g ground/minced beef
- 2 tbsp finely chopped marjoram
- 1 tbsp finely chopped parsley
- 1 egg
- 2 tbsp freshly grated Parmesan cheese
- 6 tbsp fresh bread crumbs

Preheat the oven to 400°F/200°C/gas 6. • Oil an ovenproof baking dish. • Soak the bread in the milk until absorbed completely. Squeeze out the excess. • Scrape the mushroom stalks with a knife. Wipe with a damp cloth. Coarsely chop the stalks and caps. • If using fresh grape leaves, blanch in salted, boiling water for 30 seconds. If using preserved grape leaves, blanch in salted, boiling water for 4–5 minutes, then drain and rinse well. • Drain the leaves and lay on a clean cloth. • Sauté the garlic in 2 tablespoons of oil in a large frying pan until pale gold. • Add the mushroom stalks and season with salt. Cover and cook over medium heat for 5 minutes. Add the mushroom tops and cook for 5 more minutes.

• Mix the beef, marjoram, parsley, mushrooms, egg, bread, Parmesan, and salt in a large bowl.

• Lay the vine leaves out on a clean work surface, veined surface upward. • Divide the meat mixture evenly among the leaves and carefully fold the leaves over to make parcels. • Transfer to the prepared baking dish, placing the filled leaves seam-side down. • Sprinkle with the bread crumbs and drizzle with the remaining oil. • Bake for about 35 minutes, or until the meat is cooked and the vine leaves are tender. • Serve hot.

This nutritious dish is very filling and can be served as a main course for 2–4 people.

179

MUSHROOM VOL-AU-VENTS

Sauté the mushrooms and parsley in the butter in a large frying pan over medium heat for 5 minutes. • Sprinkle with the flour and add the stock. Season with salt and pepper. Cook over low heat until the mushrooms are tender. • Beat the egg yolks with the water in a small bowl. Pour the egg mixture into the pan. Cook over low heat, stirring constantly, until well mixed. • Preheat the oven to 350°F/180°C/gas 4. • Arrange the pastry cases on a baking sheet. • Bake for 10–12 minutes, or until risen and golden. • Fill the cases with the mushroom mixture. Sprinkle with the Parmesan. • Serve warm.

Serves: 6–8
Preparation: 25'
Cooking: 30'
Level of difficulty: 2

- 1¼ lb/575 g mushrooms, coarsely chopped
- 2 tbsp finely chopped parsley
- 2 tbsp butter
- 1 tbsp all-purpose/ plain flour
- 4 tbsp Vegetable Stock (see page 224)
- salt and freshly ground black pepper to taste
- 2 egg yolks
- 1 tbsp water
- 30 frozen vol-au- vent cases
- 2 tbsp freshly grated Parmesan cheese

SHRIMP VOL-AU-VENTS

Serves: 8–10

Preparation: 25'

Cooking: 30'

Level of difficulty: 2

- 2 oz/60 g shrimp (prawn) tails
- 2 tbsp butter
- 3 tbsp all-purpose/ plain flour
- 1 cup/250 ml milk
- few drops lemon juice
- 1 tbsp chopped chives
- 1 teaspoon paprika
- salt and freshly ground black pepper to taste
- 36 small vol-au-vent cases

Preheat the oven to 400°F/200°C/gas 6. • Bring a small pan of salted water to a boil over medium-high heat. • Plunge in the shrimp tails and cook for 1 minute. Drain and let cool. Peel and coarsely chop. • Melt the butter in a pan over low heat. Add the flour and cook over low heat for 2 minutes, stirring constantly. • Remove from the heat and pour in the milk all at once. Place over a slightly higher heat and cook until thickened, stirring constantly. • Remove from the heat and stir in the chopped shrimp, lemon juice, chives, paprika, salt, and pepper. Let cool slightly.

• Fill the cases with the shrimp mixture. Arrange in a lightly greased ovenproof dish. • Bake for about 10 minutes, or until the pastry is golden brown.

• Serve hot or at room temperature.

CREAMY PEA VOL-AU-VENTS

Melt 4 tablespoons of butter in a large saucepan over low heat. • Add the flour and mix well. • Remove from the heat and add 4 tablespoons of the hot milk. • Gradually pour in the remaining milk, stirring constantly. • Return to the heat and bring to a boil over low heat. Cook for about 5 minutes, stirring constantly, until the sauce has thickened. • Remove from the heat and let cool. Mix in the egg yolks. Season with nutmeg and salt and pepper. • Sauté the onion in the remaining butter in a medium saucepan until golden. • Add the peas and cook, stirring, for 1 minute. • Pour in the stock and add the ham. Simmer over medium-high heat for 40 minutes. • Drain well. Mix the peas and ham into the Bèchamel. Add the Parmesan. • Preheat the oven to 350°F/180°C/gas 4. • Arrange the pastry cases on a baking sheet. • Bake for 10–12 minutes, or until risen and golden. • Fill the cases with the pea mixture. • Serve warm.

Serves: 6

Preparation: 40'

Cooking: 1 h

Level of difficulty: 2

- ²/₃ cup/150 g butter
- 4 tbsp all-purpose/ plain flour
- 2 cups/500 ml milk, hot
- 2 egg yolks
- ⅛ tsp freshly grated nutmeg
- salt and freshly ground black pepper to taste
- 1 small onion, finely chopped
- 3 lb/1.5 kg shelled peas
- 3 cups/750 ml Vegetable Stock (see page 224)
- ½ cup/60 g chopped ham
- ¾ cup/90 g freshly grated Parmesan cheese
- 30 frozen vol-au-vent cases

JELLIED VEGETABLES

B oil the peas in a large pot of salted, boiling water. • Drain and cool. • Soften the gelatin in cold water for 15 minutes. • Drain and dissolve in the hot water. • Stir the gelatin into the stock. • Cut four tomatoes in half and slice the remainder. • Cut the bell pepper into thin slices. • Slice the carrots into thin rounds. • Pour a little gelatin into a ring mold and freeze for 5 minutes. • Arrange a layer of the tomato halves and peas in the prepared mold. Pour in enough gelatin to cover and return to the freezer. • Arrange slices of tomato around the edges, alternating with carrot slices. • Pour in more gelatin and freeze again. • Fill with the remaining vegetables and gelatin. Freeze for at least 3 hours. • Immerse the mold in boiling water and turn out onto a serving dish.

Serves: 4–6

Preparation: 50' + 3 h 30' to freeze

Cooking: 10'

Level of difficulty: 2

- 2 cups/250 g peas
- 6 sheets leaf gelatin
- 6 tbsp hot water
- 2 cups/500 ml Vegetable Stock (see page 224)
- 8 ripe tomatoes
- 1 yellow bell pepper/capsicum, seeded and cored
- 2 carrots
- 4 tbsp dry white wine

CHILLED LAYERED VEAL AND HAM TERRINE

Put the veal between two sheets of greaseproof paper and flatten with a meat tenderizer.
• Trim them to size so that they will fit into a deep cake pan about 8 inch (20 cm) in diameter when laid out flat. Make sure that the ham and mortadella slices will also fit into it in the same way. • Butter the pan. • Layer the ingredients in the pan, starting with a slice of veal in the bottom, followed by a slice of ham and then mortadella. Sprinkle each layer liberally with freshly ground pepper and Parmesan. • Place another slice of veal on top. Pour the beaten eggs over it, then follow with another veal slice, the second ham slice, and the second slice of mortadella. Sprinkle each layer with pepper and Parmesan. Finish with the last veal slice, pressing the layers down in the cake pan. • Cover with aluminum foil and place the cake pan in a large roasting pan. Add enough boiling water to the roasting pan to come one-third of the way up the sides of the cake pan (or place in a steamer). Cook for 2 hours. • Carefully pour off the cooking juices into a shallow, straight-sided dish. Turn the molded, layered meat out onto a serving dish and place a large, flat plate on top of it. Place a weight on the plate and leave to cool to room temperature. • Chill the mold and its juices, separately, in the refrigerator for 3 hours. • Serve, carved in thin, vertical slices. Garnish with the jellied cooking juices.

Serves: 6

Preparation: 20' + 3 h to chill

Cooking: 2 h

Level of difficulty: 2

- 4 veal escalopes, each weighing about 5 oz/150 g
- 2 slices lean ham, each weighing about 5 oz/150 g
- 2 slices mortadella, each weighing about 5 oz/150 g
- freshly ground black pepper to taste
- scant 1 cup/100 g freshly grated Parmesan cheese
- 2 eggs, beaten

BRANDIED LIVER TERRINE

Serves: 8

Preparation: 25'

Cooking: 20'

Level of difficulty: 2

- 1 head red chicory or radicchio
- 7 oz/200 g chicken livers
- 7 oz/200 g calves' livers, chopped
- ⅔ cup/150 g butter
- 1 bunch thyme
- 4 leaves sage
- ⅓ cup/50 g all-purpose/plain flour
- 6 tbsp brandy
- salt and freshly ground black pepper to taste
- 7 oz/200 g red and yellow plums, pitted
- pink peppercorns, to garnish

Line a pudding mold with chicory leaves. • Pat the livers lightly with the flour. • Cook the livers in 1 tablespoon of butter with the thyme and sage in a large frying pan over high heat until browned all over. • Pour in the brandy and cook for 4–5 minutes, or until evaporated. Season with salt and pepper. Remove from the heat. • Discard the herbs and chop the livers coarsely. • Process the livers with their cooking juices and the remaining butter until smooth. • Dice the plums, reserving 1 whole for garnish. Add the diced plums to the processor. • Pour the mixture into the prepared mold. Cover with plastic wrap (cling film). • Refrigerate for at least 3 hours. • Garnish with the whole plum, cut into slices, and peppercorns.

VEGETABLE TERRINE

Soften the gelatin in the water. • Cook the green beans in a large pot of salted, boiling water for 7 minutes. • Drain and let cool. • Blanch the leek in boiling water for 1 minute. • Drain and pat dry on paper towels. • Cut the leek into thin strips. • Arrange half the celery and leek in layers in a 2-quart (2-liter) loaf pan, followed by half the zucchini, half the carrots, and the green beans. Repeat in the same order until all the vegetables are used. • Heat the water with the gelatin over medium heat, stirring often, until the mixture begins to thicken. • Let cool (but not solidify), then pour slowly over the vegetables, making sure it reaches the bottom of the pan. • Refrigerate for 2 hours. • Sauce: Blanch the tomato in boiling water for 30 seconds. Slip off the skin and gently squeeze out the seeds. Transfer to a food processor or blender and process with the oil and vinegar. Season with salt and pepper. • Serve the terrine in slices with the sauce in a separate bowl.

Serves:	6
Preparation:	40'
Chilling:	2 h
Cooking:	10'
Level of difficulty:	3

- 2 envelopes powdered gelatin
- 3¼ cups/800 ml water
- 8 oz/250 g green beans, topped and tailed
- white of 1 leek
- 3 oz/90 g celery heart, cut into thin strips
- 5 oz/150 g zucchini/ courgettes, cut into thin strips
- 7 oz/200 g carrots, cut into thin strips

SAUCE
- 1 large tomato
- 3 tbsp extra-virgin olive oil
- 1 tbsp white wine vinegar
- salt and freshly ground black pepper to taste

BULGUR AND VEGETABLE TERRINE

Preheat the oven to 325°F/170°C/gas 3. • Butter a loaf pan and sprinkle with bread crumbs. • Soak the bulgur in a large bowl of cold water for 10 minutes. • Drain and cook the bulgur in a large pot of salted, boiling water for 5 minutes. • Drain and let cool. • Cook the asparagus in salted, boiling water for 5 minutes. • Drain. • Cook the carrot in salted, boiling water for 10 minutes. • Drain. • Process the chicken, tarragon, and lemon zest in a food processor or blender until smooth. • Transfer to a large bowl and mix in the egg yolks, 4 tablespoons of cream, and bulgur. Season with salt and pepper. • Beat the egg whites in a large bowl until stiff. Gently fold them into the mixture. • Spoon the mixture into the prepared pan, alternating the bulgur mixture with the asparagus and carrots. • Cover with aluminum foil and place in a baking dish half-filled with boiling water. • Cook for 1 hour. • Let cool completely. • Turn out onto a serving platter. • Mix the mayonnaise with the remaining cream and the lemon juice and serve with the slices of terrine.

Serves: 4–6

Preparation: 40'

Cooking: 90'

Level of difficulty: 2

- 8 oz/250 g bulgur (cracked wheat)
- 7 oz/200 g asparagus tips, diced
- 1 carrot, diced
- 7 oz/200 g cooked chicken breast
- 2 sprigs tarragon
- ½ lemon
- 2 eggs, separated
- ⅔ cup/150 g heavy/double cream
- ⅔ cup/150 ml mayonnaise
- salt and freshly ground black pepper to taste

CHEESE AND SESAME PUFFS

Stir the flour, baking powder, paprika, salt, and pepper in a medium bowl. • Stir in the eggs, followed by the cheese and ham. • Use a teaspoon to shape the mixture into balls. Refrigerate for at least 4 hours. • Roll the balls in the sesame seeds. • Heat the oil to very hot in a deep fryer. • Fry the balls in batches for 5–7 minutes, or until puffed and golden brown. • Drain well on paper towels and serve hot.

Serves: 6

Preparation: 20' + 4 h to chill

Cooking: 20'

Level of difficulty: 1

- ½ cup/75 g all-purpose/plain flour
- ½ tsp baking powder
- ½ tsp paprika
- salt and freshly ground black pepper to taste
- 2 large eggs
- 1 cup/125 g freshly grated firm-textured cheese, such as Cheddar
- ½ cup/60 g coarsely chopped ham
- 6 tbsp toasted sesame seeds
- 2 cups/500 ml olive oil, for frying

COD CROQUETTES

Serves: 6

Preparation: 20'

Cooking: 1 h

Level of difficulty: 2

- 2 lb/1 kg potatoes, peeled and coarsely chopped
- 1 lb/500 g salt cod, presoaked, and crumbled
- ½ cup/125 ml milk
- 1 tbsp butter
- ⅛ tsp freshly grated nutmeg
- 2 tbsp finely chopped parsley
- 2 eggs + 1 egg, separated
- 1 cup/125 g freshly grated Parmesan cheese
- 1 cup/125 g fine dry bread crumbs
- 2 cups/500 ml olive oil, for frying

Boil the potatoes in salted water until tender, 15–20 minutes. Drain well. • Cook the cod, potatoes, milk, butter, and nutmeg in a large saucepan over low heat, stirring often, for about 5 minutes. • Remove from heat and let cool. • Stir in the parsley, 1 whole egg, 1 egg yolk, and cheese. • Shape the mixture into croquettes. • Use a fork to beat the remaining egg and egg white in a small bowl. Place the bread crumbs in a small bowl. • Dip the croquettes in the egg, then roll in the bread crumbs. • Heat the oil to very hot in a deep fryer. Fry the croquettes in batches for 5–7 minutes, or until golden brown. • Drain well on paper towels and serve hot.

197

CHICKEN BITES

Soak the bread in the milk in a small bowl for 5 minutes. Drain well, squeezing out the excess. • Mix the chicken, soaked bread, and egg in a large bowl. Season with salt and pepper. • Use your hands to bind the mixture and shape into balls the size of large marbles. • Roll the balls in the flour. • Heat the oil to very hot in a large deep frying pan. • Fry the chicken balls in batches for 5–7 minutes, or until golden brown all over. • Drizzle with the lemon juice just before serving. • Serve hot.

Serves: 4–6

Preparation: 20'

Cooking: 25'

Level of difficulty: 1

- **2 slices white sandwich bread, crusts removed**
- **4 tbsp milk**
- **2 ground/minced chicken breasts**
- **1 large egg, lightly beaten**
- **salt and freshly ground black pepper to taste**
- **½ cup/75 g all-purpose/plain flour**
- **1 cup/250 ml olive oil, for frying**
- **juice of ½ lemon**

FRIED KEFTA

Mix the beef, ginger, garlic, chiles, onion, egg, turmeric, cilantro, and mint in a large bowl until well blended. • Stir in the grated potato. Season with salt. • Shape the mixture into balls the size of golf balls. • Let rest for 30 minutes. • Heat the oil in a deep fryer to very hot. • Fry the kefta in batches for 8–10 minutes, or until brown all over. • Drain well on paper towels. • Serve hot.

Serves: 4–6

Preparation: 40' + 30' to rest

Cooking: 30'

Level of difficulty: 1

- 1 lb/500 g ground/minced beef or lamb
- 1 tbsp freshly grated gingerroot
- 2 cloves garlic, finely chopped
- 2 green chile peppers, finely chopped
- 1 small onion, finely chopped
- 1 egg, lightly beaten
- 1 tsp ground turmeric
- 2 tbsp finely chopped fresh cilantro/coriander
- 4 leaves fresh mint, finely chopped
- 1 large potato, coarsely grated
- salt to taste
- 2 cups/500 ml oil, for frying

PORK AND GRAPE BITES

Serves: 4–6

Preparation: 30'

Cooking: 20'

Level of difficulty: 2

- 1 clove garlic
- 2 leaves sage
- 2 sprigs rosemary
- 1 lb/500 g ground/ minced pork
- ½ tsp fennel seeds, crushed
- salt and freshly ground black pepper to taste
- about 16 large seedless white grapes
- ⅔ cup/100 g breadsticks, crumbled (or dried bread crumbs)
- 2 cups/500 ml olive oil, for frying

Chop the garlic, sage, and the leaves of a sprig of rosemary. • Place the pork in a bowl and add the chopped herbs and fennel seeds. Season with salt and pepper. • Wash and dry the grapes. Carefully peel each one. • Form the pork mixture into balls about the size of walnuts. Make a hollow in the center and place a grape in the center. Close up the meatball. • Finely chop the remaining rosemary and mix with the crumbed breadsticks. • Roll the meatballs in the mixture until well coated. • Heat the oil in a deep fryer to very hot. • Fry the meatballs in small batches for 5–7 minutes, or until golden all over. • Drain well on kitchen paper. • Arrange on a serving dish and serve hot.

FALAFEL (BEAN RISSOLES)

White broad beans are available in many Greek or Mediterranean specialty stores. If you can't find them, substitute with the same quantity of garbanzo beans (chickpeas). Soak the beans in a large bowl of cold water for 24 hours. • Drain well and process with the onion, garlic, potato, and parsley in a food processor until coarsely chopped. • Add the coriander, cumin, and flour, and process until well blended. • Season with salt and pepper. • Let rest for 2 hours. • Stir the baking powder into the mixture and shape into flattened patties. • Heat the oil in a deep frying pan to very hot. • Fry the patties in batches for 5–7 minutes, or until golden brown. • Drain well and pat dry on paper towels. • Serve warm with pita bread filled with sliced tomatoes and lettuce.

These rissoles, now ubiquitous throughout the Middle East, probably originated with the Copts, in Egypt.

Serves: 4–6

Preparation: 30' + 24 h to soak + 2 h to rest

Cooking: 30'

Level of difficulty: 2

- 1 lb/500 g dried white broad beans, soaked and drained
- 1 red onion
- 3 cloves garlic
- 1 medium potato, peeled
- 1 bunch parsley
- 1 tsp coriander seeds
- 1 tsp cumin seeds
- 2 tbsp all-purpose/ plain flour
- salt and freshly ground black pepper to taste
- 1 tsp baking powder
- 2 cups/500 ml olive oil, for frying

TUNA BRIK

Serves: 4

Preparation: 20'

Cooking: 15'

Level of difficulty: 3

Use a fork to crumble the tuna into a medium bowl. Stir in the onion, parsley, and capers. • Place a sheet of dough on a lightly floured surface. Place half a second sheet on top. Fold to make a square. • Use a tablespoon to place a quarter of the tuna filling in the center of the dough. Carefully break an egg over. Fold the dough over diagonally to form a triangle. Seal the edges well by folding them over repeatedly. • Heat the oil to very hot in a large frying pan. • Fry the brik in batches for 5–7 minutes, or until golden brown all over. • Drain well on paper towels. Garnish with the lemon slices and serve hot.

- ½ cup/100 g canned tuna, packed in olive oil, drained
- 1 onion, finely chopped
- 1 tbsp finely chopped parsley
- 10 salt-cured capers, rinsed and chopped
- 6 sheets frozen phyllo dough, thawed and cut into 8-inch/20-cm squares
- 4 large eggs
- ½ cup/125 ml olive oil, for frying
- 1 lemon, thinly sliced, to garnish

Serves: 8–10	
Preparation: 25' + 1 h to stand and chill	
Cooking: 50'	
Level of difficulty: 2	

- 2 lb/1 kg finely ground bulgur
- 2 lb/1 kg ground/ minced beef
- 1 large onion, finely chopped
- 1/2 tsp freshly grated nutmeg
- 1/2 tsp ground cinnamon
- salt and freshly ground black pepper to taste

FILLING

- 4 medium onions, finely chopped
- 4 tbsp extra-virgin olive oil
- 1 lb/500 g ground/ minced lamb
- salt to taste
- 1/2 tsp ground cinnamon
- 1/2 tsp ground allspice
- 2 cups/500 ml olive or sesame oil, for frying

STUFFED KIBBE BALLS

Place the bulgur in a bowl and cover with cold water. Let stand for 30 minutes. • Drain well. • Mix the beef, onion, bulgur, nutmeg, and cinnamon in a large bowl. Season with salt and pepper. • Mix well. Refrigerate for 30 minutes. • Filling: Sauté the onions in the extra-virgin oil in a frying pan for 8–10 minutes, or until lightly browned. • Add the lamb and season with salt, cinnamon, and allspice. Cook until the meat has browned. Set aside. • Scoop out enough of the bulgur mixture to form balls the size of golf balls. • Make a hollow in the center, working until you have a shell of even thickness. • Spoon in a little meat filling and close up the opening. Repeat until both mixtures are used up. • Heat the oil in a deep fryer to very hot. Fry the balls in batches for 8–10 minutes, or until browned all over. Drain on paper towels. • Serve hot.

RICE PANCAKES WITH TOMATO SAUCE

Serves: 4

Preparation: 40'

Cooking: 1 h 15'

Level of difficulty: 2

- 1 cup/200 g brown rice
- 1 (15 oz/450 g) can tomatoes
- 6 tbsp extra-virgin olive oil
- 1 clove garlic, finely chopped
- 1 sprig fresh basil, torn
- salt and freshly ground black pepper to taste
- 1 onion, finely chopped
- ½ cup/75 g all-purpose/plain flour
- 1 egg, lightly beaten
- scant ½ cup/ 100 ml milk
- ½ cup/50 g chopped walnuts
- grated zest of 1 orange
- 1 small bunch parsley, finely chopped

Cook the rice in a large pot of salted, boiling water for 45 minutes, or until tender. • Drain well and set aside. • While the rice is cooking, place the tomatoes in a medium saucepan with 2 tablespoons of oil and the garlic and basil. Season with salt and pepper and cook over medium-low heat until the oil separates from the tomatoes, about 30 minutes. • Sauté the onion in 1 tablespoon of oil in a medium frying pan until softened. • Mix the flour, egg, salt, and pepper in a medium bowl. Gradually beat in enough milk to make a thick batter. • Mix in the rice, onion, walnuts, orange zest, and parsley. • Heat the remaining oil in a frying pan. • Drop heaping tablespoons of the rice mixture into the hot oil, shaping it into slightly flattened disks with a wooden spoon. • Fry until golden on both sides. • Serve hot with the tomato sauce served separately.

BRIOUATS

Place the cheese, butter, eggs, and thyme in a saucepan. Season with salt and pepper. Cook over medium heat for 5–7 minutes, or until thickened. • Cut the dough into 4-inch (10-cm) wide sheets. • Place a spoonful of the filling about 1 inch (2.5 cm) from the top edge of each sheet. Fold over one of the corners to form a triangle over the filling, fold this triangle down over the remaining strip of dough, then fold it across, and then down again, leaving a final triangle of dough to fold onto the parcel which now consists of three layers of pastry. Brush the edges with the beaten yolk and seal. • Heat the oil to very hot in a deep fryer. • Fry the briouats in two or three batches for 5–7 minutes, or until golden brown. • Drain on paper towels and serve hot.

Serves: 6

Preparation: 20'

Cooking: 30'

Level of difficulty: 3

- 1²/₃ cups/400 g goat's cheese
- 4 tbsp butter, melted
- 7 large eggs + 1 large egg yolk, lightly beaten
- 2 tsp finely chopped fresh thyme
- salt and freshly ground black pepper to taste
- 10 sheets frozen phyllo dough, thawed
- 2 cups/500 ml olive oil, for frying

GARBANZO BEAN FRITTERS

Serves: 4

Preparation: 15'

Cooking: 40'

Level of difficulty: 1

- **2 quarts/2 liters cold water**
- **2²/₃ cups/400 g garbanzo bean/ chickpea flour**
- **salt to taste**
- **5 tbsp finely chopped parsley**
- **1 cup/250 ml olive oil, for frying**

Pour about two-thirds of the water into a blender. Add the garbanzo bean flour and process, adding more water as needed to form a pouring batter. • Pour the mixture into a saucepan. Season with salt and bring slowly to a boil, stirring almost constantly. • Continue cooking for about 30 minutes, stirring often, until it is very thick, soft, and smooth. Stir in the parsley. • Lightly oil a baking sheet or large shallow pan. • Use a spatula to spread the mixture evenly to a thickness of about $1/4$ inch (5 mm). • Let cool completely, then cut into short strips or squares. • Heat the oil to very hot in a large frying pan. • Fry the fritters in batches until golden brown on both sides.
• Drain well and serve hot.

FRIED MORTADELLA

Serves: 6–8

Preparation: 15' + 2 h
  to soak

Cooking: 10'

Level of difficulty: 1

C ut the mortadella slices into quarters and place
in a bowl. Add enough milk to cover and let
stand for 2 hours. • Drain the mortadella. Dry with
paper towels and coat with flour. • Lightly beat the
egg and season with salt, pepper, and nutmeg.
• Dip the mortadella in the egg, followed by the
bread crumbs. • Heat the oil in a deep frying pan
to very hot. • Fry the mortadella until golden
brown all over. • Drain well on paper towels
and serve hot.

- 4 slices of
  mortadella/
  Bologna sausage,
  ¼-inch/5-mm
  thick
- 2 cups/500 ml
  warm milk
- ⅔ cup/100 g all-
  purpose/plain flour
- 1 egg
- salt and freshly
  ground black
  pepper to taste
- ⅛ tsp freshly
  grated nutmeg
- ¾ cup/90 g fine
  dry bread crumbs
- 1 cup/250 ml
  sunflower oil,
  for frying

Serves: 4

Preparation: 10'

Cooking: 10'

Level of difficulty: 2

- 3 eggs
- salt and freshly ground black pepper to taste
- 8 slices sandwich bread
- 12 oz/400 g Mozzarella cheese
- 2 oz/60 g salt-cured anchovy fillets, rinsed
- 1/3 cup/50 g all-purpose/plain flour
- 1 cup/250 ml olive oil, for frying

FRIED MOZZARELLA TRIANGLES

Beat the eggs in a bowl. Season with salt and pepper. • Cut the slices of bread and the Mozzarella into triangles. Arrange an anchovy and a slice of Mozzarella on each slice of bread. Fasten them to the bread with a toothpick. • Dip the bread slices in flour and then in the beaten egg. • Heat the oil in a large frying pan to very hot. Fry the bread, Mozzarella-side down, for 30 seconds. Turn and fry until golden brown all over. • Drain well on paper towels. Remove the toothpicks before serving. • Serve hot with salad.

SEAFOOD SALAD

C lean the mussels thoroughly, removing the
beards. • Cook the mussels in a large pot over
medium heat for 5–10 minutes, or until they open
up. • Discard any that do not open. • Shell them
and set aside. • Cook the shrimp with the garlic
and 1 tablespoon of oil in a large saucepan over
medium heat for 2 minutes. Shell them and let
cool. • Steam the cod for 5 minutes, or until
tender. Let cool. • Cook the octopus in 1 cup
(250 ml) of salted, boiling water, 1 tablespoon of
oil, and the vinegar over medium heat for 20
minutes. • Drain and chop coarsely. • Beat the
lemon juice, the remaining oil, and salt in a small
bowl. • Arrange the mussels, shrimp, cod,
octopus, onion, and celery in a large salad bowl.
Drizzle with the oil and lemon. • Refrigerate until
ready to serve.

Serves: 4–6

Preparation: 30'

Cooking: 40'

Level of difficulty: 2

- **12 oz/350 g
  mussels, cleaned**
- **12 oz/350 g
  shrimp/prawns**
- **1 clove garlic,
  finely chopped**
- **4 tbsp extra-virgin
  olive oil**
- **12 oz/350 g cod
  fillets**
- **12 oz/350 g baby
  octopus, cleaned**
- **1 tbsp white wine
  vinegar**
- **1 tbsp fresh lemon
  juice**
- **salt to taste**
- **1 large onion, finely
  sliced, soaked in
  cold water for
  10 minutes,
  drained**
- **1 head celery,
  finely chopped**

OYSTERS WITH CAVIAR

A rrange the oysters on a large flat serving dish. Place on a platter covered with a layer of ice. • In a small bowl, mix the mayonnaise, puréed tomatoes, lemon juice, salt, and pepper. • Divide the sauce equally between the oysters, top with a little caviar, and serve.

This luxurious dish is a staple in the fish restaurants of southern France, between Nice and Marseilles.

Serves: 4

Preparation: 10'

Level of difficulty: 1

- **12 oysters, in half shells**
- **½ cup/125 ml mayonnaise**
- **1 tbsp puréed tomatoes (passata)**
- **few drops lemon juice**
- **salt and freshly ground black pepper to taste**
- **6–12 tbsp caviar**

VENETIAN CRAB APPETIZER

Clean the crabs by brushing them with a stiff brush under cold running water. Rinse well.
• Cook the crabs in salted, boiling water for 10 minutes. • Insert the tip of a strong knife in the underside, just under the eyes, and lever out the central section of the undershell. Keep the colored, top portions of the shells as "serving dishes." • Take all the flesh out of the shells, discarding the grayish, feathery lungs and reserving the "coral," or eggs. Cut the white flesh into small pieces. • Use special pincers or a nutcracker to break the hard shell of the legs and claws and take out all the flesh. • Mix the lemon juice, oil, parsley, and salt and pepper in a small bowl. • Wash and dry the empty shells, then arrange them upside-down on a serving dish. Fill with the crab flesh. Top with the coral as a garnish. Drizzle with the dressing and serve.

Serves: 6

Preparation: 20'

Cooking: 10'

Level of difficulty: 1

- **6 fairly small spider crabs**
- **juice of 1 lemon**
- **2 tbsp extra-virgin olive oil**
- **2 tbsp finely chopped flat-leaf parsley**
- **salt and freshly ground white pepper to taste**

220

SOUPS

BEEF STOCK

P ut all the vegetables, the meat, bones, and salt in a large pot with the water. • Bring to a boil over high heat. Lower heat to medium-low and simmer for about 2 hours. • Remove the bones and meat. Set the meat aside. • As the stock cools, fat will form on top and can be scooped off and discarded. • Use the stock as indicated in the recipes or boil with soup pasta (1–2 tablespoons per person) and serve an Italian classic— *Minestrina in brodo.*

Makes: about 2 quarts/2 liters

Preparation: 10'

Cooking: 2 h

Level of difficulty: 1

- **1 large carrot**
- **1 medium onion**
- **1 large stalk celery**
- **4 small tomatoes**
- **5 sprigs parsley**
- **10 leaves basil**
- **2 lb/1 kg lean boiling beef + 2 lb/ 1 kg beef bones**
- **1–2 tsp salt**
- **3 quarts/3 liters water**

VEGETABLE STOCK

H eat the oil in a medium saucepan. Add the onion, carrot, leek, celery, tomato, and parsley. • Cover and sauté over low heat for about 5 minutes. • Add the peppercorns, and bay leaf. Season with salt. • Pour in the water, cover, and simmer over low heat for about 1 hour. • Strain through a fine mesh strainer and discard the vegetables.

T he two stocks on this page and the ones on page 226 can be prepared in advance and frozen. Freeze in ice-cube trays so that you will always have fresh homemade stock on hand.

Makes: about 1 1/2 quarts/1.5 liters

Preparation: 10'

Cooking: 1 h

Level of difficulty: 1

- **2 tbsp extra-virgin olive oil**
- **1 medium onion**
- **1 carrot**
- **1 leek, trimmed and cut in 4 pieces**
- **2 celery stalks with their leaves**
- **1 small tomato**
- **6 sprigs parsley**
- **5 peppercorns**
- **1 bay leaf**
- **1 tsp salt**
- **2 quarts/2 liters water**

CHICKEN STOCK

Put the chicken, whole, in a very large pot. Add the carrots, onion, celery, tomatoes, parsley, salt, and peppercorns. Cover with the cold water and simmer over medium-low heat for 3 hours. The water should barely move. • Strain the stock, discarding the vegetables. • To remove the fat, in part or completely, let the stock cool, then refrigerate for about 2 hours. The fat will solidify on the top and can easily be scooped off.

Makes: about 2 quarts/2 liters

Preparation: 10' + 2 h

Cooking: 3 h

Level of difficulty: 1

- 1 chicken (about 4 lb/2 kg)
- 2 medium carrots
- 1 onion, studded with 5 cloves
- 1 large stalk celery
- 4 small tomatoes
- 5 sprigs parsley
- 1–2 tsp salt
- 5 peppercorns
- 3 quarts/3 liters water

FISH STOCK

Put the water in a large pot and add the fish trimmings, onion, carrot, celery, tomato, parsley, bay leaf, lemon slice, wine, coarse salt, and peppercorns. • Bring to a boil over medium-high heat, then lower the heat to medium and cook for 20 minutes, removing the foam at regular intervals with a slotted spoon. • Strain the stock and use as indicated in the recipes.

Makes: 1 quart/1 liter

Preparation: 15'

Cooking: 50'

Level of difficulty: 1

- 2 quarts/2 liters water
- 1 lb/500 g fish trimmings (heads, scales, skin, shells)
- 1 onion, chopped
- 1 carrot, chopped
- 1 stalk celery,
- 1 medium tomato
- 1 bunch parsley
- 1 bay leaf
- 1 large slice lemon
- ½ cup/125 ml dry white wine
- 1 tsp salt
- 6 peppercorns

COOL PEAR SOUP

Peel and core the pears. Place in a bowl with water and lemon juice to prevent them from turning brown. • Cook the peel and cores with half the stock in a large saucepan for 5 minutes. • Discard the peel and cores and return the stock to the pan. • Chop the pears coarsely (reserving a few slices to garnish) and add to the stock. Add the leek, potato, ginger, watercress, and the remaining stock. Cover and simmer over low heat for 30 minutes. • Remove from the heat and let cool. • Chop the soup in a food processor or blender until smooth. • Refrigerate for 1 hour. • Mix in the Ricotta and cream. Season with salt, pepper, and nutmeg. • Garnish with the reserved slices of pear and a few sprigs of fresh parsley.

Serve this light and tasty soup at lunch with a green salad, Pecorino cheese, and freshly baked bread.

228

Serves: 4

Preparation: 25' + 1 h to chill the soup

Cooking: 35'

Level of difficulty: 2

- **6 sweet eating pears**
- **juice of 1 lemon**
- **3 cups/750 ml Chicken Stock (see page 226)**
- **1 leek, thinly sliced**
- **1 potato, diced**
- **½ tsp finely chopped gingerroot**
- **1 bunch watercress**
- **8 tbsp very fresh Ricotta cheese**
- **1 cup/250 ml heavy/double cream**
- **salt and freshly ground black pepper to taste**
- **⅛ tsp freshly grated nutmeg**
- **fresh parsley, to garnish**

CHILLED TOMATO AND YOGURT SOUP

Serves: 4

Preparation: 20' + 1 h to chill the soup

Cooking: 1'

Level of difficulty: 1

- 3 cups/750 ml tomato juice
- 2 cups/500 ml plain yogurt
- 2 tomatoes
- 2 scallions/spring onions, thinly sliced
- 1 green bell pepper/capsicum, seeded, cored, and diced
- salt and freshly ground black pepper to taste
- 6 ice cubes

Mix the tomato juice and yogurt (straight from the fridge) in a large bowl until well blended. • Cover with plastic wrap and refrigerate for 15 minutes. • Blanch the tomatoes in boiling water for 30 seconds. • Drain, slip off the skins, and gently squeeze out as many seeds as possible. Chop coarsely. • Add the chopped tomatoes, scallions, and bell pepper to the soup. Season with salt and pepper. • Refrigerate for 45 minutes. • Add the ice cubes before serving.

CREAM OF CELERY SOUP

Sauté the leeks in the oil in a large saucepan over medium heat for 5–7 minutes, or until lightly browned. • Add the celery and pour in the stock and water. • Continue cooking for about 25 minutes, or until the celery is tender. • Process in a food processor until smooth. • Season with salt and pepper and return to the heat for 5 minutes. • Ladle the soup into serving bowls and sprinkle with the croutons. • Serve hot.

Serves: 6
Preparation: 20'
Cooking: 40'
Level of difficulty: 2

- 2 lb/1 kg leeks, white parts only, sliced
- 2 tbsp extra-virgin olive oil
- 2 lb/1 kg celery, coarsely chopped
- 3 cups/750 ml Beef Stock (see page 224)
- 3 cups/750 ml water
- salt and freshly ground black pepper to taste
- 6 tbsp croutons

CREAMY ALMOND SOUP

Serves: 4

Preparation: 15'

Cooking: 35'

Level of difficulty: 1

- **3 medium onions, finely chopped**
- **2 tbsp butter**
- **2 tbsp all-purpose/ plain flour**
- **1 quart/1 liter Chicken Stock (see page 226)**
- **½ cup/75 g finely ground almonds**
- **½ cup/125 ml heavy/double cream**
- **salt and freshly ground white pepper to taste**

Sauté the onions in the butter in a large saucepan over medium heat for 5–7 minutes, or until softened. • Add the flour and stir until well blended. • Pour in the stock and cook for 5 minutes. • Add the almonds and cook for 20 minutes more, stirring often. • Stir in the cream and season with salt and pepper. • Serve hot.

CHILLED TOMATO SOUP WITH FRESH HERBS

Blanch the tomatoes in a large pot of boiling water for 30 seconds. Drain and slip off the skins. • Cut in half and gently squeeze out as many seeds as possible. • Process the tomatoes, onion, garlic, and herbs (reserve 1–2 tsp herbs, to garnish) with the water and oil in a food processor or blender until smooth. • Season with salt and pepper. • Refrigerate for at least 2 hours. • Pour into individual bowls and garnish with the herbs. • Serve chilled.

Serve this refreshing soup for lunch during the summer with a freshly baked French baguette.

234

Serves: 4

Preparation: 20' + 2 h to chill the soup

Level of difficulty: 1

- 1 lb/500 g firm ripe tomatoes
- 1 onion, quartered
- 1 clove garlic, peeled and left whole
- 2–3 tbsp chopped fresh mixed herbs (basil, chervil, oregano, mint, tarragon, parsley, thyme)
- 2 cups/500 ml water
- ½ cup/125 ml extra-virgin olive oil
- salt and freshly ground black pepper to taste

COOL BELL PEPPER AND CUCUMBER SOUP

Remove the crusts from the slices of bread. Crumble it a little and place in a small bowl with the water. Let soak for 5 minutes. • Cut the tomatoes in half and gently squeeze out as many seeds as possible. • Chop the softened bread, tomatoes, cucumber, green bell pepper, celery, basil (reserving a few leaves to garnish), garlic, and oil in a food processor or blender until smooth. • Season with salt and pepper and stir in the sherry. • Refrigerate for 1 hour before serving. • Garnish with the yellow bell pepper and reserved basil. • Serve with toasted bread drizzled with the extra oil and sprinkled with the oregano.

Serves: 4

Preparation: 25' + 1 h to chill

Level of difficulty: 1

- 3 slices bread
- 1 cup/250 ml water
- 1 lb/500 g firm ripe tomatoes
- 1 cucumber, peeled and coarsely chopped
- 1 green bell pepper/capsicum, seeded, cored, and coarsely chopped
- 7 oz/200 g celery stalks
- 1 bunch basil
- 3 cloves garlic
- 4 tbsp extra-virgin olive oil + extra to drizzle on the toast
- salt and freshly ground black pepper to taste
- 3 tbsp sherry
- 1 small yellow bell pepper/capsicum, seeded, cored, and diced, to garnish
- 8 slices toasted bread, to serve
- 1 tsp dried oregano

CHILLED BARLEY AND RED ONION SOUP

C ook the barley in a large pot of salted, boiling water for 50 minutes. • Drain. • Sauté the onions in 3 tablespoons of oil in a large saucepan until golden. • Season with salt and add the chile powder. • Blanch the tomatoes in boiling water for 30 seconds. • Drain, slip off the skins, and remove the seeds. Chop coarsely and add to the onions. • If the mixture is too thick, add 4 tablespoons of barley cooking water. • Add the barley and refrigerate for at least 1 hour. • Sauté the garlic and sage in the remaining oil in a small saucepan over low heat until aromatic. • Remove from the heat and drizzle over the soup.

Serves: 6

Preparation: 25'

Cooking: 1 h

Level of difficulty: 2

- 1 cup/150 g pearl barley
- 5 oz/150 g red onions, coarsely chopped
- 7 tbsp extra-virgin olive oil
- salt to taste
- 1/8 tsp chile powder
- 2 lb/1 kg firm ripe tomatoes
- 1 bunch sage
- 2 cloves garlic, lightly crushed but whole

TUSCAN BREAD SOUP

Serves: 4
Preparation: 25'
Cooking: 50'
Level of difficulty: 1

- 1 lb/500 g firm ripe tomatoes
- 1 red onion
- 1 carrot
- 1 stalk celery
- 6 tbsp extra-virgin olive oil
- salt and freshly ground black pepper to taste
- 14 oz/400 g day-old bread, broken into pieces
- 1 hot red chile pepper, crumbled
- 1 quart/1 liter water
- 1 cup/125 g freshly grated Parmesan cheese

Blanch the tomatoes in boiling water for 30 seconds. • Drain, slip off the skins, and remove the seeds. Chop coarsely. • Finely chop the onion, carrot, and celery. • Sauté the onion, carrot, and celery in 4 tablespoons of oil in a large saucepan until lightly browned. • Stir in the tomatoes. Season with salt and pepper and cook over medium heat for about 15 minutes. • Add the bread and chile pepper. Pour in the water and bring to a boil. • Simmer over low heat for 30 minutes. • Drizzle with the oil and sprinkle with the Parmesan. Season generously with pepper. • Serve hot or at room temperature.

CREAM OF CARROT SOUP

Sauté the carrots in 2 tablespoons of butter in a large frying pan over medium heat for 8–10 minutes, or until lightly browned. • Pour in the water and season with salt and pepper. Sprinkle with the sugar. • Bring to a boil and lower the heat. Cover and cook for 15–20 minutes, or until the carrots are very soft. • Drain well. • Use a fork to mash the carrots. • Mix the carrots and stock in a large saucepan. • Bring to a boil and cook over low heat for 5–10 minutes, or until the carrots have almost dissolved into the stock. • Melt the remaining butter in a small saucepan over low heat. Stir in the flour until smooth and continue cooking until the mixture is lightly browned, about 5 minutes. • Pour in the milk, all at once, stirring constantly. Cook for 5–7 minutes, or until the mixture thickens. • Remove from the heat. Stir in the egg yolks, one at a time, until just blended after each addition. • Pour the egg mixture into the stock and cook for 5 minutes. • Season generously with pepper and serve hot.

Serves: 4–6

Preparation: 20'

Cooking: 50'

Level of difficulty: 2

- 1½ lb/750 g carrots, thinly sliced
- 4 tbsp butter
- 2 cups/500 ml water
- salt and freshly ground black pepper to taste
- 1 tsp sugar
- 2 quarts/2 liters Chicken Stock (see page 226)
- 2 tbsp all-purpose/ plain flour
- ⅔ cup/150 ml milk
- 3 large egg yolks

240

BLACK CABBAGE AND CORNMEAL SOUP

Serves: 4

Preparation: 10'

Cooking: 1 h 10'

Level of difficulty: 2

- **2 red onions, finely chopped**
- **2 fresh chile peppers, thinly sliced**
- **7 tbsp extra-virgin olive oil**
- **2 bunches black cabbage leaves, shredded**
- **1 tbsp tomato concentrate/purèe**
- **1 quart/1 liter hot water**
- **1²⁄₃ cups/250 g finely ground yellow cornmeal**

Sauté the onions and chile peppers in the oil in a large saucepan over medium heat for about 5 minutes, or until the onions are transparent.
- Add the cabbage and cook for 5 minutes.
- Stir in the tomato concentrate and cook for 5 minutes. Pour in the water and mix well.
- Cover and cook for 15 minutes. • Gradually sprinkle in the cornmeal, stirring constantly. Cook and stir for about 45 minutes, or until the cornmeal is well cooked. • Serve hot.

SPICY BREAD SOUP

Serves: 4

Preparation: 20'

Cooking: 45'

Level of difficulty: 1

- 2 red onions
- 1 sprig parsley
- 1 clove garlic
- 2 stalks celery
- 7 tbsp extra-virgin olive oil
- 2 anchovies in oil, chopped
- 8 tomatoes, peeled, seeded, and chopped
- 4 leaves basil, torn
- 1 finely chopped red chile pepper
- 1 quart/1 liter Vegetable Stock (see page 224)
- salt to taste
- 8 slices day-old bread, broken up into pieces
- 1 tbsp salt-cured capers, rinsed
- anchovy fillets and basil, to garnish

Finely chop the onions with the parsley, garlic, and celery. • Sauté the chopped vegetables in 6 tablespoons of oil in a large saucepan for about 5 minutes, or until the onion is transparent. • Add the anchovies, tomatoes, basil, chile pepper, 4 tablespoons of stock, and salt. • Cook for 20 minutes. • Add the remaining stock and the bread. • Cook for 20 minutes, stirring often, until the bread has broken down and blended in with the other ingredients. • Sprinkle with the capers and drizzle with the remaining oil. Garnish with basil leaves and anchovies. • Serve hot or at room temperature.

HAM AND CORN SOUP

Blanch the tomatoes in boiling water for 30 seconds. • Drain, slip off the skins, and gently squeeze out as many seeds as possible. Chop coarsely. • Process the tomatoes with 12 oz (350 g) of corn until smooth. • Sauté the onion and bell pepper in the oil in a large saucepan over low heat for 2–3 minutes, or until softened. • Pour in the stock and add the chile powder, remaining corn, and the tomato and corn mixture. Season with salt. Cook for 20 minutes. • Drizzle with the lemon and garnish with the ham. • Serve hot or at room temperature.

Serves: 4

Preparation: 20'

Cooking: 25'

Level of difficulty: 2

- 1 lb/500 g firm ripe tomatoes
- 15 oz/450 g canned corn/ sweetcorn
- 1 onion, finely chopped
- 1 small red bell pepper/capsicum, seeded, cored, and diced
- 2 tbsp extra-virgin olive oil
- 1 quart/1 liter Chicken Stock (see page 226)
- 1 tsp chile powder
- salt to taste
- 2 tbsp lemon juice
- 3½ oz/100 g ham, cut into thin sticks

MUSHROOM SOUP

Serves: 4

Preparation: 20'

Cooking: 30'

Level of difficulty: 1

Sauté the onion in the oil in a large saucepan over medium heat for 5–7 minutes, or until translucent. • Stir in the mushrooms and garlic. Cook for 3–5 minutes, or until the mushrooms have softened slightly. • Add the buckwheat and bay leaf. Pour in the water. • Bring to a boil, lower the heat, and simmer for 20 minutes. • Season with salt and pepper. Swirl in the sour cream, if using, and garnish with the thyme. • Serve hot.

- 1 medium onion, finely chopped
- 4 tbsp extra-virgin olive oil
- 6 oz/180 g mixed wild mushrooms, thinly sliced
- 2 cloves garlic, finely chopped
- 3 oz/90 g buckwheat, well-washed
- 1 bay leaf
- 1 quart/1 liter water
- salt and freshly ground black pepper to taste
- 4 tbsp sour cream, to garnish (optional)
- 1 tbsp finely chopped thyme, to garnish

Serves: 8

Preparation: 20'

Cooking: 1 h

Level of difficulty: 2

- **14 oz/400 g finely shredded green cabbage**
- **2 large red or white onions, finely chopped**
- **½ cup/125 ml extra-virgin olive oil**
- **1½ quarts/ 1.5 liters Chicken Stock (see page 226)**
- **¾ cup/125 g finely ground yellow cornmeal**
- **salt and freshly ground black pepper to taste**

CABBAGE AND CORNMEAL SOUP

B lanch the cabbage in a large pot of salted, boiling water for 3 minutes. • Drain well and set aside. • Sauté the onions in the oil in a large saucepan over medium heat for 8–10 minutes, or until lightly browned. • Stir in the cabbage and cook, stirring often, for 8 minutes. • Bring the stock to a boil in a large saucepan. Gradually add the cornmeal, stirring constantly to prevent lumps from forming. • Lower the heat and continue cooking for about 30 minutes, or until thick and smooth. • Add the cabbage mixture and cook for 10 minutes more. • Season with salt and pepper. • Serve hot.

SUMMER MINESTRONE

Blanch the tomatoes in boiling water for 30 seconds. • Drain, slip off the skins, and gently squeeze out as many seeds as possible. Chop coarsely. • Sauté the leeks in the oil in a large saucepan for 5 minutes, or until lightly golden. • Add the potatoes, carrots, celery, and peas. Sauté over high heat for 5 minutes.

Filled with light and nourishing vegetables, this is the perfect soup for hot summer days.

250

• Pour in the stock and bring to a boil. • Lower the heat and simmer for 30 minutes. • Add the bell peppers, zucchini, and tomatoes and cook for 20 more minutes. Sprinkle with the herbs and season with salt and pepper. • Sprinkle with the Parmesan flakes. • Serve hot or at room temperature.

- 2 tomatoes
- 2 leeks, finely chopped
- 4 tbsp extra-virgin olive oil
- 2 potatoes, diced
- 2 carrots, diced
- 1 stalk celery, diced
- 1¼ cups/150 g frozen peas
- 2 quarts/2 liters Vegetable Stock (see page 224)
- 1 red bell pepper/capsicum, seeded, cored, and diced
- 1 yellow bell pepper/capsicum, seeded, cored, and diced
- 2 zucchini/ courgettes, diced
- 1 sprig marjoram, finely chopped
- 1 sprig basil, torn
- 1 sprig parsley, finely chopped
- salt and freshly ground black pepper to taste
- 2 oz/60 g Parmesan cheese, flaked

COUNTRY VEGETABLE SOUP

Serves: 6

Preparation: 40' +
12 h to soak beans

Cooking: 2 h 30'

Level of difficulty: 2

- 4 cups/400 g
  dried beans
- 1 sage leaf
- 1 sprig rosemary
- 1 sprig parsley
- 1 bay leaf
- 2 potatoes,
  coarsely chopped
- 1 carrot, coarsely
  chopped
- 1 onion
- 1 stalk celery
- 1 clove garlic
- 2 quarts/2 liters
  water
- 5 oz/150 g firm
  ripe tomatoes
- ½ cup/60 g diced
  pancetta
- 2 tbsp extra-virgin
  olive oil
- salt and freshly
  ground black
  pepper to taste
- cubes of toasted
  bread, to serve
  (optional)

Soak the beans in a large bowl of cold water for 12 hours or overnight. • Drain and transfer to a large saucepan. • Tie the herbs in a bunch and place all the vegetables and garlic in the pan. Cover with the water and cook for about 2 hours. • Discard the herbs. • Blanch the tomatoes in boiling water for 30 seconds. • Drain and slip off the skins. • Transfer the vegetables and their cooking liquid to a food processor or blender with the tomatoes and process until smooth. Reserve 2 tablespoons of beans for a garnish. • Return the mixture to the saucepan. Bring to the boil and simmer for 20 minutes. • Sauté the pancetta in the oil in a small frying pan over medium heat for 2 minutes. • Season the soup with salt and pepper. • Garnish with the reserved beans and the pancetta. • Serve hot or at room temperature with the cubes of toasted bread, if liked.

NORTH AFRICAN SOUP WITH DRIED FRUIT

Serves: 4

Preparation: 30'

Cooking: 2 h

Level of difficulty: 1

- 2 lb/1 kg stewing lamb or beef, with the bone
- 2 quarts/2 liters water
- salt and freshly ground black pepper to taste
- 1 large onion, finely chopped
- 2 tbsp clarified butter (ghee)
- 2 tsp ground turmeric
- 1 cup/250 g dried prunes, pitted
- ½ cup/125 g dried apricot halves
- ½ cup/125 g coarsely chopped dried peaches
- ⅓ cup/70 g firmly packed dark brown sugar
- 2 tbsp fresh lime juice

Use a sharp knife to cut the lamb or beef into small chunks. • Place in a large pot with the bone and water. Bring to a boil and season with salt and pepper. • Cover and cook for about 1 hour 30 minutes, or until the meat is very tender. • Discard the bone. • Sauté the onion in the butter in a large frying pan over medium heat for 5–7 minutes, or until softened. Add the turmeric. • Stir the onion mixture, prunes, apricots, and peaches into the soup. • Cook for 30 minutes. • Stir in the brown sugar and lime juice. • Serve hot.

BULGUR AND LAMB SOUP

Place the bulgur in a bowl and cover with cold water. Let stand for 30 minutes. • Drain well. • Sauté the onions in the oil in a large saucepan over medium heat for 8–10 minutes, or until lightly browned. • Add the lamb and brown for 10 minutes. • Pour in the water and cook for 10 minutes more. • Stir in the tomatoes and cinnamon. Season with salt and pepper. Cook for 10 minutes. • Add the bulgur and cover and cook for 20 minutes, or until the lamb is very tender. • Remove the cinnamon sticks and season generously with pepper. • Serve hot.

Serves: 4

Preparation: 15' + 30' to stand

Cooking: 1 h

Level of difficulty: 1

- ½ cup/125 g fine-grind or medium-grind bulgur
- 2 medium onions, finely chopped
- 2 tbsp extra-virgin olive oil
- 1½ lb/750 g lamb, cut into small chunks
- 1¼ quarts/1.25 liters water
- 5 medium tomatoes, peeled and finely chopped
- 4 sticks cinnamon
- salt and freshly ground black pepper to taste

NORTH AFRICAN FISH SOUP

Serves: 6–8

Preparation: 30' + 15' to marinate the fish

Cooking: 55'

Level of difficulty: 1

P lace the fish in a large bowl and drizzle with the lemon juice. Add half the saffron and sprinkle with salt. Stir well and set aside for 15 minutes.
• Sauté the bell peppers in the oil in a large saucepan over medium heat for 8–10 minutes, or until slightly softened. • Transfer to a plate and set aside. • In the same pan, cook the onions, garlic, tomatoes, celery, carrot, fennel, bay leaf, and orange zest for 5 minutes. • Pour in the water and bring to a boil. Add the fish and simmer for 15–20 minutes, or until cooked. • Remove the fish from the pan and cover with a serving plate to keep warm. • Return the stock to a boil and add the bulgur. Cook for 15–20 minutes, or until tender.
• Remove from the heat, and stir in the capers, remaining saffron, and cumin. • Place the fish in individual soup bowls and ladle the soup over the top. • Serve hot.

- 2 lb/1 kg mixed firm-textured fish, cleaned, boned, and cut into pieces
- 1½ tbsp fresh lemon juice
- 4–6 threads saffron, crumbled
- ½ tsp salt
- 3 large red bell peppers/ capsicums, seeded and cut into strips
- 4 tbsp extra-virgin olive oil
- 2 onions, finely chopped
- 4 cloves garlic, chopped
- 4 large ripe tomatoes, finely chopped
- 1 stalk celery, chopped
- 1 carrot, chopped
- 4 sprigs wild fennel
- 1 bay leaf
- grated zest of 1 orange
- 2 quarts/2 liters water
- ¼ cup/50 g bulgur
- 20 capers
- ¼ tsp cumin seeds

Serves: 4

Preparation: 15'

Cooking: 90'

Level of difficulty: 3

- 2 oz/60 g cabbage, shredded
- scant 1/3 cup/60 g rice
- 2 large egg yolks
- generous 1/3 cup/ 100 ml sour cream
- juice of 1 lemon
- 1 lb/500 g lean lamb meat, cut into small cubes
- 1 large carrot, peeled and chopped
- 1 large parsnip, peeled and chopped
- 1 large potato, peeled and chopped
- 1 onion, chopped
- 2 cloves garlic, finely chopped
- 1 bay leaf
- salt and freshly ground black pepper to taste
- 1 tbsp allspice
- 2 tbsp finely chopped parsley
- 5 peppercorns

CROATIAN LAMB SOUP

Cook the cabbage in a pot of salted boiling water for 5–10 minutes, or until tender.
• Drain well. • Cook the rice in a small saucepan of salted, boiling water until al dente. • Drain well.
• Beat the egg yolks, sour cream, and lemon juice in a large bowl. • Place the meat in a large saucepan and cover with water by about 1 inch (2.5 cm). Bring to a boil over medium heat. Skim off any froth. • Add the carrot, parsnip, potato, onion, garlic, bay leaf, salt, pepper, and allspice. Mix well and bring to a boil. Lower the heat and simmer for 35–40 minutes, or until the meat is tender. • Remove the meat and vegetables with a slotted spoon and set aside. • Add the egg mixture to the stock and beat well. • Return the meat and vegetables to the saucepan. Add the rice and cabbage. • Stir in the parsley and sprinkle with peppercorns. • Serve hot.

CHUNKY POTATO SOUP WITH PANCETTA

Sauté the onion and pancetta in the butter in a large saucepan over medium heat for 3 minutes until lightly browned. • Sprinkle with the paprika. Add the potatoes, ginger, marjoram, bay leaf, salt, and pepper. Sprinkle with the flour and mix well. • Add the water and bring to a boil. Simmer for 20 minutes, or until the potatoes are tender. • Discard the bay leaf and let cool slightly. • Stir in the sour cream, parsley, garlic, and dill and simmer for 2 more minutes over low heat. • Ladle into serving dishes and serve hot.

Serves: 4

Preparation: 10'

Cooking: 30'

Level of difficulty: 2

- 1 large onion, finely chopped
- ½ cup/60 g diced pancetta
- 4 tbsp butter
- 2 tsp paprika
- 1½ lb/750 g potatoes, peeled and chopped
- 1 tsp ground ginger
- ½ tbsp finely chopped marjoram
- 1 bay leaf
- salt and freshly ground black pepper to taste
- 2 tbsp all-purpose/ plain flour
- 1 quart/1 liter water
- generous ¾ cup/ 200 ml sour cream
- 2 tbsp finely chopped parsley
- 2 cloves garlic, finely chopped
- ½ tbsp finely chopped dill

MIXED VEGETABLE AND VEAL SOUP

Sauté the onions in the oil in a large saucepan until golden. • Add the pancetta and veal and cook for 10 minutes. • Add the peas, asparagus, artichokes, and fava beans. Pour in the stock and season with salt and pepper. • Cook over low heat for 15 minutes. • Serve hot with croutons.

Serves: 4

Preparation: 15'

Cooking: 25'

Level of difficulty: 1

- 3 small onions, thinly sliced
- 4 tbsp extra-virgin olive oil
- ¾ cup/90 g diced pancetta
- 5 oz/150 g lean ground/minced veal
- 6 tbsp peas
- 6 tbsp asparagus tips
- 4 artichokes, cut into wedges
- 4 tbsp fresh fava/broad beans
- croutons, to serve
- 2 quarts/2 liters Beef Stock (see page 224)

Serves: 6–8

Preparation: 20' +
12 h to soak beans

Cooking: 2 h 25'

Level of difficulty: 2

- 1 lb/500 g mutton or lamb, cut up into small chunks
- 2 tbsp clarified butter (ghee)
- 2 onions, chopped
- 1 stalk celery, finely chopped
- 1 tbsp finely chopped parsley
- 1 tbsp finely chopped cilantro/ coriander
- 1 stick cinnamon
- 4 threads saffron, crumbled
- ¼ tsp ginger
- salt and freshly ground black pepper to taste
- 3½ quarts/3.5 liters cold water
- 2 cups/200 g dried garbanzo beans/ chickpeas, soaked and drained
- 2½ cups/250 g brown lentils
- 2 lb/1 kg firm-ripe tomatoes, chopped
- ½ cup/100 g vermicelli or rice
- 3 tbsp all-purpose/ plain flour
- 2 tbsp lemon juice

MOROCCAN MUTTON SOUP

Place the mutton, butter, onions, celery, half the parsley and cilantro, cinnamon, saffron, and ginger in a large saucepan. Season with salt and pepper. Stir over medium heat until the butter has melted. • Pour in 1 quart (1 liter) of water. Bring to a boil and cook for 25–30 minutes, or until reduced by half. • Stir in the garbanzo beans and lentils. • Cook over medium heat for about 1 hour 15 minutes, or until the lentils are tender. • Stir in the tomatoes, 2 quarts (2 liters) of water, and the remaining parsley and cilantro. Bring to a boil, lower the heat, and simmer for 10 minutes more. • Add the vermicelli or rice. • Mix the flour and the remaining (2 cups/500 ml) of water, stirring constantly, to prevent lumps from forming. • Remove the soup from the heat and add the flour mixture, stirring constantly.
• Return to the heat and cook for 15 minutes more, stirring constantly. The soup should not be too thick. • Stir in the lemon juice. • Serve hot.

MIDDLE EASTERN SOUP WITH BEEF, RICE, AND SPINACH

Sauté the onions, garlic, and carrot in 4 tablespoons of oil in a large saucepan over medium heat for 8–10 minutes, or until lightly browned. • Add the beef and sauté for 10 minutes. • Pour in the water and tomatoes. Lower the heat, cover, and cook over low heat for 1 hour 30 minutes, or until the beef is tender. • Stir in the rice and cook for 15 minutes. • Add the spinach and cinnamon. Season with salt and pepper. Cook for 10 minutes more. • Add the parsley and remaining oil just before serving.

Serves: 4

Preparation: 30'

Cooking: 2 h 15'

Level of difficulty: 1

- 2 onions, finely chopped
- 4 cloves garlic, finely chopped
- 1 small carrot, sliced
- 6 tbsp extra-virgin olive oil
- 1½ lb/750 g stewing beef, cut into small chunks
- 3 quarts/3 liters cold water
- 2 tomatoes, chopped
- ¾ cup/150 g long-grain rice
- 2 lb/1 kg fresh or 1 lb/500 g frozen spinach
- 1 tsp cinnamon
- salt and freshly ground black pepper to taste
- 6 tbsp finely chopped parsley

PASTA

PASTA SALAD WITH BABY MOZZARELLAS AND TOMATOES

Cook the pasta in a large pot of salted, boiling water until al dente. • Drain and place under cold running water. Drain again and dry on a clean cloth. • Place in a salad bowl and toss with 2 tablespoons of oil. • Add the Mozzarella, tomatoes, scallions, and celery to the bowl. • Mix the remaining oil, lemon juice, salt, and plenty of pepper in a small bowl. Pour over the salad and toss well. • Sprinkle with the oregano, toss again, and serve.

Serves:	4–6
Preparation:	20'
Cooking:	15'
Level of difficulty:	1

- 1 lb/500 g farfalle pasta
- 6 tbsp extra-virgin olive oil
- 14 oz/400 g baby Mozzarellas (bocconcini)
- 8 oz/250 g cherry tomatoes, halved
- 2 scallions/spring onions, finely chopped
- 1 celery heart, thinly sliced
- juice of 1 lemon
- salt and freshly ground black pepper to taste
- ½ tsp dried oregano

PASTA SALAD WITH SUNDRIED TOMATOES

Serves: 4–6

Preparation: 20' + 30' to soak tomatoes

Cooking: 25'

Level of difficulty: 1

- 2 oz/60 g sundried tomatoes
- 1 lb/500 g farfalle pasta
- 6 tbsp extra-virgin olive oil
- 12 oz/350 g green beans, topped and tailed
- 3 onions, chopped
- ⅛ tsp chile powder
- 1 clove garlic, finely chopped
- juice of 1 lemon
- salt and freshly ground black pepper to taste
- 4 tbsp pine nuts

Soak the tomatoes in warm water for 30 minutes. Drain and chop coarsely. • Cook the pasta in a large pot of salted, boiling water until al dente. • Drain and place under cold running water. Drain again and dry on a clean cloth. • Place in a salad bowl and toss with 2 tablespoons of oil. • Cook the green beans in salted, boiling water for 7–10 minutes, or until crunchy-tender. • Drain and run under cold water. Drain again and add to the pasta, along with the onions and tomatoes. • Place the remaining oil in a small screw-top jar. Add the chile powder, garlic, lemon juice, and salt and pepper. Close and shake well. • Toast the pine nuts in a nonstick frying pan until browned. • Add the pine nuts to the pasta. Mix well. • Drizzle with the dressing, toss well, and serve.

MELONS WITH PASTA SALAD

Wash and dry the outside of the melons, then cut in half. Discard the seeds. • Remove the flesh, leaving about $1/2$ inch (1 cm) attached to the peel. • Chop the flesh coarsely and place in a large bowl. • Beat the oil, lemon zest, pink pepper, and salt in a small bowl. Pour over the chopped melon. Cover with plastic wrap (cling film) and refrigerate for 30 minutes. • Cook the pasta in a large pot of salted, boiling water until al dente. • Drain and place under cold running water. Drain again and dry on a clean cloth. • Add the pasta to the melon mixture and toss well. • Spoon the mixture into the melon halves. Garnish with the flakes of Pecorino. • Set aside for 10 minutes before serving.

Serves: 4

Preparation: 25' + 30' to marinate melons

Cooking: 15'

Level of difficulty: 1

- **2 small cantaloupe/ rock melons**
- **4 tbsp extra-virgin olive oil**
- **grated zest of $1/2$ lemon**
- **1 tsp ground pink peppercorns**
- **$1/4$ tsp salt**
- **14 oz/400 g tube pasta**
- **2 oz/60 g aged Pecorino cheese, flaked**

GREEK PASTA SALAD

C ook the pasta in a large pot of salted, boiling water until al dente. • Drain and place under cold running water. Drain again and dry on a clean cloth. • Place in a salad bowl and toss with 2 tablespoons of oil. • Place the eggplant in a colander. Sprinkle with salt and let drain for 30 minutes. • Toast the pine nuts in a nonstick frying pan until browned. • Heat 1 tablespoon of oil with the vinegar, wine, and peppercorns in a large frying pan. • Add the eggplant and cook over medium heat for 5 minutes. • Set aside. • In the same pan, sauté the bell peppers over high heat for 5 minutes. • Add the eggplant, bell peppers, celery, olives, and golden raisins to the pasta.
• Drizzle with the remaining oil and sprinkle with the oregano. Toss well. • Cover with plastic wrap and refrigerate for 1 hour before serving.

Serves: 4–6

Preparation: 30' + 30' to drain eggplants + 1 h to chill

Cooking: 20'

Level of difficulty: 2

- 1 lb/500 g sedani or penne pasta
- 3 tbsp extra-virgin olive oil
- 1 eggplant/ aubergine, diced
- salt and freshly ground black pepper to taste
- 1/3 cup/60 g pine nuts
- 4 tbsp white wine vinegar
- 4 tbsp dry white wine
- 1 tbsp black peppercorns
- 3 bell peppers/ capsicums, mixed colors, seeded, cored, and cut in thin strips
- 12 oz/350 g celery, diced
- 1/2 cup/50 g black olives, pitted
- 1/3 cup/60 g golden raisins/sultanas, soaked in warm water and drained
- 1 tbsp finely chopped oregano

PASTA SALAD WITH BELL PEPPERS AND TUNA

Serves: 4–6

Preparation: 20' + 15' to chill

Cooking: 15'

Level of difficulty: 1

- 1 lb/500 g penne
- 6 tbsp extra-virgin olive oil
- 1¼ cups/250 g tuna in oil
- 5 oz/150 g cherry tomatoes, halved
- 1 yellow bell pepper/capsicum, seeded, cored, and cut in thin strips
- 1 onion, finely sliced in rings
- 2 cloves garlic, finely chopped
- 1 tsp dried oregano
- salt and freshly ground black pepper to taste

Cook the pasta in a large pot of salted, boiling water until al dente. • Drain and place under cold running water. Drain again and dry on a clean cloth. • Place in a salad bowl and toss with 2 tablespoons of oil. • Drain the tuna, breaking it up with a fork. • Add the tomatoes, tuna, bell pepper, onion rings, garlic, and oregano to the pasta. • Drizzle with the remaining oil and season with salt and pepper. Toss well. • Cover with plastic wrap (cling film) and refrigerate for 15 minutes before serving.

This salad is delicious with penne, but can also be made with fusilli or spirals or other short pasta types.

SPAGHETTI WITH KIWI FRUIT

C ook the pasta in a large pot of salted, boiling water until al dente. • Meanwhile, peel the kiwi fruit and chop two of them coarsely. Mash the others with a fork. • Warm the yogurt in a small saucepan. • Add the garlic, chopped kiwi fruit, and lemon zest. Season with salt and pepper. Cook over medium heat for 2–3 minutes, stirring constantly. • Remove from the heat and add the mashed kiwis. • Drain the pasta and toss with the sauce. • Serve immediately.

Serves: 4–6

Preparation: 15'

Cooking: 15'

Level of difficulty: 1

- **1 lb/500 g spaghetti**
- **4 kiwi fruit**
- **1 cup/250 ml thick, creamy plain yogurt**
- **2 cloves garlic, finely chopped**
- **1 tbsp finely grated lemon zest**
- **salt and freshly ground black pepper to taste**

FUSILLI WITH TUNA

Serves: 4–6

Preparation: 15'

Cooking: 20'

Level of difficulty: 1

- **1 lb/500 g fusilli**
- **2 cloves garlic, finely chopped**
- **2 tbsp finely chopped parsley**
- **2 tbsp extra-virgin olive oil**
- **3 firm-ripe tomatoes, diced**
- **4 anchovy fillets, crumbled**
- **16 black olives, pitted**
- **½ tsp dried chile pepper flakes**
- **1½ cups/300 g tuna in oil, drained and crumbled**
- **½ cup/125 ml dry white wine**
- **salt and freshly ground black pepper to taste**

Cook the pasta in a large pot of salted, boiling water until al dente. • Meanwhile, sauté the garlic and parsley in the oil in a large frying pan over medium heat until pale gold. • Add the tomatoes, anchovies, olives, and chile pepper. Cook for 10 minutes. • Add the tuna and pour in the wine. Cook over high heat until the wine has evaporated. Season with salt and pepper. • Drain the pasta and add to the pan with the sauce. • Toss well and serve.

SPAGHETTI WITH SUNDRIED TOMATO PESTO AND BEANS

Serves: 4–6

Preparation: 25' + 30' to soak tomatoes

Cooking: 20'

Level of difficulty: 1

- **5 oz/150 g sundried tomatoes**
- **salt to taste**
- **14 oz/400 g green beans, cleaned and cut in short lengths**
- **1 lb/500 g spaghetti**
- **2 cloves garlic**
- **½ cup/75 g whole almonds**
- **½ cup/125 ml extra-virgin olive oil**
- **1 tbsp finely chopped parsley**
- **4 tbsp almonds slivers**

Soak the tomatoes in warm water for 30 minutes. • Meanwhile, bring a large pot of water to a boil. Season well with salt. Add the green beans and cook for 5 minutes. • Add the spaghetti and cook until al dente. • Drain the dried tomatoes, squeezing them dry, and transfer to a food processor or blender with the garlic, whole almonds, salt, and oil. Process to make a coarse pesto. • Place the sundried tomato pesto in a large bowl. Mix in a few tablespoons of the pasta cooking water. • Drain the spaghetti and beans and toss well in the pesto. • Sprinkle with the parsley and almonds. • Serve immediately.

BUCATINI WITH CHERRY TOMATOES AND MOZZARELLA

C ook the bucatini in a large pot of salted, boiling water until al dente. • Drain and place in a large heated bowl. Add the tomatoes and Mozzarella. • Season with salt and pepper and drizzle with the oil. Sprinkle with the oregano and garlic, if using, and toss well. • Serve hot.

Serves: 4

Preparation: 15'

Cooking: 12'

Level of difficulty: 1

- 1 lb/500 g bucatini
- 14 oz/400 g cherry tomatoes, cut in half
- 14 oz/400 g buffalo Mozzarella, cut into small chunks
- salt and freshly ground black pepper to taste
- 6 tbsp extra-virgin olive oil
- 1 tsp dried oregano
- 1 clove garlic, finely chopped

SEAFOOD PASTA

Soak the mussels in a large bowl of cold water for 1 hour. • Scrub the mussels thoroughly, then rinse in several changes of water. • Cook the mussels in a large frying pan until all they have all opened, 6–10 minutes. Discard any mussels that do not open. • Filter the water from the pan and set aside. Remove the mussels from their shells (leaving just a few in the shells to garnish).

• Sauté the garlic in the oil in the same frying pan until pale gold. • Discard the garlic and add the onion, carrot, and celery. Sauté for 3 minutes.

• Chop the squid coarsely and add to the pan. Season with salt and pepper. Drizzle in the wine and cook until evaporated. • Stir in the tomatoes and cover and cook until the tomatoes begin to separate from the oil, about 35 minutes.

• Meanwhile, cook the pasta in a large pot of salted, boiling water until al dente. • Drain and add to the pan with the sauce. • Add the filtered mussel water, mussels, and parsley.

• Garnish with the mussels still in their shells and serve immediately.

Serves: 4–6

Preparation: 40' + 1 h to purge mussels

Cooking: 30'

Level of difficulty: 2

- 1¾ lb/800 g mussels, in shell
- 1 clove garlic, lightly crushed but whole
- 2 tbsp extra-virgin olive oil
- 1 small onion, finely chopped
- 1 carrot, finely chopped
- 1 stalk celery, finely chopped
- 1 lb/500 g bucatini or spaghetti
- 10 oz/300 g squid, cleaned and chopped
- salt and freshly ground black pepper to taste
- 14 oz/450 g peeled and chopped tomatoes
- 1 tbsp finely chopped parsley
- 4 tbsp dry white wine

FARFALLE WITH SHRIMP AND ZUCCHINI

Remove the zucchini flowers and rinse carefully under cold running water. Clean the zucchini and slice thinly lengthwise. • Sauté the onion in the butter in a large frying pan over medium heat for 5 minutes, or until softened. • Meanwhile, cook the pasta in a large pot of salted, boiling water until al dente. • Add the zucchini to the onions and season with salt and pepper. Cover and cook over medium heat for 10 minutes, stirring often. • Add the shrimp and zucchini flowers and cook for 5 minutes. • Mix in the cream and cook until heated through. • Drain the pasta and add to the pan with the sauce. • Sprinkle with the parsley and toss well. • Serve hot.

Serve this springtime pasta with a glass of chilled, sparkling dry white wine.

288

Serves: 4–6
Preparation: 20'
Cooking: 30'
Level of difficulty: 1

- 14 oz/400 g zucchini/ courgettes with flowers attached
- 1 onion, finely chopped
- 4 tbsp butter
- 1 lb/500 g farfalle pasta
- salt and freshly ground black pepper to taste
- 14 oz/400 g shrimp/prawns
- 1/2 cup/125 ml heavy/double cream
- 2 tbsp finely chopped parsley

VEGETARIAN FARFALLE

Serves: 4–6

Preparation: 25'

Cooking: 35'

Level of difficulty: 1

- **2 small red and yellow bell peppers/ capsicums, seeded, cored, and cut in thin strips**
- **6 tbsp extra-virgin olive oil**
- **salt and freshly ground black pepper to taste**
- **6 oz/180 g green beans, topped and tailed**
- **1 lb/500 g farfalle pasta**
- **2 carrots, julienned**
- **²/₃ cup/150 g Ricotta cheese**
- **6 tbsp freshly grated Parmesan cheese**

S auté the bell peppers in the oil in a large frying pan over medium heat for 5 minutes. • Season with salt. Cook over low heat for 15 minutes more. • Meanwhile, cook the green beans and pasta in a large pot of salted, boiling water for 10 minutes. Add the carrots and continue cooking until the pasta is al dente. • Mix the Ricotta with 2 tablespoons of the pasta cooking water in a large bowl. Add the bell peppers and their cooking liquid. • Drain the pasta and vegetables and add to the bowl with the Ricotta. Add half the Parmesan. Toss well. • Sprinkle with the remaining Parmesan and season generously with pepper. • Serve hot.

SPAGHETTI WITH OLIVE PESTO AND CRISPY FRIED TOMATOES

Blanch the tomatoes in boiling water for 30 seconds. • Slip off the skins, gently squeeze out as many seeds as possible, and slice thinly. Drain on paper towels. Set aside in the refrigerator, changing the paper a couple of times to drain as much liquid as possible. • Process the parsley, olives, pine nuts, and sea salt in a food processor or blender until smooth. Add the Parmesan. Set the blender to low speed and gradually add the extra-virgin olive oil. • Heat the frying oil in a large frying pan until very hot. Dip the tomato slices in flour until well coated. Fry in small batches until crisp and golden. • Drain on paper towels and sprinkle with salt. • Meanwhile, cook the pasta in a large pot of salted, boiling water until al dente. • Drain and toss in the olive pesto. • Transfer to a serving dish and arrange the tomato slices on top. • Serve immediately.

Serves: 4–6

Preparation: 40'

Cooking: 20'

Level of difficulty: 2

- 14 oz/400 g firm-ripe tomatoes
- 1 small bunch parsley
- 1 cup/100 g green olives, pitted
- 6 tbsp pine nuts
- 1 tbsp sea salt
- 6 tbsp freshly grated Parmesan cheese
- 6 tbsp extra-virgin olive oil
- ½ cup/125 ml olive oil, for frying
- ½ cup/75 g all-purpose/plain flour
- salt to taste
- 1 lb/500 g spaghetti

TAGLIATELLE WITH PANCETTA AND BLACK TRUFFLE

Pasta: Sift the flour onto a work surface and make a well in the center. Break the eggs into the well. Use a fork to gradually stir them into the flour. At the same time incorporate enough of the water to make a firm dough. • Knead for 15–20 minutes, until smooth and elastic. Cover and let rest for 20 minutes. • Roll the pasta dough through a pasta machine to the thinnest setting. Cut the pasta into tagliatelle in the machine. • If rolling by hand, roll out very thinly on a pasta board and cut into large rectangles. Fold the sheets of pasta into loose rolls and cut into tagliatelle using a sharp knife. • Place the tagliatelle on a clean cloth and let dry. • Sauce: Sauté the pancetta, garlic, and chile pepper in the butter in a large frying pan over low heat for 5 minutes. • Add the mushrooms and season with salt. Cook for 5–10 minutes, or until the mushrooms are tender. • Cook the pasta in a large pot of salted, boiling water for 2–3 minutes, or until al dente. • Drain and transfer to a large serving dish. • Add the sauce and toss gently.
• Sprinkle with the Parmesan and season with pepper. Top with the truffle and serve.

Serves: 4

Preparation: 40' + 20'
to rest the dough

Cooking: 20'

Level of difficulty: 3

PASTA
- 2⅓ cups/350 g all-purpose/plain flour
- 3 large eggs
- 2 tbsp warm water

SAUCE
- ¾ cup/90 g diced pancetta or bacon
- 3 cloves garlic, finely chopped
- 1 fresh red chile pepper, seeded and finely chopped
- 3 tbsp butter
- 14 oz/400 g mushrooms, sliced
- salt and freshly ground black pepper to taste
- 2–4 tbsp freshly grated Parmesan or Pecorino cheese
- 1 small black truffle, finely grated

PICI WITH SAUSAGE AND GREENS

Clean the turnip greens, removing any large leaves and tough stems. • Cook the greens in a large pot of salted, boiling water until tender. • Drain, reserving the cooking water. Let the greens cool slightly. Squeeze out the excess moisture and coarsely chop. • Sauté the garlic and chile pepper in the oil in a large frying pan until the garlic is pale gold. Discard the garlic. • Add the sausage and sauté over high heat for 4 minutes, breaking up with a fork. • Add the wine and cook until evaporated. • Add the turnip greens and cook for 2 minutes. Season with salt. • Cook the pasta in the reserved cooking water until still al dente. • Drain and transfer to the pan with the sauce. Cook over high heat for 5 minutes. • Sprinkle with the Pecorino and serve hot.

Pici are a thick homemade Tuscan spaghetti. Substitute with bucatini or tagliatelle if unobtainable.

Serves: 4

Preparation: 25'

Cooking: 15'

Level of difficulty: 1

- 1¼ lb/600 g turnip greens
- 2 cloves garlic, lightly crushed but whole
- 1 fresh red chile pepper, thinly sliced
- 2 tbsp extra-virgin olive oil
- 5 oz/150 g Italian sausage, crumbled
- 2 tbsp dry white wine
- salt to taste
- 14 oz/400 g pici pasta
- ¾ cup/90 g freshly grated Pecorino cheese

PAPPARDELLE WITH DUCK SAUCE

Sauté the onion, prosciutto, carrot, celery leaves, bay leaf, sage, and parsley in the oil in a large frying pan over medium heat for about 15 minutes. • Add the duck and cook over high heat for about 10 minutes. • Pour in the wine and cook for 15 minutes. • Stir in the tomatoes and stock and season with salt and pepper. • Cover and cook for 1 hour, or until the duck is tender. • Remove the bones and cut into small pieces. • Return the meat to the sauce and cook for about 15 minutes. • Cook the pasta in a large pot of salted, boiling water until al dente. • Drain and transfer to the pan with the sauce. Sprinkle with the Parmesan and serve.

Serves: 6–8
Preparation: 30'
Cooking: 2 h
Level of difficulty: 2

- 1 red onion, finely chopped
- 3 oz/90 g diced prosciutto/Parma ham
- ½ carrot, chopped
- 1 small sprig celery leaves, chopped
- 1 bay leaf
- 1 sprig sage
- 1 tbsp finely chopped parsley
- 5 tbsp extra-virgin olive oil
- 1 duck, cleaned, with giblets, and quartered
- ⅔ cup/150 ml dry red wine
- 2 cups/500 g peeled, chopped tomatoes
- 1 cup/200 ml Beef Stock (see page 226)
- salt and freshly ground black pepper to taste
- 1 lb/500 g fresh egg pappardelle
- ¾ cup/90 g freshly grated Parmesan cheese

Serves: 4–6

Preparation: 30'

Cooking: 2 h 30'

Level of difficulty: 2

PASTA WITH DUCK SAUCE

PASTA
- 3⅓ cups/500 g all-purpose/plain flour
- 1 large egg
- 4 tbsp warm water

SAUCE
- 1 duck, cleaned, with giblets, and quartered
- 1 stalk celery
- 1 carrot
- 1 onion
- 1 clove garlic, finely chopped
- 2 leaves fresh sage
- 2 tbsp extra-virgin olive oil
- 2 tbsp dry white wine
- 2 cups/500 g peeled and chopped tomatoes
- salt and freshly ground black pepper to taste

Pasta: Sift the flour onto a surface and make a well in the center. Break the egg into the well and mix in enough water to make a stiff dough.
• Knead for 15–20 minutes, until smooth and elastic. Cover and let rest for 20 minutes. • Roll the pasta dough out to very thin and cut into thin strips. Sauce: Finely chop the duck giblets with the vegetables. Sauté the giblets and vegetables in the oil in a large frying pan until browned. • Add the duck and brown all over. • Add the wine and cook until evaporated. • Stir in the tomatoes. Season with salt and pepper and cook for at least 2 hours, or until the duck is tender. • Cook the pasta in a large pot of salted, boiling water for 5 minutes.
• Use a slotted spoon to drain and transfer to the pan with the sauce. Serve the meat separately.

TAGLIATELLE CARBONARA

Blanch the bell pepper, zucchini, eggplant, and potato in salted, boiling water for 2 minutes. Use a slotted spoon to remove the vegetables and pat dry on kitchen paper. • Sauté all the vegetables with the onion in the oil in a large frying pan over high heat for 5 minutes, or until lightly browned.

300

This modern version of Carbonara uses fresh spring vegetables. Use whatever is in season.

• Beat the eggs and 1 tablespoon of Pecorino in a large bowl. Season with salt and pepper. • Cook the pasta in a large pot of salted, boiling water until al dente. • Drain and transfer to the vegetables in the pan. • Pour in the beaten eggs and toss gently over medium-low heat for 2 minutes. • Add the tomato and herbs. Sprinkle with the remaining Pecorino and serve.

- 1 yellow bell pepper/capsicum, seeded, cored, and coarsely chopped
- 1 zucchini/courgette, coarsely chopped
- 1 eggplant/aubergine, coarsely chopped
- 1 medium potato, diced
- 1 onion, cut into segments
- 4 tbsp extra-virgin olive oil
- 2 large eggs
- 4 tbsp freshly grated Pecorino cheese
- salt and freshly ground black pepper to taste
- 14 oz/400 g fresh store-bought tagliatelle
- 1 large tomato, halved, seeded, and coarsely chopped
- 1 bunch mixed herbs (basil, oregano, chives), finely chopped

TAGLIATELLE WITH SAUSAGE

Serves: 4

Preparation: 15'

Cooking: 20'

Level of difficulty: 1

P eel the sausages. Crumble the pork sausages with a fork. Cut the wild boar sausages into small pieces. Sauté the sausage meat in the oil in a large frying pan over medium heat for about 10 minutes, or until browned all over. • Season with salt, pepper, and nutmeg. • Beat the eggs and milk in a large bowl. Season with salt and pepper. • Meanwhile, cook the pasta in a large pot of salted, boiling water until al dente. • Drain and add to the pan with the sauce. • Pour in the beaten eggs and stir gently over low heat for 2 minutes. • Season with pepper and sprinkle with the Parmesan. • Serve immediately.

- **2 Italian pork sausages**
- **2 wild boar sausages**
- **2 tbsp extra-virgin olive oil**
- **salt and freshly ground black pepper to taste**
- **⅛ tsp freshly grated nutmeg**
- **2 large eggs**
- **4 tbsp milk**
- **14 oz/400 g fresh store-bought tagliatelle**
- **½ cup/60 g freshly grated Parmesan cheese**

Serves: 4

*Preparation: 15' + 10'
to marinate*

Cooking: 10'

Level of difficulty: 1

- **1 carrot, coarsely chopped**
- **2 scallions/spring onions, finely chopped**
- **4 pieces bell pepper in oil, coarsely chopped**
- **4 ripe tomatoes, seeded and coarsely chopped**
- **1 celery heart, coarsely chopped**
- **3 zucchini/ courgettes, coarsely chopped**
- **7 tbsp extra-virgin olive oil**
- **juice of 1 lemon**
- **2 drops Tabasco**
- **1 clove garlic, finely chopped**
- **1/8 tsp salt**
- **2 tbsp finely chopped mixed herbs (such as basil, mint, and marjoram)**
- **14 oz/400 g fresh store-bought tagliolini**

TAGLIOLINI WITH RAW VEGETABLES

Mix the vegetables with the oil, lemon juice, Tabasco, garlic, and salt in a large bowl.
• Mix in the chopped herbs and let marinate for at least 10 minutes. • Cook the pasta in a large pot of salted, boiling water until al dente. • Drain and toss with the marinated vegetables.

PAPPARDELLE WITH BEAN CREAM AND CHARD

S auté the celery, 1 shallot, and bacon fat in 2 tablespoons of oil in a large frying pan over medium heat for 5 minutes. • Add the beans and cook for 3 minutes. • Pour in the stock and add the bay leaf. Cook over low heat for about 40 minutes, stirring often with a wooden spoon. • Remove from the heat and discard the bay leaf and bacon fat. Transfer to a food processor and process until thick and smooth. Season with salt and pepper. • Sauté the remaining shallot in 1 tablespoon of oil in a frying pan until golden. • Add the bacon and Swiss chard. Cook over high heat for 5 minutes. Season with salt and pepper. • Cook the pasta in a large pot of salted, boiling water until al dente. • Drain and toss in the bean sauce. Add the bacon and chard and season with pepper. • Drizzle with the remaining oil and serve.

Serves: 4
Preparation: 30'
Cooking: 1 h
Level of difficulty: 2

- 1 stalk celery, finely chopped
- 2 shallots, finely chopped
- 1 thick slice of bacon, fat and meat separated, finely chopped
- 4 tbsp extra-virgin olive oil
- 8 oz/250 g fresh shelled borlotti beans
- 1 cup/250 ml Vegetable Stock (see page 224)
- 1 bay leaf
- salt and freshly ground black pepper to taste
- 7 oz/200 g Swiss chard or spinach
- 14 oz/400 g fresh store-bought pappardelle

PASTA RAGS WITH EGGPLANT AND GARBANZO BEANS

Serves: 4

Preparation: 30' + 30' to drain

Cooking: 20'

Level of difficulty: 1

- 2 eggplants/ aubergines, thinly sliced
- 2 cloves garlic, finely chopped
- 1 tsp coriander powder
- 1 tsp cumin
- ½ tsp cardamom pods
- ⅛ tsp ground cinnamon
- 3 tbsp extra-virgin olive oil
- 8 oz/250 g canned garbanzo beans/ chickpeas
- salt and freshly ground black pepper to taste
- 14 oz/400 g fresh store-bought lasagne
- ¾ cup/180 ml plain yogurt
- 1 sprig mint, finely chopped

Place the eggplant in layers in a colander. Sprinkle with salt and let drain for 30 minutes.

- Pat dry with kitchen paper and chop coarsely.
- Sauté the garlic with the coriander, cumin, cardamom, and cinnamon in the oil in a large frying pan for 3–4 minutes. • Add the eggplant and sauté over high heat for 3 minutes. Lower the

If you are using dried beans, soak overnight and cook for 1–2 hours, or until tender.

heat, add the garbanzo beans, and cook for 3 minutes. Season with salt and pepper. • Cut the pasta into irregular pieces. • Cook the pasta in a large pot of salted, boiling water until al dente.

- Use a slotted spoon to drain and transfer to the pan with the sauce. • Mix in the yogurt and mint.
- Serve immediately.

Serves: 6–8

Preparation: 45' + 20'
to rest pasta

Cooking: 35'

Level of difficulty: 2

PASTA

- 2⅓ cups/350 g all-purpose/plain flour
- 1 large egg and 1 large egg yolk, lightly beaten with 6 tbsp water

PESTO

- 2 cups/45 g fresh basil leaves
- 2 tbsp pine nuts
- 2 cloves garlic
- ½ cup/125 ml extra-virgin olive oil
- 4 tbsp freshly grated Parmesan
- 2 tbsp boiling water
- salt and freshly ground black pepper to taste

FILLING

- 2 lb/1 kg potatoes, peeled
- ½ cup/125 ml dry white wine
- 1 cup/250 ml water
- 5 oz/150 g sausage meat
- 2⅔ cups/400 g all-purpose/plain flour
- ½ cup/125 ml milk
- 2 tbsp freshly grated Parmesan
- 3 large eggs
- ⅛ tsp marjoram

POTATO RAVIOLI WITH PESTO

Pasta: Sift the flour onto a surface and make a well in the center. Break the egg mixture into the well and mix to make a stiff dough. • Knead for 15–20 minutes, until smooth and elastic. Cover and let rest for 20 minutes. • Pesto: Place the basil, pine nuts, garlic, oil, salt, and pepper in a food processor or blender and chop until smooth. • Transfer the mixture to a medium bowl and stir in the cheese and water. • Filling: Boil the potatoes in a large pot of salted, boiling water for 20 minutes, or until tender. • Drain and mash in a large bowl. • Bring the wine and water to a boil in a small saucepan. • Add the sausage meat and cook for about 5 minutes to remove the fat. • Drain and add to the potatoes. Mix in the flour, milk, Parmesan, eggs, and marjoram. • Roll the dough out on a lightly floured surface until very thin. Cut into 1½ x 3-inch (4 x 8-cm) rectangles. • Put a teaspoonful of the filling on each rectangle, fold each one in half, and seal, pinching the edges together. • Cook the pasta in small batches in a large pot of salted, boiling water until al dente. • Use a slotted spoon to drain the pasta and toss gently with the pesto. • Serve immediately.

POTATO AND MUSHROOM RAVIOLI

B oil the potatoes in a large pot of water for 40 minutes. • Drain, peel, and mash the potatoes. • Pasta: Sift the flour onto a surface and make a well in the center. Break the eggs into the well and mix in enough water to make a stiff dough. • Knead for 15–20 minutes, until smooth and elastic. Cover and let rest for 20 minutes. • Clean the mushrooms and chop one-third of them coarsely. • Sauté the garlic in the butter in a large frying pan until pale gold. Add the chopped mushrooms and parsley and cook for 5 minutes. Season with salt. • Remove from the heat and let cool. • Roll the dough out on a lightly floured surface to $^1/_4$-inch (5-mm) thick. Use a pastry cutter to cut out $2^1/_2$-inch (6-cm) rounds. • Mix the Ricotta, Parmesan, the remaining mushrooms, and nutmeg in a large bowl. • Place a little of the mixture on each pasta round. Fold in half to make crescents and seal the edges well. • Cook the pasta in a large pot of salted, boiling water until al dente. • Use a slotted spoon to drain and transfer to the pan with the mushroom sauce.

Serves: 6

Preparation: 40' + 20' to rest the pasta

Cooking: 1 h

Level of difficulty: 2

- 1¼ lb/575 g potatoes
- 1²/₃ cups/250 g all-purpose/plain flour
- 2 eggs
- 2 tbsp warm water
- 1 lb/500 g mixed mushrooms
- 1 clove garlic, finely chopped
- 3 tbsp butter
- 1 tbsp finely chopped parsley
- salt to taste
- ²/₃ cup/150 g Ricotta cheese
- ½ cup/60 g freshly grated Parmesan cheese
- ⅛ tsp freshly grated nutmeg

Serves: 4

Preparation: 40' + 20'
to rest the dough

Cooking: 25'

Level of difficulty: 3

PASTA
- 3¹⁄₃ cups/500 g all-purpose/plain flour
- 4 large eggs
- 2 tbsp warm water

FILLING
- 14 oz/400 g ground/minced beef
- 2 tbsp extra-virgin olive oil
- 1 tbsp butter
- 10 oz/300 g boiled Swiss chard or spinach
- 3¹⁄₂ oz/100 g mortadella, diced
- 3 large eggs
- 1¹⁄₂ cups/150 g freshly grated Parmesan cheese
- ¹⁄₈ tsp freshly grated nutmeg
- ¹⁄₈ tsp dried thyme
- salt and freshly ground black pepper to taste
- 1 quantity Meat Sauce (see page 50)

BEEF AND CHARD TORTELLI

Pasta: Sift the flour onto a work surface and make a well in the center. Break the eggs into the well and mix in enough water to make a stiff dough. • Knead for 15–20 minutes, until smooth and elastic. Cover and let rest for 20 minutes. • Roll the pasta dough out (by hand or using a pasta machine) to very thin and cut into 2-inch (5-cm) wide strips. • Sauté the beef in the oil and butter in a large frying pan over high heat until browned all over. • Add the Swiss chard, mortadella, eggs, ³⁄₄ cup (90 g) of Parmesan, nutmeg, and thyme. Season with salt and pepper. Mix well and set aside. • Place a small quantity of filling at 2-inch (5-cm) intervals along the center of the strips of pasta. Top with another pasta strip and use your fingertips to seal the tortelli well, making sure that no air bubbles remain. Use a fluted pasta or cookie cutter to cut out the tortelli. Place on a floured cloth ready to cook. • Cook the pasta in a large pot of salted, boiling water for 3–4 minutes, or until al dente. • Use a slotted spoon to drain them carefully. • Top with the meat sauce and sprinkle with the remaining Parmesan. • Serve immediately.

BAKED ORECCHIETTE

Serves: 6

Preparation: 30'

Cooking: 1 h 20'

Level of difficulty: 2

- 1 carrot, finely chopped
- 1 onion, finely chopped
- 1 stalk celery, finely chopped
- 5 tbsp extra-virgin olive oil
- 14 oz/400 g ground/minced pork or veal
- 1½ lb/750 g canned tomatoes
- salt and freshly ground black pepper to taste
- 7 oz/200 g mushrooms
- 1 lb/500 g orecchiette pasta
- ½ cup/60 g freshly grated Parmesan cheese
- 2 egg yolks
- ¾ cup/180 ml Bèchamel Sauce (see page 55)

Sauté the carrot, onion, and celery in 3 tablespoons of oil in a large frying pan until lightly golden. • Add the meat and cook until browned all over. • Stir in the tomatoes and season with pepper. Cook over medium heat for 30 minutes. • Preheat the oven to 350°F/180°C/gas 4. • Sauté the mushrooms in the remaining oil in a large frying pan until lightly browned. • Cook the pasta in a large pot of salted, boiling water for 15 minutes, or until al dente. • Drain. • Spread a little of the meat sauce on the bottom of a baking dish. Add a layer of pasta, cover with the meat sauce and mushrooms, and continue alternating layers until all the ingredients are used, finishing with pasta. • Add the Parmesan and egg yolks to the Béchamel. Pour the Béchamel over the top of the pasta. • Bake for 30 minutes, or until browned on top. • Serve hot.

BAKED CANNELLONI

Serves: 6–8

Preparation: 45'

Cooking: 40'

Level of difficulty: 2

- **2 cups/500 ml Ricotta cheese**
- **1¼ cups/150 g freshly grated Pecorino cheese**
- **1 tbsp finely chopped basil**
- **1 egg + 1 egg yolk**
- **salt and freshly ground black pepper to taste**
- **2 lb/1 kg tomatoes**
- **½ cup/125 ml extra-virgin olive oil**
- **10 oz/300 g cannelloni pasta**
- **5 oz/150 g buffalo Mozzarella, diced**

Preheat the oven to 350°F/180°C/gas 4.
• Butter a baking dish. • Mix the Ricotta, half the Pecorino, half the basil, and the egg and egg yolk in a large bowl. Season with salt and pepper and mix well. • Cut the tomatoes in half horizontally. Arrange half of them in the prepared baking dish. Drizzle with 2 tablespoons of oil and season with salt, pepper, and the remaining basil. Sprinkle with 2 tablespoons of Pecorino. • Spoon the Ricotta mixture into the cannelloni. Arrange the cannelloni on top of the tomatoes, one next to the other. Season with salt and pepper and drizzle with 2 tablespoons oil. Sprinkle with 2 tablespoons of Pecorino. • Arrange the Mozzarella on top of the cannelloni. Cover with the remaining halved tomatoes, cut-side down. Drizzle with the remaining oil and season with salt and pepper. Cover with aluminum foil and bake for 20 minutes. • Remove the foil and sprinkle with the remaining Pecorino. Bake for 20 minutes, or until golden. • Serve hot.

RICE &
GRAINS

RICE WITH PEAS AND PROSCIUTTO

C ook the rice in a large pot of salted, boiling
water for 12–15 minutes, or until tender.
• Drain and let cool under cold running water.
Drain well and transfer to a large bowl. • Cook the
peas in salted, boiling water for 8 minutes. Drain
and let cool. • Cut the prosciutto into thin strips.
• Peel the bananas and slice into thin rounds.
Drizzle with the lemon juice to prevent them from
turning black. • Mix the peas, tomatoes,
prosciutto, celery, and bananas into the rice.
Set aside in a cool place. • Sauce: Mix the Ricotta,
mayonnaise, milk, mustard, and lemon juice in a
small bowl. Season with salt and add the curry and
sugar. • Spoon the rice mixture onto serving plates
and place the egg slices in the center. Drizzle with
the sauce and serve.

Serves: 4

Preparation: 25'

Cooking: 25'

Level of difficulty: 1

- 1½ cups/300 g long-grain rice
- salt to taste
- 1¾ cups/215 g peas
- 7 oz/200 g prosciutto/Parma ham
- 2 bananas
- 1 tbsp lemon juice
- 2 firm ripe tomatoes, seeded and coarsely chopped
- 3½ oz/100 g celery, peeled and diced

SAUCE
- 4 tbsp Ricotta cheese
- 5 tbsp mayonnaise
- 2 tbsp milk
- 1 tsp mustard
- 1 tsp lemon juice
- salt to taste
- 1 tbsp curry powder
- ⅛ tsp sugar

- 2 hard-boiled eggs, shelled and cut into wedges, to garnish

CLASSIC PAELLA

S oak the mussels in cold water for 1 hour. Scrub the mussels thoroughly, removing any beards. Rinse well. • Preheat the oven to 400°F/ 200°C/gas 6. • Sauté the garlic in the oil in a paella pan or large frying pan (about 18 inches/ 45 cm in diameter) over medium heat until pale gold. • Discard the garlic. • Brown the chicken in the same pan for 5 minutes. • Add the rice and stir until well coated with oil. • Pour in the water and bring to a boil. • Add the snails, artichokes, green beans, peas, mussels, and eel. Season with salt and pepper. Add the bay leaf and saffron. • Continue cooking over medium-high heat until the liquid has almost all been absorbed. The rice grains should still be slightly crunchy but there should still be some liquid in the pan. • Bake in the oven, uncovered, for 10 minutes. • Cover the pan with foil or parchment paper and let stand for 10 minutes before serving.

Paella comes from Valencia, in Spain. The classic recipe combines meat, fish, rice, vegetables, and saffron.

Serves: 8–10

Preparation: 35' + 1 h to soak mussels

Cooking: 35'

Level of difficulty: 2

- 1 lb/500 g mussels, in shell
- 3 cloves garlic, peeled and lightly crushed
- 4 tbsp extra-virgin olive oil
- 1 chicken (or rabbit), cleaned, boned, and cut into small chunks
- 3 cups/600 g short-grain rice
- 1½ quarts/1.5 liters boiling water
- 2 lb/1 kg snails, cleaned and boiled
- 2 artichoke hearts, cleaned and chopped
- 7 oz/200 g green beans, cut in short lengths
- 7 oz/200 g peas
- 1 lb/500 g eel, cleaned and ready to cook
- salt and freshly ground black pepper to taste
- 1 bay leaf
- 8–10 strands saffron, crumbled

SAFFRON SEAFOOD RICE

S oak the mussels and clams in cold water for
1 hour. Scrub the mussels thoroughly,
removing any beards. Rinse well. • Cook the
mussels and clams in a large frying pan over
medium-high heat until they are all open. Discard
any that do not open. Set aside. • Sauté the onion,
garlic, and tomato in the oil in a large frying pan
over medium heat for 8–10 minutes, or until the
onion is lightly browned. • Add the squid and rice.
Sauté over high heat for 3 minutes. • Lower the
heat to medium. Pour in the stock and bring to a
boil. Add the chile, parsley, and saffron and season
with salt. • Cook for 20 minutes. • Stir in the tuna,
shrimp, and fish and cook for 5–10 minutes, or
until the fish begins to flake. • Stir in the clams
and mussels and cook until heated through.
• Serve hot.

Serves: 6

*Preparation: 15′ + 1 h
to soak shellfish*

Cooking: 35′

Level of difficulty: 2

- 1 lb/500 g
  mussels, in shell
- 1 lb/500 g clams,
  in shell
- 1 medium onion,
  finely chopped
- 5 cloves garlic,
  finely chopped
- 1 medium tomato,
  coarsely chopped
- 4 tbsp extra-virgin
  olive oil
- 10 oz/300 g squid
  or cuttlefish, cut
  into rings
- 1 cup/200 g long-
  grain rice
- 1 dried red chile
  pepper, finely
  chopped
- 1 tsp finely
  chopped parsley
- 4–6 threads
  saffron, crumbled
- salt to taste
- 6 oz/180 g canned
  tuna in oil, drained
  and crumbled
- 3 oz/90 g shrimp
  tails/prawn, peeled
- 4 oz/125 g firm-
  textured white fish
  fillets, cut in bite-
  sized pieces
- 1 quart/1 liter
  Fish Stock
  (see page 226)

SPICED RICE WITH CURRIED MUSHROOMS AND SHRIMP

Remove the earthy part of the mushroom stems. Wash and quarter the mushrooms. • Sauté the shallots in the oil in a large frying pan over medium heat until softened. • Add the mushrooms and sauté for 2 minutes. • Season with salt and sprinkle with the flour, stirring constantly. • Pour in the curried stock and cook for 15 minutes, stirring occasionally. • Cook the rice in salted, boiling water with the cumin, coriander, and cardamom for 10–12 minutes, or until tender. • Drain and set aside. • Steam the shrimp tails for 3 minutes, or until cooked and pink. • Spoon the rice onto individual serving plates and top with the shrimp. Add the curried mushrooms and serve.

Serves: 4

Preparation: 25'

Cooking: 30'

Level of difficulty: 1

- 1¼ lb/575 g button mushrooms
- 3 shallots, finely chopped
- 4 tbsp extra-virgin olive oil
- salt to taste
- 1 tbsp all-purpose/ plain flour
- 1 tbsp hot curry powder dissolved in ¾ cup/180 ml Vegetable Stock (see page 226)
- 1 cup/200 g long-grain rice
- ½ tsp cumin seeds
- ½ tsp coriander seeds
- 4 cardamom pods
- 14 oz/400 g shrimp tails/ prawns

RICE WITH VEGETABLES

Place the rice, peas, tomatoes, carrots, zucchini, onions, and garlic in a large saucepan. • Add the water, salt, pepper, and saffron. • Bring to a boil, then lower the heat, and cover and cook for about 20 minutes, or until the water has been completely absorbed. • Spoon the rice and vegetables onto a serving dish. • Garnish with the parsley and serve hot. • Pass the yogurt on the side.

Serves: 6–8

Preparation: 10'

Cooking: 20'

Level of difficulty: 1

- **3 cups/600 g short-grain rice**
- **2 cups/250 g peas**
- **4 firm-ripe tomatoes, coarsely chopped**
- **2 carrots, coarsely chopped**
- **3 zucchini/ courgettes, coarsely chopped**
- **2 onions, finely chopped**
- **2 cloves garlic, finely chopped**
- **1 quart/1 liter water**
- **salt and freshly ground black pepper to taste**
- **4–6 threads saffron, crumbled**
- **1 tbsp finely chopped parsley**
- **1 cup/250 ml plain yogurt**

EGGPLANT PILAF

Serves: 8

Preparation: 15'
+ 1 h 15' to drain
and stand

Cooking: 40'

Level of difficulty: 1

- **3 eggplants/**
  aubergines, each
  weighing about
  1 lb/500 g, peeled
  and cut into small
  cubes
- **salt and freshly**
  ground black
  pepper to taste
- **⅔ cup/150 ml**
  extra-virgin
  olive oil
- **3 medium onions,**
  finely chopped
- **1 cup/200 g long-**
  grain rice
- **1 tbsp pine nuts**
- **2 tomatoes, peeled**
  and finely chopped
- **1 tbsp dried**
  currants
- **1 tbsp sugar**
- **1 tsp ground**
  cinnamon
- **1 tsp paprika**
- **2 cups/500 ml**
  Beef Stock
  (see page 224)

Place the eggplants in a colander. Sprinkle with salt and let drain for 1 hour. • Heat 6 tablespoons of oil in a large frying pan over medium heat. • Fry the eggplants for 5–7 minutes, or until tender. Drain well on paper towels. • Sauté the onions in the remaining oil in a large frying pan for 8–10 minutes, or until lightly browned. • Add the rice, pine nuts, tomatoes, currants, eggplants, sugar, cinnamon, and paprika. Season with salt and pepper. Pour in the stock. • Cover and cook over high heat for 5 minutes. Lower the heat and cook for 10–15 minutes, or until all the liquid has been absorbed. • Remove from the heat and cover with a clean cloth. Let stand for 15 minutes. • Mix and serve.

PROSCIUTTO AND POMEGRANATE RISOTTO

Serves: 4

Preparation: 25'

Cooking: 25'

Level of difficulty: 2

- **1 large onion, finely chopped**
- **2 tbsp extra-virgin olive oil**
- **¾ cup/90 g diced prosciutto/Parma ham**
- **1½ cups/300 g short-grain risotto rice**
- **4 tbsp dry white wine**
- **1 quart/1 liter Vegetable Stock (see page 224)**
- **12 oz/350 g pomegranate seeds**
- **salt and freshly ground white pepper to taste**
- **4 tbsp butter**
- **¾ cup/90 g freshly grated Parmesan cheese**

Sauté the onion in the oil in a large frying pan until softened, adding water if they begin to burn. • Add the prosciutto and cook for 3 minutes. • Stir in the rice and cook for 2 minutes, stirring constantly. • Stir in the wine and when this has been absorbed, begin stirring in the stock, ½ cup (125 ml) at a time. Cook and

In season from fall through early winter, pomegranates add an elegant touch to this risotto.

stir until each addition has been absorbed, until the rice is tender, about 15–18 minutes. • Add the pomegranate seeds. Season with pepper and stir in the butter and Parmesan. • Serve hot.

SQUID RISOTTO

Sauté the onion in the oil in a large frying pan until softened. • Add the squid and season with salt and pepper. Cover the pan and cook for 10 minutes. • Stir in the rice and cook for 2 minutes, stirring constantly. • Stir in the wine and when this has been absorbed, begin stirring in the water, $1/2$ cup (125 ml) at a time. Stir in the tomatoes. Cook and stir until each addition has been absorbed, until the rice is tender, about 15–18 minutes. • Add the butter, mix well, and let stand for 5 minutes. • Sprinkle with the parsley and serve hot.

Serves: 4–6

Preparation: 20'

Cooking: 50'

Level of difficulty: 2

- 1 onion, finely chopped
- 4 tbsp extra-virgin olive oil
- 14 oz/450 g squid, cut into thin strips
- salt and freshly ground black pepper to taste
- 2 cups/400 g short-grain risotto rice
- 1 cup/250 ml dry white wine
- 1 quart/1 liter boiling water
- 12 oz/300 g peeled and chopped tomatoes
- 2 tbsp butter
- 3 tbsp finely chopped parsley

BROCCOLI RISOTTO RISSOLES WITH TOMATO SAUCE

Serves: 4

Preparation: 30'

Cooking: 45'

Level of difficulty: 2

- 7 oz/200 g broccoli
- 2 cloves garlic, finely chopped
- 4 tbsp extra-virgin olive oil
- 1½ tbsp butter
- 1¾ cups/350 g short-grain risotto rice
- 7 tbsp dry white wine
- 1½ quarts/ 1.5 liters Vegetable Stock (see page 224)
- 1 lb/500 g canned tomatoes
- 1 sprig rosemary
- salt and freshly ground black pepper to taste
- ⅛ tsp sugar
- 3 tbsp freshly grated Parmesan cheese

Preheat the oven to 350°F/180°C/gas 4.
• Line a baking sheet with waxed paper.
• Blanch the broccoli in boiling water for 2 minutes. • Remove with a slotted spoon and dip in ice water. • Drain well. • Sauté 1 clove of garlic in 2 tablespoons of oil and half the butter in a large frying pan until pale gold. • Add the broccoli and cook for 5 minutes. • Add the rice and cook for 2 minutes, stirring constantly. • Stir in the wine and when this has been absorbed, begin stirring in the stock, ½ cup (125 ml) at a time. Cook and stir until each addition has been absorbed, until the rice is tender, about 15–18 minutes. • Sauté the remaining clove of garlic in the remaining butter and oil in a large frying pan. • Stir in the tomatoes and rosemary and season with salt and pepper. Cook over high heat for 10 minutes. Add the sugar. • Form the risotto into balls the size of walnuts and arrange on the prepared baking sheet. • Bake for 5 minutes, or until golden. • Spoon the tomato sauce onto a heated serving dish and place the rissoles on top.
• Sprinkle with the Parmesan and serve hot.

If you ever have any leftover risotto, this recipe is a good way of using it up.

| Serves: 4–6 |
| Preparation: 25' |
| Cooking: 40' |
| Level of difficulty: 2 |

RISOTTO

- 2 cloves garlic, finely chopped
- 4 tbsp extra-virgin olive oil
- 1½ tbsp butter
- 1¾ cups/350 g short-grain risotto rice
- 7 tbsp dry white wine
- 1½ quarts/ 1.5 liters Vegetable Stock (see page 224)

BELL PEPPER SAUCE

- 1 clove garlic, lightly crushed but whole
- 2 tbsp extra-virgin olive oil
- 3 red and yellow bell peppers/ capsicums, cored, seeded, and coarsely chopped
- 1 bay leaf
- 4 tbsp coarsely chopped canned tomatoes
- salt to taste
- 4 tbsp freshly grated Parmesan cheese
- 6 tbsp butter

RISOTTO CAKE WITH BELL PEPPER SAUCE

Sauté the garlic in the oil and butter in a large frying pan over high heat until pale gold.
• Add the rice and cook for 2–3 minutes, stirring constantly. • Stir in the wine and when this has been absorbed, begin stirring in the stock, ½ cup (125 ml) at a time. Cook and stir until each addition has been absorbed, until the rice is tender, about 15–18 minutes. • Bell Pepper Sauce: Sauté the whole garlic in the oil in a nonstick frying pan until pale gold. • Add the bell peppers and bay leaf. Cook for 10–15 minutes, or until the peppers have softened. • Stir in the tomatoes and season with salt. Cook, stirring, for 5 more minutes. Mix in the Parmesan. • Melt the butter in a nonstick frying pan and add the risotto, smoothing the surface with a spoon. Cook over high heat for 8 minutes, shaking the pan to prevent it from sticking.
• Remove the pan from the heat and cover with a large plate. Turn upside-down so that the risotto cake is on the plate. Slide it back into the pan and brown the other side for 5 minutes. It should form a crisp golden crust. • Spoon the sauce over the rice cake. • Serve hot.

RICE AND MOZZARELLA TIMBALE

Preheat the oven to 400°F/200°C/gas 6.
• Oil a springform pan. • Sauté the onion in 2 tablespoons of oil in a large frying pan until softened. • Add the canned tomatoes, chile powder, oregano, and salt. Cook for 10 minutes. • Cook the rice in a large pot of salted, boiling water until tender. • Drain well and mix with the Parmesan, tomato and onion mixture, thyme, and basil. • Spoon half the rice into the prepared pan and top with half the Mozzarella. Spoon in the remaining rice. • Bake for 12–15 minutes, or until lightly golden. • Turn out of the pan and garnish with the fresh tomatoes, remaining Mozzarella, and basil. • Serve hot.

Serves: 4

Preparation: 30'

Cooking: 35'

Level of difficulty: 1

- 1 onion, finely chopped
- 3 tbsp extra-virgin olive oil
- 15 oz/450 g coarsely chopped canned tomatoes
- ¼ tsp chile powder
- ½ tsp dried oregano
- salt to taste
- 1½ cups/300 g short-grain rice
- ½ cup/60 g freshly grated Parmesan cheese
- 1 tbsp finely chopped thyme
- 1 bunch basil, torn + extra to garnish
- 2 firm ripe tomatoes, cut into wedges
- 5 oz/150 g Mozzarella cheese, thinly sliced

BAKED RICE TERRINE WITH PESTO AND VEGETABLES

Serves: 6–8

Preparation: 30'

Cooking: 1 h 10'

Level of difficulty: 2

- ¾ cup/150 g short-grain rice
- 1 clove garlic, finely chopped
- 1 tbsp extra-virgin olive oil
- 10 oz/300 g zucchini/ courgettes, coarsely grated
- 2 eggs
- 4 tbsp Pesto (see page 309)
- 1⅓ cups/200 g all-purpose/plain flour
- ½ tsp baking powder
- 1 carrot, cut into very thin strips

Preheat the oven to 350°F/180°C/gas 4.
• Butter a 10-inch (25-cm) loaf pan. • Cook the rice in a large pot of salted, boiling water for 12–15 minutes, or until tender. • Drain and let cool under cold running water. • Sauté the garlic in the oil in a large frying pan until pale gold. • Add the zucchini and sauté over medium heat for 5 minutes. • Transfer to a large bowl and let cool. • Mix in the rice, eggs, pesto, flour, and baking powder. • Spoon half the mixture into the prepared pan, flattening the top. • Top with the carrots in a single layer. • Spoon in the remaining mixture. • Bake for 45–50 minutes, or until lightly golden on top. • Turn out onto a serving platter. • Serve warm.

SEAFOOD RISOTTO

Sauté the garlic and 2 tablespoons of parsley in 4 tablespoons of oil in a large frying pan over medium-high heat for 3–4 minutes. • Add the shrimp and mixed shellfish. Season with salt and pepper and sauté for 5 minutes. Remove the shrimp and shellfish and set aside. • Add the remaining oil with the shrimp and rice and sauté over high heat for 2–3 minutes. • Begin stirring in the stock, $^1/_2$ cup (125 ml) at a time. Cook and stir until each addition has been absorbed, until the rice is tender, about 15–18 minutes. • Add the shrimp and shellfish, mix well, and let stand for 5 minutes. • Sprinkle with the remaining parsley and serve hot.

Serves: 4–6
Preparation: 30'
Cooking: 30'
Level of difficulty: 2

- 4 cloves garlic, finely chopped
- 3 tbsp finely chopped parsley
- 4 tbsp extra-virgin olive oil
- 8–12 large shrimp/ prawns
- 12 oz/350 g mixed mussels and clams, shelled
- salt and freshly ground black pepper to taste
- 10 oz/300 g squid, cut into thin rings
- 2 cups/400 g short-grain risotto rice
- 1 quart/1 liter Fish Stock (see page 226)

BULGUR WITH LAMB AND GARBANZO BEANS

Serves: 4

Preparation: 15'

Cooking: 45'

Level of difficulty: 1

- **2 medium onions, finely chopped**
- **4 tbsp extra-virgin olive oil**
- **12 oz/350 g lamb, cut in small cubes**
- **10 oz/300 g coarse grind bulgur**
- **salt and freshly ground black pepper to taste**
- **½ tsp ground cinnamon**
- **8 oz/200 g cooked garbanzo beans/chickpeas (canned or precooked), drained**

Sauté the onion in the oil in a large frying pan over medium-high heat for 5 minutes, or until transparent. • Add the lamb and sauté for 10 minutes, or until well browned. • Add the bulgur and enough water to cover. Season with salt, pepper, and cinnamon. • Partially cover the pan and cook over medium-low heat for about 30 minutes, or until the lamb and bulgur are both tender. Stir often during cooking, adding more water as required. • Stir in the garbanzo beans and cook until heated through. • Serve hot.

Serves: 4–6

Preparation: 40'

Cooking: 30'

Level of difficulty: 2

FILLING

- **⅓ cup/60 g pine nuts**
- **6 tbsp butter**
- **1 lb/500 g onions, finely chopped**
- **7 oz/200 g lean ground/minced lamb**
- **2 tbsp ground cinnamon**
- **2 tbsp pimento**
- **1 tsp fresh lemon juice**
- **½ tsp red pepper flakes**
- **salt to taste**

KIBBE

- **1 medium onion, peeled and quartered**
- **1 lb/500 g ground/ minced leg of lamb, fat removed**
- **2 tsp cinnamon**
- **2 tsp pimento**
- **½ tsp ground black pepper**
- **salt to taste**
- **7 oz/200 g fine bulgur**

BAKED KIBBE WITH LAMB

Filling: Toast the pine nuts in the butter in a small frying pan. Pat dry on paper towels. • Sauté the onions in the same frying pan until softened. • Add the lamb, breaking it up with a fork, and cook until browned all over. • Remove from the heat. Add the pine nuts, cinnamon, pimento, and lemon juice. Season with salt. • Kibbe: Mince the onion, lamb, cinnamon, pimento, pepper, and salt in a food processor or blender. • Soak the bulgur in a large bowl of cold water for 10 minutes, or until it swells. • Drain and add to the meat. Mix until smooth. • Preheat the oven to 350°F/180°C/gas 4. • Butter a baking dish. • Divide the kibbe in half. Dampen your hands in salted water and place half the kibbe on the base of the dish. Press down to make an even layer. Spread the filling over the top and cover with a second layer of kibbe. Divide the kibbe into four sections and use a knife to make a decorative finish. • Bake for 15–20 minutes, or until lightly browned. • Serve with cucumber and yogurt salad or houmous (see page 164).

BAKED ZUCCHINI POLENTA

Preheat the oven to 350°F/180°C/gas 4. • Oil a baking dish. • Sift the cornmeal into a large bowl. • Gradually add the water and oil to make a smooth batter. • Rinse and dry the flowers and cut into strips. Add them to the batter and season with salt. • Pour the mixture in the prepared baking dish. • Bake for 30 minutes. • Spread the cheese over the top and serve.

348

Serves: 4

Preparation: 20'

Cooking: 30'

Level of difficulty: 1

- 2²/₃ cups/400 g coarsely ground yellow cornmeal
- 2 cups/500 ml warm water
- ¾ cup/180 ml extra-virgin olive oil
- 8 zucchini/ courgette flowers
- salt to taste
- 1 cup/250 ml soft creamy cheese

BULGUR WITH FETA AND EGGPLANT

Serves: 6

Preparation: 25'

Cooking: 15'

Level of difficulty: 1

- **8 oz/250 g bulgur (cracked wheat)**
- **2 eggplants/ aubergines**
- **salt and freshly ground black pepper to taste**
- **4 firm ripe tomatoes, coarsely chopped**
- **7 oz/200 g Feta cheese, diced**
- **juice of 1 lemon**
- **1 bunch mint, torn**
- **1 bunch parsley, finely chopped**
- **2 tbsp extra-virgin olive oil**

Cook the bulgur in a large pot of salted, boiling water for 10 minutes. • Turn off the heat and let swell in the water for 10 minutes. • Drain and let dry in the colander. • Broil (grill) or roast the eggplants whole until the skins are blackened. • Wrap them in a paper bag for 5 minutes, then peel them. Dice the flesh and season with salt. • Arrange the tomatoes in a colander and sprinkle with salt. Let drain for 10 minutes. • Mix the bulgur, Feta, tomatoes, eggplants, lemon juice, and herbs in a large bowl. Season with pepper and drizzle with the oil. • Serve warm.

POLENTA WITH CHANTERELLE MUSHROOMS

B ring the water to a boil in a large saucepan. Season with the coarse salt and oil.
• Gradually sprinkle in the cornmeal, stirring constantly with a wooden spoon to prevent lumps from forming. • Continue cooking over medium heat, stirring almost constantly, for 45–50 minutes. • Remove the earthy base of the mushrooms. Cut the largest ones in half, leaving the smaller ones whole. • Sauté the garlic, onion, and pancetta in the oil in a large frying pan until the garlic is pale gold. • Add the mushrooms and season with salt and pepper. Cover and cook over low heat for 20 minutes stirring often. • Add the parsley. • Spoon the polenta into individual serving plates. Arrange the mushrooms on top with their cooking juices and top with the Parmesan flakes.
• Serve immediately.

Serves: 4

Preparation: 30'

Cooking: 1 h 5'

Level of difficulty: 2

POLENTA

- 2 quarts/2 liters water
- 1 tbsp coarse sea salt
- 1 tbsp extra-virgin olive oil
- 2⅔ cups/400 g coarsely ground yellow cornmeal

MUSHROOM SAUCE

- 1 clove garlic, finely chopped
- 1 red onion, finely chopped
- ¾ cup/90 g diced pancetta
- 4 tbsp extra-virgin olive oil
- 14 oz/400 g chanterelle or white mushrooms
- salt and freshly ground black pepper to taste
- 2 tbsp finely chopped parsley
- 1½ oz/45 g Parmesan cheese, flaked

STUFFED KIBBE BALLS

Place the bulgur in a bowl and cover with cold water. Let stand for 30 minutes. • Drain well.
• Mix the beef and onion in a large bowl. Stir in the bulgur, nutmeg, and cinnamon. Season with salt and pepper. • Use your hands to knead the mixture until well mixed. Shape into a ball, return to the bowl, and refrigerate for 30 minutes. • Filling: Sauté the onions in the oil in a large frying pan over medium heat for 8–10 minutes, or until lightly browned. • Add the lamb and season with salt. Add the cinnamon and allspice. • Cook for 10–15 minutes, or until the meat has browned.
• Remove from the heat and set aside. • Use a teaspoon to scoop out enough of the bulgur mixture to form balls the size of golf balls.
• Use your index finger to make a hollow in the center, working until you have a shell of even thickness. • Spoon in the filling and close up the opening. Repeat until both mixtures are used up.
• Heat the frying oil in a large pan until hot.
• Fry the balls in batches for 8–10 minutes, or until browned all over. Drain on paper towels.
• Serve hot.

Serves: 6–8

Preparation: 25'
+ 1 h 30' to stand
and chill

Cooking: 50'

Level of difficulty: 2

- 2 lb/1 kg fine-grind bulgur
- 2 lb/1 kg ground/ minced beef
- 1 large onion, finely chopped
- ½ tsp freshly grated nutmeg
- ½ tsp ground cinnamon
- salt and freshly ground black pepper to taste

FILLING

- 4 medium onions, finely chopped
- 4 tbsp extra-virgin olive oil
- 1 lb/500 g ground/ minced lamb
- salt to taste
- ½ tsp ground cinnamon
- ½ tsp ground allspice
- 1 cup/250 ml olive or sesame oil, for frying

COUSCOUS WITH FISH SAUCE

Serves: 6
Preparation: 30'
Cooking: 1 h 30'
Level of difficulty: 2

Rinse the couscous 2 or 3 times. Transfer to a large bowl and add 1 cup (250 ml) of salted water. Rub the grains with your fingertips for a few minutes. • Place the heads and tails of the fish, the turnips, some outer cabbage leaves, and 1 stalk celery in a saucepan. Pour in 2 quarts (2 liters) cold water. • Add $1/8$ teaspoon red pepper and season with black pepper. • Bring to a boil and cook for 15–20 minutes. • Strain the stock and set aside. • Heat the oil in the lower section of a couscoussière or a two-tiered vegetable steamer. • Sauté the onions for 8–10 minutes, or until lightly browned. • Pour in the fish stock, carrots, remaining celery, saffron, cumin, and coriander. Add 2 quarts (2 liters) of water and bring to a boil. • Place the couscous in the top pot of the couscoussière and steam for 25 minutes. • Remove from heat and transfer to a large bowl. Add 1 cup (250 ml) of warm water and stir with a wooden spoon until just warm. Return to the couscoussière. • Add the tomatoes, zucchini, and remaining cabbage to the mixture in the bottom pot of the couscoussière. Season with salt and cook the stew and couscous for 20 more minutes. • Add the fish to the bottom pan, cover with the top couscous pan and cook for 15–20 more minutes. • Remove the couscous from the heat and add the butter. • Spoon the couscous onto a serving plate. Make a well in the center and arrange the fish stew on top.

- 1 lb/500 g couscous
- 4 quarts/4 liters + 2 cups/250 ml water
- 1 white-fleshed fish, weighing about 4 lb/2 kg, such as bream or snapper, cleaned and cut into thick slices
- 2 turnips, peeled and chopped
- 1 small cabbage, finely shredded (reserve some outer leaves whole)
- 2 stalks celery, chopped
- 1 tsp red pepper flakes
- salt and freshly ground black pepper to taste
- 3 tbsp extra-virgin olive oil
- 3 onions, chopped
- 2 carrots, chopped
- 6–8 threads saffron, crumbled
- 1 tsp cumin
- 1 tsp coriander
- 1 lb/500 g tomatoes, peeled and chopped
- 3 zucchini/ courgettes, sliced
- 6 tbsp butter

COUSCOUS WITH SPICY SAUCE

Mix the tomatoes, cucumber, onion, half the lemons, olives, and herbs in a large bowl.
• Process the chile pepper, garlic, 3 tablespoons of oil, cumin, and a pinch of salt in a food processor or blender until smooth and creamy.
• Mix the remaining oil, the juice of the remaining lemons, and a pinch of salt in a small bowl. Stir in 1 teaspoon of the chile mixture and beat until well blended. Pour the mixture over the vegetables.
• Place the couscous in a large bowl. Pour in the boiling water. Let stand for 10 minutes, or until the couscous has absorbed the water. • Break it up with a fork and let cool. Transfer to a serving bowl. Mix in the vegetables and serve.

Serves: 4

Preparation: 25'

Cooking: 10'

Level of difficulty: 1

- 10 oz/300 g cherry tomatoes, cut into wedges
- 1 cucumber, thinly sliced
- 1 onion, finely chopped
- 3 lemons, thinly sliced
- 2 cups/200 g black olives, pitted
- 4 sprigs parsley, finely chopped
- 4 sprigs marjoram, finely chopped
- 1 fresh red chile pepper, thinly sliced
- 2 cloves garlic
- 7 tbsp extra-virgin olive oil
- $1/8$ tsp ground cumin
- salt to taste
- 8 oz/250 g precooked couscous
- $1\frac{1}{4}$ cups/310 ml boiling water

MIXED BEANS AND BARLEY

S oak the garbanzo beans, white beans, and barley overnight in cold water. • Drain well. • Simmer the garbanzo beans, white beans, and barley in separate pots of salted water over low heat for about 1 hour, or until tender. • Drain the garbanzo beans and barley and add to the white beans. • Season with salt and continue cooking for 10 minutes. • Drizzle with the oil and season with pepper. • Serve hot.

Serves: 4–6

Preparation: 5' + 12 h to soak

Cooking: 1 h 10'

Level of difficulty: 1

- 2½ cups/250 g dried garbanzo beans
- 2½ cups/250 g dried white beans
- 1 cup/100 g barley or wheat
- salt and freshly ground black pepper to taste
- 4 tbsp extra-virgin olive oil

BULGUR WITH CHERRY TOMATOES AND WALNUTS

Serves: 6

Preparation: 20' + 15' to soak

Level of difficulty: 1

- 2 cups/250 g coarse grind bulgur wheat
- 2⅓ cups/400 g shelled walnuts
- 1 tsp salt
- 1 onion, finely chopped
- 16 cherry tomatoes, halved
- 2 tbsp finely chopped mint + 1 sprig mint, to garnish
- 4 tbsp extra-virgin olive oil
- ½ cup/125 ml plain yogurt

Soak the bulgur wheat in warm water for 15 minutes. • Drain, squeezing out the excess water. • Chop the walnuts coarsely with 1 teaspoon of salt on a chopping board. • Mix the bulgur wheat, walnuts, onion, tomatoes, and mint in a large bowl. Drizzle with the oil. • Refrigerate for 15 minutes. • Garnish with the mint and serve with the yogurt.

EGGS

OMELET WITH TRUFFLE

Beat the eggs and 1 tablespoon of butter in a large bowl. • Sauté the truffle in the remaining butter in a large frying pan over medium heat for 1 minute. • Add the eggs and cook for 4–5 minutes. Season with salt and pepper. Turn the omelet and cook the other side for 2–3 minutes. • Serve hot.

362

Serves: 4

Preparation: 5'

Cooking: 10'

Level of difficulty: 1

- 8 large eggs
- 3 tbsp butter, softened
- ½ oz/15 g black truffle, thinly sliced
- salt and freshly ground black pepper to taste

FRENCH OMELET WITH TOMATO AND ONION

Serves: 4–6

Preparation: 15'

Cooking: 30'

Level of difficulty: 1

- 1 medium red onion, halved and thinly sliced
- 6 tbsp extra-virgin olive oil
- 4 firm-ripe tomatoes, finely chopped
- salt and freshly ground black pepper to taste
- 2 cloves garlic, finely chopped
- ¼ tsp sugar
- 10 large eggs
- 1 tbsp finely chopped parsley
- 1 tbsp finely chopped basil
- 1 tbsp butter

Sauté the onion in 4 tablespoons of oil in a frying pan over medium heat for 5 minutes, or until translucent. • Add the tomatoes and season with salt and pepper. • Cook for 15 minutes. Add the garlic and sugar. Cook for 5 minutes more. • Beat the eggs in a large bowl. Season with salt and pepper and add the parsley and basil. • Heat the remaining oil in a large frying pan over medium heat. Pour in the beaten eggs. • When the bottom has set, slide a wooden spatula under the eggs to loosen them from the pan. Shake the pan with a rotating movement. Cook until nicely browned on the underside. • Spoon a layer of the tomato mixture over the top. • Roll up the omelet and top with the butter. • Serve hot.

BAKED LAMB AND SPINACH FRITTATA

Preheat the oven to 350°F/180°C/gas 4.
• Butter a deep round baking dish. • Heat
3 tablespoons of oil in a large frying pan. • Sauté
the spinach with the salt, pepper, and cinnamon
over high heat for 10 minutes. Set aside.

• Heat the remaining oil in a separate frying pan
over medium heat.
Sauté the lamb
and onion for about 10 minutes, or until lightly
browned. • Add the beans and spinach and pour
in the water. Season with salt and pepper and
sprinkle with the saffron. • Simmer over medium-
low heat for about 20 minutes, or until the sauce
has reduced. • Mix in the cheese, bread, eggs, and
season with salt. • Spoon the mixture into the
baking dish. • Bake for about 20 minutes, or until
set and lightly browned. • Serve hot.

*A frittata is like an omelet but with vegetables or other
ingredients mixed in and cooked with the eggs.*

364

Serves: 6

Preparation: 15'

Cooking: 1 h

Level of difficulty: 2

- 6 tbsp extra-virgin olive oil
- 2 lb/1 kg fresh spinach, shredded
- salt and freshly ground black pepper to taste
- 1 tsp ground cinnamon
- 12 oz/300 g boneless lamb, cut into small cubes
- 1 large onion, finely chopped
- 1 cup/100 g cooked cannellini beans or garbanzo beans/chickpeas
- 1½ cups/375 ml water
- 4–6 threads saffron, crumbled
- 1¼ cups/150 g freshly grated Parmesan cheese
- ½ cup/50 g coarsely grated day-old bread
- 6 large eggs, lightly beaten

FRITTATA ROLL WITH OLIVES AND ONION

P reheat the oven to 400°F/200°C/gas 6.
• Grease a large baking dish with oil. • Beat 8 eggs in a large bowl. Mix in the Parmesan and cream. Season with salt and pepper. • Heat the oil in a large frying pan. Pour in the batter, rotating the pan so that it covers the bottom in an even layer. Cook over low heat for 5–6 minutes. • Flip the frittata and cook over medium heat for 3 minutes more. • Remove from the heat. • Beat the remaining egg and brush over the frittata.
• Set out a large sheet of waxed paper and sprinkle with the bread crumbs. Place the frittata egg-side down on the crumbs. • Arrange alternating slices of Mozzarella and tomatoes on top. Roll up the frittata, using the paper as a guide.
• Place the roll in the prepared baking dish with the onion and olives. • Bake for about 15 minutes, or until browned all over. • Let rest for 5 minutes.
• Slice and serve hot with the onion and olives.

Serves: 4–6

Preparation: 30'

Cooking: 20'

Level of difficulty: 2

- **9 large eggs**
- **4 tbsp freshly grated Parmesan cheese**
- **2 tbsp heavy/ double cream**
- **salt and freshly ground black pepper to taste**
- **2 tbsp extra-virgin olive oil**
- **½ cup/60 g fine dry bread crumbs**
- **6 oz/180 g Mozzarella cheese, thinly sliced**
- **2 large tomatoes, thinly sliced**
- **1 onion, thinly sliced**
- **1 cup/100 g green olives, pitted and cut into rounds**

BAKED VEGETABLE FRITTATA

Serves: 6

Preparation: 25'

Cooking: 30'

Level of difficulty: 1

- 3 potatoes, diced
- 2 tbsp extra-virgin olive oil
- 1 tsp bouillon granules dissolved in 4 tbsp hot water
- 1 eggplant/ aubergine, diced
- 4 oz/125 g Swiss chard or spinach, shredded
- 9 large eggs
- salt and freshly ground black pepper to taste
- 1 tbsp finely chopped mint
- 1 tbsp finely chopped thyme

Preheat the oven to 425°F/220°C/gas 7.
• Grease an 8-inch (20-cm) baking pan with oil.
• Sauté the potatoes in the oil in a large frying pan over medium heat for 2 minutes. • Pour in the bouillon. Add the eggplant and Swiss chard and cook for 8 minutes. • Increase the heat and cook for 2 minutes more, or until the liquid has reduced by half. • Beat the eggs in a large bowl. Season with salt and pepper. Mix in the cooked vegetables, mint, and thyme. • Pour the batter into the prepared pan. Cover with aluminum foil and bake for 10 minutes. • Remove the foil, and bake for 5 minutes more. • Set aside for 2 minutes. Cut into squares to serve.

Serve this frittata at lunch or supper, or cut it into small squares and serve at a buffet party.

369

BAKED TOMATO FRITTATA

Preheat the oven to 350°F/180°C/gas 4. • Line an 8-inch (20-cm) round baking dish with waxed paper. • Beat the eggs in a bowl. Season with salt and pepper. Mix in the onion, olive pâtè, cream, Provolone, thyme, and basil. • Arrange the tomato slices on the bottom of the prepared baking dish. Season with salt and pepper and sprinkle with the bread crumbs. Pour in the batter, smoothing the top. • Bake for 25–30 minutes, or until set. • Turn out onto a heated serving dish and let rest for 5 minutes before serving.

Serves: 4

Preparation: 25'

Cooking: 30'

Level of difficulty: 1

- **6 large eggs**
- **salt and freshly ground black pepper to taste**
- **1 small onion, finely chopped**
- **2 tbsp green olive pâtè (optional)**
- **2 tbsp heavy/ double cream**
- **2 tbsp freshly grated spicy Provolone or Parmesan cheese**
- **1 tbsp finely chopped thyme**
- **4 leaves fresh basil, torn**
- **3 tomatoes, thinly sliced**
- **2 tbsp fine dry bread crumbs**

RUSTIC-STYLE FRITTATA

Preheat the oven to 400°F/200°C/gas 6.
• Grease a 9-inch (23-cm) round baking pan with oil. • Cook the tagliatelle in a large pot of salted, boiling water until al dente. • Drain and set aside. • Cook the onion in the oil in a large frying pan over medium heat until softened. • Add the bell pepper, eggplant, zucchini, and celery. Cook for 15 minutes. • Add the tomatoes and cook for 5 minutes more. Season with salt and pepper. • Beat the eggs in a bowl. Mix in the cooked vegetables, tagliatelle, basil, and mint. • Pour the mixture into the prepared baking dish. • Bake for 20 minutes, or until set. • Let cool completely.

Serves: 4

Preparation: 30'

Cooking: 55'

Level of difficulty: 1

- 10 oz/300 g tagliatelle
- 1 red onion, finely chopped
- 4 tbsp extra-virgin olive oil
- 1 green bell pepper/capsicum, seeded, cored, and diced
- 1 small eggplant/aubergine, diced
- 2 zucchini/courgettes, thinly sliced
- 1 stalk celery, finely chopped
- 6 cherry tomatoes, halved
- salt and freshly ground black pepper to taste
- 5 large eggs
- 1 tbsp finely chopped basil
- 1 tbsp finely chopped mint

BAKED CABBAGE OMELET

Serves: 4–6

Preparation: 20'

Cooking: 35'

Level of difficulty: 1

- 1 cabbage, weighing about 4 lb/2 kg
- 4 large eggs
- ²/₃ cup/150 ml crème fraîche or sour cream
- salt and freshly ground black pepper to taste
- 1 tbsp extra-virgin olive oil
- ¾ cup/90 g freshly grated Gruyère cheese

Peel away the tough outer leaves of the cabbage. Cut into quarters and rinse well.
• Cook the cabbage in a large pot of salted, boiling water for about 10 minutes, or until the leaves are tender. • Drain well and cut into thin strips.
• Preheat the oven to 400°F/200°C/gas 6.
• Beat the eggs in a large bowl until frothy. Beat in the crème fraîche. Season with salt and pepper. Add the cabbage and mix well. • Grease an ovenproof dish with the oil. • Pour in the egg mixture and sprinkle with the Gruyère. • Bake for 15–20 minutes, or until golden brown. • Serve hot.

EASY POTATO FRITTATA

Heat the oil in a large deep frying pan over medium heat. • Arrange the potatoes, overlapping slightly, in the pan. Cover and cook for 12–15 minutes, or until the potatoes are tender but not browned. • Pour off the excess oil, leaving about 1 tablespoon in the pan. • Beat the eggs in a medium bowl until frothy. Season with salt. • Pour the eggs over the potatoes. • Cook for 8–10 minutes, or until the omelet is golden brown on the bottom and set on top. • Transfer to a serving plate and cut into wedges to serve.

376

Serves: 4–6

Preparation: 20'

Cooking: 25'

Level of difficulty: 1

- ¾ cup/180 ml extra-virgin olive oil
- 4 medium potatoes, peeled and thinly sliced
- 5 large eggs
- salt to taste

PUMPKIN AND POTATO SOUFFLÉ

Serves: 4–6

Preparation: 20'

Cooking: 1 h 15'

Level of difficulty: 1

Cook the potatoes in salted, boiling water for 25 minutes, or until tender. • Drain well. • Preheat the oven to 350°F/180°C/gas 4. • Put the pumpkin in a buttered baking dish. Cover with aluminum foil and bake for about 20 minutes, or until tender. • Process the potatoes and pumpkin in a food processor (or mash with a potato masher) until smooth. • Transfer to a large bowl and mix in half the butter, the parsley, egg yolks, and half the Parmesan. Season with salt and pepper. • Beat the egg whites until stiff, then fold them into the mixture. • Grease a 9-inch (23-cm) baking dish with butter and fill with half the potato and pumpkin mixture. Cover with the Mozzarella and the remaining potato and pumpkin mixture. Sprinkle with the bread crumbs and remaining Parmesan. Dot with the remaining butter. • Bake for 45 minutes, or until puffed and golden brown. • Serve hot.

- 1 lb/500 g potatoes
- 1 lb/500 g pumpkin, peeled and cut into small cubes
- 4 tbsp butter
- 2 tbsp finely chopped parsley
- 4 large eggs, separated
- 1 cup/125 g freshly grated Parmesan cheese
- salt and freshly ground black pepper to taste
- 8 oz/250 g Mozzarella cheese, thinly sliced
- ½ cup/125 g fine dry bread crumbs

Serves: 4–6	
Preparation: 35'	
Cooking: 10'	
Level of difficulty: 1	

BAKED CRÊPES WITH MEAT SAUCE

CRÊPES

- **2 large eggs**
- **⅔ cup/100 g all-purpose/plain flour**
- **⅛ tsp salt**
- **⅔ cup/150 ml milk**

- **2 cups/500 ml Meat Sauce (see page 50)**
- **½ cup/60 g freshly grated Pecorino or Parmesan cheese**
- **⅛ tsp cayenne or chile pepper (optional)**

Crêpes: Beat the eggs in a bowl. • Sift the flour and salt into a large bowl. • Gradually pour in the milk, stirring constantly to prevent any lumps from forming. • Beat in the eggs until smooth.

• Cover with plastic wrap (cling film) and let rest for 30 minutes. • Preheat the oven to 400°F/200°C/gas 6. • Roll the crêpes loosely and arrange them in an ovenproof baking dish.

• Spoon the sauce over the top and sprinkle with the Pecorino. Season with cayenne or chile, if liked.

• Bake for 10 minutes, or until the cheese is golden brown. • Serve hot.

BAKED CRÊPES, FLORENTINE-STYLE

Preheat the oven to 350°F/180°C/gas 4.
• Butter a baking dish. • Cook the spinach with just the water clinging to the leaves for 5–7 minutes, or until wilted. • Drain, squeezing out the excess moisture, and chop coarsely. • Mix the spinach, Ricotta, 1 egg, 4 tablespoons of Parmesan, and nutmeg in a large bowl. Season with salt and pepper. • Beat the remaining eggs, milk, and half the butter in a large bowl. Beat in the flour to make a smooth batter. Season with salt.
• Melt a little butter in a crêpe pan or small frying pan. Add 1–2 tablespoons of batter and twirl the pan so that it spreads evenly across the bottom. Cook until brown, then flip to brown the other side. Repeat until all the batter is used up. • Place a little of the spinach and Ricotta mixture at the center of each crêpe and roll them up. • Arrange in the prepared dish and spoon the Bèchamel over the top. Sprinkle with the Parmesan and pour over the tomato sauce. • Bake for about 20 minutes, or until golden on top. • Serve hot.

Serves: 8

Preparation: 45'

Cooking: 35'

Level of difficulty: 2

- 5 oz/150 g young spinach leaves
- ½ cup/125 g Ricotta cheese
- 3 large eggs
- 1 cup/125 g freshly grated Parmesan cheese
- ⅛ tsp freshly grated nutmeg
- salt and freshly ground black pepper to taste
- ½ cup/125 ml milk
- 3 tbsp butter, melted
- ⅔ cup/100 g all-purpose/plain flour
- 1 cup/250 ml Bèchamel sauce (see page 55)
- 1 cup/250 ml Tomato Sauce (see page 37)

BAKED RICOTTA CRÊPES WITH SPRING VEGETABLES

Serves: 4

Preparation: 40' + time to prepare crêpes

Cooking: 1 h

Level of difficulty: 2

- **4 oz/125 g green beans**
- **4 oz/125 g carrots, thinly sliced lengthwise**
- **4 oz/125 g zucchini/ courgettes, thinly sliced lengthwise**
- **4 oz/125 g red bell peppers/capsicum, seeded, cored, and thinly sliced**
- **5 tbsp extra-virgin olive oil**
- **salt and freshly ground black pepper to taste**
- **1 quantity Crêpes (see page 384)**
- **1 cup/250 g Ricotta cheese**
- **2 tbsp freshly grated Parmesan cheese**
- **1 large egg yolk**
- **1¼ lb/575 g tomatoes**
- **10 leaves fresh basil, torn**

Preheat the oven to 350°F/180°C/gas 4.
• Grease a large baking dish with oil. • Cook the green beans in a pot of salted, boiling water for 5 minutes. • Drain and chop into short lengths.
• Sauté the green beans, carrots, zucchini, and bell pepper in 3 tablespoons of oil in a large frying pan over medium heat for 10 minutes. Season with salt and pepper. • Let cool completely. • Prepare the crêpes. • Mix the cooled vegetables into the Ricotta in a large bowl, reserving some of the vegetables as a garnish. Stir in the Parmesan and egg yolk and season with pepper. Spread the Ricotta mixture over the crêpes. • Blanch the tomatoes in boiling water for 30 seconds. • Slip off the skins, gently squeeze out as many seeds as possible, and chop coarsely. • Sauté the tomatoes in the remaining oil in a large frying pan over medium heat for 10 minutes. Add the basil. • Fold the crêpes in half and then into quarters. • Place the crêpes in the prepared baking dish, overlapping them slightly. Cover with aluminum foil and bake for 25 minutes.
• Remove from the oven and top with the tomatoes and reserved vegetables. • Bake for about 10 minutes more. • Serve hot.

CRÊPES FILLED WITH ARUGULA AND TOMATOES

Crêpes: Beat the eggs in a bowl. • Sift the flour and salt into a large bowl. • Gradually pour in the milk, stirring constantly to prevent any lumps from forming. • Beat in the eggs until smooth. • Cover with plastic wrap (cling film) and let rest for 30 minutes. • Blanch the 2 large tomatoes in boiling water. • Slip off the skins, gently squeeze out as many seeds as possible, and chop coarsely. Mix the tomatoes into the batter. • Melt 1 tablespoon of butter in an 8-inch (20-cm) frying pan. Place 1–2 tablespoons of the batter in the pan. Rotate the pan so that it covers the bottom in an even layer. Place over medium heat and cook until the bottom is golden. • Flip the crêpe and brown on the other side. • Continue until all the batter is used. • Filling: Cut the cherry tomatoes into wedges. Toss the tomatoes with the arugula in a bowl. Drizzle with the oil and season with salt and pepper. • Place a little of the arugula and tomato mixture and Parmesan on each crêpe and roll it up. • Serve hot.

Serves: 4

Preparation: 40' + 30' to rest

Cooking: 25'

Level of difficulty: 2

CRÊPES
- **2 large eggs**
- **⅔ cup/100 g all-purpose/plain flour**
- **⅛ tsp salt**
- **⅔ cup/150 ml milk**
- **2 large tomatoes**

FILLING
- **2 tbsp butter**
- **6 cherry tomatoes**
- **1 bunch arugula/ rocket**
- **2 tbsp extra-virgin olive oil**
- **salt and freshly ground black pepper to taste**
- **1 oz/30 g Parmesan cheese, flaked**

BAKED CRÊPES WITH HAM AND BRIE

Crêpes: Beat the egg yolks and salt in a bowl.
• Beat in the flour until smooth. • Gradually pour in the milk, stirring constantly to prevent any lumps from forming. • Beat the egg whites in a separate bowl until stiff. Fold them gently into the mixture. • Cover with plastic wrap (cling film) and

Serve this nutritious dish with a green salad for the perfect light lunch.

let rest for 1 hour. • Melt 3 tablespoons of butter in a small frying pan and mix the butter into the batter. • Melt 1 tablespoon of butter in an 8-inch (20-cm) frying pan. Place 1–2 tablespoons of the batter in the pan. Rotate the pan so that it covers the bottom in an even layer. Place over medium heat and cook until the bottom is golden. • Flip the crêpe and brown on the other side. • Continue until all the batter is used. • Filling: Preheat the oven to 350°F/180°C/gas 4. Place 3 slices of ham on each crêpe. Top with 2 slices of Brie and sprinkle with chives.
• Fold the crêpes into a triangle and place them in a baking dish, overlapping them slightly. • Bake for 15 minutes, or until the cheese melts. • Serve hot.

Serves: 4

Preparation: 45' + 1 h to rest

Cooking: 15'

Level of difficulty: 1

CRÊPES
- 3 large eggs, separated
- ⅛ tsp salt
- 2⅓ cups/350 g all-purpose/plain or buckwheat flour
- 2 cups/500 ml milk
- 5 tbsp butter

FILLING
- 12 slices cooked ham
- 8 slices Brie
- 2 tsp finely chopped chives

EGG, BEEF, AND ZUCCHINI FRY

Serves: 4

Preparation: 15'

Cooking: 35'

Level of difficulty: 1

- **1 large onion, finely chopped**
- **2 cloves garlic, finely chopped**
- **4 tbsp extra-virgin olive oil**
- **8 oz/250 g ground/minced beef**
- **salt and freshly ground black pepper to taste**
- **1 tsp ground cinnamon**
- **2 medium potatoes, cut into cubes**
- **2 medium zucchini/ courgettes, diced**
- **4 eggs**
- **2 tbsp finely chopped parsley**

Sauté the onion and garlic in the oil in a large saucepan over medium heat for 8–10 minutes, or until lightly browned. • Add the beef and brown for 10 minutes. Season with salt, pepper, and cinnamon. • Add the potatoes and cook for 10 minutes, stirring occasionally. • Add the zucchini and cook for 10 minutes more, stirring occasionally. • When the potatoes and zucchini are almost tender, break the eggs over the mixture, stirring carefully to break the yolks. • Cook for 5 minutes more, or until the eggs are set. • Sprinkle with the parsley and serve hot.

EGGS WITH SPICY SAUSAGE

Beat the eggs, harissa, caraway seeds, salt, and pepper in a large bowl until frothy. • Heat the oil in a large frying pan over medium heat. • Brown the mergez. Add the chilies and cook for 5–7 minutes, or until the chilies have softened slightly. Add the tomato concentrate. • Pour in the beaten egg mixture. • Cook over low heat, stirring often, until the eggs are cooked but still soft. • Serve hot.

Serves: 6

Preparation: 10'

Cooking: 20'

Level of difficulty: 1

- **6 large eggs**
- **1 tbsp Harissa (see page 52)**
- **1 tsp caraway seeds**
- **salt and freshly ground black pepper to taste**
- **3 tbsp extra-virgin olive oil**
- **6 mergez or spicy lamb sausages, cut into 1½-inch/ 4-cm slices**
- **3 fresh red chile peppers, thinly sliced**
- **2 tbsp tomato concentrate/purèe**

390

TOMATO AND EGG BAKE

Serves: 4

Preparation: 25'

Cooking: 35'

Level of difficulty: 1

- **12–16 cherry tomatoes**
- **6 breadsticks, broken up into crumbs**
- **3 large eggs and 1 large egg yolk**
- **½ cup/125 ml heavy/double cream**
- **½ cup/125 ml milk**
- **2 tbsp freshly grated Emmental cheese**
- **2 tbsp freshly grated Parmesan cheese**
- **salt and freshly ground black pepper to taste**
- **½ cup/125 ml Pesto (see page 309)**

Slice the tops off the tomatoes. Scoop out the seeds and sprinkle with salt. Drain upside-down on a chopping board or in a colander. • Toast the breadstick crumbs in a nonstick frying pan until browned. • Let cool. • Preheat the oven to 350°F/180°C/gas 4. • Oil a baking dish. • Beat the eggs and egg yolk, cream, milk, Emmental, and Parmesan in a medium bowl until frothy. Season with salt and pepper. • Mix the toasted crumbs with the pesto and spoon the mixture inside the tomatoes. • Arrange the tomatoes in the prepared baking dish, not too close together. Put the tops back on and drizzle with the remaining oil. • Pour the egg mixture into the dish around the tomatoes. • Bake for about 30 minutes, or until set. • Serve warm.

SEAFOOD

MARINATED ANCHOVIES

C lean and wash the anchovies, removing their backbones. Dry well. • Coat with flour, shaking off any excess. • Heat the frying oil in a large frying pan to very hot. Add the sardines and fry for a few minutes until cooked through. Drain on paper towels. • Place the sardines in a shallow serving dish. Season with salt and drizzle with the vinegar. Arrange the mint leaves attractively on top. Refrigerate for 24 hours. • Drizzle with the extra-virgin oil just before serving.

Serves: 4

Preparation: 30'
* + 24 h to marinate*

Cooking: 10'

Level of difficulty: 2

- **24 fresh anchovies**
- **²⁄₃ cup/100 g all-purpose/plain flour**
- **1 cup/250 ml olive oil, for frying**
- **¹⁄₄ tsp salt**
- **2 tbsp white wine vinegar**
- **bunch of fresh mint**
- **2 tbsp extra-virgin olive oil, to serve**

BAKED SCAMPI WITH ALMONDS

Serves: 6

Preparation: 30'

Cooking: 5'

Level of difficulty: 2

- **24 scampi/Dublin Bay prawns**
- **24 slices lard or pancetta**
- **2 oz/60 g flaked almonds**
- **juice and grated zest of 2 oranges + extra orange, to garnish**
- **2 pasteurized egg yolks**
- **¾ cup/180 ml sunflower oil**
- **¼ tsp salt**
- **1 small stalk celery, finely chopped**

Preheat the oven to 400°F/200°C/gas 6.
• Roll each prawn in a slice of lard. • Place in an ovenproof dish, sprinkle with the almonds, and drizzle with the orange juice. Bake for 3–5 minutes. • Prepare a mayonnaise using the egg yolks, salt, and oil (see page 19 for method), then add the orange zest and celery. • Serve the prawns with the mayonnaise passed separately. Garnish the dish with slices of orange, if liked.

SPICY MARINATED SARDINES

Dip the sardines in the flour, making sure they are well covered. • Heat the oil in a large frying pan over medium heat. Fry the sardines for 5 minutes on both sides, or until golden brown. • Drain well on paper towels and place in an earthenware dish. • In the same pan, sauté the garlic and red pepper flakes for 5–7 minutes. • Pour in the vinegar and let it reduce. • Add the bay leaf and rosemary. Season with salt and pepper. • Pour in the water and bring to a boil. Cook for 5 minutes. • Pour the sauce over the sardines and let marinate for 1 hour before serving.

Serves: 4

Preparation: 15' + 1 h to marinate

Cooking: 20'

Level of difficulty: 1

- **24 large sardines, cleaned**
- **⅔ cup/100 g all-purpose/plain flour**
- **½ cup/125 ml extra-virgin olive oil**
- **5 cloves garlic, finely chopped**
- **1 tsp red pepper flakes**
- **1 tbsp white wine vinegar**
- **1 bay leaf**
- **1 sprig rosemary**
- **salt and freshly ground black pepper to taste**
- **1 cup/250 ml water**

PRAWN AND AVOCADO SALAD

Serves: 4

Preparation: 40'

Cooking: 12'

Level of difficulty: 1

Cook the asparagus in a large pot of salted, boiling water for 6–7 minutes, or until just tender. • Drain well and pat dry with paper towels. Cut into pieces about $^1/_2$ inch (1 cm) long. • Mix the lemon juice and 6 tablespoons of oil in a small bowl. Season with salt and pepper. Set aside. • Arrange the salad greens, tomatoes, radishes, avocados, and asparagus on individual serving plates. • Sauté the prawns in the remaining oil in a large frying pan over medium heat for 5 minutes, or until just cooked. • Arrange the prawns on top of the salads. Drizzle with the oil and lemon dressing. Season with salt and pepper.

- **10–12 asparagus stalks**
- **juice of 1 lemon**
- **$^1/_2$ cup/125 ml extra-virgin olive oil**
- **salt and freshly ground white pepper to taste**
- **8 oz/250 g mixed salad greens**
- **2 large tomatoes, finely chopped**
- **1 bunch radishes, trimmed and thinly sliced**
- **3 avocados, peeled and cubed**
- **30 large prawns (lobsterettes, Dublin Bay prawns, Italian scampi) or substitute jumbo shrimp, shelled**

Serves: 4

Preparation: 30' + 30' to chill

Level of difficulty: 2

- 4 tomatoes
- 1 small bunch chives, finely chopped
- 1 cup/200 g tuna in oil, drained, broken up with a fork
- 2 avocados
- juice of ½ lemon
- salt to taste
- 4–8 slices bread, toasted

CHILLED TUNA AND AVOCADO TIMBALES

Blanch the tomatoes in boiling water for 1 minute. Slip off the skins, gently squeeze out as many seeds as possible and chop coarsely. • Mix the tomatoes and chives in a small bowl. • Add the tuna to the tomatoes. • Halve the avocados, remove the pit, and peel. Chop the avocados coarsely and place in a small bowl. Drizzle with the lemon juice and season with salt. Stir into the tuna mixture. • Grease four 1-cup (250-ml) timbale molds with oil. • Spoon the mixture into the molds, pressing down firmly with a spoon. • Refrigerate for 30 minutes. • Turn out onto individual plates, running a knife round the inside to release them. • Serve with the toast.

STUFFED SARDINE ROLLS

Preheat the oven to 400°F/200°C/gas 6.
• Grease a baking dish with oil. • Scale the sardines and remove the heads and viscera. Use kitchen scissors to slit them along their bellies, remove the bones, and open them out flat. Rinse and dry with paper towels. • Heat 4 tablespoons of the oil in a large frying pan over medium heat and add two-thirds of the bread crumbs. Stir for 1–2 minutes, then set aside in a large bowl. • Add 1 tablespoon of oil and the anchovies, crushing them with a fork over a low heat so that they turn into a paste. • Stir the anchovies into the bread crumbs with the raisins, pine nuts, capers, olives, parsley, lemon juice and zest, sugar, a little salt, and a generous sprinkling of pepper. Mix well.
• Lay the sardines out flat, skin-side downward, and spread some of the mixture on each. • Roll the sardines up, starting at the head end, and place in the prepared dish. Pack them closely together, tail downward, and wedge a bay leaf between each one. • Sprinkle with the remaining bread crumbs and drizzle with the remaining oil. • Bake for 20–25 minutes, or the fish is tender. • Serve hot or at room temperature.

Serves: 4

Preparation: 30'

Cooking: 25'

Level of difficulty: 1

- 1½–1¾ lb/700–800 g fresh large sardines
- ½ cup/125 ml extra-virgin olive oil
- 1¾ cups/100 g fresh bread crumbs
- 8–10 anchovy fillets
- 2½ tbsp golden raisins/sultanas, soaked and drained
- 2½ tbsp pine nuts
- 1 tbsp capers
- 5 large black olives, pitted and chopped
- 1 tbsp finely chopped parsley
- 1 tbsp lemon juice
- grated zest of ½ lemon
- 1 tsp sugar
- salt and freshly ground black pepper to taste
- bay leaves

SARDINES IN SWEET AND SOUR MARINADE

C arefully remove the scales from the sardines, take off their heads, then cut down the middle of their bellies and eviscerate (gut) them. Dust lightly with flour. • Heat the oil in a large frying pan until very hot. Fry the fish in small batches until golden brown. • Drain well on paper towels and season with salt. • Remove the pan from the heat, let cool slightly, and then carefully pour off the oil into a heatproof receptacle. • Sauté the onions in the olive oil in the same pan until pale golden brown. • Pour in the vinegar and let it reduce by half. • Arrange the sardines in layers in a deep dish, alternating with the onions and the liquid, making the last layer of onions and the remaining liquid. • Refrigerate for 24 hours before serving.

Serves: 6

Preparation: 20' + 24 h to marinate

Cooking: 20'

Level of difficulty: 1

- 2 lb/1 kg very fresh sardines
- ²/₃ cup/100 g all-purpose/plain flour
- 1 cup/250 ml oil, for frying
- salt to taste
- 1³/₄ lb/800 g white onions, thinly sliced
- ½ cup/125 ml extra-virgin olive oil
- 1¼ cups/310 ml white wine vinegar

SWEET AND SOUR MARINATED BABY FISH

Serves: 6

Preparation: 30' +
*   24 h to marinate*

Cooking: 40'

Level of difficulty: 1

- 2 lb/1 kg baby fish
- 1²⁄₃ cups/250 g all-purpose/plain flour
- 2 cups/500 ml sunflower oil, for frying
- salt to taste
- 1 lb/500 g white onions, very thinly sliced
- ½ cup/125 ml extra-virgin olive oil
- 2 cups/500 ml red wine vinegar

Rinse the fish under cold running water and dry well. Lightly coat with flour. • Heat the sunflower oil in a large frying pan until very hot. Fry the fish in small batches until pale golden brown. • Drain on paper towels. Season with salt. • Cook the onions in the olive oil in a small frying pan over medium heat until very tender. • Add the vinegar and season with salt. Simmer for 10 minutes more. • Arrange the fish in layers in a shallow dish, alternating with the onions. Pour the vinegar over the top.• Refrigerate for 24 hours before serving.

CLAMS WITH ONIONS AND CHILE PEPPERS

Soak the clams in cold water for 1 hour.
• Drain well. • Transfer to a large saucepan and cook over high heat until they open, about 5–10 minutes. Discard any clams that do not open. • Drain, filtering the liquid and setting it aside. • Cut the chile peppers in half lengthwise. Discard the seeds and cut into thin slices.
• Sauté the chile peppers and onions in the oil in a large frying pan over medium heat for 10 minutes. • Add the sherry, sprinkle with the paprika, and season with salt. Cook until the vegetables have softened, adding the clam cooking liquid if the mixture begins to dry.
• Add the clams to the vegetables and cook for 2 minutes. • Transfer to individual dishes and serve with the toasted bread.

Serves: 2–4

Preparation: 30' + 1 h to soak clams

Cooking: 20'

Level of difficulty: 2

- 1½ lb/750 g clams
- 2 fresh green chile peppers
- 2 onions, finely sliced
- 2 tbsp extra-virgin olive oil
- 4 tbsp dry sherry
- 1 tsp mild paprika
- salt to taste
- 4 slices toasted bread, to serve

CLAMS WITH CHILE AND PARSLEY

Serves: 4

Preparation: 5' + 1 h to soak clams

Cooking: 30'

Level of difficulty: 2

S oak the clams in cold water for 1 hour.
• Drain well. • Place the clams in a large pot with 2 tablespoons of oil and the chile pepper. Cover and cook over high heat until they open, about 5–10 minutes. Discard any clams that do not open. • Sprinkle with the parsley and garlic and drizzle with the remaining oil. • Transfer to a serving bowl and serve hot.

- 2 lb/1 kg clams
- 6 tbsp extra-virgin olive oil
- 1 fresh red chile pepper, finely sliced
- 4 tbsp finely chopped parsley
- 4 cloves garlic, finely chopped

STUFFED SARDINES

Serves: 6
Preparation: 10'
Cooking: 40'
Level of difficulty: 1

- 1 large egg, lightly beaten
- 3 cloves garlic, finely chopped
- 2 tbsp finely chopped parsley
- 2 tbsp finely chopped cilantro/coriander
- 1 tbsp Harissa (see page 52)
- ½ tsp ground cumin
- salt and freshly ground black pepper to taste
- 1 tbsp fresh lemon juice
- 2 lb/1 kg medium sardines, heads cut off and cleaned
- ⅔ cup/100 g all-purpose/plain flour + more if needed
- 1 cup/250 ml olive oil, for frying
- lemon quarters, to garnish

Mix the egg, garlic, parsley, cilantro, harissa, cumin, salt, pepper, and lemon juice in a large bowl. • Spoon the filling into each sardine. • Dredge the sardines in the flour, shaking off any excess. • Heat the oil in a large frying pan to very hot. • Fry the sardines in batches for 8–10 minutes, or until crispy. • Season with salt and garnish with lemon quarters. • Serve hot or at room temperature.

STUFFED MUSSELS

Serves: 4–6

Preparation: 30' + 1 h
to soak mussels

Cooking: 55'

Level of difficulty: 2

- 3 lb/1.5 kg
  mussels, in shell
- 2 medium onions,
  finely chopped
- ½ cup/125 ml
  extra-virgin
  olive oil
- ¾ cup/150 g
  short-grain rice
- 3 tbsp finely
  chopped tomatoes
- 1 cup/250 ml
  boiling water
- salt and freshly
  ground black
  pepper to taste
- 3 tbsp dried
  currants
- 3 tbsp pine nuts

Soak the mussels in cold water for 1 hour.
• Scrub the mussels thoroughly, removing any
beards and discarding broken shells. Rinse well.
• Sauté the onions in the oil in a large frying pan
over medium heat for 8–10 minutes, or until lightly
browned. • Add the rice and toast over high heat
for 2 minutes. • Add the tomatoes and water.
• Bring to a boil and season with salt and pepper.
Add the currants and pine nuts. • Cover and cook
over medium heat for 15–20 minutes, or until the
rice is tender. • Use a knife to open up the mussels
without separating them. Rinse again carefully to
remove any mud or sand. • Spoon the stuffing into
the mussels. Close the two halves of each mussel
securely. • Place the mussels in a large frying pan,
adding enough water to cover. Cover and cook for
15–20 minutes. • Serve hot.

MUSSELS WITH CREAM AND WHITE WINE

Soak the mussels in cold water for 1 hour.
• Scrub the mussels thoroughly, removing any beards and discarding broken shells. Rinse well.
• Sauté the onion, garlic, shallots, parsley (reserving 2 tablespoons), and bay leaves in the oil in a large frying pan over medium heat for 5 minutes. • Add the mussels and cover and cook for 15 minutes, or until all they are all open. Discard any mussels that do not open. • Pour in the wine and let it evaporate. • Stir in the cream and cook until thickened. • Sprinkle with the reserved parsley and serve hot.

Serves: 6–8

Preparation: 15' + 1 h to soak mussels

Cooking: 30'

Level of difficulty: 1

- 6 lb/3 kg mussels, in shell
- 1 large onion, finely chopped
- 2 cloves garlic, finely chopped
- 2 shallots, finely chopped
- 1 bunch parsley, finely chopped
- 2 bay leaves
- 4 tbsp extra-virgin olive oil
- 1 cup/250 ml dry white wine
- ½ cup/125 ml heavy/double cream

DRESSED OCTOPUS

Place the octopus in a large pot of cold water. Bring to a boil and simmer for about 1 hour, or until tender. If you have time, let the octopus cool in the water as this will make it more tender. • Drain and cut the octopus into small pieces. • Mix the garlic, oil, vinegar, and parsley in a small bowl. • Pour the dressing over the octopus. • Serve hot or at room temperature.

Serves: 4

Preparation: 20' + time to cool

Cooking: 1 h

Level of difficulty: 1

- 1 octopus, weighing about 3 lb/1.5 kg, cleaned
- 3 cloves garlic, finely chopped
- ½ cup/125 ml extra-virgin olive oil
- 2 tbsp white wine vinegar
- 1 tbsp finely chopped parsley

OCTOPUS AND POTATO STEW

Serves: 2–4

Preparation: 50'

Cooking: 1 h 15'

Level of difficulty: 1

- 1 octopus, weighing about 1½ lb/ 750 g, cleaned
- 2¼ quarts/2.25 liters water
- ½ onion
- ½ carrot
- ½ stalk celery
- 1 bunch parsley
- ½ cup/125 ml vinegar
- 6 tbsp extra-virgin olive oil
- 1 medium onion, finely sliced
- 2 cloves garlic, finely chopped
- ½ cup/125 ml dry white wine
- 1 lb/500 g potatoes, cut into large cubes
- 1 tbsp finely chopped parsley
- salt and freshly ground black pepper to taste

Place the octopus in a large pot and pour in 2 quarts (2 liters) of water. • Add the onion, carrot, celery, parsley, and vinegar. Bring to a boil and cook for 40–50 minutes, or until the octopus is tender. • Drain well and cut into chunks. • Sauté the onion and garlic in the oil in a large saucepan over medium heat for 5–7 minutes, or until translucent. • Pour in the wine and let it evaporate. • Add the potatoes and remaining 1 cup (250 ml) of water, and cook for 10 minutes. • Stir in the chopped octopus and parsley. • Cook for 20–25 minutes, or until the potatoes are tender. • Season with salt and pepper. • Serve hot.

SQUID WITH GREENS

Serves: 4

Preparation: 10'

Cooking: 1 h

Level of difficulty: 2

- **14 oz/400 g beet leaves, Swiss chard, or spinach**
- **1 clove garlic, finely chopped**
- **1 small onion, finely chopped**
- **2 tbsp extra-virgin olive oil**
- **1 lb/500 g cleaned squid, cut into rings**
- **5 tbsp dry white wine**
- **1 (15-oz/450-g) can tomatoes**
- **salt to taste**

Cook the greens in a large pot of salted, boiling water for 3–5 minutes. • Drain and shred finely. • Sauté the garlic and onion in the oil in a large frying pan over medium heat for 5 minutes, or until softened. • Add the squid and sauté for 5 minutes. • Add the wine and let it evaporate. • Mix in the greens and tomatoes. Cover and cook over very low heat for about 45 minutes, or until the squid is very tender. • Season with salt and serve hot.

SQUID WITH PEAS

Carefully detach the ink sacs and set aside.
• Cut the squid into 1-inch (2-cm) rings.
• Place the squid in a large frying pan with about
$^{1}/_{2}$ inch (1 cm) of boiling water. Add the oil and
cook over medium heat for 10–12 minutes, or
until the water has evaporated and the squid has
softened. • Add the onions and cook, stirring often,
for 20 minutes. • Stir in the tomatoes and cook
for 5 minutes. • Add the peas and enough
boiling water to keep the mixture moist. Cook
for 10 minutes more, or until the peas are tender.
• Sauce: Mix the ink, garlic, parsley, flour, oil, and
water in a small saucepan over medium heat for
4–5 minutes, or until dense. • Serve the squid
with the sauce passed on the side.

Serves: 4

Preparation: 20'

Cooking: 45'

Level of difficulty: 2

- 1½ lb/750 g squid
  or cuttlefish, with
  ink sacs, cleaned
- 1 tbsp extra-virgin
  olive oil
- 2 medium onions,
  finely chopped
- 2 medium
  tomatoes, finely
  chopped
- 2 lb/1 kg peas
- 1 cup/250 ml
  boiling water

SAUCE
- 1 clove garlic,
  finely chopped
- 2 tbsp finely
  chopped parsley
- 1 tbsp all-purpose/
  plain flour
- 4 tbsp extra-virgin
  olive oil
- 6 tbsp water

STUFFED BAKED SHRIMP

Preheat the oven to 400°F/200°C/gas 6. • Use sharp, pointed scissors to snip away the upper shells covering their backs. Do not remove the heads or tails. • Mix the bread crumbs, garlic, parsley, wine, and 2 tablespoons of oil in a small bowl. Season with salt and pepper. • Stuff some of this mixture into the opening in the shell of each shrimp. Drizzle the remaining oil over the shrimp. • Place the shrimp in a roasting pan and top with the remaining bread crumb mixture. • Bake for 15 minutes, or until the shrimp are cooked through. • Serve hot.

Serves: 4–6

Preparation: 20'

Cooking: 15'

Level of difficulty: 1

- **2 lb/1 kg jumbo shrimp/prawns**
- **5 tbsp fine dry bread crumbs**
- **2 cloves garlic, finely chopped**
- **1 tbsp finely chopped parsley**
- **2 tbsp dry white wine**
- **5 tbsp extra-virgin olive oil**
- **salt and freshly ground black pepper to taste**

SHRIMP WITH OLIVE OIL AND LEMON JUICE

Serves: 5–6

Preparation: 20'

Cooking: 5'

Level of difficulty: 1

- 2 lb/1 kg medium or large unshelled raw shrimp/prawns
- 2 tbsp extra-virgin olive oil
- juice of 1 lemon
- 2 tbsp finely chopped parsley
- salt and freshly ground black pepper to taste

Rinse the shrimp well under cold running water. Bring a large saucepan three-quarters full of salted water to a boil and add the shrimp. As soon as the water returns to a boil, drain the shrimp and spread out to cool. • Use sharp, pointed scissors to snip away the upper shells covering their backs. Do not remove the heads or tails. • Arrange the shrimp on a large serving platter. Drizzle with the oil and lemon juice. Sprinkle with the parsley. Season with salt and pepper and serve hot.

BROILED SQUID WITH GARLIC AND LEMON

Preheat the broiler (grill) to a high setting.
• Rinse the squid under cold running water.
Dry well on paper towels. • Beat the oil and lemon juice in a small bowl. Dip the squid in the mixture.
• Broil for 5 minutes. Turn them over and brush with the oil and lemon. • Broil for 5 minutes more.
• Transfer to a serving dish. Sprinkle with the parsley and garlic. • During the summer months, grill the squid over the embers of a barbecue.
• Serve hot.

Serves: 2–4

Preparation: 25'

Cooking: 10'

Level of difficulty: 3

- **4 very fresh medium-large squid, about 2 lb/1 kg, cleaned**
- **½ cup/125 ml extra-virgin olive oil**
- **juice of 1 lemon**
- **4 tbsp finely chopped parsley**
- **2 cloves garlic, finely chopped**

STUFFED SQUID WITH TOMATO SAUCE

Wash the squid under running water. Finely chop the tentacles. • Cook the rice with the tentacles in a large pot of salted, boiling water for 10–12 minutes, or until tender. • Drain and add the sage and rosemary. Let cool completely. • Season with salt and pepper and mix in the egg. • Stuff the squid with the rice mixture. Close with a toothpick. • Cook the shallots in the oil in a large frying pan until softened. • Add the stuffed squid and fry gently all over. • Add the wine and let it evaporate. • Stir in the tomatoes and hot water. Season with salt and pepper. Cover and cook over medium heat for 35–40 minutes, or until the squid is tender. • Slice and serve hot.

Serves: 4–6

Preparation: 40'

Cooking: 1 h

Level of difficulty: 2

- 8 medium-large squid, cleaned
- 1½ cups/300 g short-grain rice
- 4 leaves fresh sage, chopped
- 1 tsp finely chopped rosemary
- salt and freshly ground black pepper to taste
- 1 egg
- 2 shallots, finely chopped
- 4 tbsp extra-virgin olive oil
- 4 tbsp dry white wine
- 1¼ lb/600 g canned tomatoes
- 4 tbsp hot water

SQUID STUFFED WITH RICE AND ONIONS

Serves: 6

Preparation: 40'

Cooking: 55'

Level of difficulty: 3

- **8 medium-large squid, cleaned**
- **2–3 large white onions, finely chopped**
- **½ cup/125 ml extra-virgin olive oil**
- **salt and freshly ground black pepper to taste**
- **1½ cups/300 g short-grain rice**
- **2 cups/500 ml water**
- **3 tbsp finely chopped dill**

Wash the squid under running water. Finely chop the tentacles. • Sauté the tentacles and onions in 6 tablespoons of oil in a large frying pan over medium heat for 1 minute. • Season with salt and pepper. Add the rice and sauté for 2 minutes. • Pour in 1½ cups (310 ml) of water and bring to a boil. Add the dill and simmer over low heat until the rice has absorbed all the water, about 10 minutes. • Spoon the stuffing into the squid, leaving enough room for the rice to expand. Close with a toothpick. • Arrange the squid in a large baking dish. Pour in the remaining oil and enough water to half cover them. • Simmer over low heat for 45 minutes, or until they have absorbed all the water. • Serve hot.

BREAD-FILLED SQUID IN TOMATO SAUCE

Serves: 4

Preparation: 20' + 1 h to marinate

Cooking: 30'

Level of difficulty: 2

Soften the bread in the milk for 15 minutes. Drain, squeezing out the excess moisture.
• Remove the tentacles from the squid and chop finely. Mix them with the bread, parsley, 1 clove of garlic, Parmesan, and egg in a large bowl. • Stuff the squid with the mixture and close with toothpicks. • Arrange the stuffed squid in a large baking dish in a single layer. Sprinkle with the sage, rosemary, bay leaf, the remaining garlic, lemon juice, oil, and a little salt. Set aside for 1 hour.
• Preheat the oven to 400°F/200°C/gas 6. • Bake for 10 minutes. • Pour in the wine and season with salt and pepper. Spoon the tomato sauce over the squid and bake for 20 minutes more. • Serve hot.

- 7 oz/200 g soft white bread, crusts removed
- 1 cup/250 ml milk
- 1 lb/500 g squid, cleaned
- 2 tbsp finely chopped parsley
- 2 cloves garlic, finely chopped
- 2 tbsp freshly grated Parmesan cheese
- 1 egg, beaten
- 2 leaves fresh sage, finely chopped
- 1 tbsp finely chopped rosemary
- 1 bay leaf, finely chopped
- 1 tbsp lemon juice
- 4 tbsp extra-virgin olive oil
- salt and freshly ground black pepper to taste
- ½ cup/125 ml dry white wine
- 1 quantity Tomato Sauce (see page 37)

SQUID IN THEIR INK

C lean the squid by pulling the tentacles away from each body sac. Remove and discard the quill inside and snip up the center of the sac to open it out. Remove the ink sac carefully and reserve. • Wash the squid under cold running water and cut into $1/2$-inch (1-cm) wide strips. Open 4 or 5 of the ink sacs and pour the ink into a cup. • Sauté the onion and garlic in the oil in a deep saucepan until pale golden brown. • Add the squid and cook for 3 minutes. • Pour in the wine and let it evaporate. • Dilute the ink with 2–3 tablespoons of hot water and add to the squid. Cover and simmer over low heat for 40 minutes, stirring occasionally. Add 2–3 tablespoons of hot water if the mixture begins to stick to the bottom of the pan. • Season with salt and pepper and serve hot.

Serves: 6
Preparation: 25'
Cooking: 45'
Level of difficulty: 1

- 2$1/3$ lb/1.3 kg whole small squid/cuttlefish
- 1 small onion, finely chopped
- 2 cloves garlic, finely chopped
- $1/2$ cup/125 ml extra-virgin olive oil
- 1 cup/250 ml dry white wine
- 4–6 tbsp water
- salt and freshly ground black pepper to taste

Serves: 4

Preparation: 50' + 1 h
to soak mussels

Cooking: 1 h

Level of difficulty: 2

- **4 lb/2 kg mussels, in shell**
- **4 tbsp hot water**

FILLING

- **8 oz/250 g mortadella**
- **6 slices bread soaked in milk and squeezed out**
- **1 clove garlic**
- **1 sprig parsley**
- **2 eggs**
- **½ cup/60 g freshly grated Parmesan**
- **¼ tsp dried thyme**
- **⅛ tsp freshly grated nutmeg**
- **⅛ tsp red pepper flakes**

SAUCE

- **1 lb/500 g peeled and chopped tomatoes**
- **1 clove garlic, finely chopped**
- **salt and freshly ground black pepper to taste**
- **½ cup/125 ml dry white wine**
- **4 tbsp extra-virgin olive oil**

STUFFED MUSSELS WITH TOMATOES

S oak the mussels in cold water for 1 hour.
• Scrub the mussels thoroughly, removing any beards and discarding broken shells. Rinse well.
• Place the mussels and water in a large frying pan over medium heat and cook until they open. Discard any that do not open. • Remove the mussels from the shells. • Filling: Finely chop the mortadella, bread, cooked mussels, 1 clove of garlic, and parsley in a food processor or blender.
• Transfer to a large bowl and mix in the eggs, Parmesan, thyme, nutmeg, and red pepper flakes. Season with salt and pepper. • Stuff the mussel shells with the filling. • Cook the tomatoes with the remaining garlic, wine, and oil in a large saucepan until the oil separates from the tomatoes, about 30 minutes. • Place the stuffed mussels in a large frying pan and pour the tomato sauce over the top.
• Cover and cook over low heat for about 45 minutes, or until the sauce has thickened.
• Serve hot.

MUSSEL STEW

Soak the mussels in cold water for 1 hour.
• Scrub the mussels thoroughly, removing any beards and discarding broken shells. Rinse well.
• Sauté the tomatoes, 2 tablespoons of parsley, and 2 cloves of garlic in the oil in a large, deep frying pan over medium heat for 2–3 minutes. Add the mussels and cook until they open up. Discard any that do not open. • Sprinkle with the remaining parsley and garlic. Season with salt and pepper and cook for 4–5 minutes more. • Arrange the toasted bread in individual serving dishes and spoon the mussels and the cooking juices over the top. • Serve hot.

432

Serves: 4

Preparation: 10' + 1 h to soak clams

Cooking: 5'

Level of difficulty: 1

- 3 lb/1.5 kg mussels, in shell
- 4 medium tomatoes, peeled and chopped
- 3 tbsp finely chopped parsley
- 3 cloves garlic, finely chopped
- 4 tbsp extra-virgin olive oil
- salt and freshly ground black pepper to taste
- 4 large, thick slices of bread, toasted and, if liked, rubbed with garlic

BAKED SCALLOPS

Preheat the oven to 350°F/180°C/gas 4.
• Rinse the scallops under cold running water and shuck with a sharp knife (if they are not already open). • Throw away the top half of the shell and leave the scallop intact inside the other shell.
• Mix the onion, garlic, parsley, bread crumbs, lemon juice, and oil in a small bowl.

Choose only the freshest scallops with their pink coral still attached. Serve with chilled, dry white wine.

Season with salt and pepper. • Spoon a tablespoon of the mixture on top of each scallop. • Arrange the scallops in a large baking dish. • Bake for about 10 minutes, or until the topping is lightly golden. • Serve warm.

Serves: 4–6

Preparation: 25'

Cooking: 10'

Level of difficulty: 1

- **24 scallops**
- **½ onion, finely chopped**
- **2 cloves garlic, finely chopped**
- **4 tbsp finely chopped parsley**
- **8 tbsp fine dry bread crumbs**
- **juice of 1 lemon**
- **6 tbsp extra-virgin olive oil**
- **salt and freshly ground black pepper to taste**

434

GREEK FISH STEW

S•oak the mussels in cold water for 1 hour.
• Scrub the mussels thoroughly, removing any beards and discarding broken shells. Rinse well. •
• Place the mussels in a large frying pan over medium heat and cook until they open. Discard any that do not open. • Remove the mussels from the shells. • Sauté the onions, carrots, and celery in the oil in a large saucepan over low heat for 15 minutes. • Add the parsley, peppercorns, bay leaf, and garlic. • Stir in the tomatoes and cook for 10 minutes. • Pour in the water and bring to a boil. Add the rockfish. • Partially cover and cook over low heat for 1 hour. • Add the fish and lobster. Cook over low heat for 20 minutes.
• Add the shrimp and continue cooking for 5 minutes. Add the mussels. • Remove from the heat and take out the fish and the lobster. Season with salt. • Skin and fillet the fish. Shell the lobster and cut it into thick slices. • Serve hot.

Serves: 8

Preparation: 35' + 1 h
to soak mussels

Cooking: 1 h 40'

Level of difficulty: 2

- 2 lb/1 kg mussels, in shell
- 2 red onions, finely chopped
- 2 carrots, chopped
- 2 stalks celery, finely chopped
- 4 tbsp extra-virgin olive oil
- 2 tbsp finely chopped parsley
- 1 tsp black peppercorns
- 1 bay leaf
- 2 cloves garlic, finely chopped
- 1 lb/500 g tomatoes, peeled and chopped
- 2 quarts/2 liters water
- 2 lb/1 kg rockfish, cleaned and gutted
- 1 whole fish, weighing about 2 lb/1 kg, cleaned and gutted
- 1 lobster, weighing about 2 lb/1 kg
- 1 lb/500 g shrimp/ prawns, well-washed
- salt to taste

SAFFRON FISH STEW

Soak the mussels in cold water for 1 hour.
• Scrub the mussels thoroughly, removing any beards and discarding broken shells. Rinse well.
• Sauté the mussels in a large frying pan over high heat until they have all opened. Remove the mussels from the shells. • Sauté the onion in the oil in a large saucepan over medium heat for 5–7 minutes, or until translucent. • Add the garlic, bell pepper, and ham and cook for 2 minutes. • Stir in the tomatoes, bay leaf, and oregano. Cook for 10–15 minutes, or until the sauce has thickened. • Add the fish to the sauce and pour in the wine and stock. Season with salt and add the saffron. • Bring to a boil, stirring often. • Add the mussels, shrimp, and crabmeat. Cover and cook for 5 minutes. • Season with salt and pepper and transfer to a large serving dish. Garnish with the parsley and lemon.

Serves: 4

Preparation: 20' + 1 h to soak mussels

Cooking: 35'

Level of difficulty: 2

- 15 mussels, in shell
- 1 medium onion, finely chopped
- 4 tbsp extra-virgin olive oil
- 3 cloves garlic, finely chopped
- 1 red bell pepper, seeded and finely chopped
- 2 tbsp diced ham
- 1 cup/250 ml chopped tomatoes
- 1 bay leaf
- ¼ tsp oregano
- 1 lb/500 g swordfish steaks, well-washed and cut into small chunks
- ½ cup/125 ml dry white wine
- 2 cups/500 ml Fish Stock (see page 226)
- salt and freshly ground black pepper to taste
- 3 saffron threads
- 12 shrimp, shelled and cleaned
- 8 oz/250 g crabmeat
- 3 tbsp finely chopped parsley
- 1 lemon, quartered

Serves: 6

Preparation: 50'

Cooking: 1 h 30'

Level of difficulty: 2

- 4 lb/2 kg mixed fish, such as smooth hound, stargazer, eel, scorpion fish, and gurnard
- ½ onion, finely chopped
- 1 carrot, finely chopped
- 1 stalk celery, finely chopped
- 1 sprig parsley, finely chopped
- 4 cloves garlic
- 1 fresh red chile pepper, thinly sliced
- ⅔ cup/150 ml extra-virgin olive oil
- salt and freshly ground black pepper to taste
- 1 lb/500 g octopus and squid, cleaned and coarsely chopped
- ½ cup/125 ml dry white wine
- 2 lb/1 kg ripe tomatoes, peeled and seeds removed
- 12 jumbo shrimp/ king prawns
- 6 slices firm-textured bread, toasted

TUSCAN FISH STEW

Clean the large fish and remove the heads. Set them aside for later. Leave the smaller fish whole but clean inside. • Sauté the onion, carrot, celery, parsley, 3 cloves of garlic, and chile pepper in the oil in a large saucepan over medium heat until the garlic is lightly golden. Season with salt and pepper. • Add the octopus and squid

This stew comes from Livorno, a seaport on the Tuscan coast, where it is known as "cacciucco."

and cook over high heat until any liquid has evaporated. • Pour in the wine and let it evaporate. • Stir in the tomatoes. Cover and cook for 10 minutes. • Remove the octopus and squid and set aside. Add the reserved fish heads and the smaller whole fish. Cook for 25 minutes, adding a little hot water if the sauce starts to dry out and stick to the bottom of the pan. • Remove the fish and set aside. • Transfer the sauce to a food processor and process until purèed. Return the sauce to the pan and add all the fish, cut into pieces. Cook over low heat for 15 minutes, add a little water if necessary. • Put the octopus and squid back in the pan and add the shrimp. Bring to a boil and simmer for about 30 minutes. • Serve the soup in bowls, with toasted bread rubbed with garlic.

SWORDFISH WITH PINE NUTS, CAPERS, AND OLIVES

Serves: 6

Preparation: 15'

Cooking: 10'

Level of difficulty: 2

- **2 tbsp pine nuts**
- **2 cloves garlic, finely chopped**
- **½ cup/125 ml extra-virgin olive oil**
- **6 large swordfish steaks, about 2½ lb/1.5 kg**
- **½ cup/125 ml dry white wine**
- **2 tbsp capers, rinsed and chopped**
- **2 tbsp finely chopped parsley**
- **¼ tsp dried oregano**
- **30 black olives, pitted and chopped**
- **salt and freshly ground black pepper to taste**

Toast the pine nuts in a frying pan until lightly browned. • Sauté the garlic in the oil in a large frying pan over medium heat for 1 minute. • Add the swordfish and seal on both sides. • Pour in the wine and let it evaporate. • Add the pine nuts, capers, parsley, oregano, and olives. Season with salt and pepper. • Turn the fish and cook for 5 minutes. • Transfer to a serving dish and drizzle with the sauce. • Serve hot.

CREAMY SEAFOOD BAKE

S oak the mussels in cold water for 1 hour.
• Scrub the mussels thoroughly, removing any beards and discarding broken shells. Rinse well.
• Sauté the mussels in a large frying pan over high heat until they have all opened. Reserve the cooking liquid. • Remove the mussels from the shells. • Preheat the oven to 400°F/200°C/gas 6.
• Butter a baking dish. • Place the sole in the baking dish and sprinkle with the shallot. Season with salt and pepper. • Pour in the wine and add the mussels, shrimp, and mushrooms. • Bake for about 10 minutes, or until the fish is tender.
• Strain the cooking liquid and heat in a small saucepan over medium heat. Stir in the flour.
• Add the cream and stir until thickened. Season with salt. • Pour the sauce over the sole.
• Bake for 10 minutes more. • Serve hot.

Serves: 6

Preparation: 45' + 1 h to soak mussels

Cooking: 30'

Level of difficulty: 2

- **8–10 mussels, in shell**
- **½ cup/125 ml dry white wine**
- **12 fillets sole**
- **1 shallot, finely chopped**
- **salt and freshly ground white pepper to taste**
- **12 shrimp/prawns, shelled**
- **8 cultivated mushrooms, thinly sliced**
- **1 tbsp all-purpose/ plain flour**
- **1 cup/250 ml heavy/double cream**

ITALIAN-STYLE STOCKFISH

Sauté the onions in the oil in a large frying pan over medium heat for 10 minutes. • Season with salt and pepper. Add the stockfish and cook for 30 minutes. • Boil the potatoes in salted water for 15 minutes, or until tender. • Drain and add to the fish. Stir in the tomatoes and cook for 10 minutes. • Serve hot.

Serves: 4
Preparation: 40'
Cooking: 1 h
Level of difficulty: 1

- **2 onions, finely chopped**
- **4 tbsp extra-virgin olive oil**
- **salt and freshly ground black pepper to taste**
- **1 lb/500 g presoaked stockfish, cut into small pieces**
- **5 oz/150 g new potatoes, halved**
- **8 oz/250 g tomatoes, coarsely chopped**

446

PIOMBINO STOCKFISH

447

Serves: 4–6

Preparation: 25'

Cooking: 1 h

Level of difficulty: 1

- 1¼ lb/600 g white onions, finely chopped
- 1 hot chile pepper
- 4 tbsp extra-virgin olive oil
- 1 cup/250 ml dry white wine
- 1 lb/500 g presoaked stockfish, cut into small pieces
- 2 cups/500 ml Tomato Sauce (see page 37)
- 14 oz/400 g potatoes, diced
- salt and freshly ground black pepper to taste

Sauté the onions and chile pepper in the oil in a large frying pan over medium heat for 10 minutes, or until golden. • Pour in the wine and let it evaporate. • Add the fish. Cover and cook over low heat for 30 minutes. • Stir in the tomato sauce and potatoes. Season with salt and pepper. Cook for 20 minutes, or until the fish and potatoes are tender and well cooked. • Serve hot.

BAKED SALT COD WITH PARSLEY SAUCE

Soak the salt cod in the milk in a large bowl for 3 hours. • Cook the potatoes in a large pot of salted, boiling water for 20 minutes, or until tender. Drain and slice thinly. • Sauté the celery, carrot, onion, garlic, parsley, and anchovies in 4 tablespoons of oil in a large frying pan over low heat for 10 minutes, mashing the anchovies with a fork. • Finely chop the capers, pine nuts, and mushrooms in a food processor or blender. Pour in the wine and mix well. • Add this mixture to the pan and cook for 10 minutes. • Preheat the oven to 350°F/180°C/gas 4. • Remove the cod from the milk and dip in the flour until well coated. Add to the pan and season with salt and pepper. Cook for 20 minutes. • Oil a large baking dish and arrange the potatoes in the bottom of the dish. Season with salt and pepper and drizzle with the remaining oil. Top with the cod and sauce. • Bake for about 15 minutes, or until well cooked. • Serve hot.

Salt cod is now rare. If only available unsoaked, soak in cold water for 24 hours, changing the water regularly.

448

Serves: 4

Preparation: 20' + 3 h to soak salt cod

Cooking: 1 h 20'

Level of difficulty: 2

- 2 lb/1 kg salt cod, presoaked
- 1 quart/1 liter milk
- 1 lb/500 g potatoes
- 1 stalk celery, finely chopped
- 1 carrot, peeled and finely chopped
- 1 onion, finely chopped
- 2 cloves garlic, finely chopped
- 6 tbsp finely chopped parsley
- 6 anchovy fillets
- 4 tbsp extra-virgin olive oil
- 1 tbsp capers
- 2 tbsp pine nuts
- 1 oz/30 g dried mushrooms, soaked in warm water for 15 minutes, drained
- ½ cup/125 ml dry white wine
- 2 tbsp all-purpose/plain flour
- salt and freshly ground black pepper to taste

SOLE WITH MUSHROOMS, TOMATOES, AND POTATOES

Preheat the oven to 350°F/180°C/gas 4.
• Grease a baking dish with oil. • Halve the tomatoes, gently squeeze out as many seeds as possible, and coarsely chop. • Arrange the potatoes and shallots in the prepared baking dish. • Remove the earthy part of the mushroom stalks. Wash and quarter the mushrooms and arrange them on top of the potatoes. • Place the sole fillets on top of the vegetables. Top with the tomatoes. Sprinkle with half the parsley and season with salt and pepper. • Pour in the vegetable stock and wine. • Bake for 25 minutes. • Melt the butter in a medium saucepan . Add the flour and stir until smooth. Gradually pour in the fish stock. Cook, stirring constantly, until the sauce is smooth. Season with salt and pepper. • Pour the sauce over the fish. Bake for 10 minutes more. • Season generously with pepper and garnish with the remaining parsley.

Serves: 6

Preparation: 30'

Cooking: 35'

Level of difficulty: 3

- 2 tomatoes
- 2 medium potatoes
- 6 shallots, finely sliced
- 12 button mushrooms
- 12 sole fillets
- 1 tbsp finely chopped parsley
- salt and freshly ground black pepper to taste
- 1½ quarts/ 1.5 liters hot Vegetable Stock (see page 224)
- ½ cup/125 ml dry white wine
- 2 tbsp butter
- 2 tbsp all-purpose/ plain flour
- 1 cup/250 ml Fish Stock (see page 234)

MICRO-WAVED TUNA WITH BELL PEPPERS

Serves: 4

Preparation: 25'

Cooking: 12'

Level of difficulty: 1

- 1 red bell pepper/capsicum, seeded, cored, and thinly sliced
- 1 yellow bell pepper/capsicum, seeded, cored, and thinly sliced
- 1 onion, thinly sliced
- 1 fresh red chile pepper, thinly sliced
- 4 tbsp extra-virgin olive oil
- salt to taste
- 7 oz/200 g peeled and chopped tomatoes
- 1½ lb/750 g fresh tuna slices
- 1 tbsp mild paprika

Place the bell peppers, onion, chile pepper, and oil in a heatproof bowl, suitable for microwaves. Season with salt. • Cook in the microwave at high power for 4 minutes. • Add the tomatoes and cook for 3 minutes. • Arrange the tuna slices in the bowl, making sure they do not overlap. Cover and cook in the microwave at high power for 3 minutes. • Turn over the tuna and cook for 2 minutes more. • Let stand for 2 minutes. • Place the tuna slices on a large serving plate. Top with the bell peppers and onions. Drizzle with the cooking liquid, sprinkle with the paprika, and serve warm.

453

SOLE MEUNIÈRE

Dip the sole in the flour until well coated, shaking off the excess. • Melt the butter in a large frying pan over low heat. • Add the fish to the pan and cook over low heat for 5 minutes. • Flip over the fish and cook on the other side for 5 minutes. • Season with salt. Drizzle with the lemon juice and cook for 1 minute more. • Garnish with the parsley and serve.

454

- 4 whole sole, skinned
- 6 tbsp all-purpose/plain flour
- 6 tbsp butter
- salt to taste
- juice of 1 lemon
- 2 tbsp finely chopped parsley

Serves: 4

Preparation: 20'

Cooking: 15'

Level of difficulty: 1

- 2 lb/1 kg pike
- 1⅓ cups/200 g bread crumbs
- ¾ cup/200 ml extra-virgin olive oil
- 3 tbsp finely chopped parsley
- 1 clove garlic, finely chopped
- salt and freshly ground black pepper to taste
- 1 tbsp white wine vinegar
- 4 oz/125 g pickled vegetables, chopped
- 3 oz/90 g green olives, pitted and chopped

PIKE IN OLIVE SAUCE

Clean and eviscerate (gut) the pike. Prepare fillets. (If preferred, ask your fish vendor to clean the fish). Rinse well and pat dry. • Preheat the broiler (grill) to very hot. • Coat the pike with the bread crumbs. Drizzle with a little of the oil. • Cook under the broiler, turing often, until the fish is cooked, about 5–10 minutes. • Meanwhile, mix the parsley and garlic with the remaining oil and season with salt and pepper. • Divide the cooked pike into 4 portions and drizzle each one with the sauce and vinegar and sprinkle with the chopped vegetables and olives. • Serve hot.

BAKED FISH AND POTATOES

Preheat the oven to 325°F/170°C/gas 3.
• Set out a large baking dish. • Season the fish with salt and pepper. Sprinkle with oregano.
• Place the garlic, parsley, and 4 tablespoons of oil in the dish. • Drizzle the potatoes with 4 tablespoons of oil and season with salt and pepper. Sprinkle with oregano. • Spoon the potatoes on top of the parsley and garlic.
• Bake for 20 minutes. Remove from the oven and arrange the fish on top. • Return to the oven and bake for 15–20 minutes, or until the fish is tender. • Mix the lemon juice, wine, and remaining oil and baste the fish while baking. • Serve hot.

Serves:	4
Preparation:	15'
Cooking:	40'
Level of difficulty:	1

- 2 lb/1 kg firm-textured fish (sea bass, carp, mullet, or tuna, cleaned)
- salt and freshly ground white pepper to taste
- ¼ tsp oregano
- 5 cloves garlic, finely chopped
- 3 tbsp finely chopped parsley
- ¾ cup/180 ml extra-virgin olive oil
- 2 lb/1 kg potatoes, cut in small cubes
- 3 tbsp lemon juice
- 1 cup/250 ml dry white wine

Serves: 4

Preparation: 25'

Cooking: 45'

Level of difficulty: 1

- 1 cup/120 g diced bacon
- 1 cup/180 g golden raisins/ sultanas
- 2 trout, weighing about 1½ lb/ 750 g, cleaned
- 4 cloves garlic, finely chopped
- 2 tbsp finely chopped parsley
- ½ cup/125 ml extra-virgin olive oil
- ½ cup/125 ml white wine vinegar
- 1 cup/250 ml water
- 2 large eggs, lightly beaten
- juice of 1 lemon
- salt and freshly ground black pepper to taste

TROUT WITH GOLDEN RAISINS

Preheat the oven to 400°F/200°C/gas 6.
• Set out a large baking dish. • Mix the bacon and ¼ cup (45 g) of raisins in a medium bowl. Stuff the fish with the raisin mixture. • Use a sharp knife to make a number of small cuts on the backs of the fish. • Arrange the garlic and parsley in the baking dish. Place the fish in the dish and drizzle with the oil, vinegar, and water. • Bake for 40–45 minutes, or until the fish is tender. • Transfer to a heated serving dish. • Place the eggs, remaining raisins, and lemon juice in a small saucepan. Cook over medium heat for 2–3 minutes, then pour over the fish. Season with salt and pepper. • Serve hot.

FISH WITH ONIONS AND RAISINS

Preheat the oven to 325°F/170°C/gas 3.
• Use a sharp knife to cut the fish skin diagonally in the thicker parts. • Heat 2 tablespoons of oil in a large frying pan over medium heat. • Sauté the onions for 8–10 minutes, or until lightly browned. Season with salt and pepper. • Drizzle the fish with the remaining oil. Sprinkle with the cinnamon, ginger, and nutmeg. • Transfer to a large ovenproof dish. Sprinkle with the parsley and top with the onion mixture and raisins. Pour in the water. • Bake for 40–45 minutes, or until the raisins and onions form a golden crust. • Serve hot.

458

Serves: 6	
Preparation: 20'	
Cooking: 45'	
Level of difficulty: 1	

- 1 sea bass, weighing about 3 lb/1.5 kg, cleaned
- 4 tbsp extra-virgin olive oil
- 2 large onions, finely chopped
- salt and freshly ground black pepper to taste
- 1 tsp ground cinnamon
- 1 tsp ground ginger
- ¼ tsp freshly grated nutmeg
- 1 tbsp finely chopped parsley
- 1⅔ cups/240 g raisins
- 4 tbsp water

SOLE WITH ASPARAGUS AND LEMON SAUCE

Serves: 6

Preparation: 25'

Cooking: 25'

Level of difficulty: 2

- **30 asparagus stalks**
- **12 sole fillets, each weighing about 3 oz/90 g**
- **2 shallots, finely chopped**
- **1 cup/250 ml dry white wine**
- **1 cup/250 g butter, cut into pieces**
- **5 tbsp finely chopped mixed herbs (parsley, basil, tarragon, and chervil)**
- **juice of 1 lemon**

Cook the asparagus in a large pot of salted, boiling water for 6–7 minutes, or until tender. • Trim the asparagus stalks so that they are a little longer than the width of the fish fillets. • Roll the fish fillets up around 12 asparagus stalks. • Place the shallots in a large frying pan over medium heat. Arrange the sole rolls on top. • Pour in the wine and let it evaporate. • Cover and cook over low heat for 10–15 minutes, or until the fish is cooked. Carefully remove the fish and asparagus and set aside on a heated serving plate. • Continue cooking until the sauce has reduced by half. • Cut the remaining asparagus into small pieces. • Add the butter to the pan a few pieces at a time, beating with a wire whisk. • Add the remaining asparagus, mixed herbs, and lemon juice and cook over medium heat for 2–3 minutes, or until well blended. • Spoon the sauce over the fish and serve hot.

TROUT WITH BELL PEPPERS AND BLACK OLIVES

S auté the tomatoes and bell pepper in 4 tablespoons of oil in a large frying pan over medium heat for 15–20 minutes, or until the bell pepper is tender and the tomatoes have reduced a little. Season with salt and pepper. Set aside in a warm oven. • Fry the trout in the remaining oil for 5 minutes on each side. • Arrange the trout on a large serving platter and spoon the sauce over the top. Garnish with the olives and serve.

462

Serves: 4

Preparation: 15'

Cooking: 25–30'

Level of difficulty: 1

- **6 tbsp extra-virgin olive oil**
- **1 lb/500 g tomatoes, peeled, seeded, and finely chopped**
- **1 red bell pepper/ capsicum, seeded, cut in thin strips**
- **salt and freshly ground black pepper to taste**
- **4 medium trout, skinned and gutted**
- **1 cup/100 g pitted and chopped black olives**

SWORDFISH WITH TOMATO SAUCE AND GREEN OLIVES

Serves: 4

Preparation: 15'

Cooking: 15'

Level of difficulty: 1

- **4 thick slices swordfish**
- **2 tbsp all-purpose/ plain flour**
- **4 tbsp extra-virgin olive oil**
- **2 cloves garlic, finely chopped**
- **salt and freshly ground white pepper to taste**
- **4 tbsp dry white wine**
- **2 tbsp pine nuts**
- **2 tbsp raisins**
- **1 cup/100 g pitted and chopped green olives**
- **1 quantity Tomato Sauce (see page 37)**
- **1 tbsp sugar**
- **1 tbsp white wine vinegar**

Sprinkle the swordfish with flour. • Heat 2 tablespoons of oil in a large frying pan over high heat. Add the garlic and sear the fish on both sides. • Season with salt and pepper. Pour in the wine and let it evaporate. Remove the fish from the pan and transfer to a heated serving platter. • Heat the remaining oil in a large saucepan over medium heat. Stir in the pine nuts, raisins, olives, tomato sauce, sugar, and vinegar. Cook for 5 minutes, or until the sauce has reduced. Season with salt and pepper. • Serve the swordfish with the sauce.

463

Serves: 6–8

Preparation: 30'

Cooking: 35'

Level of difficulty: 2

- **2 medium onions, finely chopped**
- **2 leeks, trimmed and finely sliced**
- **½ cup/125 ml extra-virgin olive oil**
- **1 lb/500 g tomatoes, peeled, seeded, and finely chopped**
- **6 small potatoes**
- **2 cups/500 ml dry white wine**
- **6 cloves garlic, finely chopped, + 2 cloves, peeled**
- **1 bunch fennel**
- **2 bay leaves**
- **½ tsp crumbled saffron threads**
- **salt and freshly ground black pepper to taste**
- **1½ quarts/1.5 liters Fish Stock (see page 226)**
- **24 small clams**
- **2 lb/1 kg shellfish (scallops, shrimp, lobster, crab)**
- **2 lb/1 kg fish fillets or boneless steaks (halibut, cod, sea bass, red snapper), cut into chunks**
- **6–8 thick slices firm-textured bread**

BOUILLABAISSE

Sauté the onions and leeks in 4 tablespoons of oil in a large saucepan over low heat for 5–7 minutes, or until lightly browned. • Add the tomatoes, potatoes, wine, chopped garlic, fennel, bay leaves, saffron, and the remaining oil. Season with salt and pepper. • Pour in the stock and simmer for 10 minutes. • Add the clams to the stock and cook until they begin to open, 5 minutes. Discard any that do not open. Add the remaining seafood and the chunks of fish. Simmer over low heat for 10–15 minutes, or until the fish begins to flake. • While the fish is cooking, toast the bread in the oven until it dries out but is not too brown. Rub each piece of toast with garlic and set aside. • Ladle the fish stock into the soup bowls and place the toast on top of the soup.

• Place the pieces of fish and seafood on a large heated serving platter and serve hot.

This classic stew from the French riviera is always a winner. Vary the fish according to availability.

BAKED FISH AND VEGETABLES

Serves: 4–6

Preparation: 20'

Cooking: 45'

Level of difficulty: 1

- 4 tbsp extra-virgin olive oil
- 5 cloves garlic, finely chopped
- 1 tsp ground cumin
- ¾ cup/180 ml fresh lemon juice
- salt and freshly ground black pepper to taste
- 4 medium potatoes, with skins, thinly sliced
- 4 medium carrots, thinly sliced
- 2 large tomatoes, finely chopped
- 2 lb/1 kg fresh or frozen fish fillets, thawed if frozen, such as sole or plaice
- ½ cup/90 g pine nuts
- 1 bunch parsley

Preheat the oven to 350°F/180°C/gas 4.
• Place the oil, 4 cloves garlic, cumin, 4 tablespoons of lemon juice, salt, and pepper in a baking dish. • Place a layer of potatoes, carrots, and tomatoes on top and cover with the fish fillets. Arrange the remaining vegetables over the fish.
• Bake for 40–45 minutes, or until the fish and vegetables are tender. • Just before the fish comes out of the oven, process the pine nuts, parsley, the remaining lemon juice, and remaining clove garlic in a food processor until smooth. • Spoon the sauce over the fish and vegetables. • Serve hot.

MARINATED FISH WITH CHERMOULA

Chermoula: Mix the garlic, onion, cilantro, cumin, paprika, oil, lemon juice, and salt in an oval dish into which the fish will fit snugly. • Add the fish, ensuring that some of the sauce penetrates the belly. Cover with aluminum foil and marinate for 2 hours. • Preheat the oven to 425°F/220°C/gas 7. • Arrange the parsley in an overproof baking dish and place the fish on top. Cover completely with the tomato slices. Spoon the chermoula over the top. • Bake for 25 minutes, then arrange the olives around the sides of the fish. • Bake for 10–15 minutes more, or until very well cooked. • Serve hot.

Serves: 6

Preparation: 15' + 2 h to marinate

Cooking: 40'

Level of difficulty: 1

CHERMOULA

- **5 cloves garlic, finely chopped**
- **1 small onion, finely chopped**
- **15 leaves cilantro/ coriander, finely chopped**
- **1 tsp freshly ground cumin**
- **2 tsp paprika**
- **6 tbsp extra-virgin olive oil**
- **3 tbsp fresh lemon juice**
- **1/8 tsp salt**

- **1 white-fleshed fish, weighing about 3 lb/1.5 kg, such as sea bass or bream, cleaned**
- **2 tbsp finely chopped parsley**
- **1 1/2 lb/750 g firm-ripe tomatoes, thinly sliced**
- **2 cups/200 g pitted green olives**

ADRIATIC FISH STEW

Serves: 6

Preparation: 20' + 2 h to marinate

Cooking: 45'

Level of difficulty: 1

- 2 lb/1 kg fresh fish fillets (red mullet, scorpion fish)
- salt and freshly ground black pepper to taste
- juice of 1 lemon
- ½ cup/75 g all-purpose/plain flour
- 6 tbsp extra-virgin olive oil
- 2 medium onions, finely chopped
- 2 cups/500 g chopped tomatoes
- ¾ cup/180 ml dry white wine
- 1 tbsp torn basil
- 3 bay leaves
- 1 tsp chopped rosemary
- 1 sprig parsley

Sprinkle the fish with salt and drizzle with the lemon juice. Marinate for at least 30 minutes.
• Drain well and dip the fish in the flour, making sure it is well coated. • Fry the fish in the oil in a large saucepan over medium heat for 5–7 minutes, or until golden brown. Set aside. • Sauté the onions in the same saucepan for 8–10 minutes, or until lightly browned. Stir in the tomatoes. • Lower the heat and pour in the wine. Add the basil, bay leaves, and rosemary. Season with salt and pepper. • Cook for 5–7 minutes, or until the wine has reduced. • Place the fish in the sauce, shaking the pan gently. • Cook over very low heat for 20–25 minutes, or until the sauce has thickened.
• Sprinkle with the parsley and serve hot.

BAKED FISH WITH BEANS

Soak the beans in cold water overnight. • Drain.
• Preheat the oven to 400°F/200°C/gas 6.
• Cook the beans in a large pot of water for
about 1 hour, or until tender. Drain well, reserving
4 tablespoons of liquid. • Set out a large ovenproof
dish. • Sauté the onion in the oil in a small
saucepan for 8–10 minutes, or until lightly
browned. • Pour into the dish and place the carp
on top. • Cover with the cooked beans and the
reserved liquid. Season with salt and pepper and
sprinkle with the chile. • Bake for 15–20 minutes,
or until the fish is tender. • Serve hot.

Serves: 4

Preparation: 20' +
    12 h to soak beans

Cooking: 1 h 10'

Level of difficulty: 2

- 4 oz/125 g dried
  cannellini beans
- ½ cup/125 ml
  extra-virgin
  olive oil
- 1 large onion, thinly
  sliced
- 2 carp or trout,
  weighing about
  14 oz/400 g each,
  cleaned
- salt and freshly
  ground black
  pepper to taste
- 1 red chile pepper,
  finely chopped

470

FRIED CALAMARI AND SHRIMP

Serves: 6

Preparation: 20'

Cooking: 30'

Level of difficulty: 2

- **1 lb/500 g fresh or frozen calamari rings, thawed if frozen**
- **2 cups/500 ml olive oil, for frying**
- **12 oz/350 g small shrimp/prawn tails**
- **8 oz/250 g baby octopus, cleaned**
- **1 cup/150 g all-purpose/plain flour**
- **salt to taste**

Rinse the calamari rings and shrimp under cold running water and dry well with paper towels. • Heat the oil in a large frying pan or deep fryer to very hot. • Dip the calamari, shrimp, and octopus in the flour and fry in batches until pale golden brown. Scoop out the first batch and drain on paper towels. Clean the oil by scooping out any pieces of fish and fry the next batch. • Season with salt and serve immediately.

ROAST GROUPER WITH POTATOES

Preheat the oven to 400°F/200°C/gas 6. •
Rinse the fish in cold running water and dry
with paper towels. • Fill the cavity with the garlic,
half the rosemary and sage, and the lemon slices.
Season with salt and pepper. • Pour half the oil into
the bottom of a roasting pan. Add the potatoes
and the remaining rosemary and sage. Turn the
potatoes in the oil until well coated. • Place the fish
in the pan, making sure that it touches the bottom.
• Arrange the potatoes around the fish. Drizzle with
the remaining oil. • Bake for 30 minutes, turning
the potatoes every 10 minutes and basting them
and the fish with the oil. • Transfer the fish to a
serving platter with the potatoes and serve.

Serves: 4

Preparation: 20'

Cooking: 30'

Level of difficulty: 1

- 1 grouper, about
  2½ lb/1.25 kg,
  cleaned
- 2 cloves garlic,
  peeled and cut in
  half
- 2 tbsp chopped
  rosemary leaves
- 6 leaves fresh sage
- 1 lemon, thickly
  sliced
- salt and freshly
  ground black
  pepper to taste
- ¾ cup/180 ml
  extra-virgin
  olive oil
- 2 lb/1 kg potatoes,
  cut into bite-sized
  pieces

472

SWORDFISH STEAKS WITH RICE

Serves: 4

Preparation: 15'

Cooking: 35'

Level of difficulty: 2

- 2 tbsp butter
- 1 small onion, finely chopped
- 1½ cups/300 g short-grain rice
- 1 bouillon cube, crumbled
- 4 swordfish steaks, weighing about 8 oz/250 g each
- salt and freshly ground black pepper to taste
- 1 tbsp finely chopped oregano
- 1 tbsp capers
- 2 tbsp finely chopped parsley
- 4 tbsp extra-virgin olive oil

Preheat the oven to 300°F/150°C/gas 2.
• Place the butter and onion in a baking dish. Cook in the oven for 10 minutes, stirring often.
• Add the rice, enough boiling water to cover the rice by 2 inches (5 cm), and the bouillon cube. Cover and cook for 15 minutes, stirring often, or until the rice is tender. • Cook the swordfish in a grill pan (or under the broiler or on a barbecue) over high heat for 4–5 minutes on each side. • Season with salt and pepper and transfer to a serving platter. Sprinkle with the oregano and capers. • Mix the parsley and oil into the rice and arrange on the platter with the fish. • Serve hot.

Butter small timbales and spoon in the rice, pressing down firmly. Tap out and serve warm.

FRIED SWORDFISH STEAKS WITH HERBS

Rinse the swordfish steaks and dry them carefully with paper towels. • Heat 4 tablespoons of oil in a large frying pan over high heat. • Dip the swordfish into the flour until well coated. • Fry the fish for 10 minutes, or until golden brown on both sides. Drain well on paper towels. • Mix the remaining oil with the garlic, parsley, oregano, thyme, and chile pepper in a small saucepan. Season with salt and pepper and cook over medium heat for 15 minutes. • Pour the sauce over the swordfish steaks and serve hot.

- 6 swordfish steaks, about 8 oz/250 g each
- ⅔ cup/150 ml extra-virgin olive oil
- ½ cup/75 g all-purpose/plain flour
- 2 cloves garlic, finely chopped
- 2 tbsp finely chopped parsley
- 1 tbsp finely chopped oregano
- 1 tbsp finely chopped thyme
- 1 dried red chile pepper, crumbled
- salt and freshly ground black pepper to taste

BROILED SWORDFISH WITH LEMON SAUCE

- 2/3 cup/150 ml extra-virgin olive oil
- 4 tbsp hot water
- 6 tbsp fresh lemon juice
- 1 tbsp finely chopped parsley
- 1 clove garlic, finely chopped
- 2 tsp finely chopped oregano
- salt and freshly ground black pepper to taste
- 4 steaks or slices swordfish, weighing about 5–6 oz/ 150–180 g each

Pour half the oil into a blender and gradually add the hot water and lemon juice, pulsing until well blended. • Transfer to a small heatproof bowl. Mix in the parsley, garlic, and oregano. Season with salt and pepper. • Place the bowl over barely simmering water for 3–4 minutes before serving. • Drizzle the swordfish with the remaining oil and broil/grill or barbecue them for 4–5 minutes on each side. • Serve immediately, with the sauce passed on the side.

477

SALT-BAKED PORGY

Preheat the oven to 400°F/200°C/gas 6.
• Place half of the salt into the bottom of a roasting pan in which the fish will fit snugly. Place the fish on top and cover with the remaining salt. The fish should be completely covered — adjust the quantity of salt as required. • Bake for 30 minutes. • Serve the fish directly from the roasting pan, breaking the crust at the table. Peel off the skin, spoon the fish off the bone, and serve hot.

478

Serves: 4–6

Preparation: 10'

Cooking: 30'

Level of difficulty: 1

- **1 whole porgy (or sea bass, red snapper, or rockfish), about 3 lb/1.5 kg, cleaned**
- **5 lb/2.5 kg coarse sea salt**

POACHED SALMON WITH THREE SAUCES

Serves: 4–6

Preparation: 10'
  + time to prepare
  sauces

Cooking: 25'

Level of difficulty: 2

- 1 salmon, about
  4 lb/2 kg, cleaned
- 1 leek, thickly
  sliced
- 1 carrot, thickly
  sliced
- 1 stalk celery,
  thickly sliced
- 1 bunch parsley
- 10 peppercorns
- 2 tsp salt
- 1 quantity Rouille
  (see page 18)
- 1 quantity
  Pine Nut Sauce
  (see page 24)
- 1 quantity
  Tarragon Sauce
  (see page 29)

F ill a pan just large enough to hold the salmon
with cold water. Add the leek, carrot, celery,
parsley, peppercorns, salt, and salmon. Simmer
gently for about 25 minutes, or until the fish is
tender. • Transfer to a large heated plate and
remove the head, skin, and backbone. • Place on
a heated serving platter and serve with the sauces.

HAKE PALERMO-STYLE

Preheat the oven to 375°F/190°C/gas 5.
• Place the anchovies with $1^1/_2$ tablespoons of oil in a small saucepan over low heat. Stir and crush them with a fork until they dissolve in the oil.
• Spread half this mixture inside the cavities of the hake and over their skins. • Mix the bread crumbs, parsley, rosemary, and a generous sprinkling of pepper in a small bowl and coat the fish all over.
• Grease a roasting pan with $1^1/_2$ tablespoons of oil and place the fish in it. Drizzle with the remaining oil. • Bake for 25 minutes. • Garnish with the lemon and serve hot.

Serves: 4–6

Preparation: 20'

Cooking: 25'

Level of difficulty: 1

• 4 salted anchovies (rinsed and boned) or 6–8 anchovy fillets
• 4 tbsp extra-virgin olive oil
• 2 whole, small hake, each weighing about $1^1/_2$ lb/750 g, cleaned
• 4 tbsp bread crumbs
• 1 tbsp finely chopped parsley
• 1 tsp chopped rosemary leaves
• freshly ground black pepper to taste
• lemon slices or wedges

BROILED TUNA STEAKS

Serves: 4

Preparation: 5' + 40'
to marinate

Cooking: 10'

Level of difficulty: 1

- **4 tuna steaks,**
  weighing about
  7 oz/200 g each
- **⅔ cup/150 ml**
  extra-virgin
  olive oil
- **1½ tbsp finely**
  chopped oregano
- **salt and freshly**
  ground black
  pepper to taste

Rinse the tuna steaks and dry on paper towels.
• Mix the oil, oregano, salt, and pepper in a
large bowl. Add the tuna and let marinate for
40 minutes. • Take the steaks out of the marinade
just before they are to be cooked. • Heat the
broiler (grill) or barbecue to very hot and cook the
steaks for 4–5 minutes each side, basting them
with the marinade during cooking. • Spoon more
marinade over the top and serve very hot.

TUNA WITH OREGANO AND TOMATOES

Serves: 4

Preparation: 10'

Cooking: 30'

Level of difficulty: 1

- 14 oz/400 g fresh or canned tomatoes, skinned and chopped
- 1 clove garlic, finely chopped
- 1 tbsp capers
- 1 tsp oregano
- salt and freshly ground black pepper to taste
- 4 slices fresh tuna, weighing about 6 oz/180 g each
- scant $^1/_2$ cup/ 100 ml extra-virgin olive oil

Preheat the oven to 350°F/180°C/gas 4. • Mix the tomatoes, garlic, capers, oregano, a pinch of salt, and a generous grinding of pepper in a large bowl. • Rinse the tuna and dry with paper towels. • Pour just over half the oil into a wide ovenproof dish and arrange the tuna slices in a single layer. • Cover with the tomato mixture and drizzle with the remaining oil. • Cook for about 30 minutes, or until the fish is tender. • Serve hot.

BAKED SALT COD WITH POTATOES

Preheat the oven to 350°F/180°C/gas 4. •
Grease a wide, shallow ovenproof dish with half
the oil. • Arrange the cod in a single layer and top
with the potatoes. • Top with the parsley, onion,
garlic, and oregano. Season with salt and a
generous grinding of pepper. Sprinkle with the
bread crumbs and drizzle with the remaining oil.
• Bake for about 45 minutes, or until the potatoes
and fish are tender. • Serve hot.

Serves: 4

Preparation: 15'

Cooking: 45'

Level of difficulty: 1

- 4 tbsp extra-virgin olive oil
- 1½ lb/750 g pre-soaked salt cod, cut into pieces
- 1½ lb/750 g potatoes, cut into bite-sized cubes
- 1 tbsp finely chopped parsley
- 1 medium onion, thinly sliced
- 2 cloves garlic, finely chopped
- 1 tsp finely chopped oregano
- salt and freshly ground black pepper to taste
- 4 tbsp fine dry bread crumbs

| Serves: 4–6 |
| Preparation: 10' |
| Cooking: 1 h 30' |
| Level of difficulty: 1 |

- 1½ lb/750 g pre-soaked stockfish, cut into small pieces
- ½ cup/125 ml extra-virgin olive oil
- 1 medium onion, finely chopped
- 1 clove garlic, lightly crushed but whole
- 2½ tbsp all-purpose/plain flour
- salt and freshly ground black pepper to taste
- 14 oz/400 g fresh or canned tomatoes, peeled and chopped
- 1¼ lb/625 g potatoes, peeled and thinly sliced
- 2 pears, peeled, cored, and sliced
- 1¼ cups/150 g pitted green olives
- 2 stalks celery, finely chopped
- 1–2 tbsp capers
- 2½ tbsp pine nuts
- 2½ tbsp golden raisins/ sultanas, soaked and drained

STOCKFISH WITH POTATOES

Rinse the stockfish and dry with paper towels.
• Pour the oil into a large saucepan and sauté the onion and garlic. Do not let them color. • Coat the stockfish lightly with flour and cook for 3 minutes over medium heat, turning them once. • Season with salt and pepper. • Stir in the tomatoes and enough hot water to just cover the fish. • Cover and simmer over medium heat for 45 minutes. • Add the potatoes, pears, olives, celery, capers, pine nuts, and raisins. • Cover and cook for another 40 minutes. • There should be plenty of liquid left when the fish is cooked. If not, moisten with hot water as required.

STOCKFISH, VICENZA-STYLE

Remove the skin from the fish without breaking up the flesh. Carefully remove all the bones.
• Sauté the onions and garlic in the oil in a large frying pan until the garlic is pale gold. • Add the anchovies and parsley, breaking them up completely. • Taking care to keep the fish in one piece, open out the sides a little. Spoon the anchovy mixture into the cavity. Sprinkle with half the flour and half the Parmesan. Season with salt and pepper. Gently press the fish closed again.
• Slice across the length of the fish, cutting it into 2-inch (5-cm) thick steaks. Sprinkle with the remaining flour and Parmesan. • Place the steaks snugly next to one another in a heavy-bottomed flameproof casserole which will just fit them in one layer. Pour in the milk. • Cook over low heat for 4 hours; they must not be stirred, but you can shake the dish or pan gently at intervals to prevent the fish from sticking. • Serve very hot.

Serves: 6

Preparation: 30'

Cooking: 4 h 20'

Level of difficulty: 1

- 2 lb/1 kg presoaked stockfish
- 1 lb/500 g onions, finely chopped
- 2 cloves garlic, finely chopped
- 6 tbsp extra-virgin olive oil
- 4 salted anchovies, rinsed, boned, and finely chopped (or 8 anchovy fillets)
- 2 tbsp finely chopped parsley
- 2/3 cup/100 g all-purpose/plain flour
- scant 1 cup/100 g freshly grated Parmesan cheese
- salt and freshly ground black pepper to taste
- 2 cups/500 ml milk

STOCKFISH WITH RAISINS AND ANCHOVIES

Serves: 6

Preparation: 20'

Cooking: 40'

Level of difficulty: 1

- 1¾ lb/800 g presoaked stockfish, cut into small pieces
- ⅔ cup/100 g all-purpose/plain flour
- 1 large Bermuda/Spanish onion, finely chopped
- ½ cup/125 ml extra-virgin olive oil
- 2 tbsp butter
- 2 bay leaves
- 4 anchovy fillets
- ⅓ cup/60 g golden raisins/sultanas
- ⅓ cup/60 g pine nuts
- 2 tsp sugar
- ⅛ tsp ground cinnamon
- ⅛ tsp freshly grated nutmeg
- salt and freshly ground black pepper to taste
- 1 cup/60 g fresh bread crumbs

Preheat the oven to 350°F/180°C/gas 4.
• Coat the stockfish lightly with flour. • Sauté the onion in the oil and butter in a large saucepan until softened. • Add the stock fish and pour in enough water to cover it completely. Add the bay leaves, anchovies, raisins, pine nuts, sugar, cinnamon, and nutmeg. • Simmer over medium heat until the fish has absorbed almost all of the liquid. • Season with salt and pepper. Cover with a sprinkling of bread crumbs. • Bake for 15–20 minutes, or until golden brown. • Serve hot.

RED MULLET WITH TOMATO SAUCE

Sauté the garlic and parsley in the extra-virgin olive oil in a large frying pan for 2–3 minutes, or until the garlic is pale gold. • Discard the garlic. • Stir in the tomatoes and season with salt and pepper. Simmer for 15 minutes. • Heat the olive oil in a large, deep frying pan until very hot. • Dip the fish in the flour until well coated. Fry the fish in small batches until golden brown. • Drain well on paper towels. • Add the fish to the sauce and cook for 5 minutes. • Serve hot.

Serves: 4

Preparation: 20'

Cooking: 30'

Level of difficulty: 1

- 1 clove garlic, lightly crushed but whole
- 2 tbsp finely chopped parsley
- ½ cup/125 ml extra-virgin olive oil
- 12 oz/350 g ripe tomatoes, peeled, and coarsely chopped
- salt and freshly ground black pepper to taste
- 1 cup/250 ml olive oil, for frying
- 1 lb/500 g young red mullet, cleaned
- ¾ cup/125 g all-purpose/plain flour

Serves: 4	
Preparation: 10'	
Cooking: 25'	
Level of difficulty: 1	

SALT COD WITH BELL PEPPERS

- 1 cup/250 ml olive oil, for frying
- 1¾ lb/800 g presoaked salt cod, cut into small pieces
- ⅔ cup/100 g all purpose/plain flour
- 1 large onion, finely chopped
- 4 tbsp extra-virgin olive oil
- 1⅔ cups/400 g peeled and diced fresh or canned tomatoes
- 3 large bell peppers/ capsicums, mixed colors
- salt and freshly ground black pepper to taste

Heat the olive oil in a large, deep frying pan until very hot. • Dip the cod in the flour until well coated. Fry the fish in small batches until golden brown. • Drain well on paper towels and keep warm. • Sauté the onion in the extra-virgin olive oil in a large frying pan until softened. • Add the tomatoes and cook over medium heat for 15 minutes, or until the sauce has reduced by half. Season with salt and pepper. • Clean the bell peppers, removing the seeds and core. Cut into quarters and place under the broiler (grill) until the skin blackens. Peel the blackened skin away with your fingers. Rinse the bell peppers and pat them dry. Cut into thin strips. • Add the bell peppers and salt cod to the pan with the tomato sauce. Cook for 5 minutes. • Serve hot.

CRAYFISH WITH TOMATO SAUCE

Serves: 4
Preparation: 15'
Cooking: 30'
Level of difficulty: 2

Cook the crayfish in a large pot of salted, boiling water for 10 minutes. Set aside. • Sift 1 cup (150 g) of flour into a large bowl. Make a well in the center and stir in the water and egg until well blended. • Peel the crayfish carefully, twisting off and discarding the heads. • Dip in the batter. • Heat the oil in a large frying pan to very hot. • Fry the crayfish in batches for 8–10 minutes, or until golden brown. • Drain on paper towels. Transfer to a large serving plate and set aside in a warm place. • Stir the remaining flour into the oil. Add the tomatoes, vinegar, bay leaf, and rosemary. Season with salt and pepper. Spoon the sauce over the crayfish. • Serve hot.

- 2 lb/1 kg crayfish, washed
- 1⅓ cups/200 g all-purpose/plain flour
- 6 tbsp water
- 1 large egg, lightly beaten
- 1 cup/250 ml olive oil, for frying
- 2 firm-ripe tomatoes
- 1 cup/250 ml vinegar
- 1 bay leaf
- 1 tbsp finely chopped rosemary
- salt and freshly ground black pepper to taste

Serves: 6

Preparation: 20' + 1 h to stand

Cooking: 45'

Level of difficulty: 1

- 3 lb/1.5 kg red snapper or other white firm-textured fish, cleaned
- salt and freshly ground black pepper to taste
- 2 cups/500 ml olive oil, for frying
- 1 cup/250 ml tahini (sesame seed paste)
- 4 tbsp fresh lemon juice
- 2 cups/500 ml water
- 3 onions, finely chopped
- ¼ tsp ground cinnamon

FRIED FISH WITH TAHINI

Sprinkle the fish with salt and let stand for 1 hour. • Preheat the oven to 350°F/180°C/gas 4. • Heat the oil in a large, deep frying pan to very hot. • Fry the fish for 5–7 minutes, or until golden brown. • Drain well on paper towels. • Transfer to a large baking dish, reserving ¹/2 cup (125 ml) of oil. • Mix the tahini, lemon juice, and water in a small bowl. Season with salt. • Sauté the onions in the reserved oil in a large frying pan over medium heat for 8–10 minutes, or until lightly browned. • Add the tahini mixture and bring to a boil for 1 minute. • Pour the onion mixture over the fish. Sprinkle with the cinnamon and season with pepper. • Bake for 10 minutes, or until well cooked. • Serve hot.

Serves: 6–8	
Preparation: 25'	
Cooking: 40'	
Level of difficulty: 1	

- 1 carrot, finely chopped
- 1 leek, finely chopped
- 4 cloves garlic, finely chopped
- 1 medium tomato, finely chopped
- 1 bay leaf
- 6 tbsp extra-virgin olive oil
- ½ cup/125 ml dry sherry
- 1 quart/1 liter water
- 1 lb/500 g presoaked salt cod, cut into small pieces
- 1⅔ cups/400 ml milk
- ⅔ cup/100 g all-purpose/plain flour
- ⅓ cup/50 g cornstarch/cornflour
- 3 large eggs, separated
- salt and freshly ground white pepper to taste
- 1 tbsp finely chopped parsley
- 1 cup/125 g fine dry bread crumbs
- 2 cups/500 ml olive oil, for frying

SALT COD CROQUETTES

S oak the salt cod in a large bowl of cold water
for 2–3 days, changing the water every few
hours. This will remove the excess salt. • Drain well
and set aside. • Sauté the carrot, leek, 3 cloves
garlic, tomato, and bay leaf in 4 tablespoons of oil
in a large frying pan over medium heat for 5–7
minutes, or until
lightly browned. •

*This recipe comes from Barcelona, the vibrant
capital of the Spanish Catalunya region.*

499

Pour in the sherry and water. Bring to a boil, then
simmer over medium heat for 10 minutes. • Lower
the heat and add the salt cod. Cook for 2 minutes.
• Remove from the heat and transfer the cod to a
food processor. • Add the milk, flour, cornstarch,
and 3 egg yolks and process until smooth. Season
with salt and pepper. • Heat the remaining oil in a
large saucepan over medium heat. Sauté the
remaining 1 clove garlic and parsley until aromatic.
• Add the cod mixture and cook, stirring
constantly, until the mixture is thick, about 4
minutes. • Remove from the heat and let cool
completely. • Beat the egg whites in a small bowl
until frothy. • Place the bread crumbs in a small
bowl. • Use your hands to shape the cod mixture
into small croquettes. Dip first in the beaten egg
whites, then in the bread crumbs. • Heat the oil in a
deep frying pan to very hot. • Fry the croquettes in
batches for 5–7 minutes, or until golden brown and
crispy. • Drain well on paper towels. • Serve hot.

POULTRY
& GAME

CHICKEN AND ZUCCHINI TAJINE

Serves: 6–8

Preparation: 40'

Cooking: 1 h 20'

Level of difficulty: 2

- 3 firm-ripe tomatoes
- ½ cup/125 ml extra-virgin olive oil
- 1½ lb/750 g chicken breasts, cut into chunks
- 3 large zucchini/ courgettes, cut into bite-sized cubes
- 3 onions, finely chopped
- 1¼ cups/125 g black olives, pitted
- 2 Preserved Lemons (see page 958)
- 1 small bunch parsley, finely chopped
- 1 small bunch cilantro/coriander, finely chopped
- 1 cup/250 ml Chicken Stock (see page 226)
- 2 cloves
- ¼ tsp ground cinnamon
- salt and freshly ground black pepper to taste

Preheat the oven to 325°F/170°C/gas 3.
• Blanch the tomatoes in salted, boiling water for 30 seconds. Slip off the skins, gently squeeze out as many seeds as possible, and chop coarsely.
• Drizzle 3 tablespoons of oil into a tajine or earthenware pot. Add the chicken and sauté over high heat until golden all over. • Remove the chicken and set aside. • Add the remaining oil and sauté the zucchini until browned. • Remove the zucchini and set aside. • In the same oil, sauté the onions over medium heat for 5 minutes. • Stir in the tomatoes and cook for 5 minutes. • Add the chicken, zucchini, olives, preserved lemons, half the parsley, half the cilantro, stock, cloves, and cinnamon. Season with salt and pepper. Cover with aluminum foil or the tajine lid and bake for 1 hour.
• Garnish with the remaining parsley and cilantro. Serve hot.

CHICKEN WITH BELL PEPPER AND COCONUT

Sauté the onion and garlic in the oil over medium heat for 5 minutes, or until lightly browned. • Add the chicken pieces and sauté for 5–10 minutes, or until nicely browned. • Add the bell peppers and tomatoes and season with salt and pepper. Cover and cook over low heat for 15 minutes. • Stir in the coconut milk and parsley and cook for about 10 minutes more, or until the chicken is tender. • Serve hot with boiled rice, polenta, or couscous.

504

Serves: 4

Preparation: 20' + 12 h to soak beans

Cooking: 1 h 40'

Level of difficulty: 2

- 4 tbsp extra-virgin olive oil
- 1 large white onion, coarsely chopped
- 2 cloves garlic, finely chopped
- 2 red bell peppers/ capsicums, seeded and cut in strips
- 2 large tomatoes, peeled and chopped
- 3 lb/1.5 kg chicken pieces
- salt and freshly ground black pepper to taste
- ½ cup/125 ml coconut milk
- 1 tbsp finely chopped parsley

CHICKEN AND PINEAPPLE KEBABS

Peel and dice the pineapple. Place the juice in a small saucepan. • Cut the chicken into 3/4-inch/2-cm wide strips. Thread alternate pieces of chicken and pineapple onto wooden skewers. • Mix the garlic and oil in a small bowl. Brush the kebabs with the flavored oil and let marinate for 30 minutes. • Mix the vinegar and brown sugar with the pineapple juice. Bring to a boil and stir into the tomato sauce. Season with salt and pepper and simmer for 5 minutes. • Stir in the cornstarch mixture and let the sauce thicken. • Turn on the broiler (grill) to the high setting. • Season the kebabs with salt and pepper. • Cook for 4–5 minutes on each side, or until the chicken is cooked through. • Pour the sauce into a serving dish and top with the kebabs. • Serve hot.

Serves: 4–6

Preparation: 30' + 30' to marinate

Cooking: 20'

Level of difficulty: 1

- 1 small fresh pineapple
- 2 lb/1 kg chicken breasts
- 1 clove garlic, finely chopped
- 4 tbsp extra-virgin olive oil
- 2 tsp cider vinegar
- 2 tsp brown sugar
- 1 quantity Tomato Sauce (see page 37)
- salt and freshly ground black pepper to taste
- 1 tsp cornstarch (cornflour) dissolved in 2 tbsp warm water

BRAISED CHICKEN WITH BLACK OLIVES

Sauté the garlic in the butter in a large frying pan until pale gold. • Discard the garlic. Add the chicken and cook until browned all over. • Season with salt and pepper. Pour in the wine and vinegar and let evaporate. • Add the olives and anchovies, if using. Partially cover and cook over medium heat for about 40 minutes, or until the chicken is tender. • Transfer to a heated serving dish and serve hot.

508

Serves:	4
Preparation:	30'
Cooking:	50'
Level of difficulty:	1

- 2 cloves garlic, lightly crushed but whole
- 4 tbsp butter
- 1 chicken, weighing about 3 lb/1.5 kg, cut into 6–8 pieces
- salt and freshly ground black pepper to taste
- ½ cup/125 ml dry white wine
- 2 tbsp white wine vinegar
- 1 cup/100 g pitted and chopped black olives
- 6 anchovy fillets (optional)

BRAISED CHICKEN WITH PANCETTA AND SAGE

Serves: 4

Preparation: 30'

Cooking: 50'

Level of difficulty: 1

- 2 cloves garlic, finely chopped
- 2 tbsp butter
- 2 tbsp extra-virgin olive oil
- 1 chicken, weighing about 3 lb/1.5 kg, cut into 6–8 pieces
- salt and freshly ground black pepper to taste
- ½ cup/125 ml dry white wine
- ½ cup/60 g diced pancetta
- 8 leaves fresh sage

Sauté the garlic in the butter and oil in a large frying pan until pale gold. • Add the chicken and cook until browned all over. • Season with salt and pepper. Pour in the wine and let it evaporate. • Add the pancetta and sage. Partially cover and cook over medium heat for about 40 minutes, or until the chicken is tender. • Transfer to a heated serving dish and serve hot.

CHICKEN CHASSEUR

Serves: 4

Preparation: 25'

Cooking: 1 h

Level of difficulty: 1

- 1 carrot, coarsely chopped
- 1 stalk celery, coarsely chopped
- 1 onion, coarsely chopped
- 2 tbsp extra-virgin olive oil
- 1 chicken, weighing about 3 lb/1.5 kg, cut into 6–8 pieces
- ¾ oz/20 g dried mushrooms, soaked in warm water for 15 minutes, drained
- salt and freshly ground black pepper to taste
- 6 tbsp Chicken Stock (see page 226)
- ¾ cup/180 g peeled and chopped tomatoes
- 1 bunch parsley, finely chopped

Sauté the carrot, celery, and onion in the oil in a large saucepan over low heat until softened. • Remove the vegetables with a slotted spoon and set aside. • Add the chicken pieces and fry over high heat in the same oil for 10 minutes. • Chop the soaked mushrooms and add to the pan along with the vegetables. • Season with salt and pepper and add the stock. Cover and cook over medium heat for 20 minutes. • Stir in the tomatoes and cook, half-covered, over low heat for 20 minutes, or until the chicken is tender. Turn the chicken two or three times during cooking. • Transfer to a serving dish and sprinkle with the parsley. Season with salt and pepper and serve hot.

511

CHICKEN POT-AU-FEU

Place the chicken in 6 quarts (6 liters) of water in a large pot over medium heat. • Broil (grill) the 3 unpeeled onions and garlic until very dark brown. Add the onions and garlic to the chicken. Cook over low heat for 45–50 minutes. • Add the bouquet garni. Season with salt and pepper. •

512

Pot-au-feu (literally, pot on the fire), is a classic French dish made by boiling meat and vegetables. Cook for 2 hours. • Add the carrots, leeks, turnips, and remaining 3 onions. • Simmer for 1 hour 30 minutes more. • About 1 hour before the chicken is done, boil the cabbage in a large pot with 2 cups (500 ml) of chicken stock over medium heat until tender. • About 30 minutes before the chicken is done, boil the potatoes in a large pot with the remaining chicken stock until tender. • Remove the chicken from the pot and carve. Serve with the vegetables and stock.

Serves: 8–10

Preparation: 1 h

Cooking: 4 h 30'

Level of difficulty: 1

- 1–2 chickens, weighing about 6 lb/3 kg total
- 6 onions, 3 unpeeled
- 1 whole head garlic
- 1 bouquet garni or mixed herbs
- salt and freshly ground black pepper to taste
- 6 carrots
- 6 leeks, white parts only, trimmed
- 6 turnips
- 1 cabbage, cut into wedges
- 1 quart/1 liter Chicken Stock (see page 226)
- 4 lb/2 kg potatoes

BRAISED CHICKEN WITH BELL PEPPERS

Season the flour with 1 teaspoon of salt and 1 teaspoon of pepper. • Roll the chicken thighs in the seasoned flour, shaking each piece to remove any excess. • Sauté the chicken in the oil in a large frying pan over medium heat for 5 minutes, or until browned all over. • Add the onion, garlic, bay leaf, sage, thyme, and rosemary. Pour in half the wine and let it evaporate. • Cook over high heat for 30 minutes, adding the remaining wine to keep the chicken moist.
• Discard the herbs and add the bell peppers. Cover and cook over low heat for 15 minutes, or until the bell peppers are tender. • Serve hot.

Serves: 4

Preparation: 20'

Cooking: 1 h

Level of difficulty: 2

- 3 tbsp all-purpose/ plain flour
- salt and freshly ground black pepper to taste
- 8 chicken pieces
- 4 tbsp extra-virgin olive oil
- 1 large onion, finely chopped
- 2 cloves garlic, finely chopped
- 1 bay leaf
- 2 leaves sage
- 1 sprig thyme
- 1 sprig rosemary
- 1 cup/250 ml dry white wine
- 1 red bell pepper/ capsicum, seeded, cored, and thinly sliced
- 1 green bell pepper/capsicum, seeded, cored, and thinly sliced
- 1 yellow bell pepper/capsicum, seeded, cored, and thinly sliced

VENETIAN SWEET AND SOUR CHICKEN

Serves: 4

Preparation: 15'

Cooking: 15'

Level of difficulty: 1

Flatten the chicken with a meat tenderizer.
• Sauté the chicken in the oil in a large frying pan until browned all over. Season with salt.
• Remove the chicken and set aside. • In the same oil, sauté the onion and garlic until softened.
• Add the pineapple and bell peppers and sauté over high heat for 5 minutes. • Mix the tomato purèe, vinegar, sugar, and water in a small bowl.
• Add the mixture to the pan. Add the chicken and season with pepper. Cook for 3 minutes.
• Garnish with the parsley and serve.

- 1 lb/500 g chicken breasts, sliced
- 4 tbsp extra-virgin olive oil
- salt and freshly ground black pepper to taste
- 1 small onion, finely chopped
- 1 clove garlic, finely chopped
- 2 slices of canned pineapple, drained and finely chopped
- 1 red bell pepper/capsicum, seeded, cored, and cubed
- 1 yellow bell pepper/capsicum, seeded, cored, and cubed
- 2 tbsp tomato purèe
- 2 tbsp white wine vinegar
- 1 tsp sugar
- 1 tbsp water
- 1 tbsp finely chopped parsley

Serves: 4

Preparation: 15'

Cooking: 30'

Level of difficulty: 1

- 1 small onion, finely chopped
- 1 tsp cumin seeds
- 4 tbsp extra-virgin olive oil
- 8 chicken pieces
- salt and freshly ground black pepper to taste
- ¾ cup/200 ml white wine
- 1 cup/250 ml Chicken Stock (see page 226)
- 8 oz/250 g fresh fava/broad beans
- 8 oz/250 g fresh peas
- 14 oz/400 g precooked couscous
- fresh mint and cilantro/coriander, to garnish

CHICKEN STEW WITH COUSCOUS

Sauté the onion and cumin in the oil in a large frying pan over medium heat for 5–10 minutes, or until transparent. • Add the chicken and sauté for 10 minutes, or until well browned all over. • Season with salt and pepper. Pour in the wine and let evaporate. • Add the stock with the fava beans and peas and cook for 15 minutes, or until the chicken and vegetables are tender. • Meanwhile, prepare the couscous according to the instructions on the package. • Place in a heated serving bowl and cover with the chicken stew. • Garnish with the mint and cilantro and serve hot.

BAKED MARINATED CHICKEN WITH ORANGE SALAD

Serves: 4

Preparation: 30' + 1 h to marinate

Cooking: 45'

Level of difficulty: 2

- 4 oranges
- 1 tbsp tamarind sauce
- 2 tbsp slivered almonds
- salt and freshly ground black pepper to taste
- 1 chicken, weighing about 3 lb/1.5 kg, cut into 6–8 pieces
- 4 scallions/spring onions, thinly sliced
- 6 tbsp extra-virgin olive oil

Squeeze the juice from one of the oranges and grate the zest. Mix the orange juice and zest with the tamarind sauce and almonds in a small bowl. Season with salt and pepper. • Pour the mixture over the chicken and let marinate in the refrigerator for 1 hour. • Preheat the oven to 400°F/200°C/gas 6. • Arrange the chicken pieces in aluminum foil and pour over the marinade. • Bake for 40 minutes. Open the foil and cook for 5 minutes under the broiler (grill). • Soak the scallions in ice-cold water for 10 minutes. • Peel the remaining oranges. Slice them and add to a salad bowl. Mix in the drained scallions and oil. Season with salt and pepper. • Garnish the chicken with orange zest and serve hot with the orange salad.

LEMON AND HERB ROAST CHICKEN

Preheat the oven to 400°F/200°C/gas 6.
• Season the cavity of the chicken with salt and pepper. Stuff with the thyme. Cover the outside with prosciutto and bay leaves and tie the legs and thighs against the body with kitchen string.
• Season the outside of the chicken with salt and pepper and rub with half the lemon. Brush with the oil and cover the breast with a sheet of aluminum oil. • Place the chicken in a baking dish (it should fit snugly). • Bake for 20 minutes. • Discard the foil. Place the lemon slices, tarragon, and garlic around the chicken. • Roast for about 45 minutes, turning once and basting with the cooking juices. • Take the chicken out of the oven, remove the kitchen string, and place in a warm oven. • Add the brandy to the cooking juices and cook over low heat until it evaporates. • Serve the chicken hot with the sauce.

Serves: 4
Preparation: 30'
Cooking: 1 h 15'
Level of difficulty: 2

- 1 chicken, weighing about 3 lb/1.5 kg
- salt and freshly ground black pepper to taste
- 1 sprig thyme
- 5 slices prosciutto/ Parma ham
- 3 bay leaves
- ½ lemon + 12 lemon slices
- 1 tbsp extra-virgin olive oil
- 3 sprigs tarragon
- 8 cloves garlic
- 1 tsp brandy

CHICKEN AND GRAPEFRUIT KEBABS

C hop the chicken and pancetta on a chopping board into bite-sized pieces. • Cut one of the grapefruits in half and squeeze out the juice. • Beat the grapefruit juice and oil in a small bowl. Season with salt and pepper. • Add the chicken and pancetta and let marinate for 2 hours. • Peel the remaining grapefruit, removing as much of the white inner skin as possible. • Thread a piece of chicken onto a skewer, followed by a piece of pancetta and grapefruit. Repeat until the skewers are full. • Heat a lightly oiled, nonstick frying pan over medium heat. • Cook the skewers for about 15 minutes, turning them often during cooking. Season with salt and serve.

Serves: 4

Preparation: 20' + 2 h to marinate

Cooking: 15'

Level of difficulty:

- 2 chicken breasts, weighing about 1 lb/500 g
- 7 oz/200 g pancetta or bacon
- 2 large grapefruit
- 6 tbsp extra-virgin olive oil
- salt and freshly ground black pepper to taste

Serves: 2–4

Preparation: 30'

Cooking: 35'

Level of difficulty: 2

- 1 cup/200 g black rice
- ½ onion studded with 1 clove
- 3 cups/750 ml water
- salt to taste
- 12 large shrimp/ prawn tails
- 12 oz/350 g chicken breasts, cut into 12 equal-sized chunks
- 1 cup/250 ml olive oil, for frying
- ½ onion, finely chopped
- 1 tbsp butter
- 1 apple, peeled and diced
- ½ tsp cumin seeds
- 4 tbsp heavy/ double cream

CHICKEN AND SHRIMP KEBABS

Preheat the oven to 350°F/180°C/gas 4. • Place the rice and studded onion in a large baking pan with the water. • Season with salt. • Bake for 15–20 minutes, or until the rice is tender. • Thread the shrimp and chicken onto 4 wooden skewers. • Heat the oil in a large frying pan to very hot. Fry the skewers for 7–10 minutes, turning often, until the chicken is golden. • Soften the chopped onion in the butter in a small saucepan. • Add the apple and sauté over high heat until tender. • Stir in the cumin and cream. Cook over medium heat until the sauce begins to thicken. Season with salt. • Transfer to a food processor and chop until smooth. • Serve the skewers with the rice and apple sauce.

CHICKEN WITH SPICED CITRUS JUICE

Serves: 4

Preparation: 40' + 2 h to marinate

Cooking: 1 h 30'

Level of difficulty: 2

- ¾ cup/180 ml fresh orange juice
- juice of 1 lemon
- 1 clove garlic, finely chopped
- 1 tsp oregano
- ½ tsp cumin seeds
- ½ tsp ground cinnamon
- 1 clove, crushed
- salt and freshly ground black pepper to taste
- 1 chicken, weighing about 3 lb/1.5 kg, cut into 6–8 pieces

Mix the orange and lemon juice, garlic, oregano, cumin, cinnamon, and clove in a small bowl. Season with salt and pepper. • Place the chicken pieces in a large bowl and pour over the mixture. Let marinate for 2 hours. • Cover a metal colander with two sheets of foil in a cross shape. Place the chicken and the marinade on top. Wrap the foil around the chicken, leaving it inside the colander. Place the colander over a pan half-filled with barely simmering water. • Steam for 1¹/₂ hours, or until the chicken breaks away from the bones. • Serve the chicken with the cooking juices.

CHICKEN STEW WITH RICE

Sauté the onion and bell pepper in the oil in a large frying pan over medium heat for 3 minutes. • Add the turmeric and chile pepper paste and sauté over medium heat for 2 minutes. • Add the chicken and sauté for 10 minutes, or until browned all over. • Add the vinegar and let it evaporate. • Add the tomatoes, golden raisins, and a pinch of salt. Mix well and pour in the water. Cook over low heat for 1 hour 20 minutes, or until the chicken is tender. • Cook the rice in a large pot of salted, boiling water for 12–15 minutes, or until tender. • Serve the stew hot with the rice.

Serves: 4

Preparation: 25'

Cooking: 2 h

Level of difficulty: 2

- **1 large onion, finely chopped**
- **1 bell pepper/ capsicum, seeded, cored, and thinly sliced**
- **2 tbsp extra-virgin olive oil**
- **1 tsp turmeric**
- **1–2 tsp chile pepper paste or Harissa (see page 52)**
- **3 lb/1.5 kg chicken pieces**
- **3 tbsp vinegar**
- **2 large tomatoes, finely chopped**
- **6 tbsp golden raisins/sultanas, soaked in warm water and drained**
- **salt to taste**
- **1 cup/250 ml cold water**
- **1¾ cups/350 g long-grain rice**

CHICKEN WITH PASTA

Sauté the onions in the oil in a large saucepan over medium heat for 8–10 minutes, or until lightly browned. • Stir in the garlic, cinnamon, and cloves. Add the chicken and brown over high heat. • Add the tomatoes and season with salt and pepper. Lower the heat and cook for 25–30 minutes, or until the chicken is tender. • Cook the tagliatelle in a large pot of salted, boiling water until al dente. • Drain well and add to the pan with the chicken. • Toss over medium heat for 2 minutes and serve hot.

Serves: 4

Preparation: 10'

Cooking: 55'

Level of difficulty: 1

- 2 onions, finely chopped
- 4 tbsp extra-virgin olive oil
- 2 cloves garlic, finely chopped
- 1 stick cinnamon
- 2 cloves
- 1 chicken, weighing about 3 lb/1.5 kg, cut into 6–8 pieces
- 6 firm-ripe tomatoes, coarsely chopped
- salt and freshly ground black pepper to taste
- 1 lb/500 g dried tagliatelle, broken up

CHICKEN WITH RICE

Serves: 4

Preparation: 25'

Cooking: 50'

Level of difficulty: 1

- 1¼ cups/250 g short-grain rice
- 1 chicken, weighing about 3 lb/1.5 kg, cut into 6–8 pieces
- 4 tbsp extra-virgin olive oil
- 1 medium onion, finely chopped
- 1 chicken liver, trimmed and coarsely chopped
- 1 tomato, peeled and coarsely chopped
- 2 tbsp dried currants
- salt to taste
- 2½ cups/625 ml Chicken Stock (see page 226) + more as needed
- 2 tbsp pine nuts
- 1 small bunch dill, finely chopped

Cook the rice in a large pot of salted, boiling water for 10 minutes. • Drain well. • Brown the chicken in 3 tablespoons of oil in a large frying pan over high heat for 5 minutes. • Add the onion, chicken liver, tomato, and currants. Season with salt and pour in the stock. • Lower the heat, cover, and cook for 15 minutes. • Heat the remaining oil in a large frying pan over medium-high heat. Add the rice and toast for 2 minutes. Add the pine nuts. • Transfer to the pan with the chicken, adding more stock if the mixture begins to dry. • Cover and cook over low heat for 15–20 minutes, or until the chicken and rice are tender. • Garnish with the dill and serve hot.

CHICKEN PROVENÇAL

Sauté the chicken in the oil in a large frying pan over medium-high heat until lightly browned.
• Season with salt and pepper. Remove the chicken from the pan and set aside. • In the same pan, sauté the onion, garlic, and tomatoes for 8–10 minutes, or until the tomatoes begin to break down. Season with salt. • Lower the heat and pour in the wine. Stir in the rosemary, thyme, and olives. Cook for 10 minutes. • Return the chicken to the pan and season with salt and pepper. • Cover and cook over medium-low heat for 30 minutes, or until the chicken is very tender. • Serve hot.

Serves: 4

Preparation: 30'

Cooking: 1 h

Level of difficulty: 2

- 1 chicken, weighing about 3 lb/1.5 kg, cut into 6–8 pieces
- 4 tbsp extra-virgin olive oil
- salt and freshly ground black pepper to taste
- 1 onion, finely chopped
- 3 cloves garlic, finely chopped
- 6 firm-ripe tomatoes, peeled and coarsely chopped
- 2 cups/500 ml dry white wine
- 1 tbsp finely chopped rosemary
- 1 tbsp finely chopped thyme
- 1 cup/100 g black olives

CHICKEN WITH SPANISH HAM

Mix the butter, garlic, and oregano in a small bowl. Season with salt and pepper. • Use a knife to spread half the butter mixture evenly over each piece of chicken. • Place 2 slices of jamón serrano on each piece of chicken. • Roll the chicken up and secure with toothpicks. • Spread the remaining butter mixture over the rolls. • Turn on the broiler (grill). • Broil the chicken rolls 4–6 inches (10–15 cm) from the heat source for 15–20 minutes, turning them often, or until the chicken is cooked. • Transfer to serving plates and remove the toothpicks before serving.

Serves: 4

Preparation: 15'

Cooking: 20'

Level of difficulty: 1

- ½ cup/125 g butter, softened
- 2 cloves garlic, finely chopped
- 1 tsp dried oregano
- salt and freshly ground black pepper to taste
- 4 boneless, skinless chicken breasts, sliced in half to make 8 pieces
- 16 slices jamón serrano or prosciutto/ Parma ham

CHICKEN WITH ALMONDS AND SAFFRON

Serves: 4

Preparation: 20'

Cooking: 50'

Level of difficulty: 1

- 1 chicken, weighing about 3 lb/1.5 kg, cut into 6–8 pieces
- 4 tbsp extra-virgin olive oil
- 1 large onion, finely chopped
- 2 cups/500 ml dry white wine
- 1 quart/1 liter Chicken Stock (see page 226)
- 2 hard-cooked egg yolks
- ¾ cup/120 g whole almonds
- 2 cloves garlic, peeled but whole
- 4–6 saffron threads
- 1 small bunch parsley

Sauté the chicken in the oil in a large, deep frying pan over medium heat for 10–12 minutes, or until golden brown. Remove from the pan. • In the same pan, sauté the onion for 8–10 minutes, or until lightly browned. • Pour in the wine and let it evaporate. Return the chicken to the pan. • Pour in 3 cups (750 ml) of stock. Cover and cook over medium heat for 20 minutes, or until the chicken is almost tender. • Process the egg yolks, almonds, garlic, saffron, parsley, and the remaining stock in a food processor until smooth. • Add this mixture to the chicken and cook for 10 minutes more. • Serve hot.

CHICKEN TAJINE WITH PRUNES

Place the chicken, onions, butter, cinnamon, saffron, salt, pepper, and water in a large saucepan. • Cover and cook over low heat for 40–45 minutes, stirring occasionally. • Remove the chicken from the saucepan and cover with a serving plate to keep warm. • Add the prunes to the liquid and continue cooking for 10–15 minutes, or until the prunes have softened. • Add the honey and lemon juice and cook over low heat until reduced by half. • Return the chicken to the saucepan and cook for 10 minutes more.
• Sprinkle with the sesame seeds and almonds and serve hot.

Serves: 4

Preparation: 15'

Cooking: 1 h 10'

Level of difficulty: 1

- **1 chicken, weighing about 3 lb/1.5 kg, cut into 6–8 pieces**
- **3 large onions, chopped**
- **6 tbsp butter**
- **1 stick cinnamon**
- **¼ tsp saffron threads**
- **salt and freshly ground black pepper to taste**
- **1½ cups/375 ml water**
- **1 cup/250 g pitted prunes**
- **2 tbsp honey**
- **2 tbsp fresh lemon juice**
- **1 tbsp sesame seeds**
- **¾ cup/120 g almonds**

CHICKEN WITH BELL PEPPERS

Serves: 4

Preparation: 1 h

Cooking: 45'

Level of difficulty: 1

Melt 2 tablespoons butter with 1 tablespoon of oil in a large frying pan over medium heat. Add the rosemary and, after 30 seconds, the chicken and bay leaf. • Increase the heat and fry the chicken pieces for 6–8 minutes until browned. • Add half the stock and cover. Cook for 20–25 minutes, or until tender, adding more hot stock if needed. • Melt the remaining butter in a saucepan. Add the anchovies, crushing them so that they dissolve in the butter. • Add the bell peppers and garlic. Season with salt and pepper. • Simmer over medium heat for 15 minutes, then drizzle with the vinegar. • Discard the garlic and bay leaf. • Add the bell pepper mixture to the chicken and simmer for 10 minutes more. • Serve hot.

- **4 tbsp butter**
- **6 tbsp extra-virgin olive oil**
- **1 tbsp finely chopped rosemary**
- **1 chicken, weighing about 3 lb/1.5 kg, cut into 6–8 pieces**
- **1 bay leaf**
- **1¾ cups/400 ml hot Chicken Stock (see page 226)**
- **6–7 anchovy fillets**
- **4 green or yellow bell peppers/ capsicums, seeded and cut in thin strips**
- **2 cloves garlic, lightly crushed**
- **salt and freshly ground black pepper to taste**
- **4 tbsp white wine vinegar**

Serves: 4
Preparation: 15'
Cooking: 50'
Level of difficulty: 2

LIGURIAN-STYLE CHICKEN

- 1 large onion, finely chopped
- 4 tbsp extra-virgin olive oil
- 2 cloves garlic, finely chopped
- 1 tsp fennel seeds
- 1 chicken, weighing about 3 lb/1.5 kg, cut into 6–8 pieces
- ½ cup/125 ml dry white wine
- 2 tbsp finely chopped herbs, such as rosemary, sage, thyme, or marjoram
- grated zest and juice of ½ lemon
- ½ cup/50 g black olives
- salt and freshly ground black pepper to taste

Sauté the onion in the oil in a saucepan over medium heat for 8–10 minutes, or until translucent. • Stir in the garlic and fennel seeds. • Add the chicken and sear it all over. • Pour in the wine and let evaporate. • Add the herbs, lemon zest, olives, salt, and pepper. Cover and cook over low heat for 35–40 minutes, or until the chicken is tender. • Drizzle with the lemon juice and serve immediately.

CHICKEN WITH OLIVES

S auté the onions, leeks, bay leaf, thyme, and oregano in 4 tablespoons of oil in a saucepan over medium heat for 8–10 minutes, or until the onions and leeks are lightly browned. • Pour in the vinegar, water, and remaining oil. • Add the chicken to the pan. Cover and cook over low heat for 45 minutes. • Add the olives and cook for 5 minutes more. • Discard the bay leaf. • Bone the chicken and serve hot with beans.

Serves: 4–6

Preparation: 20'

Cooking: 1 h

Level of difficulty: 1

- 2 medium onions, finely chopped
- 2 leeks, white parts only, finely chopped
- 1 bay leaf
- 1 tsp finely chopped thyme
- 1 tsp finely chopped oregano
- ½ cup/125 ml extra-virgin olive oil
- ¾ cup/180 ml sherry vinegar
- 1 quart/1 liter water
- 1 chicken, weighing about 3 lb/1.5 kg, cut into 12 pieces
- 1 cup/100 g green olives
- 1 cup/100 g black olives

Serves: 4

Preparation: 20'

Cooking: 2 h

Level of difficulty: 2

- 1 chicken, weighing about 3 lb/1.5 kg, cut into 6–8 pieces
- salt and freshly ground white pepper to taste
- ½ cup/125 g + 2 tbsp butter
- 1 medium onion, finely chopped
- 1 cup/250 ml dry white wine
- 2 tbsp water
- 8 oz/250 g tomatoes, peeled and thinly sliced
- 8 oz/250 g peas
- 8 oz/250 g carrots, peeled and thinly sliced
- 1 lb/500 g potatoes, peeled and thinly sliced
- 2 tbsp finely chopped parsley

BAKED CHICKEN WITH VEGETABLES

Preheat the oven to 350°F/180°C/gas 4. • Set out a large roasting pan. • Season the chicken with salt and pepper. • Melt 4 tablespoons of butter in a large, deep frying pan over medium heat. Sauté the chicken and onion for 8–10 minutes, or until lightly browned. • Pour in the wine, water, and tomatoes. • Transfer the chicken to the roasting pan. • Bake for 30 minutes. • While the chicken is baking, sauté the peas, carrots, and potatoes in the remaining butter in a large frying pan. • Remove the chicken from the oven and add the sautéed vegetables. Sprinkle with the parsley and season with salt and pepper. • Cover with aluminum foil. • Bake for about 1 hour, or until the juices run clear and the vegetables are tender. • Serve hot.

GARLIC FRIED CHICKEN

S eason the chicken with salt and pepper. Place in a large bowl and drizzle with the lemon juice.
• Let marinate in the refrigerator for 2 hours.
• Squeeze the pieces of marinated chicken to remove the excess lemon juice. Dip them in the flour and then in the egg. • Sauté the garlic in the oil in a large, deep frying pan until pale gold. Discard the garlic. • Fry the chicken in small batches for 4–5 minutes, or until deep golden brown. • Drain well on paper towels. Season with salt, if liked, and serve hot.

544

Serves: 4

Preparation: 15' + 2 h to marinate

Cooking: 20'

Level of difficulty: 1

- **1 chicken, weighing about 3 lb/1.5 kg, cut into 6–8 pieces**
- **salt and freshly ground black pepper to taste**
- **juice of 3 lemons**
- **½ cup/75 g all-purpose/plain flour**
- **2 eggs, lightly beaten**
- **2 cloves garlic, peeled but whole**
- **2 cups/500 ml olive oil, for frying**

BARBECUED CHICKEN

Serves: 4–6

Preparation: 10'

Cooking: 40'

Level of difficulty: 1

- **2 spring chickens, about 1½ lb/ 750 g each, cleaned**
- **salt and freshly ground black pepper to taste**
- **½ cup/125 ml extra-virgin olive oil**

Rinse the chickens under cold running water and dry with paper towels. • Place the chickens on their backs and, using a sharp knife, cut down the middle so that they can be opened out like a book but are still in one piece. • Season the chickens generously with salt and pepper. • Heat 2 tablespoons of oil in a large frying pan and brown the chickens on both sides over high heat for 8–10 minutes. • Place the chickens on the barbecue (or under the broiler/grill) and drizzle with more oil. Cook for 30 minutes, or until tender, turning often and basting with oil. Season with salt and pepper, if liked. • Serve hot.

FRIED CHICKEN WITH SAGE

546

Place the chicken in a large bowl and sprinkle with the parsley. Drizzle with the lemon juice and season with salt and pepper. • Let marinate for 1 hour, turning occasionally. • Combine the sage and bread crumbs in a bowl. • Beat the eggs in a small bowl. • Dip the chicken pieces first in the egg, then in the bread crumb and sage mixture. • Heat the oil with the sage in a large, deep frying pan until very hot. • Fry the chicken for 15 minutes over medium-low heat until cooked through. Turn up the heat and fry for 5 minutes more until golden and crunchy. • Drain well on paper towels. • Garnish with the parsley and serve hot.

Serves: 4

Preparation: 10' + 1 h to marinate

Cooking: 20'

Level of difficulty: 2

- **1 chicken, weighing about 3 lb/1.5 kg, cut into 6–8 pieces**
- **4 tbsp finely chopped parsley**
- **juice of 2 lemons**
- **salt and freshly ground black pepper to taste**
- **4 tbsp finely chopped fresh sage leaves**
- **1 cup/120 g fine dry bread crumbs**
- **2 large eggs**
- **1 cup/250 ml sunflower oil, for frying**
- **1 sprig sage**
- **1 sprig parsley, to garnish**

FRIED CHICKEN WITH FRESH THYME

Serves: 4

Preparation: 25' + 1 h to marinate

Cooking: 20'

Level of difficulty: 1

- 1 chicken, weighing about 3 lb/1.5 kg, cut into 6–8 pieces
- 4 tbsp finely chopped parsley
- juice of 1 lemon
- salt and freshly ground black pepper to taste
- 2 eggs, lightly beaten
- 2 tbsp finely chopped thyme
- 2 cups/120 g fresh bread crumbs
- ⅓ cup/50 g all-purpose/plain flour
- 2 cups/500 ml olive oil, for frying
- lemon wedges, to garnish

Place the chicken in a large bowl and sprinkle with the parsley. Drizzle with the lemon juice and season with salt and pepper. • Let marinate for 1 hour, turning occasionally. • Beat the eggs in a small bowl. • Mix the thyme with the bread crumbs in a small bowl. • Dip the chicken pieces first in the flour, then in the beaten eggs, followed by the bread crumbs. • Heat the oil in a deep-fryer to very hot. • Fry the chicken for 15 minutes over medium heat until cooked through. Turn up the heat and fry for 5 minutes more until golden and crunchy. • Drain well on paper towels. Garnish with the lemon wedges and serve hot.

549

FRICASSÉED CHICKEN, ROAST HAM, AND VEGETABLES

Remove any fat from the chicken breasts and cut into bite-sized chunks. • Sauté the leek in the oil in a large frying pan until browned. • Add the other vegetables and season with salt and pepper. Cook for 5 minutes. • Add the chicken and sauté over high heat to seal the meat. Pour in the stock (or water) and continue to cook over medium heat. • Beat the egg yolks with the lemon juice. Add the basil, oregano, salt, and pepper. • Pour the egg mixture onto the chicken and vegetables and toss quickly over high heat. • Scatter with the tomatoes and ham, toss again, and serve.

Serves: 4–6

Preparation: 15

Cooking: 30'

Level of difficulty: 1

- 1 lb/500 g chicken breasts, boned
- 1 leek, finely sliced
- 6 tbsp extra-virgin olive oil
- 7 oz/200 g zucchini/ courgettes diced
- 7 oz/200 g eggplant/ aubergines, diced
- 7 oz/200 g red bell peppers/ capsicums, diced
- salt and freshly ground black pepper to taste
- 6 tbsp Beef Stock (see page 224) or water
- 3 egg yolks
- juice of 1 lemon
- 12 leaves fresh basil, torn
- dash of oregano
- 2 ripe tomatoes, diced
- 4 oz/125 g roast ham, diced

CHICKEN WITH TOMATOES AND FRESH ROSEMARY

Serves: 4

Preparation: 15'

Cooking: 35'

Level of difficulty: 2

- **1 chicken, weighing about 3 lb/1.5 kg, preferably with the liver**
- **juice of 1 lemon**
- **4 cloves garlic, finely chopped**
- **¾ cup/180 ml extra-virgin olive oil**
- **¾ cup/180 ml dry white wine**
- **1½ lb/750 g tomatoes, peeled and chopped**
- **salt and freshly ground black pepper to taste**
- **6–8 sprigs fresh rosemary**

Rinse the chicken and divide it into 8 pieces. Remove the liver and wash in a little cold water mixed with the lemon juice. • Sauté the garlic in the oil in a large frying pan for 2–3 minutes. • Add the chicken and sauté until lightly browned. • Pour in the wine and let evaporate. • Add the tomatoes. Season with salt and pepper and cook over medium heat for about 20 minutes. Chop the liver coarsely and add to the pan with the rosemary. • Cook over high heat for 5 minutes. Serve hot.

ROAST TURKEY WITH POMEGRANATE AND PANCETTA

Preheat the oven to 325°F/170°C/gas 3.
• Grease a baking dish with 2 tablespoons of oil. • Clean the turkey and set aside the giblets.
• Wrap the turkey in the pancetta and place it in the prepared baking dish. • Brown the turkey over high heat. Roast for about 2 hours, basting often with the wine and juice of 3 pomegranates so that the meat does not dry out. • Finely chop the giblets and sauté in the remaining oil until browned. • Season with salt and pepper. Add the juice of the remaining pomegranate. Cook over low heat until thickened. • Add the cooking juices from the turkey and the seeds of 2 pomegranates.
• Pour some of the sauce over the turkey and serve the remainder on the side.

Serves: 6

Preparation: 25'

Cooking: 2 h 20'

Level of difficulty: 2

- **4 tbsp extra-virgin olive oil**
- **1 turkey, weighing about 6 lb/3 kg**
- **15 slices pancetta**
- **2 cups/500 ml dry white wine**
- **4 pomegranates**
- **salt and freshly ground black pepper to taste**

Serves: 8

Preparation: 30'

Cooking: 3 h 30'

Level of difficulty: 3

- 1 small turkey, boneless, about 8 lb/4 kg, with liver
- 4 oz/125 g ground/minced beef
- 6 oz/180 g Italian sausages, peeled and crumbled
- 1 egg
- 2 apples, peeled, cored, and diced
- 12 chestnuts, boiled in chicken stock until soft, peeled and halved
- 12 prunes, soaked in warm water for 5 minutes, then pitted and chopped
- salt and freshly ground black pepper to taste
- 1/8 tsp nutmeg
- 1/2 cup/125 ml brandy
- 2 tbsp butter
- 8 strips salt pork
- 6 twigs rosemary
- 12 leaves sage
- 1/2 cup/125 ml dry white wine
- 1/2 cup/125 ml Beef Stock (see page 224)

STUFFED ROAST TURKEY

Finely chop the turkey liver and mix in a bowl with the beef, sausages, egg, apples, chestnuts, prunes, salt, pepper, nutmeg, and brandy. • Stuff the turkey with the mixture and sew up the incision with kitchen thread. • Butter a cast-iron pot that will hold the turkey snugly. Cover the bottom of the pot with the strips of salt pork, add the turkey, and place the rosemary and sage on top. • Cook over medium heat for 30 minutes, turning often so that the turkey is evenly browned. • Preheat the oven to 400°F/200°C/gas 6. • Drain the fat from the turkey and discard. • Pour in the wine and let it evaporate. • Add 4 tablespoons of stock and cover with aluminum foil. • Roast for 3 hours, basting with the cooking juices during cooking, or until very tender and crispy on top • Serve hot.

CABBAGE AND TURKEY BAKE

Preheat the oven to 400°F/200°C/gas 6. • Mix the turkey, sausage, pancetta, Parmesan, egg and egg yolk, bread crumbs, nutmeg, salt, and pepper in a large bowl. • Parboil the cabbage leaves in a large pan of salted water for 4 minutes. • Drain well and dry with paper towels. • Arrange the cabbage leaves on a work surface in a rectangle; they should be overlapping so that there is no space between the leaves. • Place the turkey mixture in the center of the leaves and shape into a loaf. • Wrap the cabbage leaves around the loaf, taking care not to tear them. Tie with kitchen string. • Transfer to a baking dish. • Mix the onion, tomatoes, and oil and pour over the top. • Bake for 75 minutes, basting with the wine and stock, or until the turkey is cooked through. • Slice and serve.

Serves: 6

Preparation: 20'

Cooking: 1 h 15'

Level of difficulty: 2

- 1¼ lb/575 g ground/minced turkey breast
- 8 oz/250 g Italian pork sausage, skinned and crumbled
- ¼ cup/30 g diced pancetta
- 1 cup/125 g freshly grated Parmesan cheese
- 1 egg + 1 egg yolk
- 1 cup/60 g fresh bread crumbs
- ⅛ tsp nutmeg
- salt and freshly ground black pepper to taste
- 10 leaves Savoy cabbage
- 1 small onion, finely chopped
- 14 oz/400 g peeled and chopped tomatoes
- ½ cup/125 ml extra-virgin olive oil
- ½ cup/125 ml dry white wine
- ½ cup/125 ml Beef Stock (see page 224)

TURKEY WITH OLIVES AND SUNDRIED TOMATOES

Cut the turkey into thin strips about $2^1/_2$ inches (6 cm) long. • Sauté the shallots with the chile pepper in the oil in a large frying pan over medium heat for 5 minutes. • Add the turkey and sauté over high heat for 3 minutes. Season with salt and pepper. • Add the olives and tomatoes. • Drizzle in the wine and let it evaporate. • Add the stock and rosemary. Cook over low heat for 15 minutes more. • Serve hot.

Serves: 4

Preparation: 20'

Cooking: 25'

Level of difficulty: 1

- 1 lb/500 g turkey breast
- 2 shallots, halved
- 1 fresh red chile pepper, finely sliced
- 2 tbsp extra-virgin olive oil
- salt and freshly ground black pepper to taste
- 15 green olives, pitted
- 10 black olives, pitted and coarsely chopped
- 5 sundried tomatoes in oil
- 4 tbsp dry white wine
- 4 tbsp Chicken Stock (see page 226)
- 1 sprig rosemary

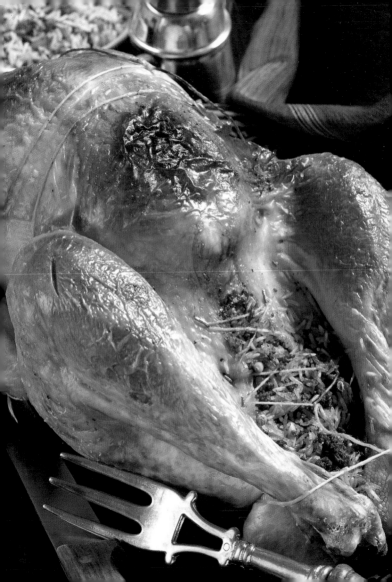

STUFFED TURKEY

Serves: 8–10

Preparation: 30'

Cooking: 3 h

Level of difficulty: 1

- 1 turkey, weighing about 8 lb/4 kg
- salt and freshly ground black pepper to taste
- 1 tsp ground allspice
- 2 cloves garlic, finely chopped
- 2 tbsp finely chopped parsley
- ½ cup/90 g pine nuts
- 4 tbsp extra-virgin olive oil
- 1 lb/500 g ground/ minced beef
- 2 cups/400 g long-grain rice
- 1 tsp freshly grated nutmeg
- 1 tsp ground cinnamon
- ½ tsp cumin seeds
- 2 cups/500 ml water
- 4 tbsp butter, cut up

Preheat the oven to 325°F/170°C/gas 3.
• Set out a large roasting pan. • Rinse the turkey and dry well. Rub inside and out with a generous seasoning of salt and pepper. Rub in the allspice. • Sauté the garlic, parsley, and pine nuts in the oil in a large frying pan over medium heat for 5 minutes. • Brown the beef for 10 minutes. • Stir in the rice, nutmeg, cinnamon, cumin, and 1 cup (250 ml) of water. Season with salt and pepper.
• Bring to a boil and simmer, uncovered, for 15–20 minutes, or until the rice is tender. • Spoon the mixture into the turkey cavity and sew up the cavity with kitchen string. • Rub the turkey with butter and place in the pan. • Pour the remaining water into the pan and cover with aluminum foil.
• Roast for 1 hour 30 minutes. Remove the foil and roast for 30 minutes more, or until tender. • Serve hot or at room temperature.

ROAST DUCK WITH FRESH FIGS

Serves: 6–8

Preparation: 40'

Cooking: 4 h

Level of difficulty: 2

- 2 ducks, weighing about 3 lb/1.5 kg each, cleaned
- salt and freshly ground black pepper to taste
- 2 onions, finely chopped
- 1 clove garlic, finely chopped
- 2 bay leaves
- 1 sprig thyme
- 1 cup/250 ml dry sherry
- 1 cup/150 g all-purpose/plain flour
- 6 tbsp Chicken Stock (see page 226)
- 1 lb/500 g fresh figs
- 4 tbsp butter

Preheat the oven to 250°F/130°C/gas 1/2. • Season the ducks with salt and pepper. Pierce the skin all over to encourage the slow release of fat during roasting. • Place the ducks in a large baking dish. Roast for 3 hours. • Add the onions, garlic, bay leaves, and thyme and cook until the onions have softened. • Increase the oven temperature to 350°F/180°C/gas 4. • Pour the sherry over the ducks and cook for about 45 minutes, or until the meat is very tender. • Remove the ducks from the pan. Cut into halves or quarters. Set aside. • Drain the cooking juices in the pan into a saucepan. Stir in 3 tablespoons of the flour and cook over low heat until thickened. • Stir in the stock and cook for 5 minutes. • Return the ducks to the baking dish. Spoon the sauce over the top. • Peel the figs and roll in the remaining flour until well coated. • Fry the figs in the butter in a large frying pan over medium heat for 5 minutes. • Add the figs to the ducks and cook over low heat for 5 minutes. • Serve hot.

This dish comes from Sicily, where it is made in late summer when fresh figs are at their succulent best.

563

STUFFED ROAST DUCK WITH RED WINE

Preheat the oven to 400°F/200°C/gas 6. • Rinse the duck under cold running water and dry with paper towels. • Mix the pork, chicken livers, parsley, amaretti cookies, bread crumbs and Marsala, half the oil, the egg, and Parmesan in a large bowl. Stuff the duck with the mixture and sew up the incision with kitchen thread. • Transfer the duck to a large roasting pan. • Mix the salt pork, rosemary, and the remaining oil in a small bowl. Drizzle the mixture over the duck. Season with salt and pepper. • Roast for $1^3/4$ hours, basting with the wine during cooking. • Place the duck on a serving dish and slice. • Serve hot.

Serves: 4–6

Preparation: 20'

Cooking: 1 h 45'

Level of difficulty: 2

- 1 duck, weighing about $4^1/2$ lb/ 2.5 kg, boneless
- 4 oz/125 g ground/minced pork
- 4 oz/125 g chicken livers, finely chopped
- 2 tbsp finely chopped parsley
- 4 amaretti cookies
- 1 cup/60 g fresh bread crumbs mixed with 2 tbsp Marsala wine
- 2 tbsp extra-virgin olive oil
- 1 egg
- 2 tbsp freshly grated Parmesan cheese
- 1 oz/30 g salt pork, chopped
- 2 tbsp finely chopped rosemary
- salt and freshly ground black pepper to taste
- 1 cup/250 ml dry red wine

ROAST DUCK WITH SAUSAGE

Preheat the oven to 350°F/180°C/gas 4. • Mix the sausage meat, liver, Parmesan, egg, and parsley in a large bowl. Season with salt and pepper. • Shape into a large rissole which will fit into the duck's cavity and coat it with the bread crumbs. • Season the duck inside and out with salt and pepper and place the rissole of stuffing in the cavity. Use a trussing needle and kitchen thread to sew up the bird. Truss the duck by tying the legs to its sides neatly with kitchen string. • Dot the surface of the duck with the pork fat and rosemary. • Transfer to a roasting pan or ovenproof dish with the oil, butter, and sage. • Roast for 1 hour 45 minutes, or until the duck is tender. • Cut the duck into at least 6 portions and slice the stuffing. • Arrange on a serving dish, spoon some of its cooking juices over the top, and serve.

Serves: 6

Preparation: 40'

Cooking: 1 h 45'

Level of difficulty: 1

- ¼ cup/60 g Italian sausage meat, crumbled
- scant ½ cup/100 g finely chopped duck (or chicken) liver
- ½ cup/60 g freshly grated Parmesan cheese
- 1 egg
- 2 tbsp finely chopped parsley
- salt and freshly ground black pepper to taste
- 1 duck, weighing about 4 lb/2 kg, cleaned
- ½ cup/60 g fine dry bread crumbs
- 2 tbsp finely chopped pork fat
- 1 sprig rosemary
- 5 tbsp extra-virgin olive oil
- 4 tbsp butter
- 2 leaves sage

DUCK IN SWEET AND SOUR SAUCE

Serves: 6

Preparation: 20'

Cooking: 20'

Level of difficulty: 1

- 6 duck breasts, weighing about 7 oz/200 g each
- salt and freshly ground black pepper to taste
- 1/2 cup/125 g butter
- 1/2 tsp fennel seeds
- 1/2 tsp ground aniseed
- 1/2 tsp cumin seeds
- 1/2 tsp ground coriander
- 1/2 tsp cinnamon stick
- 1 tbsp sesame seeds
- small piece fresh gingerroot, peeled and finely chopped
- 1 tbsp clear, runny honey
- 3 1/2 cups/800 ml best red wine vinegar
- 1 1/4 cups/310 ml Beef Stock (see page 224)

Rinse the duck breasts and dry them well. Season with salt and pepper. • Melt one-third of the butter in a frying pan and fry the duck breasts over medium heat for 5–6 minutes each side. Take them out and keep warm. • Spoon off and discard some of the excess fat from the surface of the juices. Stir in the spices, sesame seeds, and gingerroot. • Add the honey and cook for 1 minute. • Add the vinegar and let it evaporate. • Pour in the stock. Cook over high heat until the sauce has reduced by half. • Remove from the heat and stir in the remaining butter. Beat lightly with a fork. • Cut the duck breasts into strips about 1 inch (2.5 cm) wide and arrange on a serving dish. • Spoon the sauce over the top and serve hot.

DUCK WITH ORANGE

Preheat the oven to 375°F/190°C/gas 5.
• Wash and dry the duck and place the garlic, rosemary, salt, pepper, and the zest of 1 orange into the cavity. • Pour half the oil into a large roasting pan. Add the duck and sprinkle with more pepper. Arrange the onion, carrot, and celery around the duck and drizzle with the remaining oil. Roast for 10 minutes. • Pour the wine over the duck and roast for 1 hour and 20 minutes. • Peel the zest off the remaining 2 oranges and cut it into very thin strips. Place the zest in a small saucepan with cold water and bring to a boil. Drain. Repeat the process twice to remove any bitterness.
• Heat the sugar, water, and lemon juice in a small, nonstick saucepan over medium heat until the sugar melts and caramelizes until pale golden brown. • Add the strips of zest and stir over low heat for 2 minutes. Set aside. • Thirty minutes into the roasting time, squeeze the juice from 2 oranges over the duck. • When the duck is done (test by inserting a sharp knife into the thigh, if the juices run clear the duck is well done), remove the garlic, rosemary, and orange zest from the cavity.
• Transfer the duck to a casserole with the cooking juices and vegetables and spoon the caramelized orange zest over the top. Place over medium heat for 5 minutes, turning the duck once or twice.
• Serve hot.

Serves: 4

Preparation: 25'

Cooking: 1 h 30'

Level of difficulty: 1

• 1 duck, weighing about 3 lb/1.5 kg, cleaned
• 2 cloves garlic, whole
• sprig of rosemary
• salt and freshly ground black pepper to taste
• 3 oranges
• 5 tbsp extra-virgin olive oil
• 1 onion, coarsely chopped
• 1 carrot, coarsely chopped
• 1 stalk celery, coarsely chopped
• ½ cup/125 ml dry white wine
• ½ cup/100 g granulated sugar
• 1½ tbsp water
• 1 tbsp fresh lemon juice

BRAISED DUCK WITH GREEN OLIVES

Serves: 4

Preparation: 20'

Cooking: 1 h 15'

Level of difficulty: 1

- 1 duck, weighing about 3 lb/1.5 kg
- 1 bay leaf
- 1 clove garlic, finely chopped
- 1 small carrot, finely chopped
- 1 stalk celery, finely chopped
- 1 small onion, finely chopped
- 2 tbsp finely chopped parsley
- 2 tbsp butter
- 2 tbsp extra-virgin olive oil
- salt and freshly ground black pepper to taste
- 1½ cups/375 ml Beef Stock (see page 224)
- 20 giant green olives, pitted, 10 of which coarsely chopped and 10 whole
- 4 large ripe tomatoes, peeled and chopped

Rinse the duck under cold running water and dry with paper towels. • Sauté the bay leaf, garlic, carrot, celery, onion, and parsley in the butter and oil in a large frying pan until the vegetables have softened. • Season with salt and pepper. Add the duck and cook, turning often, until browned all over. • Pour in the stock and add the olives and tomatoes. • Cover and cook over medium-low heat for 45 minutes. • Uncover and cook for 15 more minutes, or until the liquid has reduced and the duck is tender. • Serve hot.

573

DUCK AND FIG TAJINE

Serves: 6

Preparation: 10'

Cooking: 1 h 10'

Level of difficulty: 1

- **6 tbsp butter**
- **1 duck, weighing about 4 lb/2 kg, cut into 8 pieces**
- **2 onions, finely chopped**
- **2 cloves garlic, finely chopped**
- **1 tsp chopped gingerroot**
- **1 tsp ground turmeric**
- **salt to taste**
- **1½ cups/375 ml water**
- **2 tbsp honey**
- **1 tsp ground cinnamon**
- **1¾ lb/850 g fresh figs, chopped, or 1⅔ cups/400 g dried figs, quartered**

Melt the butter in a tajine or saucepan over medium heat. • Sauté the duck, onions, and garlic for 8–10 minutes, or until nicely browned. • Add the ginger, turmeric, and salt. Pour in the water. • Cover and cook over very low heat for 40–45 minutes, or until the duck is tender. • Add the honey and cinnamon and cook for 10 minutes. • Stir in the figs and cook for 5 more minutes.

BRAISED MIXED POULTRY AND GAME

S auté the garlic in the oil in a large saucepan until pale gold. • Discard the garlic. • Add the onion and sauté until softened. • Add the basil and parsley. Add the meat and sauté until well browned. Season with salt and pepper. • Pour in the wine and let it evaporate. • Stir in the tomatoes. Partially cover and cook over medium-low heat for 2 hours, stirring often, adding stock to keep the stew moist. • Place the toasted bread on individual serving plates and spoon over the stew. • Serve hot.

Serves: 6

Preparation: 30'

Cooking: 2 h 15'

Level of difficulty: 2

- 2 cloves garlic, lightly crushed but whole
- 4 tbsp extra-virgin olive oil
- 1 onion, finely chopped
- 6 leaves basil, torn
- 2 tbsp finely chopped parsley
- 2½ lb/1.25 kg mixed poultry and game (chicken, rabbit, wild boar, squab pigeon, hare), cut in pieces
- salt and freshly ground black pepper to taste
- 1 cup/250 ml full-bodied red wine
- 1 cup/250 ml Beef Stock (see page 224)
- 1¼ lb/600 g tomatoes, peeled and chopped
- 6 slices toasted bread

576

CASSEROLED GUINEA FOWL

Serves: 4

Preparation: 20'

Cooking: 1 h

Level of difficulty: 1

- **1 guinea fowl, weighing about 2 lb/1 kg, cleaned**
- **2 tbsp butter**
- **scant ½ cup/ 100 ml extra-virgin olive oil**
- **½ cup/60 g diced pancetta**
- **salt and freshly ground black pepper to taste**
- **½ cup/125 ml dry white wine**
- **scant 1 cup/200 g guinea fowl or chicken livers**
- **1 slice soft, fresh Italian sausage**
- **4 anchovy fillets**
- **zest and juice of 1 lemon**
- **1 clove garlic**
- **2 tbsp finely chopped parsley**
- **1–2 tbsp white wine vinegar**

Rinse and dry the guinea fowl and cut into 6 pieces. • Melt the butter in a flameproof casserole and add half the oil and pancetta. • Add the guinea fowl and cook over high heat until browned all over. • Season with salt and pepper. Pour in the wine and let it evaporate. • Cover and cook over low heat for 1 hour, turning the pieces at intervals. • Chop the livers with the sausage, anchovy fillets, lemon zest, and garlic. Sauté the chopped mixture in the remaining oil in a small frying pan until lightly browned. Add the parsley and lemon juice. • Drizzle with the vinegar and season with a little salt. Season generously with pepper and remove from the heat. • Garnish the guinea fowl with the liver mixture and serve very hot.

ROAST STUFFED PHEASANT

Serves: 4

Preparation: 30'

Cooking: 1 h

Level of difficulty: 2

- 1 pheasant, weighing about 2 lb/1 kg, gutted with liver
- 3½ oz/100 g ground/minced pork
- 3½ oz/100 g ground/minced veal
- 4 tbsp butter
- 5 oz/150 g bread soaked in 4 tbsp dry red wine and squeezed dry
- ⅛ tsp ground cinnamon
- ⅛ tsp freshly grated nutmeg
- 2 cloves, crushed
- salt and freshly ground black pepper to taste
- 4 tbsp extra-virgin olive oil
- 2 bay leaves
- ½ cup/125 ml dry red wine

Preheat the oven to 350°F/180°C/gas 4.
• Wash and dry the pheasant. Chop the liver finely. • Mix the liver, pork, veal, butter, bread, cinnamon, nutmeg, and cloves in a large bowl. Season with salt and pepper. • Stuff the pheasant with the mixture. Tie the bird with kitchen string.
• Transfer to the baking dish and drizzle with the oil. Top with the bay leaves. • Roast for 30 minutes. Baste with the wine and roast for 30 minutes more, basting often with the cooking juices. • Cut the pheasant in four and serve with the stuffing.

ROAST PHEASANT WITH PANCETTA

Serves: 4–6
Preparation: 10'
Cooking: 1 h
Level of difficulty: 1

P reheat the oven to 400°F/200°C/gas 6. •
Rinse the pheasants under cold running water and dry with paper towels. • Wrap each bird in half the pancetta and tie them with kitchen string. Dot with the butter and season with salt and pepper (not too much salt, as the pancetta is already salty). Transfer to a large roasting pan. • Bake for 40 minutes, basting occasionally with the cooking juices. • Remove the pancetta and return the pheasants to the oven for 10 minutes so that they become crisp and golden. • Chop the pancetta and place on a heated serving dish. • Place the pheasants on top of the pancetta. • Place the roasting pan over medium heat and add the water. Cook for 2–3 minutes, then pour over the pheasants. • Serve hot.

- **2 young roasting pheasants**
- **8 slices pancetta**
- **4 tbsp butter, melted**
- **salt and freshly ground white pepper to taste**
- **4 tbsp cold water**
- **6 slices firm-textured bread, toasted**

Serves: 4	
Preparation: 25'	
Cooking: 1 h 30'	
Level of difficulty: 2	

- 1 guinea fowl, weighing about 2½ lb/1.25 kg
- salt and freshly ground black pepper to taste
- 1 lb/500 g seedless white grapes
- 4 oz/125 g sliced pancetta
- 2 tbsp butter
- 2 tbsp extra-virgin olive oil
- ½ cup/125 ml brandy
- 1 sprig rosemary

BRAISED GUINEA FOWL WITH GRAPES

Remove the heart and liver from the guinea fowl and set aside. • Season the cavity with salt and pepper and stuff with half the grapes. • Wrap the bird with the pancetta and tie with kitchen string. • Brown the guinea fowl in the butter and oil in a large saucepan. • Pour in the brandy and let it evaporate. • Chop the heart and liver with the rosemary. Add to the pan and cook for 1 minute. • Crush the remaining grapes. • Spoon the grapes into the pan. Season with salt. Cook over low heat for 1 hour, or until the bird is cooked through. • Remove the pancetta and set aside. Cook the guinea fowl over high heat for 5 minutes. • Serve with the cooking liquid and pancetta.

RABBIT IN SWEET AND SOUR SAUCE

Place the wine, parsley, onion, bay leaf, and peppercorns in a small saucepan and bring slowly to a boil. Boil for 1 minute and let cool.
• Place the pieces of rabbit in a large bowl. Pour the marinade over them and let marinate for 6–8 hours. • Remove the rabbit from the marinade and dry with paper towels. Season with salt and pepper and coat with flour, shaking off the excess.
• Heat the oil in a large frying pan until very hot. Add the pieces of rabbit and cook until browned all over, about 10 minutes. • Remove the rabbit from the pan and set aside. • In the same oil, sauté the celery, carrot, capers, raisins, and olives over medium heat for 5 minutes. • Add the rabbit and sprinkle with sugar. Pour in the vinegar and cook for 2 minutes. • Pour in the remaining marinade. Cover and simmer over low heat until very tender.
• Serve hot.

Serves: 4–6	
Preparation: 30' + 6–8 h to marinate	
Cooking: 1 h 15'	
Level of difficulty: 1	

- 1¼ cups/310 ml dry red wine
- 3 tbsp finely chopped parsley
- 1 medium onion, thinly sliced
- 1 bay leaf
- 1 tsp black peppercorns
- 1 young, tender rabbit, cleaned and cut into 6–8 pieces
- salt and freshly ground black pepper to taste
- 3 tbsp all-purpose/plain flour
- 6 tbsp extra-virgin olive oil
- 2 stalks celery, coarsely chopped
- 1 small carrot, thinly sliced
- 1 tbsp capers
- 2½ tbsp golden raisins/sultanas, soaked and drained
- 15 large green olives, pitted and coarsely chopped
- 2 tbsp sugar (or honey)
- 4 tbsp red wine vinegar

RABBIT AND ZUCCHINI CASSEROLE

Serves: 4

Preparation: 15'

Cooking: 1 h 15'

Level of difficulty: 1

- 1 tbsp butter
- 3 tbsp extra-virgin olive oil
- 1 rabbit, weighing about 3 lb/1.5 kg, cut into 6 pieces
- 5 oz/150 g salt pork, cut into cubes
- 6 zucchini/ courgettes, thickly sliced
- 6 cloves garlic, finely chopped
- 3 onions, quartered
- 1 small bunch thyme, finely chopped
- 2 bay leaves
- 6 medium tomatoes, peeled and coarsely chopped
- salt and freshly ground black pepper to taste

Melt the butter with the oil in a large saucepan over medium heat. Sauté the rabbit and salt pork until browned. • Add the zucchini, garlic, onions, thyme, bay leaves, and tomatoes. Season with salt and pepper. • Cover and cook over low heat for about 1 hour, or until the rabbit is tender. Stir often to prevent the rabbit from sticking. • Serve hot.

SWEET AND SOUR HARE

C ut the hare into small pieces and let soak in salted water overnight. • Finely chop the vegetables, prosciutto, and lard. • Sauté the chopped mixture in the oil in a large frying pan over medium heat until lightly browned. • Pour in the wine and let it evaporate. • Add the hare and cook over high heat until browned all over. • Pour in the stock and cook over medium heat for about 45 minutes, or until the hare is almost cooked. • Add the vinegar, chocolate and raisins and cook over low heat until the chocolate has melted. • Serve with the polenta.

Serves: 6–8

Preparation: 25' + 12 h to soak

Cooking: 1 h

Level of difficulty: 2

- 1 hare, weighing about 3 lb/1.5 kg, cleaned
- 1 onion
- 1 stalk celery
- 1 carrot
- 5 oz/150 g prosciutto/ Parma ham
- 3 oz/90 g lard
- 3 tbsp extra-virgin olive oil
- 4 tbsp dry white wine
- ½ cup/125 ml Chicken or Beef Stock (see pages 224, 226)
- 2 tsp sugar dissolved in 4 tbsp red wine vinegar
- ½ cup/90 g golden raisins/sultanas, soaked in cold water for 15 minutes and drained
- 7 oz/200 g semisweet/dark chocolate, coarsely chopped
- 1 quantity Polenta (see page 350)

VEAL

FRENCH VEAL STEW

Sauté the veal in the butter in a large saucepan over medium heat for 4 minutes. • Add the shallots, carrots, leeks, garlic, wine, and enough water to cover the veal. Add the bay leaf and nutmeg. Cook over low heat for 45 minutes.
• Cook the mushrooms in a large saucepan over medium heat for 5–7 minutes. Drain the juices they release and add them to the stew. Season with salt and pepper. • Beat the cream, lemon juice, cornstarch, egg yolks, and 2 tablespoons of the cooking juices from the stew in a medium bowl. Add this mixture to the stew together with the mushrooms and mix well. Cook for 2 minutes, or until the sauce is thickened. • Serve hot with boiled rice.

Serves: 6–8

Preparation: 20'

Cooking: 1 h

Level of difficulty: 2

- 3 lb/1.5 kg boned veal shoulder, cut into cubes
- 4 tbsp butter
- 4 shallots, finely chopped
- 4 carrots, cut into thin strips
- 4 leeks, finely sliced
- 3 cloves garlic, thinly sliced
- ½ cup/125 ml dry white wine
- 1 bay leaf
- ⅛ tsp freshly grated nutmeg
- 8 oz/250 g mushrooms, thinly sliced
- salt and freshly ground black pepper to taste
- ¾ cup/ 200 ml heavy/double cream
- juice of 1 lemon
- 2 tbsp cornstarch/ cornflour
- 2 large egg yolks
- boiled rice, to serve

VEAL ESCALOPES WITH BALSAMIC VINEGAR

Lightly pound the veal with a meat tenderizer so that it is thin and of even thickness. • Season the veal with salt and pepper. • Heat the oil in a large frying pan over high heat. Cook the veal for 2 minutes on each side. • Add the balsamic vinegar and let it evaporate. • Add the arugula and let it wilt for 1 minute. • Remove from the heat and let rest for 3 minutes. • Sprinkle with the Parmesan and season with salt and pepper. • Serve hot.

594

Serves: 4–6

Preparation: 3'

Cooking: 7'

Level of difficulty: 2

- 1½ lb/750 g veal escalopes
- salt and freshly ground black pepper to taste
- 2 tbsp extra-virgin olive oil
- 3 tbsp balsamic vinegar
- 4 oz/125 g arugula/rocket, shredded
- 5 oz/150 g Parmesan cheese, cut into flakes

VEAL ESCALOPES WITH MARSALA

Serves: 4–6

Preparation: 15'

Cooking: 10'

Level of difficulty: 2

- 1½ lb/750 g veal escalopes
- salt and freshly ground black pepper to taste
- ½ cup/100 g all-purpose/plain flour
- 3 tbsp butter
- 4 tbsp Vegetable Stock (see page 224)
- 6 tbsp Marsala wine

Lightly pound the veal with a meat tenderizer so that it is thin and of even thickness. • Season the veal with salt and pepper. • Dip the veal in the flour until well coated, shaking off the excess. • Melt the butter in a large frying pan over high heat. Cook the veal for 2 minutes on each side. Remove from the pan and keep warm. • Reserve the meat juices in the pan. Add the stock and bring to a boil, stirring with a wooden spoon. • Add the Marsala and let it evaporate. • Season with salt and pepper. Return the veal to the pan and cook for 2 minutes more before serving.

VEAL ESCALOPES WITH ORANGE

Serves: 4–6

Preparation: 15'

Cooking: 10'

Level of difficulty: 2

- 1½ lb/750 g veal escalopes
- salt and freshly ground black pepper to taste
- ½ cup/100 g all-purpose/plain flour
- 2 tbsp extra-virgin olive oil
- juice of 2 oranges
- ½ cup/125 ml Vegetable Stock (see page 224)
- 2 large oranges, finely sliced

Lightly pound the veal with a meat tenderizer so that it is thin and of even thickness. • Season the veal with salt and pepper. • Dip the veal in the flour until well coated, shaking off the excess. • Heat the oil in a large frying pan over high heat. Cook the veal for 2 minutes on each side. Remove from the pan and keep warm. • Add the orange juice, stock, and orange slices to the pan. Season with salt and pepper. Lower the heat and cook for 4 minutes. • Return the veal to the pan and cook for 2–3 minutes. • Transfer to a serving dish and drizzle with the sauce. • Serve hot.

SHREDDED VEAL WITH PEAS

Dip the veal in the flour until well coated, shaking off the excess. • Melt the butter in a large frying pan over high heat. Cook the veal for 2 minutes on each side. Remove from the pan and keep warm. • Add the Marsala, stock, and peas. Season with salt and pepper. • Cook for 2–3 minutes, or until the sauce has thickened. • Return the veal to the pan and heat through. • Serve hot.

Serves: 4–6

Preparation: 5'

Cooking: 10'

Level of difficulty: 2

- 1½ lb/750 g veal, cut into thin strips
- ½ cup/100 g all-purpose/plain flour
- 3 tbsp butter
- 6 tbsp Marsala wine
- 4 tbsp Vegetable Stock (see page 224)
- 3 cups/375 g peas
- salt and freshly ground black pepper to taste

BRAISED VEAL WITH BELL PEPPERS AND PEAS

Serves: 4–6

Preparation: 15'

Cooking: 25'

Level of difficulty: 1

- 1½ lb/750 g veal, cut into thin strips
- 4 oz/125 g carrots, diced
- 3 red bell peppers/ capsicums, seeded, cored, and diced
- 1 onion, finely chopped
- 2 tbsp extra-virgin olive oil
- salt to taste
- 4 tbsp sherry
- ½ cup/125 ml dry white wine
- 1 cup/250 ml Vegetable Stock (see page 224)
- 8 oz/250 g mushrooms, finely sliced
- 1¾ cups/215 g peas

Sauté the veal, carrots, bell peppers, and onion in the oil in a large saucepan over high heat until lightly browned. Season with salt. • Pour in the sherry and wine and let them evaporate. • Add the mushrooms, peas, and stock and cook over medium heat for 15 minutes, or until the veal and vegetables are both tender. • Serve hot.

VEAL COUSCOUS WITH MIXED VEGETABLES AND MEATBALLS

Place the veal and half the vegetables in a two-tiered vegetable steamer. Pour in enough water to cover and bring to a boil. • Place the couscous in the top pot of the steamer and steam for 25 minutes. • If using instant couscous, make the veal and vegetable stew in a large frying pan or Dutch oven and prepare the couscous according to the instructions on the package. • Sauté the remaining vegetables and chile peppers in the oil in a large frying pan over medium heat for 5 minutes. Season with salt and add the tomatoes. Cook over medium heat for about 10 minutes, or until the tomatoes break down. • Meatballs: Mix the lamb, egg, bread, and salt and pepper in a large bowl. Form into small balls the size of walnuts. • Cook the meatballs in the tomato sauce for about 15 minutes, turning them often, or until cooked through. • Add the meatballs to the vegetables and cook for 5 minutes. • Remove the couscous from the steamer and break up the grains with a fork. Transfer to serving dishes and garnish with the meatballs and the hard-boiled egg. • Cut up the veal and add to the vegetables. • Top with the couscous with the veal and vegetables. • Serve hot.

Serves: 6–8

Preparation: 30'

Cooking: 1 h

Level of difficulty: 2

- 2 lb/1 kg boned veal shoulder or shank
- 1 lb/500 g coarsely chopped mixed vegetables (onions, carrots, celery, peas, zucchini/courgettes, cabbage, bell peppers/capsicums, eggplant/aubergines, green beans)
- 12 oz/350 g couscous
- 2 fresh red chile peppers, sliced
- 4 tbsp extra-virgin olive oil
- salt to taste
- 4 tomatoes, finely chopped

MEATBALLS

- 7 oz/200 g ground/minced lamb
- 1 egg + 1 hard-boiled egg, coarsely chopped
- 7 oz/200 g bread, soaked in warm water and squeezed dry

VEAL ROAST WITH POLENTA

Serves: 4–6

Preparation: 25'

Cooking: 1 h 20'

Level of difficulty: 2

- **2 lb/1 kg boned veal roast**
- **7 oz/200 g sliced pancetta**
- **6 leaves fresh sage**
- **1 tbsp rosemary leaves**
- **1 clove garlic, finely sliced**
- **salt and freshly ground black pepper to taste**
- **4 tbsp extra-virgin olive oil**
- **1 quantity Polenta (see page 350)**

Preheat the oven to 450°F/225°C/gas 8.
• Wrap the veal in the slices of pancetta. Sprinkle with sage, rosemary, and garlic. Season with salt and pepper. Tie firmly with kitchen string.
• Transfer the veal to a large roasting pan and drizzle with the oil. • Roast for 20 minutes.
• Lower the oven temperature to 275°F/140°C/gas 1 and cook for 1 hour, or until cooked through. • Turn off the oven but leave the veal in the oven for 20 minutes more. • Slice thinly and serve with polenta.

ROAST VEAL WITH ORANGES

P reheat the oven to 400°F/200°C/gas 6.
• Heat the oil in a roasting pan over medium heat. Brown the veal all over. Season with salt and pepper. • Add the orange liqueur and let it evaporate. • Add the orange juice and bay leaf.
• Roast for 1 hour, turning occasionally and basting often with the cooking juices. • Add the orange zest and roast for 30 minutes more, or until the meat is well cooked. • Transfer to a serving dish. Slice and drizzle with the sauce. • Serve hot.

Serves: 4–6

Preparation: 10'

Cooking: 1 h 45'

Level of difficulty: 1

- **4 tbsp extra-virgin olive oil**
- **2 lb/1 kg boned veal roast**
- **salt and freshly ground black pepper to taste**
- **4 tbsp orange liqueur**
- **juice of 2 oranges**
- **1 bay leaf**
- **shredded zest of 2 oranges**

ROAST VEAL WITH LEEKS

Preheat the oven to 350°F/180°C/gas 4.
• Arrange the sprigs of rosemary on top of the veal and tie with kitchen string. • Heat the oil in a roasting pan over medium heat. Brown the veal all over. • Add the leeks and cook for 10 minutes, or until tender. • Pour the stock over the meat. Season with nutmeg, salt, and pepper. • Roast for about 1 hour 15 minutes, or until the meat is tender, basting often with the cooking juices. • Discard the rosemary. • Slice the veal thinly and arrange on a serving dish with the sauce.

Serves: 4–6

Preparation: 20'

Cooking: 1 h 30'

Level of difficulty: 2

- 6 sprigs rosemary
- 2 lb/1 kg boned veal roast
- 2 tbsp extra-virgin olive oil
- 3 medium leeks, cut into rounds
- 1 cup/250 ml hot Vegetable Stock (see page 224)
- ¼ tsp freshly grated nutmeg
- salt and freshly ground black pepper to taste

VEAL POT ROAST WITH WALNUTS

Serves: 6–8

Preparation: 5'

Cooking: 2 h 10'

Level of difficulty: 2

- 4 tbsp butter
- 2½ lb/1.25 kg boned veal roast
- 5 oz/150 g prosciutto/Parma ham, chopped
- salt and freshly ground black pepper to taste
- ½ cup/125 ml milk, hot
- 1 cup/100 g finely chopped walnuts
- 2 tbsp dry red wine

Melt the butter in a large saucepan over medium heat. Brown the veal and add the prosciutto. Season with salt and pepper. • Pour in the hot milk. Cover and cook over very low heat for 1 hour. • Add the chopped nuts and cook for 1 hour. • Remove the meat from the pan and set aside. • Process the sauce in a food processor or blender until smooth. Return the meat and the sauce to the pan. Add the wine and let it evaporate. • Transfer the meat to a serving dish and slice thinly. Serve the veal with the sauce passed on the side.

VEAL AND PORCINI STEW

609

Serves: 4–6

Preparation: 15'

Cooking: 50'

Level of difficulty: 2

- 1 lb/500 g porcini mushrooms, cleaned and chopped
- 1 large onion, finely chopped
- 2 cloves garlic, finely chopped
- ⅛ tsp chile powder
- 4 tbsp extra-virgin olive oil
- 4 tbsp Vegetable Stock (see page 224)
- 4 large ripe tomatoes, seeded and finely chopped
- salt to taste
- 1½ lb/750 g boned veal shoulder, cut in cubes
- 2 tbsp all-purpose/plain flour
- 4 tbsp dry white wine
- 4 leaves fresh sage, chopped
- 1 tsp finely chopped rosemary
- 1 tbsp finely chopped parsley

Blanch the mushrooms in boiling water for 2 minutes. Drain and set aside. • Cook the onion, garlic, and chile powder in 1 tablespoon of oil and the stock in a large saucepan over medium-low heat for 5 minutes. • Add the mushrooms and tomatoes and mix well. Season with salt and cook for 15 minutes. • Dip the veal in the flour until well coated, shaking off the excess. • Heat the remaining oil in a large frying pan over high heat. Sauté the veal for 3–4 minutes, or until well browned. • Remove the veal from the pan. Add the wine and let it evaporate. • Add the veal and its cooking juices to the pan with the sauce and cook for about 30 minutes, or until the meat is very tender. • Remove from the heat and add the sage, rosemary, and parsley. • Serve hot.

ROAST VEAL WITH LEMON

Preheat the oven to 350°F/180°C/gas 4.
• Season the veal with salt and pepper and cover with the slices of lemon. Tie with kitchen string. • Place a large sheet of parchment paper in a roasting pan. Place the veal on the paper and drizzle with the oil. Wrap the joint loosely with the paper. This stops the juices from evaporating during cooking and keeps the meat moist.
• Roast for 1 hour. • Remove from the oven and discard the paper. Turn the oven up to 400°F/200°C/gas 6. • Roast for 15 minutes, turning halfway through to brown evenly. • Remove from the oven and let rest for 5 minutes. • Slice and serve hot.

Serves: 6

Preparation: 20'

Cooking: 1 h 15'

Level of difficulty: 2

• 3 lb/1.5 kg boned veal roast
• salt and freshly ground black pepper to taste
• 2 large lemons, finely sliced
• 4 tbsp extra-virgin olive oil

VEAL ESCALOPES WITH ANCHOVIES

Lightly pound the veal with a meat tenderizer so that it is thin and of even thickness. • Season the veal with salt and pepper. • Heat the oil in a large frying pan over high heat. Cook the veal for 2 minutes on each side. • Add the garlic, capers, prosciutto, and anchovies. Turn the meat and add the lemon juice, lemon zest, and sage. Cook for 2 minutes. • Turn and cook for 2 minutes on the other side. • Serve hot.

612

- 1½ lb/750 g veal escalopes
- salt and freshly ground black pepper to taste
- 6 tbsp extra-virgin olive oil
- 12 veal escalopes, weighing about 1½ lb/750 g
- 2 cloves garlic, finely chopped
- 1 tbsp capers, rinsed, drained, and chopped
- ¾ cup/90 g diced prosciutto/Parma ham
- 4 anchovy fillets, finely chopped
- juice and zest of 1 lemon
- 3 leaves fresh sage, chopped

- **2 cloves garlic, lightly crushed but whole**
- **8 leaves fresh sage**
- **4 tbsp extra-virgin olive oil**
- **salt and freshly ground black pepper to taste**
- **1½ lb/750 g boned veal roast**
- **⅔ cup/150 ml dry red wine**
- **1 large onion, finely chopped**
- **2 bay leaves**
- **15 oz/400 g canned tomatoes**

VEAL WITH TOMATO SAUCE

Sauté the garlic and sage in the oil in a large casserole for 5 minutes. Season with salt and pepper. • Add the veal and brown all over. • Pour in the wine and let it evaporate. • Add the onion, bay leaves, and tomatoes. Cover and cook over low heat for about 1 hour, or until the meat is tender, stirring occasionally to make sure the sauce does not stick to the pan. • Slice thinly and serve hot.

613

GENOVESE POT ROAST

Serves: 4–6

Preparation: 10'

Cooking: 2 h 10'

Level of difficulty: 2

- **2 lb/1 kg boned veal roast**
- **4 tbsp all-purpose/ plain flour**
- **6 medium onions, finely chopped**
- **4 tbsp extra-virgin olive oil**
- **1 cup/250 ml Vegetable Stock (see page 224)**
- **salt and freshly ground black pepper to taste**
- **4 tbsp dry white wine**

Coat the veal with 3 tablespoons of flour.
• Sauté the veal and onions in the oil in a large saucepan over high heat for 5 minutes to seal the meat. • Lower the heat and pour in the stock. Season with salt. Cook over very low heat for about 2 hours, or until the meat is very tender. Turn the meat occasionally during cooking.
• Remove the meat and slice. • Process the onions and cooking juices in a food processor or blender until smooth. Return the sauce to the pan. Mix in the remaining flour, the wine, and season with pepper. Cook for 2–3 minutes, or until slightly thickened and smooth. • Transfer the meat to a serving dish and serve with the sauce passed on the side. • Serve hot.

STEWED VEAL IN MUSHROOM SAUCE

Sauté the garlic and mushrooms in half the butter in a large saucepan over medium heat for 5 minutes. • Pour in the stock and add the thyme. Cook over low heat for 15 minutes.
• Discard the thyme. Season with salt and add the Parmesan. • Process one-third of the mushrooms in a food processor or blender until smooth. Return to the pan and keep warm. • Dip the veal in the flour until well coated, shaking off the excess. • Melt the remaining butter in a large frying pan over medium heat. Cook the veal with the juniper berries until browned all over. • Stir in the mushroom mixture and parsley. Cover and cook over low heat for 40 minutes, adding a little hot water if the sauce begins to stick to the pan.
• Blanch the tomatoes in boiling water for 30 seconds. Slip off the skins, gently squeeze out as many seeds as possible, and chop coarsely.
• Spoon the stew into serving dishes and top with the tomatoes. • Serve hot.

Serves: 4–6

Preparation: 30'

Cooking: 1 h 40'

Level of difficulty: 2

- 1 clove garlic, finely chopped
- 14 oz/400 g mixed mushrooms, thinly sliced
- 4 tbsp butter
- 1²⁄₃ cups/400 ml hot Vegetable Stock (see page 224)
- 2 sprigs thyme
- salt to taste
- 2 tbsp freshly grated Parmesan cheese
- 2 lb/1 kg boned veal shoulder or shank, diced
- ¹⁄₃ cup/50 g all-purpose/plain flour
- 2 juniper berries
- 1 tbsp finely chopped parsley
- 2 large tomatoes

VEAL ESCALOPES WITH BLACK GRAPES

Serves: 4–6

Preparation: 20'

Cooking: 15'

Level of difficulty: 2

- 1½ lb/750 g veal escalopes
- salt and freshly ground black pepper to taste
- 1 lb/500 g black grapes
- 2 sprigs rosemary
- 1 clove garlic, thinly sliced
- 4 tbsp butter
- ⅓ cup/50 g all-purpose/plain flour
- ½ cup/125 ml grape juice mixed with juice of ½ lemon

Lightly pound the veal with a meat tenderizer so that it is thin and of even thickness. • Season the veal with salt and pepper. • Remove the grapes from the bunch. Cut the largest ones in half and remove the seeds. • Sauté the rosemary and garlic in 2 tablespoons of butter in a large frying pan until aromatic. • Add the grapes and sauté for 4 minutes, stirring gently with a wooden spoon. • Remove the grapes from the pan and set aside. • Add the remaining butter to the cooking juices. • Dip the veal in the flour until well coated, shaking off the excess. Add the veal to the pan and cook for 2 minutes on each side. • Season with salt and pepper. Add the grape juice and cook until thickened. • Add the grapes to the pan. Season with salt and cook for 1 minute.
• Serve hot.

619

VEAL SHANK WITH PLUMS

Preheat the oven to 350°F/180°C/gas 4.
• Sauté the shallots in 3 tablespoons of butter in a roasting pan until golden. Remove the shallots and set aside. • In the same pan, sauté the veal shank, turning frequently, until browned all over.
• Add the brandy and let it evaporate. Season with salt and pepper. • Add the rosemary, myrtle, and the sautéed shallots. • Roast for 1 hour 30 minutes, basting occasionally with the stock.
• Sauté the plums in the remaining butter in a large frying pan for 5 minutes. • Add the plums to the meat and roast for 5 minutes more. • Transfer the plums to a serving platter and arrange the veal shank on top. • Reduce the cooking juices in a frying pan with the cream over high heat. Add the egg yolk and cook until the sauce begins to simmer. • Pour over the meat and serve hot.

Serves: 6

Preparation: 30'

Cooking: 1 h 45'

Level of difficulty: 2

- **4 shallots, thinly sliced**
- **6 tbsp butter**
- **1 veal shank**
- **4 tbsp brandy**
- **salt and freshly ground black pepper to taste**
- **1 sprig rosemary**
- **1 sprig myrtle (optional)**
- **1 cup/250 ml Vegetable Stock (see page 224)**
- **1¼ lb/600 g yellow plums, pitted and cut in half**
- **1 cup/250 ml heavy/double cream**
- **1 egg yolk**

FRIED VEAL CUTLETS WITH TOMATO AND BASIL

Blanch the tomatoes in boiling water for 30 seconds. • Slip off the skins, remove the seeds, and coarsely chop. Place them in a colander and sprinkle with salt. Add the basil and let drain for 15 minutes. • Make a few cuts on the outside of the cutlets. Dip the cutlets in the eggs and then in the bread crumbs. Press down well so that the bread crumbs stick all over. • Melt the butter in a large frying pan. Add the cutlets and cook for 4 minutes on each side, or until cooked through and golden. • Drain well on kitchen towels and season with salt and pepper. Top with the tomato. Drizzle with the oil and serve hot.

622

Serves: 4

Preparation: 30'

Cooking: 10'

Level of difficulty: 2

- 2 tomatoes
- salt and freshly ground black pepper to taste
- 1 bunch basil
- 4 veal cutlets with bone about 1/3 inch/1 cm thick
- 2 eggs, lightly beaten
- 1 cup/125 g fine dry bread crumbs
- 7 tbsp butter
- 1 tbsp extra-virgin olive oil

VEAL ESCALOPES WITH TOMATO AND MINT

Serves: 4–6	
Preparation: 20'	
Cooking: 10'	
Level of difficulty: 2	

- 1½ lb/750 g veal escalopes
- salt and freshly ground black pepper to taste
- 1 lb/500 g peeled and chopped tomatoes
- 4 tbsp dry white wine
- 1 clove garlic, thinly sliced
- ⅓ cup/50 g all-purpose/plain flour
- 1 tsp dried oregano
- 5 tbsp extra-virgin olive oil
- fresh mint, to garnish

Lightly pound the veal with a meat tenderizer so that it is thin and of even thickness. • Season the veal with salt and pepper. • Dip the veal in the flour, shaking off the excess. • Heat the oil in a large frying pan over medium heat. Cook the veal for 2 minutes on each side. • Season with salt and pepper and keep warm. • In the same pan, sauté the garlic until pale gold. • Add the wine and let it evaporate. • Stir in the tomatoes and cook over high heat for 5 minutes. • Add the veal and sprinkle with the oregano. Cook for 1 minute more. • Set aside for 5 minutes. • Transfer the veal to serving plates and top with the sauce. Garnish with the mint and serve.

TOMATOES AND ONIONS STUFFED WITH VEAL

Serves: 4

Preparation: 25'

Cooking: 50'

Level of difficulty: 2

- • 4 round tomatoes
- • 4 onions
- • 4 tbsp extra-virgin olive oil
- • 10 oz/300 g ground/minced veal
- • 3½ oz/100 g sausage meat, crumbled
- • 2 eggs
- • 3 tbsp freshly grated Parmesan cheese
- • ⅓ cup/80 g boiled rice
- • 1 tbsp finely chopped parsley
- • ⅛ tsp freshly grated nutmeg
- • salt and freshly ground black pepper to taste
- • 4 tbsp Beef Stock (see page 224)

Preheat the oven to 350°F/180°C/gas 4.
• Blanch the onions in salted boiling water for 5 minutes. Drain well. • Slice "lids" off the tops of the tomatoes and onions. Carefully scoop the insides and chop finely. • Sauté the tomato and onion flesh in 2 tablespoons of oil in a large frying pan over low heat for 5 minutes. • Transfer to a large bowl. Mix in the veal, sausage meat, eggs, Parmesan, rice, parsley, and nutmeg. Season with salt and pepper. • Stuff the tomatoes and onions with the mixture. Place the "lids" on top of the vegetables. • Arrange the stuffed vegetables in a large baking dish. • Drizzle with the remaining oil and the stock. Cover with aluminum foil. • Bake for 25 minutes. Remove the foil and baste the vegetables with the cooking juices. • Bake for 20 minutes more. • Serve hot or warm.

VEAL IN MUSHROOM AND WINE SAUCE

S eason the veal with salt. Dip in the flour until well coated, shaking off the excess. • Heat the oil in a large frying pan over medium heat. Sauté the veal for 5–7 minutes, or until the meat is cooked. • Transfer to a plate and keep warm.
• Sauté the onion and tomato in the same oil for 8–10 minutes, or until the onion is lightly browned.
• Pour in the wine and let it evaporate. Season with salt. • Add the mushrooms and their liquid and cook for 5 minutes, or until tender. • Add the veal slices and cook for 5 minutes more, or until the veal is heated through. • Serve hot.

Serves: 4–6

Preparation: 15'

Cooking: 30'

Level of difficulty: 1

- 1½ lb/750 g veal, thinly sliced
- salt to taste
- ⅓ cup/50 g all-purpose/plain flour
- 4 tbsp extra-virgin olive oil
- 1 medium onion, finely chopped
- 1 medium tomato, coarsely chopped
- 1 cup/250 ml dry white wine
- 2 tbsp dried mushrooms, soaked in warm water for 15 minutes

VEAL ESCALOPES WITH MARSALA AND MARJORAM

Serves: 4

Preparation: 15'

Cooking: 15'

Level of difficulty: 1

- 1½ lb/750 g veal, thinly sliced
- salt and freshly ground black pepper to taste
- ½ cup/75 g all-purpose/plain flour
- 4 tbsp extra-virgin olive oil
- ½ cup/125 ml Beef Stock (see page 224)
- ½ cup/125 ml Marsala wine
- 2 tbsp finely chopped marjoram

Lightly pound the veal with a meat tenderizer so that it is thin and of even thickness. • Season the veal with salt and pepper. • Dip the veal in the flour until well coated, shaking off the excess. • Sauté the veal in the oil in a large frying pan over high heat, turning often until browned all over. Season with salt and pepper. • Cook over medium heat for 10–12 minutes, adding a little stock to moisten. • Transfer to a heated serving dish and keep warm. • Add the Marsala wine and marjoram to the juices left in the pan. Cook over medium-high heat until reduced by half. • Pour the sauce over the veal and serve.

STUFFED VEAL

Cut a pocket into the piece of veal or beef. • Mix the ground veal, pork, lard, bread, Parmesan, Swiss chard, marjoram, pistachios, eggs, nutmeg, salt, and pepper in a large bowl. • Stuff the meat with the mixture. • Use a trussing needle and thread to stitch up the pocket. • Place in a large saucepan and cover with hot stock. Place over high heat and bring the stock to a boil. • Lower the heat and simmer gently for about 2 hours, or until the meat is very tender. • Cool the veal completely in the stock. • Slice thinly and transfer to a serving plate.

Serves: 6

Preparation: 25'

Cooking: 2 h

Level of difficulty: 2

- 2 lb/1 kg boneless tenderloin veal or beef, in 1 piece
- 8 oz/200 g ground/minced veal
- 8 oz/200 g ground/minced pork
- 4 oz/125 g lard or pancetta, very finely chopped
- 8 slices day-old bread, soaked in milk and squeezed dry
- 3 tbsp freshly grated Parmesan cheese
- 7 oz/200 g cooked Swiss chard, squeezed and finely chopped
- 2 tbsp finely chopped marjoram
- 2 tbsp pistachios, blanched and peeled
- 4 large eggs, lightly beaten
- 1/8 tsp freshly grated nutmeg
- salt and freshly ground white pepper to taste
- 3 quarts/3 liters Vegetable Stock (see page 224)

VEAL CUTLETS WITH ANCHOVY SAUCE

Serves: 4	
Preparation: 20'	
Cooking: 10'	
Level of difficulty: 1	

Make little cuts around the edges of the cutlets to stop them from curling up during cooking.
• Coat the cutlets with flour, shaking off the excess. • Beat the eggs in a bowl with the salt. Dip the cutlets in the eggs, then coat with the bread crumbs, pressing them so they stick well.
• Heat the oil in a large frying pan until very hot. Fry the cutlets for 10 minutes, or until golden brown on both sides. • Drain well on kitchen towels. • Melt the butter in a small saucepan over low heat. Stir in the anchovies, crushing them with a fork until they dissolve. Spoon the sauce over the cutlets.
• Serve hot.

- 4–8 veal cutlets, about 1 lb/500 g total
- ½ cup/75 g all-purpose/plain flour
- 2 eggs
- salt to taste
- 2 cups/250 g fine dry bread crumbs
- ½ cup/125 ml olive oil, for frying
- ½ cup/125 g butter
- 8 anchovy fillets

Serves: 6–8

Preparation: 25' + 6 h to chill

Cooking: 2 h

Level of difficulty: 2

- 2 lb/1 kg lean veal roast, preferably rump
- 1 carrot
- 1 stalk celery
- 1 bay leaf
- 1 onion studded with 2 cloves
- salt and freshly ground black pepper to taste
- 6 oz/180 g tuna, packed in oil
- 1 cup/250 ml mayonnaise
- 2 tbsp capers
- juice of 1 lemon + ½ lemon to garnish
- 4 tbsp extra-virgin olive oil

CHILLED VEAL WITH TUNA SAUCE

Remove any fat from the meat and tie firmly with kitchen string. • Place the meat, carrot, celery, bay leaf, and onion in a pot with just enough boiling water to cover the meat. Season with salt and cover and simmer for 2 hours. Let the veal cool in its cooking water. • Drain the oil from the tuna. Process the tuna, mayonnaise, 1 tablespoon of capers, lemon juice, oil, salt, and pepper in a food processor until smooth. • Slice the veal thinly, transfer to a serving dish, and top with the sauce. Garnish with the capers and slices of lemon.
• Cover and refrigerate for at least 6 hours.
• Serve at room temperature.

STEWED VEAL ROLLS WITH OLIVES

Serves: 4

Preparation: 25'

Cooking: 30'

Level of difficulty: 1

- 3 tbsp freshly grated Parmesan cheese
- 2 tbsp finely chopped parsley
- 1 clove garlic, finely chopped
- 1½ lb/750 g veal, thinly sliced
- 2 onions, finely chopped
- 2 carrots, cut in small cubes
- 5 tbsp extra-virgin olive oil
- 14 oz/400 ml peeled and chopped tomatoes
- salt and freshly ground black pepper to taste
- 10 green olives, pitted

Process the Parmesan, parsley, and garlic powder in a food processor or blender until very finely chopped. Spread the mixture over the slices of veal. Roll up and tie with kitchen string.
• Sauté the onions and carrots in the oil in a large frying pan for 10 minutes, or until softened. • Add the veal rolls and brown all over.

For veal rolls and escalopes, always use thinly sliced topside (top round). Pound lightly before use.

633

• Pour in the tomatoes and season with salt and plenty of pepper. Add the olives. Cover and cook over medium heat for 20 minutes. • Serve hot.

LOIN OF VEAL WITH LEEKS

Tie the veal firmly with kitchen string. Season with salt and pepper. • Sauté the veal in the oil and butter in a large saucepan just large enough to contain the veal until browned all over. • Add the leeks and cook for 5 minutes, stirring often. Season with salt and pepper. • Pour in the milk to cover the meat and cook for about 1 hour, or until the milk has evaporated. • Remove the meat, slice, and transfer to a heated serving dish. • Process the leek sauce in a food processor until smooth. Reheat and spoon the sauce over the meat.
• Serve hot.

Serves: 6

Preparation: 20'

Cooking: 1 h

Level of difficulty: 1

- **2 lb/1 kg veal loin**
- **salt and freshly ground black pepper to taste**
- **6 tbsp extra-virgin olive oil**
- **2 tbsp butter**
- **4 leeks, thinly sliced**
- **1 quart/1 liter whole milk**

VEAL ROLLS

M elt half the butter and mix with the parsley, garlic, bread crumbs, Parmesan, eggs, salt, and pepper in a large bowl. • Spread this mixture over the slices of veal. Roll each slice up, securing with kitchen thread or toothpicks. • Sauté the onion in the remaining butter in a large frying pan until softened. • Add the tomato passata and season with salt and pepper. • Place the veal rolls in the pan in a single layer. Cover and cook over low heat for about 15 minutes, turning them occasionally. • Serve hot.

636

Serves: 4–6
Preparation: 20'
Cooking: 15'
Level of difficulty: 1

- scant ½ cup/ 100 g butter
- 1 tbsp finely chopped parsley
- 1 clove garlic, finely chopped
- 1 cup/125 g fine dry bread crumbs
- 1¼ cups/150 g freshly grated Parmesan cheese
- 2 eggs
- salt and freshly ground black pepper to taste
- 1½ lb/750 g thinly sliced veal
- 1 small onion, finely chopped
- 2 tbsp tomato passata diluted with ½ cup/125 ml water

VEAL ESCALOPES WITH PARMESAN

Lightly pound the veal with a meat tenderizer so that it is thin and of even thickness. • Season with salt and pepper. • Beat the egg with a pinch of salt in a small bowl. • Dip the veal in the eggs. • Melt the butter in a large frying pan over medium heat. Cook the veal for 2 minutes on each side. • Arrange in a single layer in an earthenware pot which has been greased with butter. Top with the Parmesan. Pour in the stock. Cover and cook over low heat until the cheese has melted. • Serve hot.

Serves: 4–6

Preparation: 15'

Cooking: 25'

Level of difficulty: 1

- 1½ lb/750 g thinly sliced veal
- salt to taste
- 1 egg
- 6 tbsp butter
- ¾ cup/90 g Parmesan cheese, in flakes
- ½ cup/125 ml hot Beef Stock (see page 224)

VEAL ESCALOPES WITH PROSCIUTTO

Serves: 4–6

Preparation: 20'

Cooking: 25'

Level of difficulty: 1

- **6–8 thin slices veal, about 1½ lb/750 g**
- **1 egg**
- **salt to taste**
- **1 cup/125 g fine dry bread crumbs**
- **½ cup/125 g butter**
- **8 thin slices of prosciutto/Parma ham**
- **3½ oz/100 g Parmesan cheese, in flakes**
- **scant 1 cup/200 ml tomato passata**
- **½ cup/125 ml Beef Stock (see page 224)**

Lightly pound the veal with a meat tenderizer so that it is thin and of even thickness. • Beat the egg with a pinch of salt in a small bowl. • Dip the slices of veal into the egg and then coat with the bread crumbs, pressing them so that stick well.
• Melt the butter in a large frying pan over medium heat. Cook the veal for 2 minutes on each side.
• Arrange the veal in a single layer in a flameproof casserole. Place a slice of prosciutto on each and top with the Parmesan. • Mix the tomato passata with the meat stock and pour over the veal. Cover and simmer over medium heat for about 15 minutes, or until the cheese has melted.
• Serve hot.

BRAISED VEAL AND PROSCIUTTO SLICES

Serves: 4

Preparation: 10'

Cooking: 6'

Level of difficulty: 1

- **8 thin slices of veal, weighing about 1 lb/500 g**
- **8 leaves fresh sage**
- **4 thin slices of prosciutto/Parma ham, weighing about 3½ oz/ 100 g, cut in half**
- **4 tbsp butter**
- **salt and freshly ground black pepper to taste**
- **4 tbsp dry white wine**

Put the veal between two sheets of greaseproof paper and flatten with a meat tenderizer.
- Place a leaf of sage at the center of each slice and cover with half a slice of prosciutto. Attach them to the veal using a toothpick. • Melt the butter in a large frying pan over medium heat. Cook the veal for 3 minutes on each side. Season with salt and pepper. • Drizzle with the wine and let it evaporate. • Transfer the veal to a heated serving dish. Boil the remaining cooking juices for 1 minute and pour over the veal. • Serve hot.

This succulent dish comes from Emilia-Romagna, in central Italy, the home of Parma ham.

641

CREAMY VEAL CASSEROLE

S eason the veal with salt and pepper. • Melt 1 tablespoon of butter in an earthenware pot. Add the veal and cook over medium heat, stirring often, for 15 minutes. • Melt the remaining butter in a small saucepan over medium heat. Add the flour and stir with a wooden spoon until it starts to color. • Add the flour mixture to the meat and cook for 3 minutes, stirring constantly. • Pour in the cream and mix well. Cover and simmer over low heat for at least 1 hour, stirring occasionally.
• If the liquid reduces too much, add 2 tablespoons of milk or water. There should be plenty of sauce.
• Taste and season with more salt if necessary.
• Serve hot.

Serves: 4–6

Preparation: 5'

Cooking: 1 h 30'

Level of difficulty: 1

- 1½ lb/750 g veal shank or shoulder, cut into 1¼-inch/ 3-cm cubes
- salt and freshly ground white pepper to taste
- 4 tbsp butter
- 2 tbsp all-purpose/ plain flour
- 1½ cups/375 ml light/single cream

VEAL CUTLETS WITH MELTED CHEESE FILLING

Serves: 4

Preparation: 10'

Cooking: 20'

Level of difficulty: 1

- 4 veal cutlets, with bone, each weighing about 7 oz/200 g
- 4 oz/125 g Fontina or Cheddar cheese, thinly sliced
- wafer-thin slices of fresh truffle (optional)
- salt and freshly ground black pepper to taste
- 1 tbsp all-purpose/ plain flour
- 1 egg, lightly beaten
- 5 tbsp fine dry bread crumbs
- 6 tbsp butter

Use a very sharp, pointed knife to cut horizontally into the meat of the cutlets toward the bone to form a pocket. • Place a quarter of the Fontina slices inside each pocket, together with a few slivers of truffle, if using. • Beat the edges of the pockets lightly to make the cut edges stick together, enclosing the contents. • Season the cutlets with salt and pepper and coat with flour. Dip into the egg and then coat with bread crumbs. • Melt the butter over high heat in a large frying pan over high heat. • Add the cutlets and fry for 6–8 minutes, or until golden brown all over. • Serve very hot.

643

BEEF

BEEF ESCALOPES WITH CAPERS AND OREGANO

Blanch the tomatoes in boiling water for 30 seconds. • Slip off the skins, gently squeeze out as many seeds as possible, and chop coarsely. • Sauté the garlic in 2 tablespoons of oil in a large frying pan until pale gold. Discard the garlic. • Stir in the tomatoes and season with salt and pepper. Cook over high heat for 10 minutes, stirring often. • Melt the butter with the remaining oil in a large frying pan. Add the beef and fry for 3–4 minutes on each side until cooked through. • Add the tomato sauce and capers and cook for 2 minutes more. • Transfer to a serving plate, sprinkle with the oregano, and serve hot.

646

Serves: 4–6

Preparation: 20'

Cooking: 25'

Level of difficulty: 1

- 6 large tomatoes
- 1 clove garlic, lightly crushed but whole
- 4 tbsp extra-virgin olive oil
- salt and freshly ground black pepper to taste
- 1 tbsp butter
- 1½ lb/750 g thinly sliced beef topside
- 2 tbsp salted capers, rinsed
- ¼ tsp oregano

FILLET STEAK WITH MADEIRA SAUCE

Serves: 6

Preparation: 15'

Cooking: 15'

Level of difficulty: 2

- 4 tbsp butter
- 6 thick fillet steaks
- salt to taste

SAUCE

- 6 tbsp Madeira wine
- 1 cup/250 ml Vegetable Stock (see page 224)
- 3 tbsp butter
- ⅓ cup/50 g all-purpose/plain flour

Steaks: Melt the butter over high heat in a large frying pan. • Add the steaks and cook for 3–5 minutes on each side. Season with salt and transfer to a serving dish. • Sauce: Add half the wine and the stock to the pan and bring to a boil. Cook over medium heat for about 3 minutes, or until the sauce has reduced by half. • Add the butter. • Beat in the flour and cook for 2 minutes. Add the remaining wine and mix well. • Pour the sauce over the steaks and serve hot.

BEEF AND PANCETTA MEATBALLS

B oil the potatoes for 12–15 minutes, or until tender. • Drain, slip off the skins, and mash. • Cook the beef in the butter in a large frying pan for 8–10 minutes, or until cooked through. • Finely chop the beef with the pancetta. • Mix the potatoes, chopped meat, 2 eggs, parsley, and walnuts in a large bowl. Season with salt and pepper. • Shape the mixture into balls the size of golf balls and flatten slightly. Dip in the flour until well coated, then in the remaining beaten eggs. • Heat the oil in a large frying pan until very hot. Fry in small batches for 5–7 minutes, or until golden. • Drain well on paper towels. • Place the meat sauce in a large frying pan over medium heat. Add the meatballs and cook for 5 minutes. • Serve hot.

Serves: 4

Preparation: 25'

Cooking: 40'

Level of difficulty: 2

- 2 large potatoes
- 7 oz/200 g sliced beef
- 4 tbsp butter
- 1 cup/125 g diced pancetta
- 4 eggs
- 2 tbsp finely chopped parsley
- 2 tbsp chopped walnuts
- salt and freshly ground black pepper to taste
- 1/3 cup/50 g all-purpose/plain flour
- 1 cup/250 ml olive oil, for frying
- 1 quantity Meat Sauce (see page 50)

Serves: 4–6

Preparation: 20'

Cooking: 75'

Level of difficulty: 1

- 1½ lb/750 g ground/minced beef
- 1 cup/150 g fine dry bread crumbs
- 1 tbsp finely chopped parsley
- 1–2 tsp red pepper flakes
- salt and freshly ground black pepper to taste
- 1 tbsp cumin seeds
- 2 eggs
- 1 cup/250 ml olive oil, for frying
- boiled rice, to serve

SPICY CUMIN MEATBALLS

Place the beef, $^2/_3$ cup (100 g) of bread crumbs, parsley, red pepper flakes, salt, pepper, cumin seeds and 1 egg in a large bowl and mix until well blended. • Shape the mixture into balls the size of golf balls. • Lightly beat the remaining egg. Dip the meat balls in the egg, then roll in the remaining bread crumbs. • Heat the oil to very hot in a large frying pan. Fry the meatballs in small batches for 5–7 minutes, or until cooked through and well browned. • Drain well on paper towels. • Serve hot with rice.

BEEF AND MUSHROOM STEW

Cut the beef into bite-sized pieces. • Sauté the garlic in the oil in a large frying pan until pale gold. • Discard the garlic. Add the beef and sauté over high heat until browned all over. • Pour in the wine and let it evaporate. • Mix in the tomatoes and season with salt. Cover and cook over low heat for 30 minutes. • Remove the earthy stem of the mushrooms and clean well. Chop the mushrooms and add them to the beef. • Cook for 20–30 minutes more, or until the beef is tender, adding the stock if the sauce begins to stick to the pan. • Season with salt and pepper and add the thyme. • Serve with boiled new potatoes.

If chanterelle mushrooms are not available, use a mixture of other wild or cultivated mushrooms.

650

Serves: 4–6

Preparation: 30'

Cooking: 1 h 20'

Level of difficulty: 2

- 1½ lb/750 g boneless beef chuck
- 1 clove garlic, lightly crushed but whole
- 4 tbsp extra-virgin olive oil
- 4 tbsp dry white wine
- 15 oz/450 g canned tomatoes
- salt and freshly ground black pepper to taste
- 8 oz/250 g chanterelle mushrooms
- 8 oz/250 g porcini mushrooms
- ½ cup/125 ml Beef Stock (see page 224)
- 2 tbsp finely chopped thyme
- boiled new potatoes, to serve

BEEF AND RICE KOFTE

Serves: 6

Preparation: 20'

Cooking: 55'

Level of difficulty: 1

- 2 red onions, finely chopped
- 2 tbsp butter
- 1 cup/200 g short-grain rice
- salt and freshly ground black pepper to taste
- ¾ cup/180 ml water
- 1½ lb/750 g ground/minced beef
- 1 tsp finely chopped dill
- ½ tsp ground cumin seeds
- 2 large eggs + 2 large egg yolks, lightly beaten
- ½ cup/125 ml olive oil, for frying

Sauté the onions in the butter in a large frying pan over medium heat for 8–10 minutes, or until lightly browned. • Add the rice, season with salt, and pour in the water. • Cover and cook for 10–15 minutes, or until the liquid has all been absorbed. • Mix the beef, rice, dill, cumin, and 2 whole eggs in a large bowl. Season with salt and pepper. • Shape the mixture into balls the size of golf balls. Flatten them slightly. • Dip in the egg yolks. • Heat the oil in a large frying pan until very hot. Fry the kofte in small batches for 5–7 minutes, or until golden brown all over. • Drain well on paper towels and serve hot.

BEEF AND PINE NUT ROLLS

Preheat the oven to 400°F/200°C/gas 6. • Set out a large baking dish. • Mix the beef, onions, and eggs in a large bowl. Season with salt and pepper. • Use your hands to knead the mixture until well mixed. • Turn out onto a lightly floured work surface and flatten into twelve rectangles. • Place pine nuts about $1/2$-inch (1-cm) from one of the long sides of each rectangle. Roll up into a sausage shape, starting from the edge lined with pine nuts. • Place the rolls in the baking dish. Dot with the butter and drizzle with the water. • Bake for about 1 hour, or until well browned. • Transfer to a preheated serving dish. Garnish with the parsley and slices of lemon. • Serve hot.

Serves: 6

Preparation: 15'

Cooking: 1 h

Level of difficulty: 2

- 2 lb/1 kg ground/ minced beef
- 2 onions, very finely chopped
- 2 eggs, lightly beaten
- salt and freshly ground black pepper to taste
- 4 tbsp pine nuts
- 3 tbsp butter
- 3 tbsp water
- fresh parsley, coarsely chopped
- slices of lemon, to garnish

BEEF CASSEROLE WITH ORANGE

Serves:	6–8
Preparation:	30'
Cooking:	4 h
Level of difficulty:	2

Preheat the oven to 325°F/170°C/gas 3. •
Sauté the salt pork in the oil in a large
ovenproof casserole over medium heat until lightly
browned. • Add the beef and cook for 8–10
minutes, or until browned. • Stir in the onions and
cook for 10 minutes more. • Drain off any excess
fat. • Pour in one-third of the wine and let it
evaporate. Repeat twice until all the wine has been
added. • Add the water, celery, bay leaves, and
carrots. Season with salt and pepper. • Bring to a
boil and cover and cook for 5 minutes. Add the
thyme, olives, tomatoes, garlic, and orange zest.
• Cover with the lid and bake in the oven for about
3 hours, or until the meat is very tender.
• Serve hot.

- 6 oz/180 g salt pork or bacon, diced
- 4 tbsp extra-virgin olive oil
- 3 lb/1.5 kg chuck steak, cut in chunks
- 5 medium onions, finely chopped
- 2 cups/500 ml dry white wine
- 1 quart/1 liter water
- 2 stalks celery, diced
- 2 bay leaves
- 3 carrots, sliced
- salt and freshly ground black pepper to taste
- 1 tbsp finely chopped thyme
- 20 black and 20 green olives, pitted
- 4 tomatoes, peeled, seeded, and finely chopped
- 6 cloves garlic, finely chopped
- grated zest of 1 orange

Serves: 6

Preparation: 15'

Cooking: 2 h

Level of difficulty: 1

- **2 tbsp extra-virgin olive oil**
- **2 lb/1 kg lean stewing beef, cut into cubes**
- **1 lb/500 g fresh fava/broad beans, shelled**
- **2 cloves garlic, peeled and finely chopped**
- **1 tsp freshly ground coriander seeds**
- **salt and freshly ground black pepper to taste**
- **2 quarts/2 liters water**

BEEF STEW WITH FAVA BEANS

Heat the oil in a large saucepan over medium heat. Brown the beef for 10 minutes. • Add the fava beans, garlic, and coriander. Season with salt and pepper. Pour in the water. • Bring to a boil, cover, and cook over low heat for about 2 hours, or until the beef and fava beans are very tender. • Serve hot.

POT-AU-FEU

Serves: 6–8

Preparation: 25'

Cooking: 3 h

Level of difficulty: 1

- **2 lb/1 kg beef tenderloin**
- **2 lb/1 kg chicken**
- **1 lb/500 g lamb shoulder roast**
- **4 oz/125 g salt pork**
- **2 quarts/2 liters water**
- **1 cup/250 ml dry white wine**
- **2 cloves**
- **2 medium onions**
- **4 cloves garlic, finely chopped**
- **3 turnips, halved**
- **4 tomatoes, halved**
- **1 lb/500 g carrots**
- **whites of 2 leeks**
- **1 bouquet garni (celery, bay leaves, chervil, thyme)**
- **salt and freshly ground black pepper to taste**
- **6–8 slices firm-textured bread, toasted**

Place the beef, chicken, lamb, and salt pork in a large pot with enough water to cover. Add the wine and bring to a boil. • Press a clove into each onion and add to the meat with the garlic, turnips, tomatoes, carrots, leeks, and the bouquet garni. Season with salt and pepper. • Bring to a boil and skim off any foam. Cook over low heat for 2–3 hours, or until the meat is very tender. • Place the toast in individual soup bowls and ladle the stock over the top. • Serve the meat and chicken, sliced, and vegetables on a large platter as a second course.

GROUND MEAT SKEWERS

Process the beef and onion in a food processor until finely chopped. Add the cumin, cinnamon, and egg. Season with salt and pepper. Process again briefly. • Transfer the mixture to a large bowl. • Rinse your hands in cold water and knead the mixture until very smooth. Add the pine nuts. • Shape the mixture into sausage shapes and wrap around the skewers. • Cook under the broiler (grill) or over the glowing embers of a barbecue for 15–20 minutes, or until browned and cooked through. • Serve hot with fresh, plain yogurt, boiled rice, and a green salad.

- 2 lb/1 kg ground/ minced beef
- 1 large onion, very finely chopped
- 1 tsp freshly ground cumin seeds
- 1 tsp ground cinnamon
- 1 large egg, lightly beaten
- salt and freshly ground black pepper to taste
- 2 tbsp coarsely chopped pine nuts
- hot boiled rice, to serve
- yogurt, to serve
- green salad, to serve

| Serves: 4 |
| Preparation: 25' |
| Cooking: 1 h 30' |
| Level of difficulty: 1 |

- **2 large onions,
  coarsely chopped**
- **2 cloves garlic,
  finely chopped**
- **4 tbsp extra-virgin
  olive oil**
- **1 lb/500 g stewing
  beef, cut into small
  chunks**
- **2 lb/1 kg green
  beans, trimmed
  and cut into
  short lengths**
- **1½ cups/375 ml
  water or more if
  needed**
- **15 oz/450 g
  chopped tomatoes**
- **½ tsp ground
  cinnamon**
- **salt and freshly
  ground black
  pepper to taste**
- **hot boiled rice,
  to serve**

GREEN BEAN AND MEAT STEW

S auté the onions and garlic in the oil in a large frying pan over medium heat for 8–10 minutes, or until lightly browned. • Add the beef and brown for 10 minutes. • Add the beans and pour in the water. Bring to a boil, cover, and cook over low heat for 40–45 minutes, or until the beans are tender. Add more water if the pan dries out. • Add the tomatoes and cinnamon and season with salt and pepper. • Cook over low heat for 30 minutes more. • Serve hot on a bed of boiled rice.

TENDERLOIN BEEF WITH BALSAMIC VINEGAR

Serves: 4–6

Preparation: 10'

Cooking: 10'

Level of difficulty: 1

- 2 tbsp butter
- ½ shallot, finely chopped
- 1½ lb/750 g tenderloin beef, cut in 4 slices
- ½ cup/125 ml balsamic vinegar
- salt and freshly ground black pepper to taste
- 1 tbsp cornstarch/ cornflour

Melt the butter in a large frying pan over high heat. When it is foaming, add the shallot and beef. Cook for about 4 minutes on each side.

• Pour in the balsamic vinegar and season with salt and pepper. Cook for 1–2 minutes more.

• Set the meat aside on a heated serving dish and keep warm. • Return the cooking juices to the heat and cook until they foam. Add the cornstarch and stir until thickened. • Pour the sauce over the meat and serve hot.

BEEF WITH PRUNES

Serves: 6–8
Preparation: 15'
Cooking: 1 h 40'
Level of difficulty: 1

Heat the oil in a large frying pan over high heat. Brown the beef for 5 minutes. • Add the onions and bay leaves and sauté until lightly browned, 8–10 minutes. • Pour in the wine and let it evaporate. • Season with salt and pepper. Stir in the tomatoes, cinnamon, and sugar. • Cook for 55–65 minutes, or until the beef is tender, adding water if the sauce begins to dry. • Remove the beef from the saucepan and add the prunes. Cover with the meat. • Cook over low heat for 15 minutes more. • Arrange the beef and prunes on a serving plate. Serve hot.

- 4 tbsp extra-virgin olive oil
- 2 lb/1 kg lean beef, cut into cubes
- 2 onions, finely chopped
- 2 bay leaves
- ½ cup/125 ml dry red wine
- salt and freshly ground black pepper to taste
- 1 lb/500 g peeled and chopped tomatoes
- 1 tsp ground cinnamon
- 1 tsp sugar
- water (optional)
- 1½ lb/750 g pitted prunes

MEDITERRANEAN POT ROAST

Serves: 8

Preparation: 30' +
12 h to marinate

Cooking: 3 h

Level of difficulty: 1

- 4 lb/2 kg topside of beef
- 4 cloves garlic, finely chopped
- 2 quarts/2 liters dry red wine
- 4 large onions, finely chopped
- 1 tbsp finely chopped thyme
- 1 bay leaf
- 1 tbsp finely chopped rosemary
- 3 stalks celery, finely chopped
- salt and freshly ground black pepper to taste
- ½ cup/125 ml extra-virgin olive oil
- 8 oz/250 g finely chopped bacon
- 2 tbsp finely chopped parsley
- 4 large carrots, peeled and thinly sliced
- 1 lb/500 g peeled and chopped tomatoes
- 2 tsp mustard

Use a sharp knife to make slashes in the beef. Press the garlic into the slashes. • Place the beef in a deep roasting pan and pour in the wine. Add the onions, thyme, bay leaf, rosemary, and celery. Season with salt and pepper. • Cover with aluminum foil and refrigerate for 12 hours. • Heat the oil in a large saucepan over medium heat. Brown the beef and bacon for 5 minutes. • Remove the beef from the pan. Add the marinade and cook for 1 minute. • Add the beef, parsley, carrots, tomatoes, and mustard. Cover and cook over low heat for 2–3 hours, or until the beef is very tender. • Serve hot.

SEARED BEEF WITH ASPARAGUS

Wash the asparagus, trim the tough parts off the bottom of the stalks, and cut into $1/2$-inch (1-cm) long pieces. Leave the tips whole. • Sauté the shallot in the oil in a large frying pan over medium heat for 3 minutes. • Add the asparagus and season with salt and pepper. • Pour in the wine and let it evaporate. • Pour in half the stock and cook for 15 minutes, adding more stock during cooking if the pan dries out. • Remove from the heat when the asparagus is crunchy-tender. • Heat a large nonstick frying pan over medium-high heat. Cook the slices of beef, 2 or 3 at a time, by dropping them into the pan and turning them immediately. They will only take a minute or two to cook. • Arrange the beef on heated dinner plates, and season with salt and pepper • Spoon the asparagus and cooking liquids over the top and serve hot.

Serves:	4–6
Preparation:	15'
Cooking:	25'
Level of difficulty:	1

- **12 oz/300 g asparagus**
- **1 shallot, finely chopped**
- **6 tbsp extra-virgin olive oil**
- **salt and freshly ground black pepper to taste**
- **4 tbsp dry white wine**
- **$3/4$ cup/180 ml Beef Stock (see page 224)**
- **$1^{1}/_2$ lb/750 g prime beef fillet or tenderloin, very thinly sliced**

BEEF POT ROAST WITH PINK GRAPEFRUIT

Serves: 6

Preparation: 15'

Cooking: 1 h 20'

Level of difficulty: 2

- **2 tbsp butter**
- **4 tbsp extra-virgin olive oil**
- **2 lb/1 kg boneless beef roast**
- **²⁄₃ cup/150 ml dry white wine**
- **generous ¹⁄₃ cup/ 100 ml brandy**
- **salt and freshly ground black pepper to taste**
- **juice of 1 pink grapefruit**
- **2 pink grapefruit, peeled and cut into segments**

Melt the butter with the oil in a large pot over medium heat. • Add the beef and cook until browned all over. • Pour in the wine and brandy and let evaporate. • Season with salt and pepper. Cook for about 1 hour 15 minutes, or until the beef is very tender, moistening from time to time with the grapefruit juice. • Transfer the meat to a chopping board. • Add the grapefruit segments to the cooking liquids and cook until heated through. • Slice the meat and garnish with the grapefruit. Drizzle with the sauce and serve hot.

BEEF AND GARLIC STEW

Sauté the garlic in the oil in a deep saucepan or earthenware pot over high heat for 2–3 minutes, or until pale gold. • Add the beef and sauté until well browned. • Season with salt and add the peppercorns, sage, rosemary, and wine. Cover and cook over low heat for 3 hours, or until the beef is very tender. • Serve hot.

670

Serves: 4–6

Preparation: 20'

Cooking: 3 h 15'

Level of difficulty: 2

- 5 cloves garlic, whole
- 4 tbsp extra-virgin olive oil
- 2 lb/1 kg beef, cut into small chunks
- salt to taste
- 2 tbsp black peppercorns
- 1 bunch sage
- 1 twig rosemary
- 1 quart/1 liter Chianti Classico or other full-bodied red wine

MEATBALLS WITH TOMATO SAUCE

Serves: 4

Preparation: 25'

Cooking: 45'

Level of difficulty: 2

- 2 lb/1 kg canned tomatoes
- 4 tbsp extra-virgin olive oil
- 7 oz/200 g crusty white bread
- 1 lb/500 g ground/ minced lean beef
- 1 cup/125 g freshly grated Parmesan cheese
- 3 eggs
- salt and freshly ground black pepper to taste

Cook the tomatoes with the oil in a large saucepan over medium heat for 15 minutes, stirring often. • Grate the bread into a large bowl. Mix in the beef, Parmesan, and eggs. Season with salt and pepper. Mix in 4 tablespoons of the tomatoes. • Shape the mixture into balls about the size of large plums. • Add the meatballs to the tomato sauce. Cook over low heat for 20–30 minutes, or until cooked through, shaking the pan very gently from time to time. • Serve the meatballs hot with the sauce.

HAMBURGERS WITH MUSTARD SAUCE

Serves: 2–4

Preparation: 10'

Cooking: 20'

Level of difficulty: 1

- 1 large onion, finely chopped
- 1 red bell pepper/capsicum, cut into strips
- 1 green bell pepper/capsicum, cut into strips
- 4 tbsp extra-virgin olive oil
- 4 hamburgers
- salt and freshly ground black pepper to taste
- ½ cup/125 ml dry white wine
- ½ cup/125 ml Beef Stock (see page 224)
- 2 tbsp hot mustard

Sauté the onion and bell peppers in the oil in a large frying pan over medium heat until softened. • Add the hamburgers and season with salt and pepper. • Pour in the wine and let it evaporate, turning the hamburgers often. • Gradually pour in the stock and cook for 10–15 minutes, or until the hamburgers are cooked through. • Transfer the hamburgers to a heated serving dish. • Stir the mustard into the cooking juices in the pan. • Spoon the mustard sauce over the hamburgers and serve hot.

BEEF STEW WITH POTATOES

S auté the garlic, onion, carrot, celery, tomatoes, and mixed herbs in the oil in a large saucepan over medium heat for 5 minutes. • Add the beef, season with salt and pepper, and cook until browned. • Pour in the wine and let it evaporate. • Cover and simmer over low heat for about 2 hours, gradually adding the stock to stop the sauce from drying out. • Add the potatoes. Cover and simmer for 30 minutes more, or until the beef is very tender. Stir often to prevent the meat from sticking to the pan. • Serve hot.

Serves: 4–6

Preparation: 25'

Cooking: 2 h 15'

Level of difficulty: 1

- 1 clove garlic, 1 onion, 1 carrot, 1 stalk celery, all finely chopped
- 6 large tomatoes, peeled and chopped
- 1 tbsp chopped, mixed herbs (sage, parsley, oregano, rosemary, thyme)
- 6 tbsp extra-virgin olive oil
- 1½ lb/750 g beef chuck with muscle, cut into bite-sized pieces
- salt and freshly ground black pepper to taste
- 1 cup/250 ml dry red wine
- 2 cups/500 ml Beef Stock (see page 224)
- 1½ lb/750 g potatoes, peeled and cut into bite-sized chunks

BEEF STEW WITH MUSHROOMS

Serves: 4–6

Preparation: 25'

Cooking: 1 h 15'

Level of difficulty: 1

- **1 clove garlic, finely chopped**
- **1 onion, finely chopped**
- **4 tbsp extra-virgin olive oil**
- **1½ lb/750 g boneless beef chuck, cut into bite-sized pieces**
- **salt and freshly ground black pepper to taste**
- **½ cup/125 ml dry white wine**
- **1 lb/500 g canned tomatoes**
- **1 lb/500 g porcini or white mushrooms**
- **2 tbsp finely chopped parsley**
- **1 cup/250 ml Beef Stock (see page 224)**

Sauté the garlic and onion in the oil in a large pot over medium heat until the onion is translucent. • Add the beef, season with salt and pepper, and sauté until browned. • Pour in the wine and let it evaporate. • Mix in the tomatoes and cook over low heat for 40 minutes. • Clean and wash the mushrooms. Cut the caps into thick strips and the stalks into chunks. • Add the mushrooms and parsley. Partially cover and simmer over low heat for about 40 minutes more, or until the beef is cooked, stirring often, adding the stock if the sauce begins to stick to the bottom of the pan. • Serve hot.

FILLED CABBAGE LEAF ROLLS

Blanch the cabbage leaves in salted, boiling water for 2–3 minutes. Let dry on a clean cloth. • Cook the spinach with just the water clinging to the leaves in a saucepan over medium heat for 5–7 minutes. • Sauté the beef in the oil in a large frying pan until browned all over. • Transfer the beef to a large bowl. Mix in the mortadella, pancetta, spinach, eggs, Pecorino, bread, and oregano. Season with salt and pepper. • Stuff the cabbage leaves with this mixture and roll up into parcels, securing with a toothpick or kitchen string. • Cook the cabbage rolls in the tomatoes in a large saucepan over medium heat for 10 minutes. Season with salt and pepper. • Serve hot.

678

- 1 Savoy cabbage
- 5 oz/150 g spinach
- 8 oz/250 g ground/ minced beef
- 2 tbsp extra-virgin olive oil
- 3 oz/90 g mortadella, chopped
- ½ cup/60 g diced pancetta
- 3 eggs
- 1 cup/125 g freshly grated Pecorino cheese
- 7 oz/200 g bread, soaked in milk and squeezed out
- ⅛ tsp oregano
- salt and freshly ground black pepper to taste
- 1 lb/500 g canned tomatoes

Serves 4–6

Preparation: 15'

Cooking: 1 h 30'

Level of difficulty: 1

- 1½ lb/750 g beef (brisket, rump roast, or bottom round/brisket, topside)
- 1 onion, cut in half
- 1 carrot, cut in 3–4 pieces
- 1 stalk celery, cut in 3–4 pieces
- 1 sprig parsley
- 6 tomatoes
- 1 tbsp coarse sea salt
- 5 onions, thinly sliced
- 4 tbsp extra-virgin olive oil
- 1 cup/250 ml Beef Stock (see page 224)
- salt and freshly ground black pepper to taste
- 1 lb/500 g canned tomatoes

BOILED BEEF WITH ONIONS

Place the beef in a large saucepan with cold water to cover. Add the onion, carrot, celery, parsley, whole tomatoes, and sea salt and bring slowly to a boil. Simmer over low heat for about 1 hour, or until the beef is very tender. • Sauté the onions in the oil in a large saucepan over medium heat for 2–3 minutes. • Pour in half the stock. Partially cover and cook for 10 minutes, or until reduced. • Chop the beef into small pieces or thin slices. • Add to the onions, season with salt and pepper, and stir for 3–4 minutes. • Stir in the tomatoes and season with salt to taste. Cover and simmer over low heat for about 15 minutes, adding more stock if the sauce begins to stick to the bottom of the pan. • Serve hot.

ITALIAN BEEF CASEROLE

Cut the beef into very thin slices. Coat lightly with flour. • Melt the butter in an earthenware pot. Add the beef slices and brown over high heat for 2 minutes, turning them often . • Remove the beef from the pot and set aside. • Add the onions to the butter and cooking juices. Cook over medium heat until softened and lightly browned. • Add the beef. Season with salt and pepper and add 4 tablespoons of wine. Simmer over very low heat for 45–50 minutes, adding more wine at intervals. • When cooked, there should be plenty of rich, dark liquid and the onion should have almost completely dissolved. • Serve hot.

680

Serves: 4–6

Preparation: 15'

Cooking: 1 h

Level of difficulty: 1

- 1½ lb/750 g lean braising beef
- 2 tbsp all-purpose/ plain flour
- 4 tbsp butter
- 2 large onions, peeled and sliced
- salt and freshly ground black pepper to taste
- 1⅔ cups/400 ml full-bodied dry red wine

STUFFED BEEF ROLL

Serves: 6

Preparation: 30'

Cooking: 1 h 15'

Level of difficulty: 1

Mix the ground beef and sausage meat in a large bowl. • Add the egg, Pecorino, parsley, onion, and garlic. Season with salt and pepper. • Place the slice of beef flat between 2 sheets of parchment paper and flatten to $^1/_4$ inch (5 mm) thick. • Lay the meat out flat and top with the prosciutto and pancetta. Spread the ground meat mixture over the top, leaving a narrow border around the edge. • Slice the pointed ends off the eggs and place them "nose to tail" down the center. • Lay the Provolone on either side of the eggs. • Carefully roll up, bringing one "long" side over the eggs. Tie with kitchen string at regular intervals. • Heat the oil in a large earthenware pot and brown the meat roll all over. • Pour in the wine and let it evaporate. • Pour in the tomato paste mixture. Cover and simmer over very low heat for about 1 hour, turning several times. • Remove the string and transfer to a heated serving platter. • Slice about $^3/_4$-inch (2-cm) thick, spooning some of the cooking liquid over each serving.

- 4 oz/125 g ground/minced lean beef
- 7 oz/200 g Italian sausage meat
- 1 egg
- $^1/_2$ cup/60 g freshly grated Pecorino cheese
- 1 tbsp finely chopped parsley
- 1$^1/_2$ tbsp finely chopped onion
- 2 cloves garlic, finely chopped
- salt and freshly ground black pepper to taste
- 1 single, thick slice of lean beef, about 1$^1/_2$ lb/750 g
- 7 oz/200 g prosciutto/Parma ham
- 4 slices pancetta, chopped
- 3 hard-boiled eggs
- 4 oz/125 g Provolone cheese, cut into strips
- 4 tbsp extra-virgin olive oil
- $^1/_2$ cup/125 ml dry red wine
- 1 tbsp tomato paste mixed in 1 cup/ 250 ml hot water

ROMAN BEEF STEW

Serves: 4–6

Preparation: 10'

Cooking: 2 h 15'

Level of difficulty: 1

- $\frac{1}{2}$ cup/60 g pork fat or pancetta, diced
- 1 large onion, finely chopped
- 2 tbsp extra-virgin olive oil
- 2 cloves garlic, finely chopped
- 1 stalk celery, finely chopped
- 1$\frac{1}{2}$ lb/750 g boneless beef chuck, cut in bite-sized cubes
- salt and freshly ground black pepper to taste
- scant $\frac{1}{2}$ cup/ 100 ml dry white wine
- 2 large ripe tomatoes, peeled and diced
- 1 tbsp finely chopped marjoram or parsley

Heat the pork fat or pancetta in a large pot and sauté the onion until softened. • Add the oil, garlic, and celery and sauté for 5 minutes. • Add the beef and season with salt and pepper, stirring constantly until the beef is lightly browned all over. • Pour in the wine and let it evaporate. • Add the tomatoes and cook for 10 minutes, stirring often. • Pour in enough cold water to cover the meat. Cover and cook over low heat for 2 hours. The sauce should be thick and dark in color. • Remove from the heat and add the marjoram. • Serve hot.

BEEF BRAISED IN RED WINE

Wrap the pork fat around the beef and tie with kitchen string. • Season with salt and pepper and coat lightly with flour. • Heat the oil and butter in an earthenware pot large enough to accommodate the meat snugly. Add the beef and cook until browned all over, about 10 minutes. • Remove the beef from the pot and set aside. • Add the rosemary, sage, garlic, parsley, onion, carrot, and celery to the cooking juices left in the pot. Cook over medium heat for 5 minutes. • Add the beef, bay leaves, cloves, and nutmeg. Mix in 2–3 tablespoons of boiling water and cook for 1 minute. • Pour in 1 cup (250 ml) of wine. Cover and cook over low heat for 40 minutes. • Pour in the remaining wine and cover and cook for 3 hours, or until the beef is very tender. • Discard the bay leaves and cloves. Remove the beef and keep hot. • Strain the cooking liquid through a fine mesh strainer, pushing the vegetables through (or process in a blender until very smooth). • Slice the beef about $1/2$ inch (1 cm) thick. • Transfer to a heated serving platter and cover with the sauce.

Serves:	4–6
Preparation:	20'
Cooking:	4 h
Level of difficulty:	1

- 2 slices pork fat, $1/2$-inch/1-cm thick (or slices of pancetta or bacon)
- 2 lb/1 kg beef, chuck, or boneless rump roast/ silverside
- salt and freshly ground black pepper to taste
- 2 tbsp all-purpose/ plain flour
- 3 tbsp extra-virgin olive oil
- 3 tbsp butter
- 2 tsp finely chopped rosemary
- 4 leaves sage, finely chopped
- 1 clove garlic, finely chopped
- 1 tsp finely chopped parsley
- 1 medium onion, coarsely chopped
- 1 medium carrot, coarsely chopped
- 1 stalk celery, trimmed and sliced
- 2 bay leaves
- 1–2 cloves
- $1/8$ tsp ground nutmeg
- 3 cups/750 ml robust red wine

TUSCAN MIXED MEAT STEW

Sauté the onion, garlic, parsley, and basil in the oil in a large saucepan or earthenware pot until the garlic is pale gold. • Add the chile pepper and sauté until the onion has softened. • Add all the meat and cook until browned all over. • Pour in the wine and let it evaporate. • Stir in the tomatoes. Season with salt and pepper and cook for 10 minutes. • Pour in the stock and cook for 5 minutes more. • Serve hot.

Serves: 6

Preparation: 15'

Cooking: 30'

Level of difficulty: 2

- 1 onion, finely chopped
- 2 cloves garlic, finely chopped
- 1 small bunch parsley, finely chopped
- 6 leaves fresh basil, torn
- 5 tbsp extra-virgin olive oil
- 1 fresh red chile pepper
- 2 lb/1 kg mixed veal, chicken, rabbit, pork, and guinea fowl, cut in pieces
- 1 cup/250 ml dry red wine
- 1 lb/500 g peeled and chopped tomatoes
- salt and freshly ground black pepper to taste
- 1 cup/250 ml hot Beef Stock (see page 224)

BOILED MEATS, MADRID STYLE

Soak the garbanzo beans in cold water for 12 hours. Drain well. • Place the beef, beef bone, and jamón in a large pot and cover with cold water. Bring to a boil. • Add the chicken, garbanzo beans, carrot, turnip, celery, and onion. • Simmer over low heat for 2 hours. • Add the potatoes and cook for 30 minutes more. • Add the cabbage and chorizo and cook for 30 more minutes, or until tender and well-cooked. • Drain the stock from the meats and vegetables. If liked, serve as a soup as a first course. • Discard the beef bone and serve the meats and vegetables hot as a second course.

Serves: 6–8

Preparation: 40' + 12 h to soak beans

Cooking: 3 h

Level of difficulty: 2

- **1 lb/500 g garbanzo beans/ chickpeas**
- **1½ lb/750 g boneless beef brisket or chuck**
- **1 beef bone**
- **4 oz/125 g jamón serrano (or prosciutto/ Parma ham)**
- **½ chicken**
- **1 carrot**
- **1 turnip**
- **½ stalk celery**
- **1 small onion studded with 1 clove**
- **8 potatoes**
- **1 chorizo sausage**
- **1 large Savoy cabbage, cut in wedges**

LAMB

LAMB WITH RED WINE AND POLENTA

Season the lamb with salt, pepper, and cinnamon. Sprinkle with the flour. • Melt the lard in a large frying pan. Add the lamb and brown over high heat • Remove from the pan and set aside. • Drain off half the fat. Sauté the onions, garlic, and carrot in the remaining fat until softened. • Pour in the wine and stock and bring to a boil. • Return the lamb to the pan. Simmer for about 40 minutes, or until the lamb is very tender. • Serve hot with the polenta.

Serves: 4–6

Preparation: 20'

Cooking: 1 h

Level of difficulty: 2

- 2½ lb/1.2 kg lamb shoulder, cut into cubes with the bone in
- salt and freshly ground black pepper to taste
- 1 tsp ground cinnamon
- 1 tbsp all-purpose/ plain flour
- 2 tbsp lard
- 2 onions, thinly sliced
- 3 cloves garlic, finely chopped
- 1 carrot, finely chopped
- 1½ cups/375 ml robust red wine
- 1 cup/250 ml Vegetable Stock (see page 224)
- 1 quantity Polenta (see page 350)

LAMB AND PLUM TAJINE

Place the lamb in a large roasting pan. Cover with the grated onions and ras el hanout. Season with salt and pepper. Marinate in the refrigerator for 2 hours. • Melt half the butter in a large pot. Add the lamb and sauté until golden all over. • Add the water, saffron, and cinnamon and bring to a boil. Cover and simmer over low heat for about 1 hour 30 minutes, or until the lamb is tender. • Bone the meat, discarding the fat, cartilage, and bones. Season with salt and pepper. • Heat the remaining butter and oil in a medium saucepan. Add the sliced onions and sprinkle with the sugar. Season with salt and pepper. Cook over medium-high heat for 15 minutes, or until golden. • Stir in the tomatoes and meat juices. Bring to a boil. Add the lamb, garbanzo beans, and pumpkin. • Cover and simmer over low heat for 15 minutes. • Add the plums and boil until the sauce thickens, about 15–20 minutes. • Serve hot.

Serves: 4

Preparation: 30' + 2 h to marinate

Cooking: 2 h 20'

Level of difficulty: 2

- 3 lb/1.5 kg lamb shoulder
- 3 medium onions, finely grated
- 1 tbsp ras el hanout (North African spice mix)
- salt and freshly ground black pepper to taste
- 2 tbsp butter
- ½ tsp saffron
- 1 cup/250 ml water
- 1 stick cinnamon
- 1 tbsp extra-virgin olive oil
- 2 onions, coarsely chopped
- 2 tsp sugar
- 2 large tomatoes, peeled and chopped
- 1 cup/100 g canned garbanzo beans/chickpeas
- 3 cups/300 g chopped pumpkin
- 6 oz/180 g plums, halved and pitted

LAMB AND RAISIN PILAF

Serves: 4

Preparation: 20'

Cooking: 25'

Level of difficulty: 1

- **2 onions, coarsely chopped**
- **2 cloves garlic, finely chopped**
- **5 tbsp extra-virgin olive oil**
- **1½ lb/750 g lean boned lamb shoulder, diced**
- **1½ cups/300 g long-grain rice**
- **2 tomatoes, peeled and chopped**
- **½ tsp saffron dissolved in 2 cups/500 ml Vegetable Stock (see page 224)**
- **salt and freshly ground black pepper to taste**
- **1 tsp sugar**
- **⅓ cup/60 g golden raisins/sultanas, soaked in warm water and drained**
- **4 leaves fresh mint, torn**
- **3 tbsp pine nuts, toasted**

Sauté the onions and garlic in the oil in a large frying pan over medium heat for 5 minutes, or until softened. • Add the lamb and sauté for 10 minutes, or until browned all over. • Stir in the rice and cook for 2 minutes. • Add the tomatoes and the saffron stock. Season with salt and pepper and add the sugar. • Cover and cook over medium heat for about 20 minutes, or until the rice is tender. • Add the golden raisins and mint and cook for 5 more minutes. • Transfer to serving dishes and garnish with the pine nuts. • Serve hot.

LAMB WITH EGGS AND CHIVES

Sauté the lamb, leeks, rosemary, bay leaves, and sage in the oil in a large saucepan over high heat for 5 minutes. • Pour in the wine and water. Season with salt. Cover and cook over low heat for about 50 minutes, or until the lamb is tender. • Beat the eggs, chives, and Pecorino in a medium bowl. Season with salt and pepper. Add to the pan with the lamb and toss over medium-high heat for 5 minutes so that the eggs are cooked through. • Serve at once.

Serves: 6

Preparation: 15'

Cooking: 1 h

Level of difficulty: 1

- 2 lb/1 kg boned lamb shoulder, cut in cubes
- 3 leeks, thinly sliced
- 1 tbsp dried rosemary
- 2 bay leaves
- 1 tsp dried sage
- 6 tbsp extra-virgin olive oil
- 1 cup/250 ml dry white wine
- ½ cup/125 ml water
- 6 eggs
- 1 tbsp chopped chives
- ½ cup/60 g freshly grated Pecorino cheese
- salt and freshly ground black pepper to taste

LAMB STEW WITH CUMIN AND FAVA BEANS

Serves: 6–8

Preparation: 30'

Cooking: 2 h 20'

Level of difficulty: 2

- $\frac{1}{3}$ cup/50 g all-purpose/plain flour
- 2 lb/1 kg boned lamb shoulder, cut into pieces
- 4 tbsp extra-virgin olive oil
- 2 onions, thinly sliced
- 1 clove garlic, finely chopped
- 1 tbsp ground cumin
- 2 lb/1 kg fresh fava/broad beans, shelled
- 4 tbsp tomato purèe/paste dissolved in 1 cup/250 ml water

Lightly flour the pieces of lamb. • Sauté the lamb in the oil in a large frying pan for 5–10 minutes, or until browned all over. • Remove from the pan and set aside. • Sauté the onions, garlic, and cumin in the same oil until the onions have softened. Season with salt and pepper. • Add the fava beans and cook for 5 minutes. • Pour in the diluted tomato mixture and add the lamb. • Cover and cook over low heat, stirring occasionally, for about 2 hours, or until the meat is tender. • Serve hot.

ROAST LAMB WITH CAPERS, OLIVES, AND ANCHOVIES

Preheat the oven to 425°F/220°C/gas 7. •
Grease a baking dish with oil. • Season the
lamb with salt and pepper and sprinkle with the
rosemary and thyme. • Place the onions, garlic,
and bay leaf in the prepared dish. Place the lamb in
the dish and drizzle with the oil. • Roast for 10
minutes. • Lower the oven temperature to
350°F/180°C/gas 4 and roast for 30 minutes.
• Remove from the oven and add the anchovies,
capers, olives, and wine mixture. • Bake for
30 minutes more, or until the lamb is tender.
Baste the lamb occasionally with the cooking
juices. • Remove the meat, cover with aluminum
foil, and let rest for 10 minutes. • Remove
the lamb and place on a heated serving dish.
• Spoon the cooking juices and onions around
the lamb and serve hot.

Serves: 4–6

Preparation: 20'

Cooking: 1 h 20'

Level of difficulty: 2

- 1½ lb/750 g
  saddle of lamb
- salt and freshly
  ground black
  pepper to taste
- 1 tbsp finely
  chopped rosemary
- 1 tbsp finely
  chopped thyme
- 2 onions, thinly
  sliced
- 2 cloves garlic,
  finely chopped
- 1 bay leaf, finely
  chopped
- 2 tbsp extra-virgin
  olive oil
- 3 anchovies, finely
  chopped
- 2 tbsp capers,
  rinsed and
  chopped
- 16 black olives,
  pitted
- juice of ½ lemon
  mixed with
  ⅔ cup/150 ml
  dry white wine

LAMB WITH POTATOES AND MUSHROOMS

S eason the lamb with salt. • Transfer the lamb to a large saucepan. Add the oil, onions, and herbs. Sauté over medium heat for 10 minutes, turning the meat so that it browns all over. • Pour in the wine and let it evaporate. • Add the water, tomatoes, mushrooms, and potatoes. Season with salt. Cover and cook over medium heat for 1 hour, stirring occasionally. • Garnish with the remaining parsley and serve hot.

Serves: 4–6

Preparation: 20'

Cooking: 1 h 15'

Level of difficulty: 1

- 1½ lb/750 g lamb shoulder, cut in cubes
- salt and freshly ground black pepper to taste
- 6 tbsp extra-virgin olive oil
- 4 small onions, thinly sliced
- 1 tsp dried marjoram
- 1 tsp dried tarragon
- 1 tsp dried bay leaves
- 1 tsp dried chives
- 1 tbsp finely chopped parsley + extra, to garnish
- 1 cup/250 ml rosè wine
- ½ cup/125 ml water
- 2 tomatoes, peeled and chopped
- 1½ lb/750 g white mushrooms, thinly sliced
- 5 medium potatoes, peeled and chopped

LAMB MEATLOAF BAKED IN YOGURT

Serves: 4–6

Preparation: 20'

Cooking: 30'

Level of difficulty: 2

- 1½ lb/750 g lean ground/minced lamb
- 2 tbsp pine nuts
- 1 egg
- 15 leaves fresh mint, finely chopped
- 2 cloves garlic, finely chopped
- salt and freshly ground black pepper to taste
- 2 tbsp butter
- 1 large egg yolk
- 1¼ cups/310 ml plain yogurt

Preheat the oven to 400°F/200°C/gas 6. • Mix the lamb, pine nuts, 1 egg, mint, and garlic in a large bowl. Season with salt and pepper. • Use your hands to shape the mixture into a large loaf. • Transfer to a large baking dish and dot with the butter. • Beat the egg yolk with the yogurt in a medium bowl. Season with salt and pepper. Pour over the meatloaf. • Bake for 25–30 minutes, or until the meatloaf is cooked through. • Serve hot.

BOOZY LAMB WITH MUSHROOMS

Melt 2 tablespoons of the butter in a large earthenware pot over medium heat. • Add the mushrooms and garlic and sauté for 3 minutes. • Add half the wine and let it evaporate. • Season with salt and pepper and remove from the heat. • Dip the lamb in the flour until well coated. • Melt 1¹/₂ tablespoons of butter in a large frying pan over medium heat. Cook the lamb for 2–3 minutes on each side. • Add the remaining wine and let it evaporate. Season with salt and pepper. • Remove the lamb from the pan and add the remaining butter. • Add 1 tablespoon of flour and mix well. Add the mushrooms and Marsala. • Return the lamb to the pan and add the parsley. • Cook for 2 minutes more. • Serve hot.

706

Serves: 4–6

Preparation: 10'

Cooking: 20'

Level of difficulty: 2

- 4 tbsp butter
- 12 oz/350 g white mushrooms, thinly sliced
- 1 clove garlic, finely chopped
- ¹/₂ cup/125 ml dry white wine
- salt and freshly ground black pepper to taste
- 2¹/₂ lb/1.25 kg lamb fillet, sliced into medallions
- 2 tbsp all-purpose/ plain flour
- 4 tbsp Marsala wine

GREEK LAMB STEW WITH PASTA

P reheat the oven to 400°F/200°C/gas 6. •
Place the lamb in a large casserole dish. Dot
with 4 tablespoons of butter and season with salt
and pepper. Drizzle with the lemon juice. • Bake
for 20 minutes. If the lamb becomes too dark,
lower the oven temperature. • Sauté the onion in
the remaining butter in a large frying pan over
medium heat for 8–10 minutes, or until lightly
browned. • Add the tomatoes and season with
salt and pepper. Add the sugar. • Cook for
10 minutes over medium heat. • Add the sauce
to the lamb. Lower the oven temperature to
350°F/180°C/gas 4 and bake for 15 minutes.
• Pour the boiling water over the lamb. Add the
pasta and cover the casserole with aluminum foil.
• Bake for 15–20 minutes, or until the pasta is al
dente. • Sprinkle with the cheese and serve hot.

Serves: 6–8

Preparation: 15'

Cooking: 1 h 15'

Level of difficulty: 2

- 1 leg of lamb,
  weighing about
  5 lb/2.5 kg
- 6 tbsp butter
- salt and freshly
  ground black
  pepper to taste
- juice of 1 lemon
- 1 onion, finely
  chopped
- 1 lb/500 g
  tomatoes, peeled
  and chopped
- ¼ tsp sugar
- 1½ quarts/1.5
  liters boiling water
- 1 lb/500 g rice-
  shaped soup pasta
- 4 tbsp freshly
  grated Kefalotiri or
  Parmesan cheese

Serves: 6

Preparation: 20'

Cooking: 2 h

Level of difficulty: 1

- **3 red onions, finely chopped**
- **3 tbsp butter**
- **2 lb/1 kg boned lamb shoulder, cut into small cubes**
- **4 tomatoes, peeled and chopped**
- **salt and freshly ground black pepper to taste**
- **1½ cups/375 ml hot water, or more, as needed**

EGGPLANT PURÈE

- **2 eggplants/ aubergines, about 1 lb/500 g**
- **1 tbsp fresh lemon juice**
- **2 tbsp butter**
- **2 tbsp all-purpose/ plain flour**
- **1 cup/250 ml milk**
- **½ cup/60 g freshly grated Parmesan cheese**
- **½ tsp salt**
- **2 tomatoes, peeled and chopped, to garnish**
- **1 tbsp finely chopped parsley, to garnish**

SULTAN'S DELIGHT

S auté the onions in the butter in a large frying pan over medium heat for 8–10 minutes, or until lightly browned. • Add the lamb and brown for 5 minutes. • Stir in the tomatoes and season with salt and pepper. Pour in the water. Cover and cook over low heat for 1 hour 30 minutes, or until the lamb is tender, adding more water if the pan dries out. • Eggplant Purèe: Preheat the oven to 400°F/ 200°C/gas 6. • Arrange the eggplants in a baking pan. • Roast for about 50 minutes, turning often, until the skins have blackened and the insides are tender. • Remove from the oven and peel while still warm. • Place the eggplant in a large bowl and drizzle with the lemon juice. Use a fork to mash. • Melt the butter in a large saucepan over low heat. Stir in the flour until smooth. Stir in the milk and cook for 5 minutes. • Add the eggplants and cheese. Season with salt and cook, stirring constantly for 8–10 minutes. • Place the eggplant purèe on a heated serving dish and spoon the lamb stew over the top. • Garnish with the tomatoes and parsley and serve hot.

TURKISH LAMB WITH YOGURT SAUCE

Heat 2 tablespoons oil in a large saucepan over high heat. Brown the lamb for 5 minutes.
• Pour in the water and cook for 30 minutes.
• Meanwhile, sauté the onion and carrot in the remaining oil in a large frying pan over medium heat for 8–10 minutes, or until lightly browned.
• Add to the lamb and cook for 15–20 minutes, or until the lamb and vegetables are cooked, adding more water if the pan dries out. There should be about 2 tablespoons of liquid. • Preheat the oven to 350°F/180°C/gas 4. • Yogurt Sauce: Mix the flour and yogurt in a small saucepan. Stir in the 2 tablespoons of cooking liquid from the lamb.
• Bring to a boil and cook for 5–7 minutes, or until thickened. • Remove from the heat and stir in the egg yolks. Season with salt and pepper. • Transfer the lamb to a roasting pan and cover with the yogurt sauce. • Bake for 15–20 minutes, or until lightly browned. • Serve hot.

Serves: 4–6

Preparation: 30'

Cooking: 1 h 30'

Level of difficulty: 2

- 4 tbsp extra-virgin olive oil
- 3 lb/1.5 kg lamb shoulder, cut into 4–6 pieces, with the bone
- 2 cups/500 ml water, or more as needed
- 1 medium onion, finely chopped
- 1 carrot, finely chopped

YOGURT SAUCE

- 2 tbsp all-purpose/ plain flour
- 2 cups/500 ml plain yogurt
- 2 large egg yolks
- salt and freshly ground white pepper to taste

LAMB AND SPINACH STEW

Serves: 6–8
Preparation: 15'
Cooking: 1 h 30'
Level of difficulty: 1

- 3 lb/1.5 kg boned lamb shoulder, cut into small cubes
- 1 small onion, whole + 1 small onion, finely chopped
- 1 quart/1 liter water
- 4 tbsp butter
- 1 clove garlic, finely chopped
- 1 lb/500 g spinach, well-washed and coarsely chopped
- 1 tsp freshly ground coriander seeds, crushed
- salt and freshly ground black pepper to taste
- juice of ½ lemon
- cooked rice, to serve

Place the lamb and whole onion in a large pot over high heat. Pour in the water. • Bring to a boil and lower the heat. Cover and cook for 1 hour, or until the lamb is tender. • Sauté the chopped onion in the butter in a large saucepan for 8–10 minutes, or until lightly browned. • Add the garlic, spinach, and coriander. Season with salt and pepper. Cook, stirring occasionally, over medium heat until the spinach has wilted. • Add the lamb and stock. Cover and cook over low heat for 10–15 minutes. • Drizzle with the lemon juice. • Serve hot on a bed of rice.

LEG OF LAMB

Cook the rice in a large pot filled with the water for 15–20 minutes, or until tender. • Add the oil, salt, and 1 tablespoon of harissa. • Place the onion in a large earthenware pot. • Sprinkle the lamb with the remaining harissa. • Place the lamb on top of the onion. • Spoon the rice mixture over the lamb to cover it completely. • Cover and cook over low heat for 2 hours 30 minutes–3 hours. Do not remove the cover until the end of the second hour, or the steam will escape. Remove from the heat and set aside for 10 minutes. • Spoon the rice onto a large serving dish. Cover with the lamb and serve hot.

Serves: 4

Preparation: 25'

Cooking: 3 h

Level of difficulty: 2

- **2 cups/400 g long-grain rice**
- **1 quart/1 liter water**
- **3 tbsp extra-virgin olive oil**
- **1 tbsp salt**
- **3 tbsp Harissa (see page 52)**
- **1 large onion, thinly sliced**
- **3 lb/1.5 kg boneless leg of lamb**

LAMB AND TOMATO STEW

Sauté the rosemary, garlic, and chile pepper in the oil in a cast-iron frying pan over medium heat until aromatic. • Add the lamb and brown all over. • Pour in the wine and let it evaporate. • Stir in the tomatoes and season with salt. Partially cover and cook over low heat for 25–30 minutes, or until the tomatoes have broken down. Add the water if the stew dries out. • Place the bread in individual plates and spoon the meat and its fairly liquid sauce over the top. • Garnish with the parsley and serve hot.

Serves: 4

Preparation: 15'

Cooking: 65'

Level of difficulty: 1

- ¼ tsp finely chopped rosemary
- 4 cloves garlic, finely chopped
- 1 dried chile pepper, crumbled
- 4 tbsp extra-virgin olive oil
- 1 lb/500 g boneless lamb, cut into cubes
- ½ cup/125 ml dry white wine
- 1½ lb/750 g tomatoes, peeled and chopped
- salt to taste
- 4 tbsp water + more as needed (optional)
- 4 slices firm-textured bread, toasted and rubbed with garlic
- 1 tbsp finely chopped parsley

OVEN-BRAISED LAMB WITH OLIVES

Serves: 4–6

Preparation: 10'

Cooking: 1 h

Level of difficulty: 1

- 2 lb/1 kg lamb, cut into fairly small pieces
- 4 tbsp extra-virgin olive oil
- salt and freshly ground black pepper to taste
- 1½ cups/200 g large black olives, pitted and chopped
- 1¼ cups/310 ml dry red wine

Preheat the oven to 350°F/180°C/gas 4. • Place the lamb in a flameproof earthenware casserole. Drizzle with the oil and season with salt and a generous sprinkling of pepper. Add the olives and moisten with half the wine. • Cover and bake for about 1 hour or until the meat is very tender, basting at frequent intervals with the remaining wine. • Serve hot.

LAMB SHOULDER WITH DRIED FRUIT

Serves: 4–6

Preparation: 15'

Cooking: 1 h

Level of difficulty: 2

- 1 bone-in lamb shoulder roast, weighing about 4 lb/2 kg
- 2 twigs fresh rosemary
- freshly ground black pepper to taste
- ⅔ cup/150 g butter
- ½ cup/125 ml brandy
- ½ cup/125 ml Port
- ½ cup/125 g prunes
- ½ cup/125 g dried apricots
- 3 tbsp honey

Preheat the oven to 450°F/230°C/gas 8. • Score the lamb shoulder in four places, taking care not to cut it all the way through, only to cleave the bone. Rub the surface and interior with the rosemary and season with pepper. • Place the lamb in a baking dish and dot with the butter.
• Roast the lamb for 10 minutes, then turn it.
• Roast for 10 minutes more. • Drizzle with the brandy and Port and turn it. • Roast for 5 minutes more. • Add the prunes and apricots. Drizzle with the honey. • Return to the oven and continue roasting, basting often, for 30–35 minutes, or until the juices run clear. Transfer to a serving plate and spoon the prunes and apricots over the top.
• Reduce the sauce and pour over the meat.
• Serve hot.

BRAISED LAMB WITH POTATOES

S auté the scallions in the oil over low heat in a large flameproof casserole. • Add the pork fat and stir until it has melted. • Add the lamb and brown all over. • Pour in the wine and let evaporate. • Stir in the parsley, garlic, salt, and pepper, then add most of the stock. Cover and cook over low heat for 45 minutes. • Add the potatoes and more stock, if the lamb is too dry. • Cover and cook for 30 minutes, or until the potatoes and meat are tender, stirring occasionally. • Sprinkle with the cheese, stir, and turn off the heat. • Let stand for 4–5 minutes before serving.

- 2 scallions/spring onions
- 3 tbsp extra-virgin olive oil
- 3 tbsp pork fat
- 2 lb/1 kg lamb (from the shoulder or leg), cubed
- 1 cup/250 ml dry red wine
- 1 tbsp finely chopped parsley
- 2 cloves garlic, lightly crushed
- salt and freshly ground black pepper to taste
- 1 cup/250 ml Beef Stock (see page 224)
- 2 lb/1 kg potatoes, diced
- ¾ cup/90 g freshly grated Pecorino cheese

Serves: 4–6

Preparation: 10'

Cooking: 1 h

Level of difficulty: 1

- 4 lb/2 kg boneless leg of lamb, cut into small pieces
- 5 onions, finely chopped
- 2 cloves garlic, finely chopped
- 6 tbsp butter
- 1 tsp ground ginger
- 1 tsp ground turmeric
- salt to taste
- 1½ cups/375 ml water
- 2 lb/1 kg pitted dates
- 3 tbsp honey
- 1 tsp ground cinnamon
- 1 tbsp sesame seeds, toasted

LAMB TAJINE WITH DATES

Sauté the lamb, onions, and garlic in the butter in a large saucepan over medium heat for 8–10 minutes, or until lightly browned. • Add the ginger, turmeric, and salt. Pour in the water and cover and cook over low heat for 35–40 minutes, or until the lamb is tender. • Stir in the dates, honey, and cinnamon. • Cook over low heat for 12–15 minutes more, or until the sauce has reduced. • Sprinkle with the sesame seeds and serve hot.

LAMB COUSCOUS

Wash the couscous and soak in 2 quarts (2 liters) cold water for 30 minutes. Drain well and pat dry with paper towels. • Heat the oil in the lower section of a couscoussière or two-layered vegetable steamer. • Sauté the onion, lamb, ginger, pepper, saffron, and chile peppers for 8–10 minutes, or until lightly browned. • Add the garbanzo beans and tomatoes. Pour in the water and bring to a boil. • Place the prepared couscous in the upper section of the couscoussière and steam for 25 minutes. • Stir the couscous. • Cook the lamb mixture, covered, over low heat for 25 minutes. Remove from the heat and transfer to a large bowl. • Stir the couscous. • Add the turnip, yellow squash, and the cabbage to the lamb mixture in the lower section of the couscoussière. • Stir the couscous and continue cooking for 25 minutes. • Remove from the heat and add the butter. • Add the zucchini, eggplant, parsley, and coriander to the meat mixture. • Cook for 25 minutes more. • Spoon the couscous onto a serving plate. Make a well in the center and arrange the meat and vegetables on top. Drizzle the liquid over and serve.

Serves: 4-6

Preparation: 15' + 30' to soak couscous

Cooking: 75'

Level of difficulty: 2

- 1 lb/500 g couscous
- 4 tbsp sunflower oil
- 2 onions, chopped
- 1¾ lb/750 g lamb, cubed
- 1 tsp minced ginger
- black pepper to taste
- ⅛ tsp saffron
- 2 chile peppers
- 8 oz/250 g cooked garbanzo beans/chickpeas
- 2 firm-ripe tomatoes, peeled and puréed
- 2 quarts/2 liters water
- 2 turnips, chopped
- 8 oz/250 g yellow squash, chopped
- 8 oz/250 g Savoy cabbage, finely shredded
- 1 tbsp butter
- 2 zucchini/ courgettes, chopped
- 1 eggplant/ aubergine, chopped
- 1 bunch parsley, chopped
- 1 bunch coriander/ cilantro, chopped

COUSCOUS WITH LAMB SAUCE

Serves: 4

Preparation: 20'

Cooking: 35'

Level of difficulty: 1

- 8 oz/250 g precooked couscous
- 2 cloves garlic, finely chopped
- 4 tbsp extra-virgin olive oil
- 2 lb/1 kg boned leg of lamb, cut into bite-size chunks
- 1 tbsp mild paprika
- salt and freshly ground black pepper to taste
- 1 cup/250 ml hot Beef or Chicken Stock (see pages 224, 226)
- 1 tbsp finely chopped parsley
- 1 tbsp finely chopped chervil
- 2 tbsp butter

Prepare the couscous according to the instructions on the package. • Sauté the garlic in the oil in a large frying pan until pale gold. • Add the lamb and season with paprika, salt, and pepper. • Pour in the stock and cover and cook over low heat for 25 minutes. • Sprinkle with the parsley and chervil. *Often mistaken for a grain, couscous is a small granular pasta made from semolina.* • Dot the couscous with the butter on a serving dish. • Top with the lamb sauce and serve hot.

LAMB WITH ARTICHOKES

Clean the artichokes by pulling the tough outer leaves down and snapping them off. Cut off the top third of the leaves and trim the stalk. Cut in half and use a sharp knife to remove any fuzzy choke. Cut in quarters and place in a bowl of cold water with the lemon juice. • Finely chop the prosciutto, garlic, and parsley together and transfer to a large frying pan. • Sauté for 3–4 minutes, then add the lamb and onion. Season with salt and pepper. • When the onion is transparent, pour in the wine and let it evaporate. • Add the tomato paste and the drained artichokes. Cover and cook over medium-low heat for about 25 minutes, or until the lamb and artichokes are tender. • Serve hot.

Serves: 4

Preparation: 25'

Cooking: 45'

Level of difficulty: 1

- **4 large artichokes**
- **juice of 1 lemon**
- **2 oz/60 g prosciutto/Parma ham**
- **2 cloves garlic**
- **1 small bunch parsley or marjoram**
- **3 lb/1.5 kg lamb chops**
- **1 small onion, finely chopped**
- **½ cup/125 ml dry white wine**
- **1 tbsp tomato paste**
- **salt and freshly ground black pepper to taste**

728

GRILLED LAMB PATTIES

Place the lamb in a large bowl. • Mix in the chopped onions, egg, cumin, and paprika. Season with salt and pepper. • Shape the mixture into 12 patties. Brush with the oil. • Refrigerate for 15 minutes. • Cook the meat on a very hot grill for 4–5 minutes on each side, or until browned and cooked through. • Arrange the patties on a serving plate and place the onion rings in the center. Broil (grill) the chilies and use them as garnish.

730

Serves: 4–6

Preparation: 10'

Chilling: 15'

Cooking: 10'

Level of difficulty: 1

- 1½ lb/750 g ground/minced lamb
- 2 medium onions, very finely chopped + 1 medium onion, cut into rings
- 1 large egg, lightly beaten
- 1 tsp freshly ground cumin
- 1 tsp sweet paprika
- salt and freshly ground black pepper to taste
- 2 tbsp extra-virgin olive oil
- 1–2 green chile peppers

LAMB WITH PEAS

Serves: 4–6

Preparation: 20'

Cooking: 45'

Level of difficulty: 1

- 1 onion, thinly sliced
- ½ cup/125 ml extra-virgin olive oil
- 2½ lb/1.25 kg lamb, cut in pieces
- 14 oz/400 g fresh shelled peas
- 2 tbsp finely chopped parsley
- salt and freshly ground black pepper to taste

Sauté the onion in the oil in a large, deep frying pan until golden. • Add the lamb and fry for 15 minutes. • Drain off the excess oil. Add the peas and parsley. Season with salt and pepper. Cover and cook over medium heat for about 30 minutes, adding water if the mixture begins to dry. • Serve hot.

KEBAB WITH YOGURT

Serves: 5

Preparation: 15'

Marinating: 12 h

Cooking: 25'

Level of difficulty: 1

- 1 lb/500 g boneless lamb or mutton, cut into small cubes
- 1 onion, finely chopped
- 3 tbsp extra-virgin olive oil
- salt and freshly ground white pepper to taste
- 4 tbsp butter
- 4 tomatoes, finely chopped
- 5 slices firm-textured bread, toasted
- 2 cups/500 ml plain yogurt

Marinate the lamb in a large bowl with the onion and oil for 12 hours. Season with salt and pepper. • Carefully thread the meat onto five skewers. • Cook on a very hot grill for 15–20 minutes, or until the kebabs are cooked through, turning often. • Melt the butter in a large frying pan. Stir in the tomatoes and season with salt and pepper. Cook, stirring often, for 5 minutes. • Place the toast on a serving dish. Lay the skewers of cooked meat on the toast, spoon the tomato mixture over the top, and cover with the yogurt.

LAMB SKEWERS WITH COUSCOUS

Chop the parsley and onion in a food processor or blender. Add the lamb and season with salt, pepper, and half the cinnamon. • Shape the meat mixture into 8–12 large, slightly flattened rissoles. Thread onto 2–3 metal skewers. Drizzle with the oil and refrigerate. • Prepare the couscous according to the instructions on the package. • Place the couscous in a large bowl and mix in the remaining oil, lemon juice, pepper, mint, and remaining cinnamon. • Soak the rings of red onion in cold water for 30 minutes. • Drain and pat dry with paper towels. • Broil (grill) the meatballs and cook for 12 minutes, turning 2 or 3 times. • Add the vegetables and onion to the tabbouleh. • Mix well and serve with the hot meat still on the skewers.

Serves: 4–6

Preparation: 35' + 30' to soak the onions

Cooking: 25'

Level of difficulty: 2

- 3 sprigs parsley
- 1 onion
- 1½ lb/750 g ground/minced lamb
- salt and freshly ground black pepper to taste
- ¼ tsp ground cinnamon
- 7 tbsp extra-virgin olive oil
- 12 oz/350 g instant couscous
- juice of 3 lemons
- 2 sprigs mint
- 1 small red onion, cut into rings
- 1 yellow bell pepper/capsicum, seeded, cored, and diced
- 1 red bell pepper capsicum, seeded, cored, and diced
- 1 cucumber, thinly sliced
- 7 oz/200 g firm ripe tomatoes, diced

ROAST LAMB WITH ROSEMARY AND GARLIC

Preheat the oven to 350°F/180°C/gas 4. •
Place the lamb in an ovenproof dish large
enough to hold the lamb and the potatoes. • Use
the point of a sharp knife to make small incisions
in the meat and push the pieces of garlic in. Close
the meat around it, so that the flavor will permeate the
meat during cooking. • Sprinkle the rosemary leaves over the
lamb. Tuck the remaining sprigs in around the
meat. Drizzle with the oil. Season with salt and
pepper. • Roast for 20 minutes. • Peel the
potatoes and cut into large bite-sized chunks.
Arrange the potatoes around the meat. Roast for
1 hour more, basting the meat with the cooking
juices 2 or 3 times during roasting and turning
the potatoes so that they are evenly browned. •
Serve hot.

*Succulent baby lamb is traditionally served at
Easter in many parts of the Mediterranean.*

Serves:	4
Preparation:	10'
Cooking:	1 h
Level of difficulty:	1

- 3 lb/1.5 kg shoulder baby lamb (with some loin attached),
- 3 cloves garlic, peeled and cut in half
- 4–6 sprigs rosemary
- 4 tbsp extra-virgin olive oil
- salt and freshly ground black pepper to taste
- 2 lb/1 kg roasting potatoes

PORK

PORK COOKED IN BEER

Melt the butter with the oil in a large saucepan over medium heat. • Add the pork and garlic and sauté for 3–4 minutes, or until well browned. Discard the garlic. • Pour in the beer and add the bay leaves. Simmer over very low heat for about 2 hours, or until the meat is very tender. • Add the capers and cook for 10 minutes more. • Serve hot.

740

Serves: 4–6
Preparation: 5'
Cooking: 2 h 15'
Level of difficulty: 2

- 2 tbsp butter
- 4 tbsp extra-virgin olive oil
- 2 lb/1 kg chine of pork
- 2 cloves garlic, crushed but whole
- 1 cup/250 ml dark beer (such as Guinness)
- 2 bay leaves
- 1 tbsp salted capers, rinsed

PORK CUTLETS, MADRID-STYLE

Serves: 4

Preparation: 20'

Cooking: 20'

Level of difficulty: 1

- **2 cloves garlic, finely chopped**
- **4 sprigs parsley, finely chopped**
- **1 small onion, finely chopped**
- **1 tbsp paprika**
- **salt and freshly ground black pepper to taste**
- **4 tbsp extra-virgin olive oil**
- **4 pork cutlets weighing about 6 oz/180 g each**
- **boiled rice, polenta, or mashed potatoes, to serve**

Preheat the oven to 350°F/180°C/gas 4.
• Grease a baking sheet with oil. • Mix the garlic, parsley, onion, and paprika in a small bowl. Season with salt and pepper. Stir in half the oil.
• Season the pork cutlets with salt and pepper. Spread the sauce over the pork. Transfer to the prepared baking sheet. • Roast in the oven for about 10 minutes on each side. • Serve hot with boiled rice, polenta, or mashed potatoes.

PORK WITH CABBAGE

Sauté the onions and pork in the oil in a large saucepan over medium heat for 2–3 minutes, until the meat is browned all over. • Pour in the tomato juice and season with salt and pepper. • Pour in 1 cup (250 ml) of water and bring to a boil. Simmer over low heat for 15 minutes, or until the meat is almost cooked. • Add the cabbage and the remaining water. Return to a boil and simmer for 10–15 minutes, or until the meat and cabbage are both tender. • Serve hot with boiled rice.

Serves: 6–8

Preparation: 5'

Cooking: 35'

Level of difficulty: 2

- **2 large onions, finely chopped**
- **2 lb/1 kg pork, cut into cubes**
- **4 tbsp extra-virgin olive oil**
- **generous 1⅓ cups/350 ml tomato juice**
- **salt and freshly ground black pepper to taste**
- **2 cups/500 ml water**
- **2 lb/1 kg cabbage, shredded**
- **boiled rice, to serve**

SAUSAGES AND BEANS

S oak the beans overnight in cold water. Drain.
• Cook in a large pot of boiling water for 1
hour, or until tender. Season with salt just before
they are cooked. • Prick the sausages with a fork
and sauté in a large frying pan over high heat for
5 minutes. Remove from heat and set aside in a
warm oven. • Sauté the garlic and rosemary in the
same pan with the sausage fat and oil until the
garlic is pale gold. • Add the tomatoes and season
with salt and pepper. • Add the beans and cook
for 10 minutes. Add the sausages and cook for
5 more minutes. • Serve hot.

Serves: 4

Preparation: 10' +
12 h to soak beans

Cooking: 25'

Level of difficulty: 2

- **10 oz/300 g dry
  cannellini or white
  kidney beans**
- **salt and freshly
  ground black
  pepper to taste**
- **12 medium Italian
  sausages**
- **3 cloves garlic,
  finely chopped**
- **sprig fresh
  rosemary, finely
  chopped**
- **6 tbsp extra-virgin
  olive oil**
- **14 oz/400 g fresh
  or canned
  tomatoes, peeled
  and chopped**

SAUSAGES AND POLENTA

745

Serves: 4–6

Preparation: 10' + time to make polenta

Cooking: 25'

Level of difficulty: 2

- **1 quantity Polenta (see page 350)**
- **1 lb/500 g luganega (long, thin Italian pork sausage; substitute with any highly flavored Italian sausage)**
- **1 tbsp finely chopped rosemary**
- **2 tbsp butter**
- **1 tbsp extra-virgin olive oil**
- **1 cup/250 ml dry white or red wine**

Prepare the polenta. • About 20 minutes before the polenta is ready, prick the sausage well with a fork. • Sauté the rosemary in the butter and oil in a large frying pan over medium heat for 2 minutes. • Add the sausage and brown for 5 minutes. • Increase the heat to high and pour in the wine. Bring to a boil. Cover the pan and cook for about 10 minutes, turning once. • Cut the sausage into pieces about 2 inches (5 cm) long. • Spoon the polenta onto a serving dish and arrange the sausage on top. Drizzle the cooking juices over the top. • Serve hot.

LEMON ROASTED PORK

Serves: 4–6

Preparation: 30' + 2 h
to marinate

Cooking: 2 h 5'

Level of difficulty: 3

- 2½ lb/1.25 kg
  boned pork loin
- 2 tsp finely
  chopped rosemary
- ½ cup/125 ml dry
  white wine
- salt and freshly
  ground black
  pepper to taste
- ¼ cup/50 g sugar
- 4 tbsp lemon juice
- 2 tbsp brandy

Make several incisions in the pork. Push a pinch of rosemary into each incision, using 1 teaspoon of the rosemary. Place the pork in a bowl and sprinkle with the remaining rosemary. Pour in the wine and marinate in the refrigerator for 2 hours. • Preheat the oven to 450°F/230°C/ gas 8. • Remove the meat from the marinade and roll it into a joint. Tie securely with kitchen string. Transfer to a roasting pan and roast for 15 minutes. • Lower the heat to 350°F/180°C/ gas 4. • Roast for 30 minutes. • Remove from the oven and add the marinade. Season with salt and pepper. Return to the oven and roast for 1 hour. • Dissolve the sugar in the lemon juice and brandy in a small saucepan over low heat. Remove the meat from the oven and skim off any fat. Drizzle with the lemon mixture and return to the oven. • Roast for 20 minutes, basting often. • Remove from the oven. The sauce should be thick and the meat glossy and browned. Slice and transfer to a serving dish. • Drizzle with the sauce and serve hot.

PORK WITH APRICOTS

Preheat the oven to 425°F/220°C/gas 7. •
Season the pork with salt and pepper. Wrap the
pancetta around the pork roast. • Place a sprig of
rosemary on each and truss with kitchen string.
• Pit and quarter the apricots. • Melt the butter in a
large baking dish. • Add the pork and brown all
over. • Add the apricots and cinnamon. Season
with salt and pepper. • Drizzle with the wine and let
it evaporate. • Roast for 30–35 minutes, basting
often with the cooking juices. • Slice the meat and
serve with the apricots and cooking juices.

Serves: 4–6

Preparation: 20'

Cooking: 35'

Level of difficulty: 2

- 2 lb/1 kg pork loin
  roast, boneless, in
  one piece
- salt and freshly
  ground black
  pepper to taste
- 5 oz/150 g thinly
  sliced pancetta
  or bacon
- 2 sprigs rosemary
- 8 firm-ripe apricots
- 4 tbsp butter
- 1 stick cinnamon,
  broken up
- 4 tbsp dry white
  wine

PORK ROSETTES WITH COCONUT AND PLUMS

Grate half of the coconut and finely slice the rest. • Cut the pork into 1-inch (2.5-cm) thick slices. Season with salt and pepper and dip in the grated coconut. Press gently to make sure the coconut sticks. • Wrap the pork in the slices of pancetta. Tie with kitchen string. • Sauté the coconut slices and plums in the butter in a large frying pan over high heat until the plums have softened. • Season with salt and pepper. Add the parsley. • Add the pork and cook for 2 minutes on each side, or until cooked through. • Serve hot.

Serves: 4	
Preparation: 25'	
Cooking: 30'	
Level of difficulty: 2	

- **½ coconut**
- **1¼ lb/575 g pork fillet**
- **salt and freshly ground black pepper to taste**
- **4 oz/125 g sliced pancetta**
- **14 oz/400 g plums, pitted and sliced**
- **2 tbsp butter**
- **1 tbsp finely chopped parsley**

PAN ROASTED PORK WITH MILK AND BREAD

Serves: 4

Preparation: 10'

Cooking: 2 h

Level of difficulty: 1

- ½ cup/75 g all-purpose/plain flour
- 2 lb/1 kg pork loin roast
- 4 tbsp butter
- salt and freshly ground black pepper to taste
- 3 cups/750 ml milk
- 1 cup/250 ml heavy/double cream
- 8 slices firm-textured bread

Lightly flour the pork. Place in a heavy-bottomed pan with 3 tablespoons of butter. Cook until browned. • Season with salt and pepper and add 1 tablespoon of milk. Cover and cook over medium heat, gradually adding the remaining milk. Cook for 1 hour 30 minutes, turning from time to time.
• Add the cream 30 minutes before the pork is cooked. • After about 2 hours, when the roast is well-cooked and the sauce thick, transfer it to a chopping board and slice. • Add the remaining butter to the pan and cook until thick. Spread on the bread and arrange the slices around the meat on a heated serving dish. • Pour the remaining sauce over the meat and serve hot.

MEATBALLS WITH CHOPPED ALMONDS

Serves: 4–6

Preparation: 20'

Cooking: 30'

Level of difficulty: 2

- 8 oz/250 g ground/minced veal
- 8 oz/250 g ground/minced pork
- ½ cup/60 g finely chopped bacon
- 1 onion, finely chopped
- 2 large eggs, lightly beaten
- 1 cup/60 g fresh bread crumbs
- salt to taste
- ⅓ cup/70 g finely ground almonds
- 4 tbsp extra-virgin olive oil
- 3 large tomatoes, peeled and coarsely chopped
- 1 quart/1 liter water
- 2½ cups/375 g peas

Mix the veal, pork, bacon, half the onion, eggs, bread crumbs, and salt in a large bowl. • Place the almonds in another large bowl. Form the meat mixture into balls the size of walnuts. Roll in the almonds until well coated. • Sauté the remaining onion in the oil in a large frying pan over medium heat for 8–10 minutes, or until lightly browned. • Add the tomatoes and cook for 5 minutes. • Pour in the water and season with salt. Add the peas and meatballs. Cover and cook for 20 minutes, or until the meatballs are cooked through. • Serve hot.

ZAMPONE WITH LENTILS

Rinse the zampone and wrap it in a clean white cloth. Place in a large pot of water and bring quickly to a boil. Reduce the heat to medium-low and simmer for 4 hours. • Meanwhile, place the lentils in another large pot of cold water. Cook over medium heat for about 1 hour, or until tender. • When the zampone is cooked, remove the cloth and carefully cut into fairly thick slices. • Season the lentils with salt and pepper, drizzle with the oil, and serve with the zampone.

Serves: 4–6

Preparation: 20'

Cooking: 30'

Level of difficulty: 2

- 1 medium zampone
- 14 oz/400 g dried lentils
- salt and freshly ground black pepper to taste
- 6 tbsp extra-virgin olive oil

COTECHINO SAUSAGE WITH POTATO PURÈE

Serves: 4
Preparation: 20'
Cooking: 1 h
Level of difficulty: 2

- **1 medium leek, thinly sliced**
- **7 tbsp butter**
- **2 lb/1 kg potatoes, peeled and diced**
- **2 cups/500 ml milk**
- **1 precooked cotechino sausage, about 2 lb/1 kg**

Sauté the leek in the butter in a large pot until soft, but not browned. • Add the potatoes and sauté for a few minutes. • Pour in the milk and cook over medium heat for 40 minutes. • Meanwhile, prick the cotechino well with a fork and boil in a large pot of water according to the instructions on the package. • When the potatoes are cooked, remove from the heat and mash well. Add a little more milk if the mixture is too dense. • Remove the sausage from the pan, cut into thick slices, and serve with the potato and leek purèe.

FRIED PORK SKEWERS

Carefully thread the meat, alternating with the bell peppers, potatoes, scallions, and bacon onto four metal skewers. • Drizzle with the extra-virgin olive oil and season with salt and pepper. Roll in the cornmeal. • Heat the frying oil in a large, deep frying pan until very hot. Fry the skewers for 15–20 minutes, or until the meat is well cooked. • Serve hot.

756

Serves: 4

Preparation: 10'

Cooking: 20'

Level of difficulty: 1

- 1½ lb/750 g lean pork, cut into 16 cubes
- 2 red bell peppers/ capsicums, seeded, cored, and cut into large chunks
- 10 oz/300 g small new potatoes, parboiled
- 10 oz/300 g scallions/spring onions
- 5 oz/150 g bacon, in thick strips and cut in squares
- 2–4 tbsp extra-virgin olive oil
- salt and freshly ground black pepper to taste
- 1 cup/150 g coarsely ground cornmeal
- 2 cups/500 ml olive oil, for frying

SAUSAGE AND BEAN SALAD

S auté the garlic, rosemary, and sage in the oil in a large frying pan until the garlic is pale gold. • Add the beans, and cook for 1 minute. • Add the endive. Cover and cook over low heat for 10 minutes. • Add the soppressata and cook until the fat begins to melt. • Remove from heat and sprinkle with the vinegar and parsley. • Serve hot with thick slices of whole-wheat (wholemeal) bread.

758

Serves: 4

Preparation: 5'

Cooking: 25'

Level of difficulty: 1

- 3 cloves garlic,
  1 sprig rosemary,
  2 sage leaves,
  finely chopped
- 5 tbsp extra-virgin
  olive oil
- 1 lb/500 g canned
  cannellini or white
  kidney beans
- 1 head Belgian
  endive, diced
- 10 oz/300 g
  soppressata (large
  Italian sausage)
- 3 tbsp vinegar
- 4 tbsp finely
  chopped parsley

COTECHINO SAUSAGE WRAPPED IN VEAL

Serves: 4

Preparation: 25'

Cooking: 1 h 30'

Level of difficulty: 2

- 1 precooked cotechino sausage, about 2 lb/1 kg
- 1 slice veal, about 1½ lb/750 g
- 1¼ lb/600 g spinach, boiled, squeezed dry, and finely chopped
- 1 tsp salt
- 2 tbsp butter
- 5 oz/150 ham, cut in thin strips
- 1 cup/250 ml dry white wine

Prick the cotechino well with a fork. Boil in a large pot of water according to the instructions on the package. • Drain and set aside to cool. • Skin the sausage carefully, taking care not to break it. • Preheat the oven to 400°F/200°C/ gas 6. • Flatten the veal with a meat tenderizer. • Sauté the spinach with a pinch of salt in the butter in a large frying pan for 5 minutes. • Spread the spinach evenly over the veal and sprinkle with the ham. • Place the cotechino in the center and carefully roll up the meat. Tie firmly with kitchen string. Wrap in aluminum foil and place in an ovenproof dish. Pour the wine over the top and bake for 1 hour. • Slice thickly and spoon the cooking juices over the top. • Serve hot.

PORK SKEWERS

Serves: 4

Preparation: 5'

Cooking: 20'

Level of difficulty: 1

- **2 lb/1 kg boned leg or shoulder of pork**
- **16 button mushrooms**
- **16 cherry tomatoes**
- **4 Italian sausages, cut in 3**
- **16 leaves fresh basil**
- **salt and freshly ground black pepper to taste**
- **4 tbsp extra-virgin olive oil**

C hop the pork into bite-sized pieces. • Wash the mushrooms and tomatoes and pat dry with paper towels. • Thread eight skewers with the pork and other ingredients. • Season with salt and pepper and cook over the glowing embers of a barbecue or under the broiler (grill) until the meat and vegetable are cooked. • Drizzle with extra-virgin olive oil as required during cooking. • Serve hot.

Serve these hearty skewers at a barbecue with plenty of mixed salad and pita bread.

HAM AND CABBAGE STEW

Serves: 4

Preparation: 15'

Cooking: 80'

Level of difficulty: 2

C ook the ham and cabbage in a large pot of salted, boiling water for 15–20 minutes, or until the cabbage is tender. • Cook the beans in a large pot of salted, boiling water for 25–30 minutes, or until tender. • Cook the potatoes in a large pot of salted, boiling water for 15–20 minutes, or until tender. • Add the beans and their liquid to the cabbage mixture. Use a fork to mash the potatoes and add them to the cabbage.
• Sauté the onions in the oil in a large frying pan over medium heat for 8–10 minutes, or until lightly browned. • Add the onions to the cabbage. • Stir in the garlic, tomato paste, and bay leaf. Season with salt and pepper. • Serve hot.

- 1 lb/500 g ham on the bone
- 1 lb/500 g cabbage
- 2½ cups/250 g fresh or frozen (not dried) cannellini beans
- 12 oz/350 g potatoes, peeled and cut into large chunks
- 2 medium onions, finely chopped
- 4 tbsp extra-virgin olive oil
- 1 clove garlic, finely chopped
- 1 tbsp tomato paste/puree
- 1 bay leaf
- salt and freshly ground black pepper to taste

762

PROSCIUTTO WITH SHERRY SAUCE

- **8 slices prosciutto/ Parma ham, weighing about 2 oz/60 g each**
- **½ cup/125 ml dry sherry**
- **1 tsp finely ground cornmeal**
- **1 cup/250 ml hot Beef Stock (see page 224)**
- **mashed potatoes and parsley, to garnish**

Preheat the oven to 400°F/200°C/gas 6.
• Arrange the slices of prosciutto in a baking dish. • Drizzle with the sherry and cover with waxed paper. • Cook in the oven for 1 minute.
• Drain the sherry into a bowl and let cool.
• Stir the cornmeal into the sherry and mix into the stock. Boil for 1 minute. • Place the prosciutto on a serving dish and spoon the sauce over the top.
• Decorate with curls of mashed potato and sprigs of parsley.

763

VEGETABLES

BELL PEPPERS WITH GARLIC

Sauté the onions and garlic in the oil in a large frying pan over medium heat for 5 minutes, or until lightly browned. • Add the bell peppers and season with salt and pepper. • Cover and cook over low heat for 25–30 minutes, or until the bell peppers are tender. • Serve hot.

Serves: 4

Preparation: 20'

Cooking: 35'

Level of difficulty: 1

- **2 large onions, finely chopped**
- **2 cloves garlic, finely chopped**
- **4 tbsp extra-virgin olive oil**
- **4 medium red bell peppers/ capsicums, seeded and cut into thin strips**
- **salt and freshly ground black pepper to taste**

GREEN BEANS WITH ANCHOVIES

Serves: 4

Preparation: 5'

Cooking: 20'

Level of difficulty: 2

- 1½ lb/750 g green beans
- 1 clove garlic, finely chopped
- 2 tbsp finely chopped parsley
- 4 anchovy fillets, rinsed and coarsely chopped
- 4 tbsp extra-virgin olive oil
- 4 tbsp butter
- salt and freshly ground black pepper to taste

Cook the beans in a large pot of salted, boiling water for 5–7 minutes, or until crunchy-tender. • Drain. • Sauté the garlic, parsley, and anchovies in the oil and butter in a large frying pan over low heat for 5–10 minutes, or until the anchovies have started to break down. • Add the beans and mix well. Season with salt and pepper. • Serve hot.

BELL PEPPERS STUFFED WITH TABBOULEH

Cook the bulgur in a large pot of salted, boiling water for 10 minutes. • Turn off the heat and let swell in the water for 10 minutes. • Drain and let cool completely. • Mix in the cucumber, tomatoes, and scallions. Drizzle with the oil and season with salt and pepper. Mix in the raisins, lemon juice, mint, and parsley.

Tabbouleh is a classic Lebanese salad made with bulgur and chopped vegetables and herbs.

Refrigerate for 2 hours. • Halve the peppers and remove the seeds and filaments. Fill with the tabbouleh. Garnish with the mint leaves and serve.

768

Serves: 4

Preparation: 25' + 2 h to chill

Cooking: 10'

Level of difficulty: 2

- 8 oz/250 g bulgur
- 1 cucumber, peeled and diced
- 8 oz/250 g cherry tomatoes, diced
- 2 scallions/spring onions, finely chopped
- 3 tbsp extra-virgin olive oil
- salt and freshly ground black pepper to taste
- $1/3$ cup/60 g golden raisins/sultanas
- juice of 2 lemons
- 2 tbsp finely chopped mint
- 4 tbsp finely chopped parsley
- 2 green bell peppers/ capsicums
- 2 red bell peppers/ capsicums
- mint leaves, to garnish

TOMATO AND POTATOES WITH FRESH BASIL

Sauté the onions in the oil in a large saucepan over medium heat until translucent. • Add the chopped garlic, potatoes, tomatoes, and half the basil. Season with salt and pepper. • Add enough water to cover the vegetables. Bring to a boil. Simmer over low heat for 1 hour 30 minutes. • Add the remaining basil just before serving. • Rub the toast with the remaining garlic. • Spoon the tomato and potato mixture over the top. • Garnish with the basil leaves. Serve hot or at room temperature.

Serves:	6
Preparation:	20'
Cooking:	1 h 45'
Level of difficulty:	1

- 2 onions, finely chopped
- 4 tbsp extra-virgin olive oil
- 3 cloves garlic, 2 finely chopped, 1 peeled and left whole
- 1½ lb/750 g potatoes, peeled and halved or quartered
- 1½ lb/750 g tomatoes, peeled and coarsely chopped
- 1 bunch fresh basil, coarsely chopped
- salt and freshly ground black pepper to taste
- 2 cups/500 ml water + more as required
- 6 slices firm-textured bread, toasted
- basil, to garnish

SICILIAN EGGPLANT MIX

S oak the eggplant in a large bowl of cold water
with the lemon juice for 15 minutes. • Drain
and pat dry with kitchen towel. • Sauté the
eggplant in 4 tablespoons of oil in a large frying
pan until lightly browned. • Sauté the onions and
celery in the remaining oil in a large frying pan
until golden. • Add
the tomatoes,
eggplant, and capers. Cover and cook for 15
minutes. • Add the sugar and vinegar and cook
until the vinegar has evaporated. • Garnish with
the mint and let cool completely.

*Eggplants are a staple throughout the long, hot
Sicilian summer. They are served in myriad ways.*

Serves: 4

Preparation: 35'

Cooking: 25'

Level of difficulty: 1

- 2 eggplants/
  aubergines, cut into
  small cubes
- juice of 2 lemons
- 8 tbsp extra-virgin
  olive oil
- 2 medium onions,
  thinly sliced
- 1 stalk celery, finely
  chopped
- 4 tomatoes, seeded
  and coarsely
  chopped
- 3 tbsp salted
  capers, rinsed
- 2 tbsp sugar
- 4 tbsp vinegar
- 2 sprigs mint,
  to garnish

ZUCCHINI AND GOAT'S CHEESE MOLD

Serves: 4

Preparation: 30' + 3 h to chill

Level of difficulty: 3

- 5 medium zucchini/courgettes
- 1 cup/250 g fresh, creamy goat's cheese
- 1 bunch parsley, finely chopped
- 1 tbsp finely chopped thyme
- 1 tbsp finely chopped marjoram
- salt and freshly ground black pepper to taste
- 1 tbsp agar-agar
- 4 tbsp dry white wine
- 1 cup/250 ml heavy/double cream

Use a potato peeler or mandolin to slice two of the zucchini very thinly lengthwise. Coarsely grate the remainder. • Oil a 1-quart (1-liter) ring mold and line with the sliced zucchini, overlapping them slightly. • Mix the goat's cheese, grated zucchini, parsley, thyme, and marjoram in a large bowl. Season with salt and pepper. • Melt the agar-agar with the wine in a small saucepan over low heat for 2 minutes, stirring constantly. • Let cool. • Beat the cream in a large bowl until stiff. Use a large spatula to fold in the gelling mixture and cream into the cheese mixture. • Spoon into the prepared mold, taking care not to move the zucchini lining. Smooth the surface. Fold in the zucchini slices that are overlapping the edges. • Refrigerate for at least 3 hours. • Dip the mold in hot water and turn out onto a serving plate.

EGGPLANT AND ALMOND MIX

Dice the eggplant and place in a colander. Sprinkle with salt and drain for 20 minutes. • Pat dry with kitchen paper. • Halve the tomatoes and scoop out as many seeds as possible. • Sauté the onion in the oil in a large frying pan until transparent. • Add the garlic and sauté for 2 minutes. • Add the eggplant and almonds and cook until golden. • Stir in the tomatoes, mint, vinegar, sugar, and chile powder. Cook over high heat for 10 minutes until the eggplant have softened but not falling apart.
• Season with salt and sprinkle with the parsley.
• Transfer to a bowl and let cool completely.
• Cover with aluminum foil and refrigerate until ready to serve.

Serves: 4

Preparation: 40'

Cooking: 15'

Level of difficulty: 1

- 1¾ lb/800 g eggplant/aubergines
- salt to taste
- 1 lb/500 g cherry tomatoes
- 1 large white onion, finely sliced
- 4 tbsp extra-virgin olive oil
- 2 cloves garlic, finely chopped
- 2 oz/60 g peeled almonds
- 2 sprigs mint, torn
- 2 tbsp white wine vinegar
- 1 tbsp sugar
- ⅛ tsp chile powder
- 1 bunch parsley, finely chopped

VEGETABLE KEBABS WITH YOGURT

Sauce: Place the cucumber in a colander. Sprinkle with salt and let drain for 1 hour.
• Transfer to a bowl and mix in the yogurt, onion, and mint. Season with pepper. Cover with plastic wrap and refrigerate for 2 hours. • Thread the vegetables onto wooden skewers. • Mix the oil with a pinch of salt and pepper in a small bowl. Brush the kebabs with the oil. • Turn on the broiler (grill) and broil the skewers, turning occasionally, for 8–10 minutes, or until the vegetables are lightly browned. • Serve hot with the sauce.

Serve these Greek kebabs as an appetizer with a glass of cool retsina.

778

Serves: 4

Preparation: 1 h + 2 h to chill

Cooking: 10'

Level of difficulty: 1

SAUCE
- 1 cucumber, peeled and finely chopped
- salt and freshly ground black pepper to taste
- 1¼ cups/310 g Greek yogurt
- 1 tbsp finely chopped onion
- 1 tbsp finely chopped mint

KEBABS
- 32 cherry tomatoes
- 1 large potato, thinly sliced
- 1 fresh corn cob, sliced
- 1 yellow bell pepper, seeded, cored, and cut into squares
- 2 zucchini/ courgettes, cut into rounds
- 1 large onion, cut into squares
- 4 tbsp extra-virgin olive oil
- salt and freshly ground black pepper to taste

SOUTHERN VEGETABLE STEW

Serves: 4

Preparation: 15'

Cooking: 35'

Level of difficulty: 1

- 3 yellow and red bell peppers/ capsicums, seeded, cored, and cut into strips
- 6 tbsp extra-virgin olive oil
- 1 clove garlic, finely chopped
- 1 onion, thinly sliced
- 2 eggplants/ aubergines, coarsely chopped
- 2 potatoes, peeled and chopped
- 2 zucchini/ courgettes, cut in rounds
- 10 oz/300 g tomatoes, quartered
- salt and freshly ground black pepper to taste
- 1 tbsp finely chopped parsley
- 1 tbsp torn basil
- 2 tbsp capers
- 3 oz/90 g black olives

Sauté the bell peppers in the oil in a large frying pan until softened. • Set aside. • In the same pan, sauté the garlic until pale gold. • Add the onion and sauté until golden. • Add the eggplant, potatoes, zucchini, and tomatoes. Season with salt and pepper. Cover and cook over low heat for 20 minutes. • Add the bell peppers, parsley, and basil. Cook for 3 minutes. • Add the capers and olives. • Serve hot or at room temperature.

PEAS WITH PANCETTA

Serves: 4

Preparation: 15'

Cooking: 10'

Level of difficulty: 1

Place the peas in a large saucepan with the garlic, parsley, and oil. Season with salt. • Pour in the water and cook over low heat for 5 minutes. • Add the pancetta. Cook until the peas are cooked and the water has reduced by half. • Serve hot.

- 1 lb/500 g shelled peas
- 1 clove garlic, finely chopped
- 1 sprig parsley, finely chopped
- 8 tbsp extra-virgin olive oil
- salt and freshly ground black pepper to taste
- 1 cup/250 ml water
- ½ cup/60 g diced pancetta

Serves: 4–6	
Preparation: 25'	
Cooking: 30'	
Level of difficulty: 1	

BRAISED GREEN BEANS WITH PAPRIKA

- 2 onions, finely chopped
- 2 cloves garlic, finely chopped
- 4 tbsp butter
- 1½ lb/750 g green beans, cut in short lengths
- 2 large tomatoes, peeled and chopped
- salt and freshly ground black pepper to taste
- 1 tbsp all-purpose/ plain flour
- 1 tsp red paprika
- ½ cup/125 ml boiling Beef Stock (see page 224)
- 1 tbsp finely chopped parsley
- 1 tbsp finely chopped mint

Sauté the onions and garlic in 2 tablespoons of butter in a large frying pan for 5 minutes until transparent. • Add the green beans and tomatoes and season with salt and pepper. Cover and cook over low heat for 15 minutes, stirring often. • Melt the remaining butter in a small saucepan and stir in the flour and paprika. • Pour in the stock and stir until thickened. • Pour the sauce into the beans and cook, stirring often, for 5 more minutes, or until the beans are tender. • Sprinkle with the parsley and mint. • Serve hot.

SWEET POTATOES WITH ONIONS AND CAYENNE

Serves: 4

Preparation: 15'

Cooking: 40'

Level of difficulty: 1

- **2 large red onions, finely chopped**
- **2 cloves garlic, finely chopped**
- **3 tbsp extra-virgin olive oil**
- **1 tbsp sweet paprika**
- **1 tsp cayenne pepper**
- **1 tbsp tomato purèe/paste**
- **3 lb/1.5 kg sweet potatoes, peeled and quartered**
- **1 cup/250 ml dry white wine**
- **1 cup/250 ml water**
- **salt and freshly ground black pepper to taste**

Sauté the onions and garlic in the oil in a large frying pan over medium heat for 8–10 minutes, or until lightly browned. • Add the paprika, cayenne pepper, and tomato purèe. • Stir in the sweet potatoes and cook for 1 minute. • Pour in $^1/_2$ cup (125 ml) of wine and the water and bring to a boil. • Cover and cook over low heat for 12–15 minutes, or until the sauce has thickened. • Season with salt and pepper. Pour in the remaining wine. • Cover and cook for 10–15 minutes, or until the sweet potatoes are tender. • Serve hot.

POTATO AND BEAN PURÈE

Serves:	4–6
Preparation:	15'
Cooking:	20'
Level of difficulty:	1

Cook the potatoes in their skins in a large pot of salted, boiling water for 15–20 minutes, or until tender. • Drain, let cool a little, and slip off the skins. • Chop the potatoes and beans in a food processor until smooth. • Sauté the onion and garlic in the oil in a small frying pan until pale gold. • Stir the onion and garlic into the purèe. • Season with salt and pepper and serve hot.

- 1 lb/500 g potatoes
- 8 oz/250 g canned white kidney or cannellini beans
- 1 medium onion, finely chopped
- 2 cloves garlic, finely chopped
- 4 tbsp extra-virgin olive oil
- salt and freshly ground black pepper to taste

Serves: 6–8	
Preparation: 15'	
Cooking: 35'	
Level of difficulty: 1	

FAVA BEANS WITH LEEKS

- whites of 3 medium leeks, sliced
- ½ cup/125 ml extra-virgin olive oil
- 4 large potatoes, peeled and cut into cubes
- 2 lb/1 kg fresh fava/broad beans, hulled
- salt and freshly ground black pepper to taste
- 2 cups/500 ml water

Sauté the leeks in the oil in a large frying pan over medium heat for 8–10 minutes, or until lightly browned. • Add the potatoes and fava beans. Season with salt and pepper. • Pour in the water and bring to a boil. Cover and cook over medium heat for 20–25 minutes, or until the fava beans and potatoes are tender. • Season with salt and pepper. Remove from the heat and serve hot.

ZUCCHINI MOUSSAKA

Sauté the onions in 2 tablespoons of oil in a large frying pan over medium heat for 8–10 minutes, or until lightly browned. • Add the beef and brown over high heat for 5 minutes. • Season with salt and pepper. Add the tomatoes and sprinkle with the parsley, cumin, and nutmeg. • Cook over low heat for 45 minutes, adding a little water if the mixture begins to dry. • Sauté the zucchini in the remaining oil in a large frying pan over high heat for 5–7 minutes, or until lightly browned. • Season with salt. Cook over medium heat for 10 minutes. • Stir the zucchini into the meat sauce. • Place a layer of zucchini on a serving plate and top with the meat sauce. Repeat the layers of zucchini and meat sauce until all the ingredients are used up. • Serve hot.

Serves: 6–8

Preparation: 15'

Cooking: 1 h 15'

Level of difficulty: 1

- **2 medium onions, finely chopped**
- **4 tbsp extra-virgin olive oil**
- **1½ lb/750 g ground/minced beef**
- **salt and freshly ground black pepper to taste**
- **2 lb/1 kg firm-ripe tomatoes, peeled and cut into cubes**
- **1 tbsp finely chopped parsley**
- **½ tsp ground cumin**
- **¼ tsp freshly grated nutmeg**
- **water (optional)**
- **2 lb/1 kg zucchini/ courgettes, thinly sliced lengthwise**

MASHED POTATOES, LEBANESE-STYLE

Cook the potatoes in a large pot of salted, boiling water for 15–20 minutes, or until tender. • Drain well, transfer to a large bowl, and mash until smooth. • Add the oil, lemon juice, garlic, and salt and mix until well blended. • Sprinkle with the mint and serve warm.

Serves: 4

Preparation: 15'

Cooking: 20'

Level of difficulty: 1

- 6–8 medium potatoes, peeled and cut in 4
- 6 tbsp extra-virgin olive oil
- 6 tbsp fresh lemon juice
- 3 cloves garlic, finely chopped
- salt to taste
- 3 tbsp finely chopped mint

GRATED CARROTS WITH CARDAMOM

Serves: 4–6

Preparation: 15'

Cooking: 25'

Level of difficulty: 1

- **1 lb/500 g carrots, finely grated**
- **1 cup/200 g sugar**
- **2 cups/500 ml milk**
- **¼ tsp ground cardamom**
- **2 tsp lemon zest**
- **2 tbsp butter**
- **2 tbsp all-purpose/ plain flour**

Cook the carrots, sugar, milk, cardamom, and 1 teaspoon of lemon zest in a large saucepan over medium heat for 10 minutes, or until the carrots are tender. • Strain the carrots, reserving the liquid. • Melt the butter in a small saucepan over medium heat. Stir in the flour. • Stir in the carrots, coating them well. Cook for 5 minutes. • Pour the reserved cooking liquid in and mix. • Cook for 5 minutes more. • Garnish with the remaining lemon zest and serve hot.

SAUTÉED SPINACH

Sauté the onion in the oil in a large frying pan over medium heat for 8–10 minutes, or until lightly browned. • Add the spinach and cook, stirring often, until it begins to wilt. • Season with salt and pepper. Stir in the tomatoes and cook until slightly softened. • Sprinkle with the almonds just before serving.

Serves: 4

Preparation: 10'

Cooking: 15'

Level of difficulty: 1

- 1 onion, finely chopped
- 2 tbsp extra-virgin olive oil
- 2 lb/1 kg spinach, well-washed and tough stems removed
- salt and freshly ground black pepper to taste
- 4 tomatoes, peeled and sliced
- ¼ cup/40 g flaked almonds

SPINACH WITH RAISINS AND PINE NUTS

Serves: 6	
Preparation: 5'	
Cooking: 20'	
Level of difficulty: 1	

- **4 lb/2 kg spinach, well-washed and chopped**
- **2 tbsp butter**
- **¾ cup/135 g golden raisins/ sultanas**
- **¾ cup/135 g pine nuts**
- **salt to taste**

Cook the spinach in a large pot of salted, boiling water for 1–2 minutes, or until just wilted. • Drain well, squeezing out excess water. • Melt the butter in a large saucepan over medium heat. Sauté the raisins and pine nuts for 5–7 minutes, or until toasted. • Add the spinach and cook for 5 minutes, stirring constantly, until the butter has been absorbed. Season with salt. • Serve hot.

ZUCCHINI COOKED WITH TOMATOES

Place the tomatoes in a colander and sprinkle with salt. Let drain for 1 hour. • Heat the oil in a large frying pan over medium heat. Add the garlic, tomatoes, and zucchini and cook for 10–15 minutes, or until softened. • Season with salt and pepper and sprinkle with the thyme. • Serve hot.

Serves: 6

Preparation: 15' + 1 h to drain tomatoes

Cooking: 15'

Level of difficulty: 1

- 2 lb/1 kg firm-ripe tomatoes, quartered and seeded
- salt and freshly ground black pepper to taste
- 4 tbsp extra-virgin olive oil
- 1 clove garlic, finely chopped
- 6 zucchini/ courgettes, cut into ½-inch/1-cm thick slices
- 1 tbsp finely chopped thyme

SAVOY CABBAGE TAJINE

Place the cabbage in a tajine or large, deep saucepan with the oil, garlic, and paprika, if using. Season with salt and pepper. • Add the preserved lemon, lemon juice, and water. • Cook over very low heat for 35–40 minutes, or until the volume of the cabbage has reduced by half. • Serve hot.

Serves: 6

Preparation: 10'

Cooking: 40'

Level of difficulty: 1

- 1 Savoy cabbage, finely shredded
- 1 tbsp extra-virgin olive oil
- 2 cloves garlic, finely chopped
- 1 tsp sweet paprika (optional)
- salt and freshly ground black pepper to taste
- 1 Preserved Lemon (see page 958), cut into small pieces
- juice of 1 lemon
- 2 tbsp water

SPICY POTATOES
WITH BELL PEPPERS

Serves: 4

Preparation: 15'

Cooking: 25'

Level of difficulty: 1

- 1½ lb/750 g new potatoes
- 6 tbsp extra-virgin olive oil
- 1 green bell pepper/capsicum, seeded and thinly sliced
- 2 cloves garlic, finely chopped
- ½ tsp red pepper flakes
- ½ tsp cumin seeds
- ¼ tsp paprika
- 2 tbsp white wine vinegar
- salt to taste

Cook the potatoes in a large pot of salted, boiling water for 15–20 minutes, or until tender. • Drain well and cut into bite-sized pieces (or leave whole if small). • Sauté the potatoes, bell peppers, garlic, red pepper flakes, cumin, and paprika in the oil in a large frying pan over high heat for 5 minutes, or until lightly browned. • Add the vinegar to the potatoes. Cook, stirring often, for 10 minutes. • Season with salt and serve hot.

EGGPLANT STUFFED WITH BEEF

Make long, deep lengthwise cuts in the eggplants and soak in salted water for 1 hour. • Pat dry on paper towels. • Heat 4 tablespoons of oil in a large frying pan over medium heat. Fry the eggplants for 10–15 minutes, or until tender. • Drain well on paper towels. • Use a spoon to scoop out the flesh. Finely chop and set aside. • Sauté the onion in the remaining oil in a large frying pan over medium heat for 8–10 minutes, or until lightly browned. • Add the garlic, cinnamon, and beef and sauté over high heat until the beef is browned. • Pour in the wine and let it evaporate. Add the tomatoes and parsley. Bring to a boil and season with salt and pepper. • Cover and cook over low heat for 40 minutes. • Preheat the oven to 400°F/200°C/gas 6. • Mix the meat sauce and the reserved eggplant flesh in a large bowl. Spoon the mixture into the hollow eggplants. • Arrange the eggplants in a large baking pan. Top with the tomato cubes and spoon the Béchamel sauce over the top. Sprinkle with the cheese. • Bake for 15–20 minutes, or until the cheese is golden brown. • Serve hot.

Serves:	3
Preparation:	30' + 1 h to soak eggplants
Cooking:	1 h 20'
Level of difficulty:	2

- 3 medium eggplants/ aubergines, weighing about 1½ lb/750 g, cut in half
- salt and freshly ground black pepper to taste
- 6 tbsp extra-virgin olive oil
- 1 onion, finely chopped
- 1 clove garlic, finely chopped
- 1 tsp ground cinnamon
- 1 lb/500 g ground/ minced beef
- ½ cup/125 ml dry red wine
- 1 cup/250 ml canned tomatoes
- 2 firm-ripe tomatoes, coarsely chopped
- 1 tbsp finely chopped parsley
- 1 cup/250 ml Béchamel sauce (see page 55)
- 2 tbsp freshly grated Kefalotiri or Parmesan cheese

LEEK GRATIN

Serves: 4–6

Preparation: 30'

Cooking: 1 h

Level of difficulty: 2

- 8–10 leeks, white parts only, halved lengthwise
- 1 cup/250 ml heavy/double cream
- 1 tsp freshly grated nutmeg
- salt and freshly ground black pepper to taste
- ¾ cup/90 g freshly grated Gruyère cheese

Preheat the oven to 400°F/200°C/gas 6. • Cook the leeks in a large pot of salted, boiling water for 5–7 minutes, or until tender. • Drain well, pressing with a fork to remove excess water, and set aside. • Beat the cream and nutmeg in a large bowl until thickened. Season with salt and pepper. • Spread 3 tablespoons of the cream in an ovenproof dish. Arrange the cooked leeks on top and pour the remaining cream over the top. Sprinkle with the Gruyère. • Bake for 25–30 minutes, or until lightly browned and the cheese is bubbling. • Serve warm.

TOMATOES STUFFED WITH EGG AND RICOTTA

Slice the "lids" off the tomatoes. Scoop out the seeds and let drain upside-down for 30 minutes. • Preheat the oven to 350°F/180°C/gas 4. • Line a baking sheet with waxed paper. • Beat the eggs and Ricotta in a large bowl. Add the torn basil. Season with salt and pepper. • Melt the butter in a large frying pan. Add the egg mixture and cook until the eggs are cooked, breaking them up with a fork. Place the tomatoes on the prepared baking sheet. Bake for 8 minutes. • Add the tomato "lids" and bake for 2 minutes more. • Spoon the eggs into the tomatoes and garnish with the basil. • Top with the "lids" and serve.

Serves: 4

Preparation: 20' + 30' to drain the tomatoes

Cooking: 15'

Level of difficulty: 2

- **8 small to medium firm-ripe tomatoes**
- **8 eggs**
- **6 tbsp Ricotta cheese**
- **1 bunch basil, torn + extra, to garnish**
- **salt and freshly ground black pepper to taste**
- **2 tbsp butter**

TURKISH EGGPLANTS

Make long, deep lengthwise cuts in the eggplants. Place in a colander and sprinkle with salt. Let drain for 1 hour. • Heat $^1/_2$ cup (125 ml) of oil in a large frying pan over medium heat. • Fry the eggplants for 10–15 minutes, or until tender. • Drain well on paper towels. • Sauté the onions in the remaining oil in a large frying pan over medium heat for 8–10 minutes, or until lightly browned. • Add the beef and brown over high heat for 5 minutes. • Add the cubed tomatoes and season with salt and pepper. • Cover and cook over low heat for 30 minutes. • Preheat the oven to 400°F/200°C/gas 6. • Arrange the eggplants in a large baking dish. • Spoon the meat sauce into the cuts in the eggplants. Cover with the tomato slices. • Pour the water into the pan. • Bake for 15–20 minutes, or until tender. • Sprinkle with the parsley and serve hot.

Serves: 3–4

Preparation: 25' + 1 h to drain eggplants

Cooking: 1 h 20'

Level of difficulty: 1

- 3 medium eggplants/ aubergines, each weighing about 1½ lb/750 g, halved lengthwise
- salt
- $^1/_2$ cup/125 ml + 3 tbsp extra-virgin olive oil
- 3 medium onions, finely chopped
- 1 lb/500 g ground/ minced beef
- 4 tomatoes, cut into cubes, and 2 tomatoes, thinly sliced
- salt and freshly ground black pepper to taste
- 1 cup/250 ml water
- 1 tbsp finely chopped parsley

BAKED POTATO AND MUSHROOM PIE

Serves: 4

Preparation: 30'

Cooking: 40'

Level of difficulty: 1

- 1¾ lb/800 g porcini (or other wild) mushrooms
- 1 bunch parsley
- 4 sprigs thyme
- 4 sprigs marjoram
- 1 clove garlic
- 5 tbsp freshly grated Parmesan cheese
- salt and freshly ground black pepper to taste
- 1¾ lb/800 g yellow-fleshed potatoes, thinly sliced
- 8 tbsp extra-virgin olive oil

Preheat the oven to 350°F/180°C/gas 4. • Oil a baking dish. • Remove the mushroom caps. Rinse and coarsely chop the stalks with the parsley, thyme, marjoram, and garlic. • Transfer to a large bowl and mix in the Parmesan. Season with salt and pepper. • Thinly slice the mushroom caps. • Arrange a layer of potato slices in the prepared baking dish, overlapping them slightly. Season with salt and pepper and sprinkle with the chopped mushroom and herb mixture. • Top with a layer of sliced mushrooms. • Drizzle with the oil and continue to layer until all the ingredients are used. • Bake for 35–40 minutes, or until the vegetables are cooked and golden. • Serve warm.

STUFFED ONIONS

Serves: 6

Preparation: 25'

Cooking: 45'

Level of difficulty: 1

810

Boil the onions in salted water for 15 minutes.
• Drain and let cool. • Scoop out the flesh and chop finely. • Mix the chopped onion, veal, sausage meat, 2 tablespoons of Parmesan, the oil, egg, and nutmeg. Season with salt and pepper. • Stuff the onions with this mixture. Arrange the onions in a single layer in a large saucepan and pour in the stock. Cover and cook over low heat for about 30 minutes, or until the sauce thickens.
• Serve hot.

- **6 large onions**
- **8 oz/250 g ground/minced veal**
- **2 sausages, peeled and crumbled**
- **4 tbsp freshly grated Parmesan cheese**
- **4 tbsp extra-virgin olive oil**
- **1 egg**
- **⅛ tsp freshly grated nutmeg**
- **salt and freshly ground black pepper to taste**
- **1 cup/250 ml Vegetable Stock (see page 224)**

Serves: 6	
Preparation: 10'	
Cooking: 50'	
Level of difficulty: 1	

POTATO AND VEGETABLE BAKE

Preheat the oven to 350°F/180°C/gas 4. • Oil a 9-inch (23-cm) baking dish. • Layer the potatoes in the dish. • Beat the flour, milk, eggs, oil, and water in a large bowl until smooth. Mix in the basil, parsley, tomatoes, and chile pepper, if using. Season with nutmeg and salt. • Pour the mixture over the potatoes. • Bake for 50 minutes, or until the potatoes are tender and lightly browned. • Serve hot.

- 3 lb/1.5 kg potatoes, peeled and finely sliced
- 2 cups/300 g all-purpose/plain flour
- ½ cup/125 ml milk
- 3 large eggs, lightly beaten
- 6 tbsp extra-virgin olive oil
- 4 tbsp water
- leaves from 1 bunch of basil, torn
- 1 tbsp finely chopped parsley
- 2 tomatoes, finely chopped
- 1 fresh red chile pepper, seeded and finely chopped (optional)
- ¼ tsp freshly grated nutmeg
- salt to taste

STUFFED ZUCCHINI

Serves: 4–6

Preparation: 20'

Cooking: 30'

Level of difficulty: 2

- **12 medium round zucchini/ courgettes**
- **2 scallions/spring onions, finely chopped**
- **1 clove garlic, finely chopped**
- **2 tbsp butter**
- **4 eggs, lightly beaten**
- **½ cup/60 g freshly grated Parmesan cheese**
- **2 cups/120 g fresh bread crumbs**
- **4 tbsp milk**
- **1 oz/30 g dried mushrooms, soaked in warm water for 15 minutes, drained, and chopped**
- **7 oz/200 g sausage meat**
- **4 tbsp extra-virgin olive oil**
- **4 tbsp finely chopped parsley**
- **salt and freshly ground black pepper to taste**

Cut the zucchini in half. • Cook the zucchini in salted, boiling water for 7–8 minutes, or until tender. • Drain and let cool. Scoop out the insides from the zucchini with a teaspoon. • Sauté the scallions and garlic in the butter in a medium frying pan over medium heat for 2 minutes until softened. • Add the zucchini flesh and cook for 2 minutes. • Preheat the oven to 350°F/ 180°C/gas 4. • Oil a baking sheet. • Mix the eggs, Parmesan, 1 cup (60 g) of bread crumbs, milk, mushrooms, sausage meat, 2 tablespoons of oil, and parsley in a large bowl. Season with salt and pepper. • Add the sautéed mixture and mix well. • Spoon the filling into the zucchini and arrange on the prepared baking sheet. Sprinkle with the remaining bread crumbs and drizzle with the remaining oil. • Bake for 15–20 minutes, or until browned. • Serve hot.

BAKED TOMATOES
AND EGGPLANT

Serves: 6

Preparation: 20'

Cooking: 40'

Level of difficulty: 1

- ½ cup/125 ml extra-virgin olive oil
- 4 eggplants/ aubergines, thickly sliced
- 8 large tomatoes, peeled and chopped
- 1 clove garlic, finely chopped
- 1 shallot, finely chopped
- 2 tsp finely chopped thyme
- 8 oz/200 g Mozzarella cheese, thinly sliced
- salt and freshly ground black pepper to taste

Preheat the oven to 350°F/180°C/gas 4. • Oil a large baking dish. • Heat 4 tablespoons of oil in a large frying pan over medium heat. Fry the eggplant in small batches for 5–7 minutes, or until golden brown all over. • Drain well on paper towels. • In the same pan, sauté the tomatoes for 5 minutes over medium heat. Add the garlic, shallot, and thyme. • Place a layer of eggplant in the bottom of the prepared dish and cover with a layer of tomato mixture. Repeat until all the eggplant and tomatoes are in the dish. • Bake for 25–30 minutes, or until the eggplants are tender. • Top with the Mozzarella and season with salt and pepper. Drizzle with the remaining oil. • Return to the oven and bake for 10 minutes more, or until the cheese has melted.

VEGETABLE ASPIC

Soften the gelatin in the water in a large saucepan. • Trim the tops off the artichokes and remove the tough outer leaves. Cut into small thin wedges and rub all over with the lemon. • Boil the potatoes in a large pot of salted, boiling water for 12–15 minutes, or until tender. • Remove with a slotted spoon and let cool. •

Serve slices of cool aspic as a summer appetizer, or as a side dish with boiled meats or fish.

Cook the carrots in the same water for 8–10 minutes, or until crunchy-tender. • Remove with a slotted spoon and let cool. • Cook the green beans and peas in the same water until tender. • Transfer all the vegetables to a large bowl and let cool completely. • Drizzle with the oil and vinegar. Season with salt and pepper. Mix in the mayonnaise until well blended. • Heat the water with the gelatin over medium heat, stirring often, until the mixture begins to thicken. • Pour a layer of the gelatin into a deep 2-quart (2-liter) mold. Refrigerate for 1 hour. • Arrange half the eggs and a layer of vegetables in the mold and pour in a layer of gelatin. • Refrigerate for 1 hour. • Repeat with the other vegetables (reserving a few for garnish) and the remaining gelatin until all the ingredients have been used. • Refrigerate for 3 hours. • Turn out the aspic onto a serving platter. • Garnish with the remaining eggs and vegetables.

Serves: 6–8

Preparation: 45' + 5 h to chill

Cooking: 30'

Level of difficulty: 3

- **1 tbsp gelatin (or 4 sheets)**
- **1 quart/1 liter water**
- **3 artichokes**
- **½ lemon**
- **2 potatoes, cubed**
- **4 carrots, cubed**
- **10 oz/300 g peas**
- **10 oz/300 g green beans, topped and tailed**
- **2 tbsp extra-virgin olive oil**
- **1 tbsp balsamic vinegar**
- **salt and freshly ground black pepper to taste**
- **1 cup/250 ml mayonnaise**
- **3 hard-boiled eggs, cut into wedges**

816

LENTILS AND POTATO MIX

Cook the lentils in a large pot of salted, boiling water for 20 minutes. • Add the potatoes and cook for 15–20 minutes more, or until the potatoes and lentils are tender. • Drain the lentil mixture and set aside. • Sauté the garlic and cilantro in the oil in a large frying pan over medium heat for 3 minutes. • Stir in the lentil mixture. • Mix the flour and water in a small bowl. Add to the lentil mixture. • Cover and cook for 20 minutes. • Season with salt. Drizzle with the lemon juice and serve hot or at room temperature.

Serves: 6

Preparation: 15'

Cooking: 1 h

Level of difficulty: 1

- 1½ lb/750 g lentils
- 2 medium potatoes, peeled and coarsely chopped
- 6 cloves garlic, finely chopped
- ¼ cup/60 g finely chopped fresh cilantro/coriander
- 2 tbsp extra-virgin olive oil
- 2 tbsp all-purpose/ plain flour
- 2 tbsp water
- salt to taste
- 4 tbsp fresh lemon juice

WHITE BEAN AND POLENTA MIX

Serves: 6–8	
Preparation: 20'	
Cooking: 1 h 40'	
Level of difficulty: 2	

- 1 lb/500 g fresh white beans, shelled
- 1 piece pork rind
- 1 carrot
- 1 onion
- 1 stalk celery
- 1 bunch parsley
- 1 clove garlic
- 4 tbsp lard
- 1 small black cabbage, cut into strips
- 3 potatoes, diced
- 1/8 tsp crushed fennel seeds
- 3 cups/450 g polenta (coarsely ground yellow cornmeal)

P lace the beans and pork rind in a large pot of cold water and simmer for 45 minutes. • Discard the pork rind. • Chop the carrot, onion, celery, parsley, and garlic. Sauté the chopped mixture in the lard in a large saucepan until aromatic. • Add the beans and their cooking liquid, cabbage, potatoes, and the fennel seeds. Cook for 15 minutes. • Gradually sprinkle in the polenta and cook for 40 minutes, stirring constantly. • Serve hot.

SOY BEAN RISSOLES

Serves: 4–6

Preparation: 45' +
overnight to soak
soy beans

Cooking: 3 h 20'

Level of difficulty: 2

Cook the soy beans in a large pot of salted water for 2 1/2 hours. • Drain and let cool. • Preheat the oven to 400°F/200°C/gas 6. • Grease a baking dish with oil. • Sauté half the onion in 2 tablespoons of oil in a large frying pan until softened. • Stir in the tomatoes and season with salt and pepper. • Add the flour mixture, thyme, bay leaf, wine, and stock. Cook over medium heat for 20 minutes. • Sauté the eggplant in the remaining oil in a medium frying pan until golden. • Remove from the pan and sauté the bell pepper and remaining onion in the same oil until softened. • Transfer the bell pepper mixture to a large bowl. Mix in the soy beans, eggplant, garlic, bread crumbs, Parmesan, and eggs. Season with salt and pepper. • Form the mixture into rissoles. • Arrange the rissoles in the prepared baking dish. • Bake for 10 minutes. • Pour over half the sauce and bake for 15 minutes, or until the rissoles are golden. • Serve hot with the remaining sauce.

- 3 1/2 oz/100 g yellow soy beans, soaked overnight and drained
- 1 onion, chopped
- 6 tbsp extra-virgin olive oil
- 4 tomatoes, peeled and chopped
- salt and freshly ground black pepper to taste
- 1 tbsp whole-wheat flour mixed in 2 tbsp water
- 2 sprigs thyme
- 1 bay leaf
- 3 tbsp dry red wine
- 1 1/4 cups/310 ml Vegetable Stock (see page 224)
- 1 eggplant/ aubergine, diced
- 1 red bell pepper, seeded, cored, and finely chopped
- 1 clove garlic, finely chopped
- 3 1/2 cups/200 g fresh bread crumbs
- 1 1/4 cups/150 g freshly grated Parmesan cheese
- 2 eggs, lightly beaten

SHRIMP AND BEANS

Place the beans in a serving dish. • Blanch the tomatoes in boiling water for 30 seconds. Slip off the skins, squeeze out as many seeds as possible, and chop coarsely. • Cook the shrimp in a large pot of salted, boiling water for 2–3 minutes, or until cooked and pink. • Drain, let cool, and peel. • Add the shrimp and tomatoes to the beans. • Sprinkle with the basil and season generously with pepper. Drizzle with the oil and serve.

Serves: 4

Preparation: 25'

Cooking: 5'

Level of difficulty: 1

- **1 lb/500 g canned cannellini beans, drained**
- **2 tomatoes**
- **1½ lb/750 g shrimp/prawns**
- **4 leaves fresh basil, torn**
- **freshly ground black pepper to taste**
- **3 tbsp extra-virgin olive oil**

STEWED CHANTERELLES AND BEANS

Serves: 4

Preparation: 30' +
12 h to soak beans

Cooking: 1 h 35'

Level of difficulty: 2

- • 8 oz/250 g dried cannellini beans, soaked overnight and drained
- • 3 cloves garlic
- • 2 sprigs calamint
- • 5 tbsp extra-virgin olive oil
- • 3 leaves fresh sage
- • 1 lb/500 g chanterelle mushrooms, washed
- • 1 tbsp tomato purèe/paste dissolved in 4 tbsp hot water
- • salt to taste

Place the beans in an earthenware pot with 1 clove of garlic and calamint. Cover with water and boil for 1 hour. • Drain. • Chop the remaining garlic. Sauté the garlic in the oil in a large frying pan until pale gold. • Add the sage and mushrooms and cook over medium heat for 10 minutes. • Add the beans and the tomato water. Cook for 20 minutes more. Season with salt. • Let cool for 10 minutes before serving.

BAKED LENTILS WITH TOMATO SAUCE

Place the lentils in a large pot. Pour in enough water to cover the lentils completely. Season with salt. • Bring to a boil and cook for 45 minutes, or until tender. • Drain well. • Process the lentils, 4 tablespoons of water, Parmesan, onion, egg, thyme, and 1 tablespoon of butter until smooth. Season with salt and pepper. • Preheat the oven to 350°F/180°C/gas 4. • Grease a baking dish with the remaining butter and sprinkle with the bread crumbs. • Pour in the lentil mixture, smoothing the top. • Bake for 30 minutes. • Cut into rectangles and serve with the hot tomato sauce.

Serves: 4

Preparation: 35'

Cooking: 3 h

Level of difficulty: 2

- 4 cups/400 g green lentils
- salt and freshly ground black pepper to taste
- ¾ cup/90 g freshly grated Parmesan cheese
- 1 onion, finely chopped
- 1 egg, beaten
- ⅛ tsp thyme
- 2 tbsp butter, melted
- 2 tbsp fine dry bread crumbs
- 1 quantity Tomato Sauce (see page 37)

SALADS

SPINACH AND PARMESAN SALAD WITH GRAPEFRUIT

Rinse the spinach leaves thoroughly under cold running water and dry well. • Remove the tough stems. Arrange the spinach on four individual serving plates. Top with the Parmesan and grapefruit. • Dressing: Mix the lemon juice, oil, and chives in a small bowl. Season with salt and pepper. • Pour the dressing over the salad and toss well.

Serve as an appetizer or with roast meats during the winter when spinach and grapefruit are in season.

828

Serves: 4

Preparation: 15'

Level of difficulty: 1

- **7 oz/200 g fresh spinach leaves**
- **4 oz/125 g Parmesan cheese, in flakes**
- **1 grapefruit, cut into segments**

DRESSING
- **juice of ½ lemon**
- **2 tbsp extra-virgin olive oil**
- **1 tbsp finely chopped chives**
- **salt and freshly ground black pepper to taste**

CHILLED CUCUMBER AND YOGURT SALAD

Peel the cucumbers. Cut them in half and use a teaspoon to scrape out the seeds. Slice very thinly. • Place the cucumber slices in a colander. Sprinkle with salt and let drain for 20 minutes. • Mix the garlic, lemon juice, yogurt, and dill in a large bowl until well blended. • Stir in the cucumbers. • Drizzle with the oil and sprinkle with the mint. • Refrigerate for at least 30 minutes before serving.

Serves: 4–6

Preparation: 15' + 50' to drain and chill

Level of difficulty: 1

- 2 large cucumbers
- 1 tsp salt
- 2 cloves garlic, finely chopped
- 2 tbsp fresh lemon juice
- 2 cups/500 ml Greek yogurt
- 1 tbsp finely chopped fresh dill
- 4 tbsp extra-virgin olive oil
- 1 tbsp finely chopped mint

TZATZIKI (GREEK YOGURT SALAD)

Serves: 4–6

Preparation: 15'
+ 2 h 30' to drain
and chill

Level of difficulty: 1

- **2 large cucumbers**
- **salt and freshly ground black pepper to taste**
- **2 cups/500 ml Greek yogurt**
- **2 cloves garlic, finely chopped**
- **4 tbsp extra-virgin olive oil**
- **1 tbsp white wine vinegar**
- **olives, to garnish**

Peel the cucumbers. Cut them in half and use a teaspoon to scrape out the seeds. Grate the flesh coarsely. • Place the grated cucumber in a colander. Season with salt and let drain for 30 minutes. • Place the yogurt in a medium bowl and stir in the garlic, oil, vinegar, and cucumber. Season with salt and pepper. • Refrigerate for at least 2 hours before serving. • Garnish with the olives and serve.

MIXED WILD SALAD GREENS

Wash all the salad vegetables very thoroughly in cold running water. • Drain well and dry in a salad spinner or wrap the leaves in a clean cloth and shake until completely dry. • Place the leaves, whole or coarsely torn, in a large salad bowl. Season with salt and pepper and drizzle with the vinegar and, lastly, the oil. • Toss vigorously and serve immediately.

Serves: 6–8

Preparation: 20'

Level of difficulty: 1

- **2 lb/1 kg mixed wild salad greens (such as endive/chicory and radicchio varieties, arugula/ rocket)**
- **7 oz/200 g tender young cabbage or spinach leaves (optional)**
- **salt and freshly ground black pepper to taste**
- **2 tbsp red wine vinegar**
- **6–7 tbsp extra-virgin olive oil**

SALAD WITH PARMESAN AND BALSAMIC VINEGAR

Serves: 4–6

Preparation: 25'

Level of difficulty: 1

- 1 lb/500 g mâche/corn salad/lamb's lettuce
- 3 oz/90 g Parmesan cheese, in flakes
- ½ cup/125 ml extra-virgin olive oil
- salt to taste
- 2 tbsp balsamic vinegar

Wash all the salad vegetables very thoroughly in cold running water. • Drain well and dry in a salad spinner or wrap the leaves in a clean cloth and shake until completely dry. • Place the leaves, whole or coarsely torn, in a large salad bowl. • Add the parmesan. • Mix the oil, salt, and balsamic vinegar together in a small, deep bowl until very well blended. • Drizzle over the salad and toss thoroughly. • Serve at once.

CARROT AND YOGURT SALAD WITH FRESH TARRAGON

Serves: 4

Preparation: 10'

Cooking: 35'

Level of difficulty: 1

- 2 cups/500 ml plain yogurt
- 6 tbsp finely chopped tarragon
- 4 tbsp butter
- 6 large carrots, thinly sliced
- 1 small onion, finely chopped
- 2 tsp sugar
- salt and freshly ground black pepper to taste

Mix the yogurt and tarragon in a medium bowl. • Melt the butter in a large frying pan. Add the carrots, onion, and sugar and cook, stirring often, over low heat for 30 minutes, or until the carrots are tender. • Season with salt and pepper. Add the yogurt mixture and stir over low heat until the yogurt has lost all its extra moisture. • Serve hot or spread on slices of warm toast.

ZUCCHINI AND PARMESAN WITH BALSAMIC VINEGAR

Rinse the zucchini thoroughly under cold running water. Dry well and trim off the ends. • Slice very thinly onto a large serving platter. • Season lightly with salt and pepper and sprinkle with the Parmesan. • Drizzle with the balsamic vinegar and serve at once.

Serves: 4

Preparation: 10'

Level of difficulty: 1

- **2 large very fresh zucchini/ courgettes**
- **salt and freshly ground black pepper to taste**
- **4 oz/125 g Parmesan cheese, flaked**
- **2 tbsp Balsamic vinegar**

TOMATO AND MOZZARELLA SALAD

Serves: 4–6

Preparation: 10'

Level of difficulty: 1

- **6–8 large ripe salad tomatoes**
- **1 lb/500 g Mozzarella cheese (preferably made with water buffalo's milk)**
- **20 fresh basil leaves, torn**
- **salt and freshly ground black pepper to taste**
- **2 tbsp balsamic vinegar (optional)**
- **6 tbsp extra-virgin olive oil**

Rinse the tomatoes thoroughly under cold running water. Dry well. • Cut the tomatoes into fairly thick slices. • Cut the Mozzarella in slices of the same thickness. • Arrange the slices alternately on an attractive serving dish. • Sprinkle with the basil and season with salt and pepper. Drizzle with vinegar, if using, and the oil.

TABBOULEH

Place the bulgur in a bowl and cover with warm water. Let stand for 20 minutes, or until the grains have softened. • Drain well, squeezing out excess moisture, and transfer to a large salad bowl. • Season with salt and pepper and drizzle with half the lemon juice and the oil. Let stand for 30 minutes.

838

Tabbouleh can be served a starter, and also as a salad with meat and fish dishes.

• Add the parsley, scallions, mint, and tomatoes. • Drizzle with the remaining lemon juice. Toss well and serve.

Serves: 4

Preparation: 15'
+ 1 h 20' to stand
and chill

Level of difficulty: 1

- 1 cup/150 g bulgur wheat
- salt and freshly ground black pepper to taste
- juice of 1–2 lemons
- 6 tbsp extra-virgin olive oil
- 5 oz/150 g finely chopped parsley
- 4 scallions/spring onions, finely chopped
- 20 fresh mint leaves, finely chopped
- 3 medium tomatoes, finely chopped

EMMENTAL AND MINT SALAD

Place the tomatoes in a colander. Sprinkle with salt and let drain for 15 minutes. • Transfer the tomatoes to a large bowl and add the mint and garlic. • Add the Emmental and season with salt and pepper. Drizzle with the oil. • Sprinkle with the basil and serve.

Serves: 4

Preparation: 15' + 15' to drain tomatoes

Level of difficulty: 1

- 1¼ lb/575 g plum tomatoes, coarsely chopped
- salt and freshly ground black pepper to taste
- 1 bunch mint, torn
- 2 cloves garlic, finely chopped
- 7 oz/200 g Emmental cheese, diced
- 3 tbsp extra-virgin olive oil
- 4 leaves fresh basil

ZUCCHINI AND BEAN SALAD WITH BASIL SAUCE

C ook the green beans in salted, boiling water for 10–15 minutes, or until tender. • Drain and chop. • Sauté the zucchini in 2 tablespoons of oil in a large frying pan over medium heat for 4 minutes. • Season with salt and pepper and let cool. • Finely chop the basil with the pine nuts and garlic. Transfer to a small bowl and add the Parmesan. Season with salt and pepper and mix in the remaining oil. • Place the green beans, zucchini, and tomatoes in a salad bowl. Add the pesto, stir gently, and serve.

842

Serves: 4
Preparation: 25'
Cooking: 20'
Level of difficulty: 2

- **14 oz/400 g green beans, topped and tailed**
- **14 oz/400 g zucchini/ courgettes, cut in rounds**
- **7 tbsp extra-virgin olive oil**
- **salt and freshly ground black pepper to taste**
- **1 bunch basil**
- **1 tbsp pine nuts**
- **½ clove garlic**
- **1 tbsp freshly grated Parmesan cheese**
- **2 ripe tomatoes, cut into wedges**

POTATO SALAD WITH MINT

Serves: 4

Preparation: 15'

Cooking: 25'

Level of difficulty: 1

- 8 medium potatoes
- 1 tbsp finely chopped mint
- 2 cloves garlic, finely chopped
- 4–6 tbsp extra-virgin olive oil
- 2 tbsp white wine vinegar
- salt and freshly ground black pepper to taste

Boil the potatoes in their skins in a large pot of salted, boiling water for 20–25 minutes, or until tender. • Drain well, let cool enough to handle, then slip off the skins. • Chop into bite-sized chunks and transfer to a large salad bowl. • Add the mint and garlic. Toss well. • Mix the oil and vinegar in a small bowl. Pour over the potatoes. Season with salt and pepper and serve.

843

GREEN BEAN, TUNA, AND EGG RICE SALAD

Cook the green beans in salted, boiling water for 7–10 minutes, or until crunchy-tender. • Drain and set aside. • Drain the tuna, breaking it up with a fork. • Place the eggs in a pan of cold water and bring to a boil. Boil for 7 minutes. • Drain and let cool completely. • Peel and set aside. • Cook the rice in a large pot of salted, boiling water with 1 tablespoon of oil for 12–15 minutes, or until tender. • Drain and let cool completely. • Mix the lemon juice, the remaining oil, garlic, and oregano in a small bowl. Season with pepper. Discard the garlic. • Drizzle the dressing over the rice. Transfer to a large serving dish and top with the tuna and beans. • Crumble the yolks from 2 eggs over the top of the rice. • Garnish with the basil and the remaining eggs (cut into wedges).

844

Serves: 4–6

Preparation: 25'

Cooking: 30'

Level of difficulty: 2

- 10 oz/300 g green beans, topped and tailed
- ¾ cup/150 g tuna in oil
- 4 eggs
- 2 cups/400 g Basmati rice
- 5 tbsp extra-virgin olive oil
- juice of 1 lemon
- 1 clove garlic, lightly crushed but whole
- ⅛ tsp oregano
- salt and freshly ground black pepper to taste
- 1 sprig basil, to garnish

PAPPARDELLE SALAD WITH SPINACH AND ROQUEFORT

Serves: 4

Preparation: 25'

Cooking: 15'

Level of difficulty: 2

- 1 shallot, finely chopped
- 1 clove garlic, finely chopped
- 3 tbsp extra-virgin olive oil
- 7 oz/200 g spinach leaves
- salt and freshly ground black pepper to taste
- 3½ oz/100 g rolled pancetta, sliced
- ½ cup/50 g chopped walnuts
- 14 oz/400 g fresh pappardelle or tagliatelle pasta
- 1 onion, finely chopped
- 3 oz/90 g Roquefort cheese, diced
- 1 tbsp finely chopped parsley

Sauté the shallot and garlic in 1 tablespoon of oil in a large frying pan until softened. • Add the spinach and season with salt. Cover and cook for 7 minutes, or until the spinach has wilted. • Chop the spinach coarsely. Transfer to a dish and set aside. • In the same oil, sauté the pancetta and walnuts until the pancetta is crispy. • Drain well on paper towels. • Cook the pappardelle in a large pot of salted, boiling water until al dente. • Drain and let cool completely. • Transfer the pasta to a large bowl and drizzle with the remaining oil. • Add the spinach, pancetta, walnuts, shallot, and Roquefort. Mix well. Season with salt and pepper and garnish with the parsley.

RICE SALAD WITH GARBANZO BEANS AND TOMATOES

Cook the rice in a large pot of salted, boiling water with 1 tablespoon of oil for 12–15 minutes, or until tender. • Drain and let cool completely. • Transfer the rice to a large bowl. • Mix the remaining oil, vinegar, and red pepper flakes in a small bowl. Pour the dressing over the rice and toss well. • Mix half the tomatoes and half the garbanzo beans into the rice. Add the mint and mix well. Season with salt. • Top the rice salad with the remaining tomatoes and garbanzo beans. Garnish with a sprig of mint.

Serves:	4–6
Preparation:	25'
Cooking:	15'
Level of difficulty:	1

- 2½ cups/500 g Italian risotto rice
- 4 tbsp extra-virgin olive oil
- 2 tbsp red wine vinegar
- ⅛ tsp red pepper flakes
- 1 lb/500 g cherry tomatoes, thinly sliced
- 3 cups/300 g canned garbanzo beans/chickpeas
- 1 bunch mint, torn + extra, to garnish
- salt to taste

BUCKWHEAT-FILLED PEARS

Serves: 5

Preparation: 20'

Cooking: 20'

Level of difficulty: 1

- 2½ oz/75 g dried apricots, soaked in warm water, drained, and chopped coarsely
- 1 clove garlic, finely chopped
- juice and zest of 2 lemons
- 5 oz/150 g buckwheat
- ¾ cup/75 g chopped walnuts
- 4 tbsp extra-virgin olive oil
- 1 tbsp mustard
- salt and freshly ground black pepper to taste
- 5 firm-ripe pears
- 10 sprigs mint, to garnish

Mix the apricots, garlic, and lemon juice (reserving 2 tablespoons) in a large bowl.
• Cook the buckwheat in a large pot of salted, boiling water for 20 minutes. • Drain and let cool completely. • Add the buckwheat and walnuts to the salad. • Mix the oil, the reserved lemon juice, and mustard in a small bowl. Season with salt and pepper. • Pour the dressing over the salad and mix well. • Halve the pears, removing the core. • Fill each half with the buckwheat mixture.
• Garnish with the mint and serve.

An attractive, palate-cleansing salad to finish a meal.

851

BULGUR SALAD WITH CHEESE ROLLS

Place the bulgur in a large bowl and cover with cold water for 30 minutes. • Peel the cucumbers and remove the seeds. Chop the flesh coarsely. Sprinkle with salt and let drain for 20 minutes. • Halve the tomatoes and remove the seeds. Chop coarsely. • Drain the bulgur, breaking up the grains with a fork. • Mix in the tomatoes, scallions, parsley, and half the mint. Season with salt and pepper and drizzle with the lemon juice and oil. • Mix well and refrigerate for 2 hours. • Mix the yogurt, cucumber, the remaining mint, garlic, cumin, and coriander in a medium bowl. Season with salt and pepper. • Cover with plastic wrap and refrigerate until ready to serve. • Cheese Rolls: Mix the goat's cheese, egg, parsley, and dill in a medium bowl. • Cut out 7 x 5-inch (18 x 13-cm) rectangles from the pastry. • Put a spoonful of cheese filling on each, leaving a 1-inch (2.5-cm) border on the short ends. • Wrap the pastry round the filling to make little horns. Dampen the edges with a little water to make sure they stick together. • Heat the oil in a large, deep frying pan until very hot. Fry the rolls in small batches for 5–7 minutes, or until golden and crispy. • Drain well on paper towels. • Spoon the bulgur into serving bowls and top with the cheese rolls. Garnish with the olives and serve with the yogurt sauce passed on the side.

Serves: 4

Preparation: 1 h 30' + 2 h to chill

Cooking: 10'

Level of difficulty: 3

- 7 oz/200 g bulgur
- 2 cucumbers
- salt and freshly ground black pepper to taste
- 3 tomatoes
- 2 scallions/spring onions, finely chopped
- 2 tbsp finely chopped parsley
- 1 tsp finely chopped mint
- juice of 2 lemons
- 1¼ cups/310 g plain yogurt
- 2 cloves garlic, finely chopped
- ⅛ tsp cumin
- ⅛ tsp coriander

CHEESE ROLLS
- ¾ cup/180 g goat's cheese
- 1 egg
- 1 tbsp finely chopped parsley
- 1 tbsp finely chopped dill
- 5 oz/150 g phyllo pastry
- 1 cup/250 ml olive oil, for frying
- 1 cup/100 g black olives

SPICY EGGPLANT SALAD

Place the eggplant in a colander. Sprinkle with salt and let drain for 1 hour. • Heat the oil in a large frying pan. Fry the eggplants in batches for 5–7 minutes, or until tender. • Drain well on paper towels. • Transfer the eggplant to a large bowl. Mix in the bell pepper, radishes, scallions, tomato, garlic, parsley, cumin, red pepper flakes, salt, lemon juice, and oil. • Toss well and serve.

854

Serves: 4

Preparation: 15' + 1 h to drain eggplants

Cooking: 20'

Level of difficulty: 1

- 1 large eggplant/ aubergine, cut into cubes
- 1 cup/250 ml olive oil, for frying
- 1 green bell pepper/capsicum, seeded, cored, and finely chopped
- 6 radishes, finely chopped
- 4 scallions/spring onions, finely chopped
- 1 firm-ripe tomato, finely chopped
- 2 cloves garlic, finely chopped
- 3 tbsp finely chopped parsley
- 1 tsp cumin seeds
- 1 tsp red pepper flakes
- ½ tsp salt
- 1 tbsp fresh lemon juice
- 4 tbsp extra-virgin olive oil

SIMPLE SUMMER SALAD

Place the onions in a salad bowl and season with salt. • Add the tomatoes, cucumber, bell pepper, and chile pepper. • Mix the oil and lemon juice in a small bowl. Season with salt and pepper. • Drizzle the dressing over the salad and toss well. • Garnish with the olives.

856

- 2 medium onions, thinly sliced
- salt and freshly ground black pepper to taste
- 2 large firm-ripe tomatoes, coarsely chopped
- 1 cucumber, cubed
- 1 green bell pepper/capsicum, seeded and cubed
- 1 fresh red chile pepper, finely sliced
- 6 tbsp extra-virgin olive oil
- 2 tbsp fresh lemon juice
- black olives, to garnish

Serves: 6
Preparation: 40'
Level of difficulty: 1

- 2 cups/200 g fine- or medium-grind bulgur
- 2 medium tomatoes, finely chopped
- 4 scallions/spring onions, finely chopped
- 1 fresh red or green chile pepper, thinly sliced
- 4 tbsp finely chopped parsley
- 1 tbsp finely chopped mint
- 4 tbsp extra-virgin olive oil
- juice of 1 lemon
- salt and freshly ground black pepper to taste

PIQUANT BULGUR SALAD

Place the bulgur in a bowl and cover with cold water. Let stand for 30 minutes. • Drain well. • Stir in the tomatoes, scallions, chile pepper, parsley, and mint. • Drizzle with the oil and lemon juice and season with salt and pepper. • Serve.

POMEGRANATE SALAD

C ut the pomegranate into quarters, reserving the seeds and juice. • Mix the oil, vinegars, and pomegranate juice in a small bowl. Season with salt and pepper. • Arrange the salad greens, onion, and scallions in layers in a large salad bowl. • Drizzle with the oil mixture and toss well. • Garnish with the pomegranate seeds.

Serves: 4

Preparation: 15'

Level of difficulty: 1

- 1 pomegranate
- 6 tbsp extra-virgin olive oil
- 2 tsp sherry wine vinegar
- 1 tbsp red wine vinegar
- salt and freshly ground black pepper to taste
- 8 oz/200 g mixed salad greens
- 1 red onion, finely chopped
- 2 scallions/spring onions, finely chopped

WARM GREEN BEAN AND TUNA SALAD

Serves: 6

Preparation: 20'

Cooking: 10'

Level of difficulty: 1

- 1½ lb/750 g green beans
- 2 tbsp extra-virgin olive oil
- 1 tbsp balsamic vinegar
- 1 medium onion, cut into thin rings
- salt and freshly ground black pepper to taste
- 1 cup/200 g canned tuna in oil, drained and broken up with a fork

Cook the green beans in salted, boiling water for 5–7 minutes, or until crunchy-tender. • Drain well and cut into short lengths. • Mix the oil, vinegar, and onion in a large salad bowl. Season with salt and pepper. • Add the green beans and tuna. • Toss carefully and serve.

FRENCH RICE SALAD

Bring the water to a boil in a large pot with the rice, bay leaf, and whole onion. • Lower the heat and simmer for 25–30 minutes, or until the rice is tender. • Drain well, discarding the bay leaf and onion. Let cool. • Mix the rice, onion rings (reserving a few rings to garnish), tomatoes, bell peppers, and green and black olives in a large salad bowl. • Mix the vinegar and oil in a small bowl. Season with salt and pepper and drizzle over the salad. Toss the salad and top with the reserved onion rings and anchovies.

Serves: 4–6

Preparation: 15'

Cooking: 30'

Level of difficulty: 1

- 2 quarts/2 liters water
- 1¼ cups/250 g short-grain rice (preferably red Camargue rice)
- 1 bay leaf
- 2 onions (1 whole, 1 thinly sliced)
- 6 tomatoes, peeled, seeded, and finely chopped
- 2 red bell peppers/ capsicums, seeded and cut into strips
- ½ cup/50 g green olives
- ½ cup/50 g black olives
- 1 tbsp white wine vinegar
- 6 tbsp extra-virgin olive oil
- salt and freshly ground black pepper to taste
- 6 anchovy fillets

POTATO SALAD WITH LEMON DRESSING

Boil the potatoes in their skins in a large pot of salted water for 20–25 minutes, or until cooked. • Drain well and let cool completely. • Slip off the skins and cut into small cubes. • Mix the potatoes, parsley, and scallions in a large salad bowl. • Mix the garlic, lemon juice, and oil in a small bowl. Pour over the potatoes and toss well. • Refrigerate for at least 1 hour before serving.

Serves: 4

Preparation: 10' + 1 h to chill

Cooking: 25'

Level of difficulty: 1

- 6 medium potatoes, well-washed
- 2 tbsp finely chopped parsley
- 2 scallions/spring onions, trimmed and finely chopped
- 1 clove garlic, finely chopped
- juice of 1 lemon
- ½ cup/125 ml extra-virgin olive oil

BAKED ZUCCHINI SALAD

Serves: 6

Preparation: 15'

Cooking: 45'

Level of difficulty: 1

- **3 lb/1.5 kg zucchini/ courgettes, peeled and thickly sliced**
- **salt and freshly ground black pepper to taste**
- **¹⁄₂ cup/125 ml extra-virgin olive oil**
- **2 tbsp finely chopped parsley**
- **2 cloves garlic, finely chopped**

Preheat the oven to 400°F/200°C/gas 6.
• Place the zucchini in a large oiled baking dish.
Season with salt and pepper and drizzle with
4 tablespoons of oil. • Bake for 40–45 minutes,
turning frequently to brown. • Remove from the
oven and let drain in a colander. • Arrange on a
deep serving plate and drizzle with the remaining
oil. Sprinkle with the parsley and garlic and toss
gently. • Refrigerate until ready to serve.

SPICY CARROT SALAD

Serves: 6

Preparation: 10'

Cooking: 25'

Level of difficulty: 1

- 1 lb/500 g carrots, cut into thin strips
- 3 cloves garlic, finely chopped
- 4 tbsp extra-virgin olive oil
- 2 tsp caraway seeds
- 1 tsp freshly ground coriander seeds
- 1 tsp finely chopped fresh sweet red chile pepper
- 1 tbsp Harissa (see page 52)
- 1 tbsp white wine vinegar or fresh lemon juice
- salt to taste
- 3 tbsp capers, to garnish

Cook the carrots in a large pot of salted, boiling water for 8–10 minutes, or until crunchy-tender. • Drain well, reserving 1 cup (250 ml) of the cooking water. • Sauté the garlic in the oil in a large frying pan over medium heat for 5 minutes, or until pale gold. • Add the carrots, reserved water, caraway seeds, coriander, chile, harissa, and vinegar. Season with salt. • Cook over high heat for 8–10 minutes, or until the sauce has reduced. • Remove from heat and let cool. • Serve at room temperature, garnished with the capers.

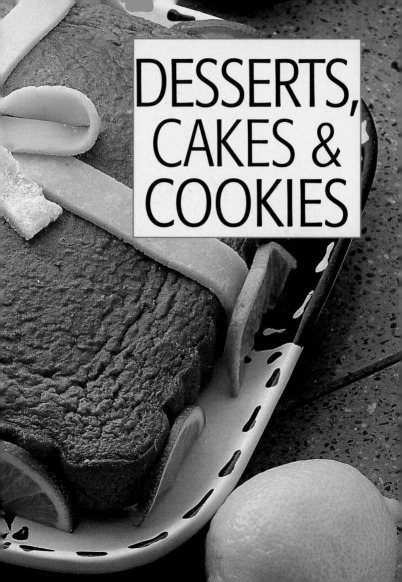

DESSERTS, CAKES & COOKIES

ORANGES WITH WHISKY

Serves: 4

Preparation: 40' + 2 h
to macerate

Cooking: 30'

Level of difficulty: 3

- 8 large oranges
- 2 cups/500 ml
  water
- 2 cups/400 g
  sugar
- 1 vanilla pod
- 6 tbsp whisky
- 1¼ cups/310 ml
  heavy/double
  cream

Peel the oranges, taking care to remove all the inner pith. Reserve the peel. • Cut the peeled oranges into segments. Arrange the segments in a single layer in a shallow bowl. • Bring the water, 1^1/$_2$ cups (300 g) of sugar, and vanilla to a boil in a small saucepan over medium heat. • Lower the heat and simmer for 10 minutes. • Remove from the heat and add the whisky. Mix well and pour over the oranges. • Macerate in a cool place for about 2 hours. • Cut the reserved peel into very thin strips and place in a small saucepan. Cover with water, bring to a boil over low heat, and simmer for 10 minutes. • Remove from the heat. Drain and rinse with cold water. • Return the zest to the saucepan with the remaining sugar and 1 tablespoon of the orange soaking syrup. • Caramelize over low heat for 3–4 minutes, or until the sugar is melted and golden. Transfer to a plate and let cool. • Beat the cream in a large bowl until stiff. • Arrange the oranges in serving dishes. Drizzle with the syrup, top with the caramelized peel, and serve with the cream.

CARAMELIZED FIGS WITH MASCARPONE

Wash and dry the figs carefully, making sure the peel is intact. Make two cuts in each one, starting from the stem as if to cut into quarters. • Arrange the figs on a baking sheet covered with oiled waxed paper. Sprinkle each fig with 1 teaspoon of sugar. • Turn on the broiler (grill). Broil for 2–3 minutes, or until the sugar has caramelized slightly. • Beat the Mascarpone, confectioners' sugar, and vin santo in a medium bowl until smooth. • Serve the figs with the Mascarpone cream.

Serves: 4

Preparation: 20'

Cooking: 3

Level of difficulty: 1

- 8 ripe green figs
- 8 tsp brown sugar
- 1¼ cups/310 ml Mascarpone cheese
- 3 tbsp confectioners'/ icing sugar
- ½ cup/125 ml vin santo or sweet sherry

PEACHES STUFFED WITH WALNUTS

Preheat the oven to 400°F/200°C/gas 6.
• Cut the peaches in half and remove the pits.
Pit the cherries and chop coarsely. • Scoop out
some of the peach flesh and chop coarsely. Place
in a bowl with $1/3$ cup (70 g) of sugar, the amaretti
cookies, walnuts, brandy, cocoa, butter, lemon
zest, and cherries. Mix well. • Fill the peaches with
the mixture. Sprinkle with the remaining sugar.
• Bake for 20 minutes. • Serve hot.

Serves: 4

Preparation: 20'

Cooking: 20'

Level of difficulty: 1

- • 4 yellow peaches
- • 12 cherries
- • $2/3$ cup/140 g
  firmly packed
  brown sugar
- • $1/2$ cup/60 g
  amaretti cookies,
  crumbled
- • $1/2$ cup/50 g
  chopped walnuts
- • 4 tbsp brandy
- • 2 tbsp unsweetened
  cocoa powder
- • 2 tbsp butter,
  softened
- • grated zest
  of 1 lemon

STUFFED DATES

Pit the dates by cutting them lengthwise down one side only. • Stir together the almonds and raw sugar in a large bowl. • Mix the orange-flower water and food coloring in a small bowl. Add to the almond mixture and stir until well mixed. • Mix the confectioners' sugar with enough water to make a thick paste. • Fill the dates with the almond paste. Dip in the confectioners' sugar paste, then roll in the sugar.

Serves: 10–12

Preparation: 15'

Level of difficulty: 1

- 1¾ lb/750 g dates
- 3 cups/300 g finely ground almonds
- 1 cup/200 g raw sugar
- 1 tbsp orange-flower water or rose water
- ¼ tsp green food coloring
- 1 cup/150 g confectioners'/icing sugar
- 2 tbsp water or more as needed
- ½ cup/100 g sugar

SPELT TART WITH RASPBERRIES

Pastry: Mix the spelt, butter, sugar, and wine in a large bowl to form a dough. • Shape into a ball, wrap in plastic wrap, and refrigerate for 30 minutes. • Preheat the oven to 400°F/200°C/ gas 6. • Roll the dough out on a lightly floured surface to ¼ inch (5 mm) thick. • Use the pastry to line a 11 x 7-inch (28 x 18-cm) shallow baking pan. Prick all over with a fork. • Cover with aluminum foil and fill with pie weights or dried beans. • Bake for 20 minutes. • Remove the foil and beans. • Filling: Mix the crème fraiche, eggs, sugar, and cinnamon in a large bowl. • Spoon the filling into the pastry case. • Bake for 25–30 minutes, or until set. • Let cool completely. • Arrange the raspberries on top and dust with the confectioners' sugar.

Serves: 6

Preparation: 40' + 30' to chill

Cooking: 50'

Level of difficulty: 2

PASTRY

- 1⅔ cups/250 g finely ground spelt
- ½ cup/125 g butter
- 2 tbsp sugar
- 2 tbsp dry white wine

FILLING

- ¾ cup/180 ml crème fraiche or sour cream
- 3 large eggs
- ½ cup/100 g sugar
- 1 tsp ground cinnamon
- 14 oz/400 g raspberries, hulled
- 2 tbsp confectioners'/ icing sugar

CHOCOLATE CREAM AND RASPBERRY DESSERT

Melt the chocolate over barely simmering water. Mix into half of the custard. • Arrange a layer of sponge cake on the bottom of a glass bowl. Drizzle with half the liqueur. • Spoon in the plain custard and top with half the raspberries. • Cover with another layer of sponge slices and drizzle with the remaining liqueur. • Add the chocolate custard and sprinkle with the hazelnuts (reserving a few for decoration). • Add the remaining raspberries. Cover with plastic wrap and refrigerate for 1 hour. • Add the whipped cream. Sprinkle with the cocoa powder and remaining chopped hazelnuts.

Serves: 6

Preparation: 25' + 1 h to chill

Level of difficulty: 2

- 8 oz/250 ml semisweet/dark chocolate, coarsely chopped
- 1 quantity Custard (see recipe Greek cinnamon pudding, page 892)
- 5 oz/150 g Sponge Cake (see recipe Italian chocolate cream roll, page 902), thinly sliced
- ²/₃ cup/150 ml raspberry liqueur
- 1¼ lb/575 g raspberries, hulled
- ½ cup/50 g chopped hazelnuts
- ¾ cup/180 ml whipped cream
- 1 tbsp unsweetened cocoa powder

CHOCOLATE MILLEFEUILLE WITH MINT CREAM

Melt the chocolate in a double boiler over barely simmering water. • Pour the melted chocolate over a large sheet of waxed paper and spread to a thickness of $1/8$ inch (3 mm). • Let stand until set. • Cut the sheet into 18 rectangles of equal size. • Finely chop the mint, reserving a few leaves to garnish. • Beat the cream and sugar in a large bowl until stiff. Mix in the chopped mint. • Refrigerate until ready to use. • Place a rectangle of chocolate on each serving plate. Top with a spoonful of cream and a few raspberries. Cover with another piece of chocolate, more cream and raspberries and finish with another layer of chocolate. • Decorate with the reserved mint leaves and raspberries. Dust with the confectioners' sugar.

Serves: 6

Preparation: 35'

Level of difficulty: 2

- 10 oz/300 g semisweet/dark chocolate
- 1 sprig mint
- $1^{1}/4$ cups/310 ml heavy/double cream
- 4 tbsp sugar
- 14 oz/400 g raspberries, hulled
- $1/3$ cup/50 g confectioners'/icing sugar

RASPBERRY CHEESECAKE

Serves: 8

Preparation: 1 h

Cooking: 1 h

Level of difficulty: 2

BASE
- 1¾ cups/215 g graham cracker crumbs/crushed digestive biscuits
- ⅔ cup/150 g butter, melted

FILLING
- 7 oz/200 g raspberries, hulled
- ⅓ cup/50 g confectioners/icing sugar
- 2 eggs, separated
- ⅓ cup/70 g sugar
- 1¼ cups/310 g Ricotta cheese
- ½ cup/125 ml heavy/double cream
- grated zest and juice of 1 lemon
- ⅛ tsp salt

Preheat the oven to 350°F/180°C/gas 4. • Line an 8½-inch (22-cm) springform pan with waxed paper. • Crumb Base: Mix the crumbs and butter in a medium bowl. • Firmly press the crumb mixture into the bottom and sides of the prepared pan. • Filling: Process the raspberries with the confectioners' sugar in a food processor or blender until puréed. Strain through a sieve to remove the seeds. • Beat the egg yolks and sugar in a medium bowl with an electric mixer at medium speed until pale and thick. • Mix in the Ricotta, cream, and lemon zest and juice. • Beat the egg whites and salt in a medium bowl until stiff. Fold them into the mixture. • Pour the mixture into the crumb base, smoothing the top. Drizzle 1 teaspoon of the raspberry purée onto the surface and drag with a toothpick to decorate. • Bake for about 1 hour, or until almost completely set. • Turn off the oven and let the cheesecake cool with the door ajar. • Loosen and remove the pan sides and bottom. Transfer the cheesecake to a serving dish and serve with the raspberry purèe.

APPLE GRATIN WITH GRAPE SAUCE

Serves: 6

Preparation: 45' + 1 h to macerate

Cooking: 1 h

Level of difficulty: 3

GRAPE SAUCE
- 10 oz/300 g black grapes
- ½ cup/100 g sugar
- 4 tbsp water

APPLES
- 1 quart/1 liter water
- 1 vanilla pod
- 1¾ cups/350g sugar
- juice of 1 lemon
- 4 apples, peeled and cut into wedges

BASE
- 1 large egg
- ½ cup/100 g sugar
- scant ½ cup/100 g butter, softened
- 1 cup/100 g slivered almonds
- 2 tbsp all-purpose/ plain flour

Crush the grapes with a fork in a medium bowl. Add ¼ cup (50 g) of sugar. Let macerate for 1 hour. • Preheat the oven to 425°F/220°C/gas 7. • Line an 8-inch (20-cm) baking pan with waxed paper. • Apples: Bring the water, vanilla pod, sugar, and lemon juice to a boil in a large saucepan. • Add the apples and return to a boil. Cook for 5 minutes, or until the apples are tender but still crunchy. • Drain on a plate. • Base: Beat the egg, sugar, and butter in a medium bowl until creamy. • Mix in the almonds and flour. • Spread the cream in the prepared pan. • Arrange the apple slices on top. • Bake for 25 minutes, or until golden. • Let cool completely. • Grape Sauce: Strain the grape mixture, eliminating the seeds and skins. • Caramelize ¼ cup (50 g) of sugar with the water in a small saucepan until it begins to turn dark. • Add the grape juice and cook over medium sauce for 15–20 minutes to make a syrup.
• Serve the apple gratin with the warm sauce passed on the side.

UPSIDE-DOWN APPLE TART

Pastry: Sift the flour and salt into a large bowl. •
Use a pastry blender to cut in the butter until
the mixture resembles fine crumbs. Add enough
water and knead quickly with your hands to form a
fairly stiff dough. • Gather the crumbs and shape
into a ball. Wrap in plastic wrap (cling film) and chill
in the refrigerator for 1 hour. • Preheat the oven to
350°F/180°C/gas 4. • Caramel: Heat the sugar
and water in a small saucepan over low heat until
caramelized. • Pour the caramel into a
9-inch (23-cm) round cake pan. • Sprinkle with
the brown sugar and dot with the butter. • Topping:
Arrange the apples in the prepared pan and
sprinkle with the brown sugar. • Roll the pastry out
on a lightly floured surface to fit the pan. Cover the
apples with the pastry. • Bake for 40–45 minutes,
or until golden brown. • Invert the tart onto a
serving plate and let cool. • Serve hot or at
room temperature.

Serves: 6

Preparation: 35' + 1 h
to chill pastry

Cooking: 45'

Level of difficulty: 2

PASTRY
- 2 cups/300 g all-
  purpose/plain flour
- ½ tsp salt
- ½ cup/125 g
  butter, cut up
- 4–6 tbsp ice water

CARAMEL
- ½ cup/100 g sugar
- 1 tbsp cold water
- 1 tbsp brown sugar

TOPPING
- 1 cup/200 g firmly
  packed dark brown
  sugar
- ½ cup/125 g
  butter, cut up
- 6 apples, peeled,
  cored and
  quartered

BERRY CLAFOUTIS

Preheat the oven to 400°F/200°C/gas 6. • Line an 8-inch (20-cm) flan dish with waxed paper. • Beat the eggs, sugar, and lemon zest in a large bowl with an electric mixer at medium speed until pale and thick. • With mixer at low speed, mix in the milk, yogurt, and flour. • Arrange the bilberries and blackberries in the prepared dish.
• Pour the egg mixture over the berry fruit. • Bake for about 45 minutes, or until browned and set.
• Serve warm.

This classic French clafoutis is served in the summer as a light dessert.

Serves: 4

Preparation: 25'

Cooking: 45'

Level of difficulty: 1

- **3 eggs**
- **¹⁄₃ cup/70 g firmly packed brown sugar**
- **grated zest of 1 lemon**
- **1¹⁄₂ cups/375 ml milk**
- **¹⁄₂ cup/125 ml low fat yogurt**
- **¹⁄₂ cup/75 g all-purpose/plain flour**
- **8 oz/250 g bilberries**
- **8 oz/250 g blackberries**

GREEK CINNAMON PUDDING

Syrup: Place the water, sugar, brandy, and honey in a medium saucepan over medium-low heat and bring to a boil. Simmer for 15 minutes. Set aside to cool. • Custard: Place the milk and sugar in a saucepan and whisk in the egg yolks, flour, and cornstarch. Place over medium-low heat and stir with a wooden spoon until thickened. • Remove from heat, let cool a little, then cover with plastic wrap to prevent a skin from forming on the top (or stir often). • Rusk Base: Line a glass trifle dish with the rusks. Pour the cooled syrup over the top. The syrup should cover the rusks completely. Dust with the cinnamon. • Spoon the cooled custard over the rusks. Refrigerate for 2 hours. • Topping: Beat the cream and sugar in a large bowl until stiff. • Decorate the pudding with the cream. Dust with the cinnamon and sprinkle with the nuts just before serving.

Serves: 6

Preparation: 40' + 2 h to chill

Cooking: 30'

Level of difficulty: 2

SYRUP
- 1 cup/250 ml water
- 1 cup/200 g sugar
- ½ cup/125 ml brandy
- 4 tbsp honey

CUSTARD
- 3 cups/750 ml milk
- ¾ cup/150 g sugar
- 2 large egg yolks, lightly beaten
- 2 tbsp all-purpose/plain flour
- 2 tbsp cornstarch/cornflour

RUSK BASE
- 1 package square rusks
- 2 tsp ground cinnamon

TOPPING
- 1 cup/250 ml heavy/double cream
- 2 tbsp sugar
- 1 tsp ground cinnamon
- ½ cup/50 g slivered almonds

SICILIAN CASSATA

Serves: 6

Preparation: 25' + 2 h to chill

Cooking: 10'

Level of difficulty: 3

Line a 9-inch (23-cm) cake pan with waxed paper. Line with the cake slices. • Warm the preserves and water in a small saucepan until liquid. • Fill the spaces in the pan with the preserves. • Filling: Warm the sugar, water, and vanilla in a saucepan over medium heat, stirring constantly, until the sugar has dissolved. • Place the Ricotta in a large bowl and gradually beat in the sugar mixture until stiff. • Use a large rubber mixture to mix in the candied fruit peel and pistachios. Add the kirsch. • Pour the mixture over the cake slices. • Refrigerate for 2 hours. • Dip the pan briefly in cold water and invert onto a plate. • Orange Glaze: Mix the confectioners' sugar, preserves, and orange flower water in a saucepan over medium heat until smooth. • Drizzle over the cake. • Decorate with the remaining candied fruit.

- 1 Sponge Cake (see recipe Italian chocolate cream roll, page 902), cut into ½-inch/1-cm thick slices
- 6 tbsp apricot preserves
- 2 tsp water

FILLING

- 1¼ cups/250 g sugar
- 1 tbsp water
- ½ tsp vanilla extract/essence
- 2 cups/500 ml Ricotta cheese
- 3 cups/300 g mixed candied peel, chopped
- 2 tbsp chopped pistachios
- 2 tsp kirsch

ORANGE GLAZE

- 1⅓ cups/200 g confectioners'/ icing sugar
- ½ cup/160 g apricot preserves
- 2 tsp orange flower water
- 1 cup/100 g mixed candied peel, to decorate

SEMOLINA DESSERT

Serves: 4

Preparation: 15'

Cooking: 30'

Level of difficulty: 1

- ½ cup/125 g butter
- ¾ cup/125 g semolina
- ⅓ cup/70 g sugar
- 1 tsp almond extract/essence
- 2 cups/500 ml milk
- 1 tbsp golden raisins/sultanas
- 1 tbsp slivered almonds

Melt the butter in a small saucepan. • Gradually sprinkle in the semolina, stirring constantly. Cook over low heat until golden. • Add the sugar and almond extract. • Pour in the milk and cook over low heat until thick and creamy. • Spoon into a bowl and sprinkle with the golden raisins and slivered almonds. • Serve at room temperature or chilled.

APRICOT CRÊPES

Serves: 4

Preparation: 40' + 30' to rest

Cooking: 20'

Level of difficulty: 2

CRÊPES
- ²/₃ cup/100 g all-purpose/plain flour
- ⅛ tsp salt
- 2 large eggs
- 1 tbsp sugar
- ²/₃ cup/150 ml whole milk
- 2 tbsp butter, melted

FILLING
- 8 apricots
- ⅓ cup/80 g Ricotta cheese
- 2 oz/60 g semisweet/dark chocolate, chopped
- 1 tbsp brown sugar
- ½ tsp ground cinnamon
- 1 cup/250 ml peanut oil, for frying

Sift the flour and salt into a medium bowl. • Beat in the eggs and sugar. • Gradually pour in the milk and beat the batter until smooth. • Set aside for 30 minutes. • Brush a small, heated frying pan with the butter, and add a small ladleful of batter. Spread evenly by tipping the pan, so that it forms a thin film. Cook each crêpe on both sides, taking care not to let them color too much. When the edges curl slightly, it is done. • Filling: Halve and pit the apricots. • Mix the Ricotta, chocolate, sugar, and cinnamon in a small bowl. Stuff the apricots with the mixture and put the halves back together. Wrap each apricot in a crêpe and tie with cooking string. • Heat the oil in a small, deep frying pan until very hot. Fry the crêpes, two or three at a time, for 2–3 minutes, or until golden all over. • Drain well on paper towels. • Serve warm.

COCONUT AND CHOCOLATE SEMIFREDDO

Serves: 4

Preparation: 25' + 4 h to freeze

Level of difficulty: 2

- 1 tsp orange flower water
- 1¼ cups/310 g Ricotta cheese
- ¾ cup/150 g sugar
- ¾ cup/90 g shredded/desiccated coconut
- ½ tsp vanilla extract/essence
- 4 oz/125 g semisweet/dark chocolate, chopped
- 2 cups/500 ml heavy/double cream
- 2 kiwi fruit
- 2 star anise
- 1 ripe mango
- 1 ripe papaya/pawpaw

Dampen a sheet of waxed paper with the orange flower water. Use the paper to line a loaf pan.
• Process the Ricotta, sugar, coconut, and vanilla in a food processor or blender until smooth. • Stir in the chocolate. • Beat the cream in a large bowl until stiff, then carefully fold it into the mixture. • Spoon the mixture into the prepared pan. • Freeze for 4 hours. • Cut the kiwi fruit and star anise into slices and the mango and papaya into thin segments. • Turn the semifreddo out onto a serving platter. • Decorate with the fruit and serve in thick slices.

Serve this cooling dessert to finish a meal during the hot summer months. Vary the fruit as liked.

901

ITALIAN CHOCOLATE CREAM ROLL

S ponge Cake: Preheat the oven to 350°F/
180°C/gas 4. • Line a 11 x 15-inch
(28 x 38-cm) jelly roll pan with parchment paper.
• Sift the flour, cornstarch, and baking powder into
a large bowl. • Beat the egg yolks and sugar in a
large bowl with an electric mixer at high speed until
pale and frothy. • Use a large rubber spatula to fold
in the dry ingredients and melted butter. • Beat the
egg whites and salt in a separate large bowl with
mixer at high speed until stiff peaks form. • Fold
the whites into the batter. • Spoon the batter into
the prepared pan. Bake for about 15 minutes, or
until a toothpick inserted into the center comes out
clean. • Lay out a large clean cloth. Sprinkle with
the confectioners' sugar. • Cool the cake in the pan
for 10 minutes, then turn out onto the cloth.
Carefully remove the parchment paper and use a
sharp knife to trim away the crisp edges. • Using
the cloth as a guide, roll the cake up. Leave, seam-
side down, until completely cooled. • Filling: Melt
the chocolate in a double boiler over barely
simmering water. • Unroll the cake and brush all
over with the Alchermes. • Stir the chocolate into
the custard. • Spread the cake with the chocolate
custard. Re-roll the cake. • Dust with the
confectioners' sugar just before serving.

Serves: 6	
Preparation: 45'	
Cooking: 15'	
Level of difficulty: 2	

SPONGE CAKE

- 1 cup/150 g all-purpose/plain flour
- ⅓ cup/50 g cornstarch/cornflour
- 1 tsp baking powder
- 5 large eggs, separated
- 4 tbsp butter, melted
- 1¼ cups/250 g sugar
- ⅛ tsp salt
- ⅓ cup/50 g confectioners'/icing sugar

FILLING

- 4 oz/125 g semisweet/dark chocolate
- 4 tbsp Alchermes liqueur (or few drops of red food coloring in 4 tbsp orange liqueur)
- 1 quantity Custard (see recipe Greek cinnamon pudding, page 892)
- ⅓ cup/50 g confectioners'/icing sugar

FRESH FRUIT ROULADE

Prepare the sponge cake. • Soften the gelatin in the water. • Bring the sugar, lemon juice, and pineapple juice to a boil in a small saucepan. • Simmer over medium heat until reduced by half. • Remove from the heat and mix in the lemon zest and the pineapple. • Mix in the egg yolks and and return to the heat. Cook, stirring constantly, over low heat until the mixture begins to thicken. • Add the gelatin mixture and let cool. • Beat the cream in a large bowl until stiff. • Refrigerate for 15 minutes. • Unroll the cake and spread with the pineapple cream. Cover with a layer of fruit. Re-roll the sponge. • Refrigerate for 30 minutes. • Dust with the confectioners' sugar just before serving. • Serve with the remaining fruit and the cream passed on the side.

Serves: 6–8

Preparation: 30' + 45' to chill

Cooking: 15'

Level of difficulty: 2

- 1 Sponge Cake (see recipe Italian chocolate cream roll, page 902)
- 1¼ tbsp gelatin (or 5 sheets gelatin)
- ½ cup/125 ml cold water
- ½ cup/100 g sugar
- grated zest and juice of 1 lemon
- 1 cup/250 ml pineapple juice
- 1 slice fresh pineapple, finely chopped
- 3 large egg yolks
- 2 cups/500 ml heavy/double cream
- 8 oz/250 g mixed fresh fruit (strawberries, melon, and kiwi fruit), cut into small chunks
- ⅓ cup/50 g confectioners'/icing sugar

ALMOND CAKE

Serves: 6

Preparation: 25'

Cooking: 40'

Level of difficulty: 1

Preheat the oven to 350°F/180°C/gas 4.
• Butter an 8-inch (20-cm) baking pan. • Sift the flour, baking powder, and salt into a large bowl. • Beat the eggs, sugar, and lemon zest in a large bowl with an electric mixer at medium speed until pale and thick. • With mixer at low speed, beat in the dry ingredients, butter, and two-thirds of the almonds. • Spoon the batter into the prepared pan. Sprinkle with the remaining almonds. • Bake for 35–40 minutes, or until a toothpick inserted into the center comes out clean. • Turn out onto a rack and let cool completely. • Dust with the confectioners' sugar and cinnamon.

- 1⅓ cups/200 g all-purpose/plain flour
- 1 tsp baking powder
- ⅛ tsp salt
- 3 large eggs
- 1 cup/200 g sugar
- grated zest of 1 lemon
- ¾ cup/180 g butter, melted
- 1 cup/100 g chopped almonds
- ⅓ cup/50 g confectioners'/icing sugar
- 1 tsp ground cinnamon

Serves: 8–10

Preparation: 40'

Rising time: 2 h

Cooking: 45'

Level of difficulty: 2

- 1 oz/30 g fresh yeast or 2 (¹/₄-oz/ 7-g) packages active dry yeast
- ¹/₂ cup/125 ml warm water + extra
- 3¹/₃ cups/500 g all-purpose/plain flour
- ¹/₈ tsp salt
- ³/₄ cup/150 g sugar
- 1 large egg
- 2 tbsp butter, softened
- 4 tbsp milk
- ¹/₄ cup/50 g golden raisins/sultanas
- 2 tsp ground anise
- 1 tbsp diced candied peel

ANISEED AND FRUIT LOAF

Mix the yeast and water in a small bowl. Let stand until foamy. • Sift the flour and salt into a large bowl. • Stir in the sugar, egg, butter, milk, the yeast mixture and enough extra water to form a soft, elastic dough. Knead in the raisins, anise, and candied peel. • Shape the dough into a ball and place in an oiled bowl. Cover with a cloth and let rise for 1 hour. • Shape into a long loaf.
• Transfer to a baking sheet. • Set aside in a warm place for 1 hour. • Preheat the oven to 350°F/180°C/gas 4. • Bake for about 45 minutes, or until dark golden brown. • Serve hot or at room temperature.

ZESTY CITRUS CAKE

Serves: 6–8

Preparation: 40'

Cooking: 35'

Level of difficulty: 2

- 1 cup/150 g all-purpose/plain flour
- ½ tsp baking powder
- ⅛ tsp salt
- 3 large eggs, separated
- ¾ cup/150 g sugar
- 5 tbsp extra-virgin olive oil
- 8 tbsp fresh orange juice
- 2 tbsp grated lemon zest
- 1 tbsp grated orange zest

SYRUP
- ¾ cup/180 ml fresh orange juice
- 5 tbsp lime juice
- ½ cup/100 g sugar

- marzipan, to decorate
- slices of lime, orange, and lemon, to garnish

Preheat the oven to 350°F/180°C/gas 4. • Butter a 9-inch (23-cm) square baking pan. • Sift the flour, baking powder, and salt into a large bowl. • Beat the egg yolks, sugar, oil, orange juice, and orange and lemon zest in a large bowl with an electric mixer at medium speed until pale and creamy. • With mixer at low speed, beat in the dry ingredients. • Beat the egg whites in a large bowl until stiff. • Fold into the batter. • Spoon the batter into the prepared pan. • Bake for about 35 minutes, or until a toothpick inserted into the center comes out clean. • Syrup: Bring the fruit juices and sugar to a boil in a small saucepan and boil for 2–3 minutes to make a syrup. • Use a toothpick to make small holes all over the warm cake. Drizzle with the syrup and let stand until the syrup has been absorbed. • Decorate with the strips of marzipan. • Garnish with slices of the citrus fruits around the edges.

Serves: 8

Preparation: 45'

Cooking: 45'

Level of difficulty: 2

- 2 tbsp fine dry bread crumbs
- 8 eggs, separated
- 1½ cups/300 g sugar
- 1⅔ cups/250 g finely ground almonds
- 4 amaretti cookies, crumbled
- ⅓ cup/50 g cornstarch/cornflour
- 1 tbsp ground cinnamon
- 5 cloves, crushed
- 1 tsp baking powder
- ½ tsp vanilla extract/essence
- ⅛ tsp salt
- ⅓ cup/50 g confectioners'/icing sugar

CUSTARD

- 2 cups/500 ml milk
- ½ vanilla pod
- 3 large egg yolks
- ⅓ cup/70 g sugar
- 1½ tbsp cornstarch/cornflour

SPICE CAKE WITH ENGLISH CUSTARD

Preheat the oven to 350°F/180°C/gas 4. • Butter a 9-inch (23-cm) baking pan and sprinkle the base with bread crumbs. • Beat the egg yolks and sugar in a large bowl with an electric mixer at high speed until pale and thick. • With mixer at low speed, beat in the almonds, amaretti cookies, cornstarch, cinnamon, cloves, baking powder, and vanilla until smooth. • Beat the egg whites and salt in a large bowl until stiff. Gently fold them into the batter. • Spoon the batter into the prepared pan. • Bake for 35–40 minutes, or until a toothpick inserted into the center comes out clean. • Turn out onto a rack and let cool completely. • Dust with the confectioners' sugar. • Custard: Bring the milk and vanilla pod to a boil in a medium saucepan. • Discard the vanilla. • Beat the egg yolks and sugar in a medium bowl until fluffy. Add the cornstarch. • Gradually pour in the milk, whisking constantly. • Return to low heat and cook until thickened, stirring continually. • Place a sheet of plastic wrap directly on the surface and let cool completely. • Serve the cake with the custard passed on the side.

NEAPOLITAN COOKIES

Preheat the oven to 350°F/180°C/gas 4. •
Butter two cookie sheets. • Sift the flour,
cocoa, cinnamon, and salt into a large bowl. • Mix
in the almonds and confectioners' sugar. • Stir in
the eggs to form a stiff dough. • Form the dough
into balls the size of walnuts. Flatten them to about
1/4 inch (5 mm) thick. • Bake for 12–15 minutes,
or until browned. • Brush the tops of the cookies
lightly with water and decorate with the sugar
sprinkles. • Let cool completely.

Serves: 8–10

Preparation: 25'

Cooking: 15'

Level of difficulty: 1

- 1/3 cup/50 g all-purpose/plain flour
- 2 tbsp unsweetened cocoa powder
- 1 tbsp ground cinnamon
- 1/8 tsp salt
- 10 oz/300 g toasted almonds, finely chopped
- 2 cups/300 g confectioners'/icing sugar
- 2 large eggs, lightly beaten
- 2 tbsp sugar sprinkles

FRIED COOKIE BOWS

Serves: 8–10
Preparation: 15'
Cooking: 25'
Level of difficulty: 2

- 3 cups/450 g all-purpose/plain flour
- ⅛ tsp salt
- 2 large eggs
- 2 tbsp sugar
- grated zest of 1 lemon
- 1 tbsp dry white wine
- 1 tbsp extra-virgin olive oil
- 1 cup/250 ml olive oil, for frying
- ⅓ cup/50 g confectioners'/icing sugar

Sift the flour and salt into a large bowl. • Mix in the eggs, sugar, lemon zest, wine, and the extra-virgin oil to form a stiff dough. • Roll the dough out and cut into strips about 1 x 6-inches (2.5 x 15-cm). • Heat the oil in a deep fryer until very hot. • Fry the cookies in small batches for 5–7 minutes, or until crisp and golden brown. • Drain well on paper towels. • Dust with the confectioners' sugar and serve.

ALMOND MACAROONS

Serves: 12
Preparation: 35'
Cooking: 35'
Level of difficulty: 2

P reheat the oven to 350°F/180°C/gas 4.
• Line two large baking sheets with waxed paper. • Toast the almonds on a large baking sheet until golden brown. • Process the almonds with the sugar in a food processor until very finely chopped. • Beat the egg whites and salt in a large bowl until stiff. • Gently fold in the almond mixture and lemon zest. • Spoon the mixture into a pastry bag fitted with a 1/2-inch (1-cm) plain tip. • Pipe small rosettes of the mixture onto the prepared baking sheet. • Bake for 12–15 minutes, or until lightly browned. • Let cool.

- 8 oz/250 g blanched almonds
- 1 cup/200 g sugar
- 2 large egg whites
- 1/8 tsp salt
- grated zest of 1 lemon

CREAM DOUGHNUTS

Serves: 6–8

Preparation: 45'

Rising time: 5 h

Cooking: 45'

Level of difficulty: 3

- 1 oz/30 g fresh yeast or 2 (1/4-oz/7-g) packages active dry yeast
- 1/2 cup/125 ml warm milk + extra
- 3 cups/450 g all-purpose/plain flour
- 1/8 tsp salt
- 1/3 cup/70 g sugar
- grated zest of 1 lemon
- 1/8 tsp vanilla extract/essence
- 6 large egg yolks
- 6 tbsp butter
- 1 quantity Custard (see recipe Greek cinnamon pudding, page 892)
- 2 cups/500 ml olive oil, for frying
- 1/4 cup/50 g sugar, to roll

Mix the yeast and milk in a small bowl. Let stand until foamy. • Sift the flour and salt into a large bowl. • Stir in the sugar and lemon zest. Add the vanilla and egg yolks, beating until just blended. Mix in the butter, yeast mixture, and enough extra milk to form a smooth dough. • Knead for 15 minutes. Shape the dough into a ball and place in an oiled bowl. Cover with a cloth and let rise for 2 hours. • Knead and refrigerate for 2 hours. • Roll the dough out to about 1/2 inch (1 cm) thick. • Use a 2 1/2-inch (6-cm) cookie cutter to cut out rounds. Use your thumb to make a hole in the dough and fill with custard. Fold the dough around the cream. • Let rise for 1 hour. • Heat the oil in a deep fryer until very hot. Fry the doughnuts in small batches until golden. • Drain well on paper towels. • Roll in the sugar and serve hot.

DOUGHNUTS

Serves: 12–14

Preparation: 30'

Rising time: 1 h 30'

Cooking: 45'

Level of difficulty: 3

- 1½ oz/45 g fresh yeast or 3 packages (¼-oz/7-g) active dry yeast
- ½ cup/125 ml warm water
- 1 tsp sugar
- 1 cup/250 ml milk
- 1 cup/250 ml half and half cream
- ⅔ cup/150 g butter
- 6 large eggs
- 1 cup/250 ml sour cream
- ½ cup/100 g sugar
- 1 tsp salt
- 3 lb/1.5 kg all-purpose/plain flour or more if needed
- grated zest and juice of 1 lemon
- 1 quart/1 liter oil, for frying
- ½ cup/75 g confectioners'/icing sugar

Mix the yeast, water, and sugar in a small bowl. Let stand until foamy. • Heat the milk, cream, and butter in a medium saucepan. Let cool to warm. • Beat the eggs, sugar, salt, and sour cream in a large bowl with an electric mixer at high speed until creamy. Fold the milk mixture into the beaten egg mixture. • Stir in the yeast mixture, lemon zest and juice, and 2 cups (300 g) of flour. Add enough of the remaining flour to form a soft dough. • Knead until smooth and elastic. Place in a oiled bowl and cover with a clean cloth. Let rise for 1 hour, or until doubled in bulk. • Turn the dough out onto a lightly floured surface and stretch to ½-inch (1-cm) thick. Use a large cookie cutter or glass to stamp out rounds. • Place the rounds on a lightly floured cloth. Cover with a clean cloth and let rise for about 30 minutes, or until doubled in bulk. Reroll the trimmings. • Heat the oil in a deep fryer to very hot. • Fry the doughnuts in small batches for 10–15 minutes, or until golden brown. • Drain well on paper towels. • Dust with the confectioners' sugar and serve warm.

WALNUT COOKIES

Preheat the oven to 400°F/200°C/gas 6. • Butter two cookie sheets and line with waxed paper. • Sift the flour and salt into a medium bowl. Stir in $1/2$ cup (75 g) of confectioners' sugar, walnuts, lemon zest, and vanilla. • Mix in the butter to form a smooth dough. Let stand for 20 minutes. • Roll the dough out on a lightly floured surface into a 1-inch (2.5-cm) thick rectangle. Cut diagonally into slices about 1-inch (2.5-cm) thick. • Arrange the cookies on the prepared cookie sheet. • Bake for 15–20 minutes, or until lightly browned. • Cool the cookies completely on racks. • Dust with the remaining confectioners' sugar.

Serves: 8

Preparation: 20' + 20' to rest

Cooking: 20'

Level of difficulty: 1

- 1$1/2$ cups/225 g all-purpose/plain flour
- $1/8$ tsp salt
- 1 cup/150 g confectioners'/icing sugar
- 2 cups/200 g finely chopped walnuts
- grated zest of 1 lemon
- $1/2$ tsp vanilla extract/essence
- 6 tbsp butter, melted

TURKISH BAKLAVA

Serves: 8

Preparation: 20'

Cooking: 1 h

Level of difficulty: 2

- **8 sheets frozen phyllo dough, thawed**
- **1 cup/250 g butter, melted**
- **2¾ cups/280 g coarsely chopped walnuts**

SYRUP

- **2½ cups/600 ml water**
- **3 cups/600 g sugar**
- **2 tbsp fresh lemon juice**

Preheat the oven to 350°F/180°C/gas 4. • Butter a 10-inch (25-cm) square pan. • Cut the sheets of phyllo to the size of the baking pan. • Brush a sheet of phyllo with butter and place in the baking pan. Brush with more butter. Repeat with 3 more sheets of phyllo and butter. Do not butter the top of the last sheet of phyllo. • Sprinkle with the walnuts. • Cover with a sheet of phyllo and brush with butter. • Brush butter on both sides of 3 more sheets of phyllo and place them on top. • Cut the cake diagonally into 2-inch (5-cm) squares or triangles, making sure that all the layers of dough have been cut through. • Bake for 50–60 minutes, or until crisp and golden brown. • Syrup: Bring the water, sugar, and lemon juice to a boil. Boil for 20 minutes. Remove from the heat. • Pour the syrup over the baklava. • Cool completely in the pan.

CINNAMON AND CLOVE COOKIES

Serves: 15–20

Preparation: 20'

Resting: 30'

Cooking: 15'

Level of difficulty: 1

- 7 cups/750 g all-purpose/plain flour
- ½ tsp salt
- 1 cup/250 ml water
- 1 stick cinnamon
- 5 cloves
- 1½ cups/375 ml extra-virgin olive oil
- 1½ cups/300 g sugar
- 1 cup/250 ml brandy
- 2 tsp baking soda

Sift the flour and salt into a large bowl. • Bring the water, cinnamon, and cloves to a boil in a small saucepan. Discard the cinnamon and cloves and set the water aside. • Beat the oil and sugar in a large bowl with an electric mixer at high speed until creamy. • Add the brandy, spiced water, and baking soda. • Fold in the dry ingredients. • Turn out onto a lightly floured work surface and knead to form a stiff dough. • Shape into a ball, wrap in plastic wrap, and let rest for 30 minutes. • Preheat the oven to 375°F/190°C/gas 5. • Butter three cookie sheets and line with waxed paper. • Discard the plastic wrap, break off pieces of dough and shape into balls the size of walnuts. Shape into oblongs. • Place on the prepared cookie sheets. • Bake for 12–15 minutes, or until firm to the touch. • Transfer to racks and let cool completely.

FRIED CARDAMOM COOKIES

Sift the flour into a large bowl. • Beat the egg yolks and egg white, rose water, milk, and cardamom in a large bowl with an electric mixer at high speed until pale and creamy. • Use a large rubber spatula to fold in the flour. • Turn the dough out onto a lightly floured surface. Knead until smooth and elastic. • Cover with a clean cloth and let stand for 2 hours. • Shape into balls the size of walnuts. • Roll the balls out to $1/8$-inch (3-mm) thick and to 3 inches (8 cm) in diameter. • Carefully fold the disks of dough in half. • Cover with a clean cloth and let stand for 5 minutes. • Heat the oil to very hot in a deep-fryer. • Fry the cookies in batches for 2–3 minutes, or until lightly browned all over. • Drain well on paper towels. • Dust with the confectioners' sugar and serve hot.

Serves: 10

Preparation: 20' + 2 h to rest

Cooking: 15'

Level of difficulty: 2

- 2$2/3$ cups/400 g all-purpose/plain flour
- 3 large egg yolks + 1 large egg white
- 4 tbsp rose water
- $1/2$ cup/125 ml milk
- $1/2$ tsp ground cardamom
- 2 cups/500 ml olive oil, for frying
- $1/3$ cup/50 g confectioners'/icing sugar, to dust

STUFFED TARTLETS

Serves: 10–12

Preparation: 30'

Cooking: 25'

Level of difficulty: 2

DATE FILLING

- 1½ cups/150 g pitted dates, coarsely chopped
- ½ cup/125 ml water
- 1 tbsp fresh lemon juice

PASTRY

- 3⅓ cups/500 g all-purpose/plain flour
- 1 cup/250 g butter
- 2 tbsp rose water
- 4 tbsp milk
- ⅓ cup/50 g confectioners'/ icing sugar, to dust

Date Filling: Mix the dates and water in a small saucepan over low heat. Cook, stirring often, for 6–7 minutes, or the dates have softened. • Add the lemon juice. • Transfer to a food processor and process until smooth. Let cool completely. • Pastry: Preheat the oven to 325°F/170°C/gas 3. • Sift the flour into a large bowl. Use your hands to rub in the butter. Add the rose water, followed by the milk to form a soft dough. • Shape into balls the size of walnuts. Flatten slightly, pinching up the sides to form hollow rounds. • Spoon the filling into the center of the pastry rounds. Stretch the dough over the filling to enclose it. • Arrange the pastries on a large baking sheet. Use a fork to prick all over. • Bake for 20–25 minutes, or until set. While still warm they may seem soft, but on cooling they become firm. • Dust with the confectioners' sugar.

ALMOND YOGURT CAKE

Preheat the oven to 400°F/200°C/gas 6. • Oil a large baking sheet. • Melt half the butter in a large frying pan over medium heat. Sauté the almonds for 5 minutes. Transfer to a plate and set aside. • Mix the yogurt and sugar in a large bowl. • Stir in the almond mixture, semolina, and vanilla. • Pour the batter onto the prepared baking sheet. • Bake for 25–30 minutes, or until lightly browned. • Syrup: Mix the sugar, water, and lemon juice in a small saucepan over medium heat. Cook, stirring constantly, until thick enough to coat a metal spoon. Add the rose water, if using. Cook for 5 minutes more. • Remove from heat and let cool slightly. • Pour the syrup over the cake as soon as it comes out of the oven. • Cut into diamond shapes and return to the oven for 5 minutes more. • Melt the remaining butter in a small saucepan. Pour over the cake. Decorate with the whipped cream and serve.

Serves: 4

Preparation: 30'

Cooking: 30'

Level of difficulty: 1

- 1 cup/250 g butter
- 4 cups/400 g coarsely chopped almonds
- 1 cup/250 ml plain yogurt
- ½ cup/100 g granulated sugar
- 1 cup/200 g semolina
- 1 tsp vanilla extract/essence

SYRUP

- 1 cup/200 g sugar
- 6 tbsp water
- juice of 1 lemon
- 1 tbsp rose water (optional)

- 1 cup/250 ml whipped cream

EGG YOLK NOUGAT

Serves: 10

Preparation: 30' + 2 h to freeze

Level of difficulty: 2

- 2¾ cups/400 g almonds, blanched and peeled
- 2 tsp cold water
- 8 large egg yolks
- 2 cups/400 g sugar
- grated zest of 1 lemon
- ½ tsp ground cinnamon

Finely chop the almonds in a food processor and transfer to a medium bowl. Add enough water to prevent any oil from forming. • Whisk the egg yolks and ¹/₂ cup (100 g) of sugar in a double boiler until pale and creamy. Cook over low heat, stirring constantly, until the mixture lightly coats a metal spoon or registers 160°F (80°C) on an instant-read thermometer. Immediately plunge the pan into a bowl of ice water and stir until the egg mixture has cooled. • Add the egg mixture to the almonds, stirring until well blended. • Stir the remaining sugar, lemon zest, and cinnamon in a small saucepan over medium heat. • Cook for 8–10 minutes, or until golden in color. Add the almond paste and cook, stirring constantly, until the mixture is no longer sticky, about 10 minutes. • Pour the mixture into an 11 x 7-inch (28 x 18-cm) baking tray and freeze for at least 2 hours. • Remove from the freezer and cut into squares to serve.

PINE NUT COOKIES

Serves: 10–12

Preparation: 20'

Cooking: 15'

Level of difficulty: 1

- 2½ cups/500 g sugar
- 5 cups/500 g finely ground almonds
- about ½ cup/ 125 ml water
- 1 large egg, lightly beaten
- 1 cup/180 g pine nuts

Preheat the oven to 400°F/200°C/gas 6. • Butter two cookie sheets. • Mix the sugar, almonds, and water in a large bowl to form a smooth marzipan dough. • Break off pieces of dough and shape them into balls the size of walnuts. • Brush with the beaten egg. • Roll in the pine nuts, making sure that the nuts stick. • Place the cookies on the prepared cookie sheet. • Bake for 10–15 minutes, or until risen and lightly browned. • Cool the cookies completely on the baking sheet.

PRESERVES

PEAR AND LEMON MARMALADE

C ook the sugar in the water in a large saucepan over low heat until the sugar has dissolved completely. • Add the lemons and cook for 35–40 minutes, stirring constantly, until the lemon is slightly caramelized. • Add the pears and lemon juice. Bring to a boil. Remove from the heat and transfer to a bowl. • Cover with a clean cloth and let rest overnight. • Return the marmalade to a large saucepan and bring to a boil over low heat. Cook for 10 minutes, or until a teaspoon of marmalade dropped onto a cold plate will set. • Spoon into sterilized jars and seal. • Store in a cool dark place.

Serves: 10–15

Preparation: 15' + 12 h to rest

Cooking: 1 h

Level of difficulty: 2

- 2½ cups/500 g sugar
- generous ¾ cup/ 200 ml water
- 2 lemons, cut into ¼-inch/5-mm cubes
- 2.5 lb/1.25 kg ripe pears, peeled, cored, and coarsely chopped
- juice of 1 lemon

PLUM JAM

Serves: 10–15

Preparation: 20'

Cooking: 1 h 30'

Level of difficulty: 2

- **3 lb/1.5 kg plums, pitted**
- **1 cup/250 ml water**
- **3 cups/ 600 g sugar**
- **4 tbsp rum**

Cook the plums with the water in a large saucepan over medium heat for about 30 minutes, or until tender. • Let cool. • Press the plums through a fine mesh strainer and then weigh the plum purèe. • Add the same weight of sugar and return to the pan. • Cook over high heat for 15 minutes, stirring constantly with a wooden spoon. • Lower the heat and simmer for about 45 minutes, or until you can spoon a drop onto a chilled plate and it begins to set. • Remove from the heat and stir in the rum. • Mix well and spoon into sterilized jars. Let cool and seal. • Store in a cool dark place.

FOUR FRUIT CONSERVE

P ut the fruit in a large saucepan. Add the lemon juice and fruit pectin. Mix well. • Bring to a boil over medium heat and simmer for 1 minute, stirring constantly. • Add the sugar and bring to a boil, stirring constantly. • Raise the heat and boil for 15 minutes. • Remove from the heat and continue stirring for 1 minute. • Pour into sterilized jars and seal. Turn the jars upside down for 5 minutes. • Store in a cool dark place.

Serves: 10–15

Preparation: 5'

Cooking: 20'

Level of difficulty: 2

- 14 oz/400 g strawberries, chopped
- 7 oz/200 g red currants
- 7 oz/200 g grapes, chopped
- 4 oz/125 g raspberries, hulled and chopped
- juice of 1 lemon
- 1 tbsp fruit pectin
- 4 cups/800 g sugar

PEARS PRESERVED IN GRAPPA

Serves: 6–8

Preparation: 15'

Cooking: 40'

Level of difficulty: 2

- **12 small firm pears**
- **juice of 1 lemon**
- **1½ cups/300 g sugar**
- **½ cup/125 ml water**
- **2 cinnamon sticks**
- **4 cloves**
- **3 cups/750 ml grappa**

Peel the pears without removing the stems. Place in a large bowl and cover with cold water and the lemon juice to prevent browning. • Cook the sugar in the water in a large saucepan over low heat until the sugar had dissolved completely. • Bring to a boil and add the cinnamon and cloves. Simmer for 5 minutes. • Add the pears and cook for 25–30 minutes, or until the pears are opaque. • Remove from the heat and transfer the pears to sterilized jars. • Mix the grappa into the syrup and cover the pears with this mixture. • Seal and store in a cool dark place.

Use whisky or a strong lemon liqueur instead of grappa for a different flavor.

941

STRAWBERRY AND LEMON JAM

Mix the strawberries with the sugar in a large bowl and let macerate for 12 hours.
• Process the mixture in a food processor or blender until smooth. • Transfer to a large saucepan. Add the lemon juice and mix well.
• Bring to a boil over medium heat and cook for 20 minutes. • Remove from the heat and let cool slightly. • Spoon into sterilized jars and seal.
• Store in a cool dark place.

942

Serves: 4–6

*Preparation: 10' +
    12 h to macerate*

Cooking: 25'

Level of difficulty: 2

- 1 lb/500 g
  strawberries,
  chopped
- 1¾ cups/350 g
  sugar
- 2 tbsp lemon juice

FIG JAM

Serves: 6–8

Preparation: 20' +
    12 h to macerate

Cooking: 1 h 30'

Level of difficulty: 2

- 4 lb/2 kg fresh figs
- 2 lb/1 kg sugar

Wash and slice the figs. • Place the figs in a large saucepan and cover with the sugar. Let macerate for 12 hours. • Cook the figs over medium heat for about 1 hour 30 minutes, skimming off any froth that forms. The jam is ready when you can spoon a drop onto a chilled plate and it begins to set. • Spoon the jam into sterilized jars. • Store in a cool dark place.

APRICOTS IN RED WINE

Boil the wine with the sugar in a large saucepan.
• Add the whole apricots and simmer over low
heat for 8 minutes. • Add the pepper, cloves, and
the cinnamon stick. • Remove the apricots with a
slotted spoon. • Continue to boil the wine until it
reduces to a syrup. • Halve and pit the apricots.
• Transfer them in a large jar in layers and cover
with the wine syrup. • Seal the jar hermetically.
• Keep in a cool dark place. The apricots are
ready to eat after 1 week.

Serves: 6–8

Preparation: 20'

Cooking: 30'

Level of difficulty: 1

- 3 cups/750 ml full-
  bodied red wine
- 3¾ cups/750 g
  sugar
- 2¼ lb/1.25 kg ripe
  apricots
- ¼ tsp freshly
  ground black
  pepper
- 3 cloves
- 1 cinnamon stick

ONION MARMALADE

Melt the butter in a saucepan over medium heat. • Add the onions and sauté for 5 minutes, or until softened. • Add the sugar and lower the heat. Cook for 15–20 minutes, or until the onions are very soft. • Add the red wine vinegar and let it evaporate. • Add the sherry vinegar and let it evaporate. • Lower the heat and pour in the red wine. Season with salt and pepper. • Cook over low heat for 1^1/$_2$ hours, stirring occasionally, until very thick and glossy. • Let cool and spoon into sterilized jars. • Seal and store in a cool dark place.

Serves: 10–15

Preparation: 10'

Cooking: 2 h

Level of difficulty: 2

- ^{1}/$_2$ cup/125 g butter
- 1^1/$_2$ lb/750 g onions, finely sliced
- ^{3}/$_4$ cup/150 g sugar
- 2 tbsp red wine vinegar
- generous ^{1}/$_3$ cup/ 100 ml sherry vinegar
- 1 cup/250 ml dry red wine
- 1^1/$_2$ tsp salt
- 1^1/$_2$ tsp freshly ground black pepper to taste

PICKLED ONIONS

Serves: 10–15

Preparation: 15' +
24 h to stand

Cooking: 10'

Level of difficulty: 1

- **4 lb/2 kg small pickling onions**
- **1½ quarts/1.5 liters white wine vinegar**
- **6 whole black peppercorns**

Cook the onions in a large pot of salted, boiling water for 5 minutes. • Drain and transfer to sterilized jars. • Bring the vinegar to a boil and pour over the onions. • Let stand for 24 hours. • Drain the onions, returning the vinegar to a saucepan. Add the black peppercorns. Bring to a boil and pour over the onions. • Seal and store in a cool dark place for 2 months before using.

PICKLED PEPPERS

A rrange the bell peppers in sterilized jars.
• Bring the vinegar, wine, oil, sugar, salt, and
cloves to a boil in a large saucepan. • Pour the hot
vinegar mixture over the peppers in the jars. • Seal
and store in a cool dark place for 2 months
before using.

Serves: 10–15

Preparation: 20'

Cooking: 5'

Level of difficulty: 1

- **4 lb/2 kg red and
  yellow bell peppers/
  capsicums, seeded
  and sliced**
- **3 cups/750 ml
  vinegar**
- **6 tbsp dry white
  wine**
- **½ cup/125 ml
  extra-virgin
  olive oil**
- **½ cup/100 g sugar**
- **¼ cup/50 g salt**
- **6 cloves**

SUNDRIED TOMATOES

Serves: 10–15

Preparation: 40' + 4 days to dry

Level of difficulty: 2

- **4 lb/2 kg ripe tomatoes**
- **2 tbsp salt**
- **leaves from 3 large sprigs basil**
- **1 quart/1 liter extra-virgin olive oil + more if needed**

Cut the tomatoes in half and remove the seeds. Pat dry with paper towels and sprinkle each one with salt. • Arrange in a single layer on baking racks. Dry in the hot sun for 4 days. Take the tomatoes indoors at night as the damp night air will prevent them from drying. • Pack the dried tomatoes tightly in a large glass jar interspersed with basil leaves. Cover with the oil and seal. • The tomatoes will absorb the oil a little so check after 2–3 days and add more oil if necessary. • Store in a cool dark place.

PRESERVED EGGPLANTS

Serves: 6

Preparation: 20' +
2 days to steep,
drain, and rest

Cooking: 5'

Level of difficulty: 2

- 4 lb/2 kg
  eggplants/
  aubergines, cut
  into small cubes
- 1½ quarts/1.5
  liters vinegar
- 2 stalks celery,
  chopped
- 2 yellow bell
  peppers/
  capsicums,
  seeded and sliced
- 4 cloves garlic,
  lightly crushed but
  whole
- leaves from 2
  sprigs oregano
- 3 cups/750 ml
  extra-virgin
  olive oil

Place the eggplants in a large bowl and cover with water. Let steep overnight. • Drain and let stand in a colander on the draining board for 12 hours. • Transfer the eggplants to a large saucepan and cover with vinegar. Bring to a boil and cook for 4 minutes. • Drain and spread out on a cloth. • Let rest for 24 hours. • Place the eggplants in sterilized jars with the celery, bell peppers, garlic, and oregano. • Cover with oil and seal. • Store in a cool dark place for 1 month before using.

GREEN TOMATO CONSERVE

Place the tomatoes into a large saucepan.
• Add the lemon zest and fruit pectin and mix
well. Bring to a boil over medium heat, stirring
constantly. • Simmer for 1 minute. Add the sugar
and bring to a boil, stirring constantly. • Simmer
over high heat for 12 minutes. Remove from the
heat and discard the lemon zest. Stir for 1 minute.
Add the cinnamon or cloves if using. • Transfer to
sterilized jars and seal. Turn the jars upside down
for 5 minutes. • Store in a cool dark place.

Serves: 10–15

Preparation: 15'

Cooking: 20'

Level of difficulty: 2

- 2 lb/1 kg green
  tomatoes, finely
  chopped
- zest of 1 lemon,
  removed in large
  pieces with a
  sharp knife
- 1 tbsp fruit pectin
- 5 cups/1 kg sugar
- 1 cinnamon stick or
  4 cloves (optional)

PICKLED CAULIFLOWER

Serves: 8

Preparation: 20'

Cooking: 15'

Level of difficulty: 2

- **1 large cauliflower,
  cut into florets**
- **juice of 1 lemon**
- **2 white onions,
  sliced**
- **1 quart/1 liter
  white wine vinegar**
- **salt and freshly
  ground black
  pepper to taste**
- **4 fresh red chile
  peppers, seeded
  and sliced**

Cook the cauliflower in a large pot of salted, boiling water with the lemon juice for 10 minutes, or until tender. • Drain well. • Cook the onions in a large pot of salted, boiling water for 3 minutes. • Drain well. • Bring the vinegar to a boil with the salt and pepper. • Remove from the heat and let cool. • Arrange the cauliflower, chile peppers, and onions in layers in sterilized jars. Cover with the vinegar and seal. • Store the jars in a cool dark place for 2 months before using.

ZUCCHINI PRESERVED IN OIL

Cover a baking sheet with a cloth and arrange the zucchini on it. Drizzle with the vinegar and let absorb overnight. • Sprinkle with sugar and salt. Transfer to sterilized jars, add the basil, and cover with the oil. • Seal and store in a cool dark place for 1 month before using.

Serves: 10–15

Preparation: 10' + 12 h to rest

Level of difficulty: 1

- 2 lb/1 kg small zucchini/ courgettes, sliced
- 2 cups/500 ml vinegar
- 1 cup/200 g sugar
- ⅛ tsp salt
- leaves from 2 sprigs basil
- 3 cups/750 ml extra-virgin olive oil

ONIONS PRESERVED IN OIL

Serves: 10–15

Preparation: 20' + 1 h to dry

Cooking: 15'

Level of difficulty: 2

- 1 quart/1 liter white wine vinegar
- ½ cup/125 ml dry white wine
- 4 cloves
- ½ cup/100 g sugar
- 2 bay leaves
- salt to taste
- 2 lb/1 kg pickling onions
- 1 quart/1 liter extra-virgin olive oil
- 4 whole black peppercorns

Bring the vinegar, wine, cloves, sugar, bay leaves, and salt to a boil in a large saucepan. • Add the onions and bring back to a boil. • Simmer for 10 minutes. • Drain the onions and let dry on paper towels for 1 hour. • Transfer them to sterilized jars and cover with oil. Add the peppercorns and seal. • Store in a cool dark place for 1 month before using.

PRESERVED LEMONS

Soak the lemons in cold water for 3–4 days, changing the water daily. • Without slicing all the way through, cut each lemon vertically into four. Open them out carefully, salt generously, then press the quarters back together to make whole lemons. • Insert the lemons into two sterilized 1 quart (1 liter) preserving jars, packing them tightly together. Seal and store in a cool dark place for 1 month.

Preserved lemons are a classic garnish for many North African tajines and other dishes.

958

Serves: 10

*Preparation: 30' +
3–4 days to soak*

Level of difficulty: 2

- about 2 lb/1 kg lemons, preferably organic
- 1 cup/250 g coarse salt, such as kosher salt

INDEX

967

969

970

975